Pathways to Prohibition

Pathways to Prohibition

Radicals, Moderates, and Social Movement Outcomes

Ann-Marie E. Szymanski

Duke University Press Durham and London 2003

Printed in the United States of America on acid-free paper ♾
Typeset in Quadraat by Tseng Information Systems, Inc.
Library of Congress Cataloging-in-Publication Data appear
on the last printed page of this book.

To Loren, with all my love

Contents

List of Figures

List of Tables

Acknowledgments

I am indebted to a number of people who assisted in the completion of this book. As a graduate student in Cornell University's Department of Government, it was my good fortune to work under the direction of Elizabeth Sanders, Sidney Tarrow, and Martin Shefter, each of whom played a significant role in this undertaking. It was Marty Shefter's seminar on political change in the United States that first introduced me to the temperance movement and, more generally, to the study of American political development. Meanwhile, Sid Tarrow's seminar on comparative social movements inspired me to apply a different theoretical approach to my work, and I also benefited greatly from his sage advice about research methods, the process of writing, and the academic profession. Finally, Elizabeth became the chair of my dissertation committee at a crucial stage in my career as a doctoral student. She challenged me to meet her high standards, and her patience, criticism, and support were invaluable to me particularly toward the end of this process.

Other scholars who made useful suggestions include: Richard Bensel, Peter Katzenstein, Mary Katzenstein, E. W. Kelley, Jeremy Rabkin, Elisabeth Clemens, Don Maletz, and Loren Gatch. I am grateful to them for taking the time to offer me advice, and to all the Cornell graduate students who participated in the informal dissertation colloquium established by Peter Katzenstein. I learned much from my fellow students, including that my initial research design was too unwieldy.

I also acknowledge my gratitude to my colleagues at the University of Oklahoma and especially to Ron Peters, who permitted me to escape some departmental duties that might have interfered with the completion of this book. Another colleague, Jim Douglas, graciously lent me his scanner at a key moment in the book's completion.

Part of this work was supported by two Arts and Sciences Junior Faculty Research grants and by the Jonathan R. Meigs Fellowship, which defrayed the costs of traveling to various archives. Moreover, I benefited from a year-long Mellon Fellowship, which gave me the freedom to write as a graduate student.

Finally, I must express my appreciation to my family for their support and loyalty throughout the duration of this project. My parents, Richard and Edna Szymanski, have provided everything from free babysitting to travel money during these years, and my sisters-in-law, Alice Fox, Cathy Gatch, Dorothy Gatch, and June Zaragoza, opened their homes to me during some of my research trips. Suffice it to say that I could not have completed this book without their help.

Meanwhile, I thank Rosemary Gatch for her patience. She has been a remarkably good-natured child, and has adjusted well to having a perpetually stressed-out mother. Oliver and John Gatch arrived as I was completing this project, and have proved much of the conventional wisdom about twins to be wrong. Finally, my husband, Loren Gatch, sustained me through the darkest days of this book, when it seemed as though nothing was coming together. He read every chapter, helped me with my teaching, and assumed all of the household responsibilities when necessary. I will be eternally grateful for his love and understanding.

Pathways to Prohibition

1 Political Strategy and Social Movement Outcomes

Radicals and Moderates

For radical social movement activists, moderation is usually not a virtue. For example, the radical environmentalist David Brower has said that his moderate colleagues "don't seem to learn . . . that whenever they compromise they lose." Moreover, moderates are suspect because their pragmatism seems incapable of challenging the broader political, economic, and social relations that constitute the status quo. The radical pacifist Daniel Berrigan once accused moderate antiwar activists of being "obsessed by the necessity of delivering results." Instead of worrying about "efficiency," Berrigan argued, the movement had to realize that "the spiritual dismantling of the American empire is going to consume at least our lifetime, and perhaps the lifetime of the next generation." Finally, many radicals question whether modest reform efforts are worthwhile if the public has yet to adopt the "correct" beliefs. In 1840, for instance, a radical abolitionist issued this warning to his moderate counterparts: "All attempts to abolish slavery by legislation before the people of the country are converted to anti-slavery principles must of necessity be unsuccessful."[1] But is moderation really so lethal to a social movement?

Like other social movements, America's anti-liquor crusade divided along ideological lines after 1875. On one side stood the radicals, who favored state and national prohibition, particularly if these policies were incorporated into state and national constitutions. On the other side were the moderates, who believed that the movement should initially focus on restricting local liquor retailing, and only later seek prohibition on a broader scale. Both sides believed that theirs was the best approach to the liquor question, and both sought to mobilize citizens who shared their visions.

For the radicals, only the state and national governments had the power to crush the liquor traffic. "Penalties sufficient to destroy the traffic will never be made," wrote one orthodox dry, until these governments brand it "an outlaw and enemy." Furthermore, radicals preferred constitutional prohibition to mere laws, as it created "an established standard of right principles exerting its instructive influence upon public sentiment—a beacon of essential truth illuminating and guiding public thought." Conversely, they frowned on agitation for prohibition in one's neighborhood, town, or county, for "it was wrong for the state to surrender its sovereignty, evade its duty and divest itself of responsibility on a matter vitally affecting the welfare of the state by shifting the decision to localities, a procedure making it practically certain that some localities would vote to perpetuate plague centers."[2] Indeed, the radicals often dismissed local prohibition as no better than Stephen Douglas's "squatter sovereignty."[3]

Though acknowledging that many did not share their views, the orthodox drys were nevertheless confident that they could command public support for prohibition. All it took was for courageous men and women to unapologetically rally round this policy and to persuade the public of its value. As F. A. Noble put it,

> When there is a vigorous public sentiment on any question of morals, it is because somebody has taken an advanced position, and educated and drawn the people up to it. If all who think and even say [prohibition] would be a good thing . . . would only say it without any 'ifs,' and 'ands,' and 'buts,' . . . public sentiment on this liquor business would swell and press on like an incoming tide, and in a little while there would be laws looking to the suppression of this evil which would have in them the force of the right hand of God.[4]

During the 1880s the radicals had good reason to believe that prohibition measures would soon be embodied in state constitutions. By swamping the state legislatures with petitions, and by carefully navigating the quagmires of the amendment process and the party system, the drys forced referenda in eighteen states on whether to include prohibition in their constitutions.[5] In one state, North Carolina, the prohibitionists failed to frame prohibition as a constitutional issue but nonetheless compelled the legislature to hold a referendum on a state prohibition law.

Unfortunately, these referenda only revealed the lack of grassroots support for statewide prohibition. Between 1882 and 1890 voters in twelve states rejected prohibition outright; in four other states, constitutional prohibition won but fleeting victories.[6] As of 1900, Kansas, Maine, and North Dakota alone retained constitutional prohibition, and only New Hampshire and Vermont maintained statutory prohibition.[7] At the national level, prohibitionists were hardly more successful. During the winter of 1889–90, Senator Henry W. Blair (R-N.H.) and Representative John A. Pickler (R-S.D.) introduced resolutions in their respective houses that called for submitting a prohibition amendment to the states for ratification. Although reported favorably by Blair's committee (the Committee on Education and Labor), the resolution was otherwise ignored by party leaders in both houses.[8] By 1890 the crusade for state and national prohibition was at a virtual standstill.

While the Prohibition party, the Woman's Christian Temperance Union (WCTU), the Independent Order of Good Templars (IOGT), and other radicals united to support state and national prohibition during the 1880s, moderate anti-liquor activists became convinced that these groups had lost touch with the gritty reality of local liquor control. As L. Edwin Dudley recalled, "In one temperance society to which I belonged I asked the question one evening of the presiding officer: 'Will you tell me, sir, what is the law of Massachusetts relating to the liquor-traffic?' and I was answered: 'I don't know and I don't care; it is not prohibition and that is all I want to know about it.' "[9]

To Dudley, the radicals' indifference to the practical aspects of liquor control was disturbing. In pursuing nothing less than state prohibition, orthodox temperance groups offered no assistance to those who suffered daily from the saloon's illegal activities. Such prohibition may have been a noble goal, but Dudley worried about the "poor, ragged little fellows" who were enticed into Boston's saloons to drink, gamble, and mingle "with crowds of dissolute and drunken men and women, and all this in violation of the law of the state."[10] Recalling the North's mobilization for the Civil War, he concluded that the campaign against liquor would never enlist a majority of Americans without a more pragmatic battle plan:

> I remembered that at the beginning of the War of the Rebellion volunteers were called upon to enlist for the suppression of the Rebellion and the maintenance of the government of the United States. I remembered, also, . . . that if the call had been at the beginning for volunteers to go to the South to fight for the abolition of slavery, not one in ten of those who went would have been at all likely to enlist, and yet I remembered that the educating influence of the conflict carried these men . . . on, step by step, until . . . they were all abolitionists. It seemed to me that in temperance work there should be a place for the moderate as well as for the extreme man.[11]

In 1882 Dudley established the Massachusetts Law and Order League, a group devoted to enforcing extant liquor laws at the local level. Although short-lived, the Law and Order League would bequeath its law enforcement methods and, more significantly, its focus on securing modest, local goals to the Anti-Saloon League (ASL).

Like Dudley, the ASL's leaders believed that "reforms are not revolutions; they are evolutions." In their view, "every law on the statute books which tends to suppress or repress the liquor traffic is a weapon in the hands of the forces of reform, which, if used will hasten the day of permanent victory."[12] In short, the ASL had grasped an essential property of collective action: its potential to radicalize the moderate adherent of a social movement, even when the goals of such action seem limited. Instead of expecting its recruits to adopt the "correct" beliefs about prohibition before participating in the movement, the Anti-Saloon League first sought to engage Americans in local prohibition skirmishes which barely dented the profits of the liquor industry, but which socialized them into the militancy of the broader movement.

The capacity of movement participation to radicalize adherents has often been noted by social scientists. For example, Doug McAdam found that Freedom Summer activists eventually shifted to the left ideologically, while others who had applied to take part in the project but ultimately did not maintained moderate political views.[13] Unlike the Freedom Summer participants, however, the reformers who traveled the path from "damp" to "bone dry" were generally not involved in high-risk behavior which threatened their lives.[14] Rather, dry radicalism was forged when individuals confronted the intransigence of the liquor interests, which refused to accept even the most modest restraints on the saloon. Hence, the Anti-Saloon League deliberately instigated local prohibition conflicts, and advocated state laws which authorized local prohibition referenda—commonly known as "local option" laws. Such laws brought nascent drys face to face with the obstinate saloon, and unleashed the democratic potential of the decentralized American state. As one League leader described it:

> [Local option] is a law that enables a community opposed to saloons to keep them out, even though other places in the state may allow them to exist. . . . Its essential element is the rule of popular government. There can be no principle of legislation more American, or more democratic. To refuse the right of the people to determine such a question for themselves by communities, and thus permit saloons to be forced upon neighborhoods . . . against the popular will . . . is to proclaim an autocracy of rum that is thoroughly at variance with our American usages.[15]

League strategy was not only locally based but also gradual in character. By attaining partial but positive victories in the legislative, electoral, and judicial arenas and then building on those victories, the ASL drew its adherents into an escalating conflict which eventually scaled the walls of American federalism. Engaged in an ever-widening battle that lasted twenty years (from about 1900 to 1920), a proponent of municipal prohibition could become an advocate of county prohibition, then an advocate of statewide prohibition, and finally an advocate of national constitutional prohibition. By 1919 the ASL and its allies had amassed an enormous dry army which obtained statewide prohibition in thirty states and sustained it in three more (Maine, Kansas, and North Dakota).[16] In short, the league's crowning achievement—the Eighteenth Amendment—cannot be understood without appreciating the ASL's extraordinary capacity to involve moderates in temperance agitation and then keep them in a state of perpetual motion.

The prohibitionists of the 1880s gained limited success, while their Progressive Era counterparts achieved a remarkable—albeit temporary—accomplishment in American politics: the passage of an amendment to the U.S. constitution. How can such divergent outcomes be explained?

This book argues that choice of strategy—or how a social movement defines and pursues its goals—is important in determining whether the movement will succeed. Of course, the political system must be somewhat vulnerable to the challenge posed by a social movement for it to have a chance of winning concessions. Indeed, unstable political alignments would prove vital to both the prohibition movement's limited success in the 1880s and its ultimate triumph in the early twentieth century. Once movements have gained some access to the policymaking process, however, their fate cannot be explained solely in terms of their access. In other words, political opportunities were necessary for dry success in both the 1880s and the Progressive Era, but they do not sufficiently account for why outcomes differed across these two periods.

Instead, these divergent outcomes reflected the shift in the movement's strategy from promoting state constitutional amendments to advocating "local gradualism," the strategy which produced greater success in the Progressive Era. Local gradualism is "local" in that it initially focuses on local issues before targeting the state and national levels of government. It is "gradualist" in that it emphasizes achieving moderate goals before pursuing more radical goals. In the prohibition crusade these two aspects of strategy produced both a potent grassroots component and the capacity to transcend the limited scope of local politics. Well-suited to the porous, federal structure of the American state, local gradualism has been effectively used by other social movements in the United States, including the civil rights movement and the Christian Right.

Finally, this research suggests that a social movement's choice of strategy reflects both changes in state structure and new ideas about the appropriate distribution of political power. While novel institutional arrangements may channel a movement's energies in unprecedented directions, such innovations are often the byproduct of evolving ideas about the distribution of political authority. In the case of the prohibition movement, it adopted local gradualism partly in response to recent modifications of the political system, namely the devolution of the state legislatures' liquor licensing power to the localities, and the judiciary's growing acceptance of these licensing regimes. Moreover, these developments reflected a collective belief that the people, rather than the state legislatures, were best situated to resolve controversial issues affecting their localities—a view which gave many judges a coherent rationale for upholding local option laws and other types of local referenda. Meanwhile, whereas the moderates heartily embraced critiques of legislatures prevalent during the Gilded Age and adopted a strategy to exploit devolution, the radicals were more ambivalent about the emasculation of state legislatures and hence, its strategic implications. In short, social movements may only capitalize on new statutes, bureaucratic configurations, or judicial decisions if their leaders share the philosophy which animates them.

Explaining Outcomes: Internal Dynamics versus External Environment

According to social movement theorists, a social movement's outcome may reflect its internal dynamics and resources, its external political environment, or both. Analysts who have peered into the internal machinery of social movements link a movement's chances of success with its capacity to construct viable organizations, raise money, exploit the expertise of professional activists, recruit from existing groups, devise an effective repertoire of collective action for confronting political élites, pursue narrow goals, and articulate an ideology with widespread appeal. In contrast, social scientists who have concentrated on external factors claim that the success of social movements stems from opportunities created by political crises and unstable political alignments, and from the process by which state structures channel mobilization.

Before examining these two approaches, I should note that scholars have long disputed the definition of success and how to classify movement outcomes. Among other things, "success" may refer to a movement's attainment of tangible benefits that meet its goals, its formal acceptance by political élites, the legitimization of its goals, and the transformation of individual or group consciousness.[17] In this study, "success" will be defined instrumentally because that is how the drys themselves measured success. In other words, the prohibitionists succeeded when their participation in collective action produced tangible benefits that met their goals.[18] Of course, segments of the prohibition movement—such as the dry fraternal orders—also focused on consciousness raising and the transformation of social attitudes about drinking. However, as chapter 2 shows, the temperance fraternities declined in strength during the late 1800s, and by the Progressive Era played a lesser role in the movement than groups which sought to influence political institutions.[19]

Success and the Internal Dynamics of Social Movements

In the early 1970s sociologists turned to organizations as the appropriate focus of social movement research, and articulated what came to be known as resource mobilization theory. Some proponents of this theoretical framework claim that successful social movement organizations tend to possess a formalized structure with a clear division of labor, which increases combat readiness by reducing internal conflicts.[20] Other resource mobilization theorists link a group's capacity to mobilize support with its command of financial resources,[21] access to a pool of movement professionals,[22] and ability to recruit from existing solidarity groups.[23] Such assets, they argue, help the challenging group overcome the costs of collective action and sustain its mobilization efforts.

While these insights contribute to our understanding of social movements, they seem more concerned with illustrating the dynamics of mobilization than with accounting for movement success as defined above. Indeed, adherents of these views have been accused of equating movement success with the ability of particular social movement organizations to mobilize people.[24] For the most part, I second this criticism,[25] and would add that while resource mobilization theory may describe what an established social movement organization looks like, it cannot explain why some organizations are successful in their campaigns for policy change and others are not.

For example, the Anti-Saloon League fits the classical resource mobilization model quite well. First, the ASL's upper echelons exhibited both hierarchical organization and professional staff. In addition, the organization drew upon the vast financial and organizational resources of the evangelical Protestant churches, which promoted the league's highly productive fundraising and recruitment efforts.[26] However, the Anti-Saloon League only perfected this form after years of struggle, and did not differ markedly from other temperance organizations in terms of structure and resource base.[27] Almost every dry group sought to create a bureaucratic organization; several groups were staffed by career activists and could afford to hire movement organizers; and many organizations attempted to harness the Protestant churches' resources.[28] With these resources, anti-liquor organizations often mobilized hundreds of thousands of followers, and yet only the ASL led an effective charge for prohibition.[29] In short, if the league was not unique in its organizational structure or resource base, then one must look beyond resource mobilization theory to explain why this organization was more successful than its competitors.

While resource mobilization theorists stress the role of organizational resources, other scholars have sought to gauge the impact of violence, disruptive protest, and other forms of collective action on the success of social movements. According to some analysts, movement leaders may decide their movement's fate when they select their protest forms. For example, Frances Fox Piven and Richard Cloward argue that poor people's movements advance solely through disruptive protest and that constructing permanent movement organizations is inherently counterproductive.[30] In a similar fashion, Lee Ann Banaszak has discovered that the aggressive use of organizational, lobbying, and confrontational tactics were associated with early success by both the Swiss and American woman suffrage movements.[31] In contrast, other social scientists believe that movement success cannot be ascribed to a single protest form, and instead underscore the efficacy of "multiform movements," which maintain diversified repertoires of collective action. As Sidney Tarrow notes, multiform movements often "combine the demands and the participation of broad coalitions of actors in coalitional campaigns of collective action."[32]

In a way, these discussions of "collective action form" capture part of what I mean by "strategy." Indeed, some analysts distinguish between "confrontational" social movement strategies (which are contentious forms of collective action), and "assimilative" ones (which are more conventional).[33] However, if "strategy" means "a method for obtaining a specific goal," then these authors only emphasize how particular methods are chosen, rather than how goals are defined. This theoretical lapse may be crucial, for the leadership of a social movement would presumably determine its intermediate and long-term goals when making decisions about how to achieve them.

In any event, the prohibition movement used any number of collective action forms throughout its long history. As participants in a multiform movement, the drys employed petition campaigns, parades, mass meetings, electoral pressure, court actions, and occasionally even violence to destroy the saloons and their contents. While some movements succeed by being unruly, the prohibition movement, with the exception of the Women's Crusade,[34] usually preferred conventional protest forms to more contentious ones.[35] In addition, as chapter 3 maintains, there is no compelling evidence that the Progressive Era drys improved upon the means of collective action used by their nineteenth-century predecessors. Hence, the form of collective action had no significant impact on the prohibition movement's disparate outcomes in these two periods.

To reiterate, if "strategy" is defined as "a method for obtaining a specific goal," then social scientists have generally emphasized the "means" over the "ends" in discussing this concept. One exception to this imbalance is William Gamson, who asked whether challenging groups which pursue narrow goals are more likely to succeed than groups with broader aims.[36] In his study of fifty-three social movement organizations, Gamson measured the magnitude of movement goals on three fronts:

1. Did the group make single-issue or multiple-issue demands?

2. Did the group make radical demands or demands that did not attack the legitimacy of present distributions of wealth and power?

3. Did the group intend to influence élites or to replace élites?

He found that groups with single-issue demands were more successful than those having multiple-issue demands, and that groups which tried to displace an established member of the polity usually failed. Once Gamson controlled for the effect of élite displacement, his analysis of radicalism's impact revealed that the success rate of groups with radical demands and that of groups with moderate demands were virtually indistinguishable.[37]

At first glance, Gamson's conclusions suggest that the prohibition movement should have been equally likely to succeed in the 1880s and the Progressive Era. Both the campaigns for prohibition amendments and those for local option concentrated on one issue and did not attempt to displace political élites. Nonetheless, historians are correct in saying that the most prominent national dry organizations of the 1880s, namely the Prohibition party and the Woman's Christian Temperance Union, both possessed broader and more radical agendas[38] than the Anti-Saloon League, which focused primarily on prohibition during the early twentieth century.[39] Perhaps the former groups expended their scarce resources on various unrelated campaigns and slighted their efforts to pass state prohibition. In addition, Gamson might say that the Prohibition party was doomed to failure, given its goal of seizing the reins of government from the "corrupt" Republicans and Democrats.

One should not be too hasty, however, in accepting the conventional wisdom that the ASL succeeded because it adopted a single-issue position, in contrast to the earlier prohibitionists. For one thing, it must be noted that Gamson ultimately discovered no *independent* effect of multiple-issue demands on group outcomes, because virtually all the groups in his sample with multiple-issue demands also sought to replace political élites.[40] Second, most historical accounts of the nineteenth-century state referendum campaigns do not indicate that the drys linked their demand for statewide prohibition with other issues.[41] In fact, though local branches of the WCTU and Prohibition party participated in statewide campaigns, these campaigns were typically directed by local single-issue prohibition groups which were nonpartisan and unaffiliated with the national party and the national union.[42] Finally, single-issue drys attempted to organize two national groups in the mid-1880s (the nonpartisan National League for the Suppression of the Liquor Traffic, 1885, and the Anti-Saloon Republican Movement, 1886), but these efforts nonetheless failed to advance their cause.[43]

While rejecting the single-issue explanation for the prohibition movement's greater success after 1900, this book nevertheless emphasizes the significance of goal selection as an integral part of political strategy. To be sure, many social movement *organizations* (e.g., the WCTU and the General Federation of Women's Clubs) thrive as groups by embracing a wide range of causes.[44] However, as chapters 3, 4, and 8 suggest, social *movements* often flounder if their constituent groups fail to coalesce around shared goals when defining their political strategies. In the prohibition movement, which encompassed thousands of local groups and operated in a federal system, finding a unifying purpose was a prerequisite for the development of a national—rather than a parochial—political strategy. Furthermore, as the Anti-Saloon League demonstrated, there may be definite advantages to focusing on local issues rather than state and national ones.

Other scholars who focus on internal movement dynamics have examined how movement ideology influences social movement outcomes. In particular, Jane Mansbridge has outlined a particularly cogent model of how a group's expression of its ideology affects movement development. According to Mansbridge, movements organized on the basis of ideological incentives typically follow an "iron law of involution." As the very "dynamic that binds activists to the movement," movement ideology tends to be idealistic, radical, and exclusive, which in turn "works against the inclusive policy of accommodation and reform." In the end, the movement's own exclusivity isolates it from the rest of society, rendering it ineffectual.[45]

Over all, Mansbridge's model contributes more to an understanding of social movement failure than to an explanation for movement success. Since it was organized on the basis of nonmaterial incentives, the prohibition movement should have been subject to the iron law of involution, and there is some evidence to this effect. As this book shows, the leading prohibitionists of the 1880s were indeed more ideologically pure than their counterparts in the Progressive Era, and that purity helped ensure their defeat. Still, Mansbridge's framework cannot explain why the drys of the early twentieth century not only escaped the "iron law of involution" but also achieved extraordinary success. Her own discussion of ideology and the ERA movement indicates that a social movement may mount an effective mobilization effort which temporarily evades the iron law, but which nevertheless fails to accomplish its primary goal.[46]

Reversing Mansbridge's argument, Suzanne M. Marilley suggests that social movements are more likely to succeed when they construct inclusive ideological appeals that promote political alliances. In her account of America's woman suffrage movement, it was only when a new generation of pragmatic leaders forged a "feminism of personal development" after 1906 that the movement formed a winning coalition. This ideology downplayed the exclusive nativist and racist positions of some suffragists, and instead built support for suffrage by promoting the vote as crucial to securing woman's full opportunities to pursue happiness. In the end, such feminism appealed to a variety of groups—from trade unionists to settlement workers—because each group believed that its own particular causes would be promoted by suffrage.[47]

This book reinforces Marilley's broader point about the advantages of inclusive movements. However, it specifically underscores the significance of moderation as a source of inclusivity. Indeed, as chapters 6 and 7 show, the moderate drys' willingness to lower the ideological barriers to movement participation meant that they could mobilize new adherents to the dry cause who might otherwise have remained uninvolved. In contrast, the radical prohibitionists energized a core group of supporters but failed to win over many potential drys. Still, moderation alone cannot explain why the Progressive Era drys were able to navigate their political environment so successfully. For that, one must look beyond the internal dynamics of social movements.

Success and the External Environment of Social Movements

Advocates of the "political process" approach have criticized theorists who focus on internal movement dynamics for neglecting the political context of social movements. In general, these scholars contend that social movements can obtain "some measure of success when they are able to take advantage of the weakness of their opponents, in particular the state and political authorities."[48] If such weaknesses exist, the social movement is said to confront a favorable political opportunity structure, and the dimensions of its success will be shaped by the contours of that structure.

Political opportunities may reflect an enduring, dynamic process of social and political change, or they may be embedded in state institutions. For example, some analysts claim that movements profit from broad political crises, such as depressions, wars, and other periods when established interests are more likely to accommodate the claims of challenging groups.[49] Similarly, other social scientists argue that the instability of political alignments has contributed significantly to the success of many social movements. According to this view, a political party (faction or actor) operating in a closely contested electoral arena may be more willing to respond to the demands of a social movement if it will gain votes by doing so.[50] Alternatively, some proponents of this theoretical framework maintain that the institutional arrangements which characterize state structure determine a movement's ability to affect both public policy and its implementation. For instance, a social movement may face enormous obstacles in influencing the policy of a highly centralized state, but still might not realize its goals in a less centralized state which lacks the capacities for implementation.[51]

Two versions of the political process approach have been used to explain the prohibition movement's success during the Progressive Era. First, historians have often suggested that America's entry into World War I in April 1917 significantly increased the support for prohibition among political élites, thus contributing to the claim that political crises shape movement outcomes.[52] To bolster this argument, they note that the wartime government strictly regulated liquor production for the purposes of food conservation and also disseminated anti-German propaganda, which undoubtedly weakened the political power of wet groups like the German-American Alliance. However, the timing of prohibition victories casts doubt on this argument. By 1917 twenty of the thirty states that would adopt state prohibition during the Progressive Era had already done so. In addition, though accelerated by the wartime atmosphere, the Eighteenth Amendment's ratification "was completed suddenly by the actions of twenty-one state legislatures during the month of January 1919, more than six weeks after the war's end."[53]

A second political process explanation has been proposed by J. Christopher Soper, who attributes prohibition's success in America to particular features of the American state. In his comparison of the British and American prohibition movements, he asserts that "the weakness of the American national state and the absence of a coherent alcohol policy opened up myriad opportunities for meaningful local activism," whereas "the relative strength of the British state meant that local regions had very little political autonomy which, in turn, discouraged local activism." State weakness would prove to be the key to the Americans' success, since dry access to the federal system "generated membership and interest in the ASL, which was situated to provide the expertise necessary to organize a successful campaign."[54] While Soper is correct to point to federalism as one cause of the American prohibitionists' success, his comparison cannot explain why federalism mattered more during the Progressive Era than it did during the 1880s. Indeed, he provides virtually no evidence to support the contention that American institutions abruptly became more conducive to local activism in the early twentieth century than in the late nineteenth.[55]

A third variant of the political process approach, which underscores the role of unstable political alignments, does help account for both the prohibition movement's limited success in the 1880s and its impressive triumph in the Progressive Era. However, political instability only creates an opportunity to succeed, not success itself. For this reason, my study of the prohibition movement will ultimately contend that the classic version of the political process model cannot explain why a movement sometimes succeeds in taking advantage of its opportunities, and why another movement might fail when presented with the same or similar opportunities.

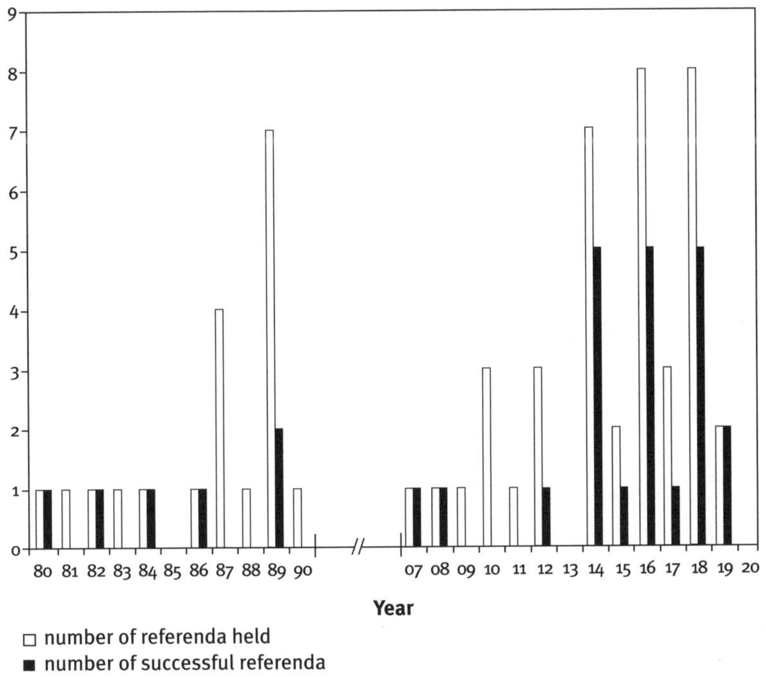

Figure 1 Use of All Forms of Referendum by the Prohibition Movement to Achieve Statewide Prohibition, 1880–1920. Source: Ernest H. Cherrington, *The Evolution of Prohibition in the United States of America* (Westerville, Ohio: American Issue Press, 1920).

As can be seen in figure 1,[56] unstable political alignments left political élites vulnerable to dry demands during the 1880s, and they thus furnished the prohibition movement with opportunities to advance their cause. In nineteen states, policymakers granted the drys nineteen chances to use direct legislation[57] to further their cause at the state level; only six (or 31.6%) of these attempts succeeded.[58] Likewise, the Progressive Era drys also made use of statewide direct legislation to achieve their goals. Once these prohibitionists believed that local option had been fully exploited, they too sought to pass referenda at the state level. Between 1907 and 1919, the drys managed to use direct legislation in twenty-nine states, again owing to political instability.[59] Of the forty referenda that they proposed to establish statewide prohibition,[60] twenty-two (or 55%) would pass.

In general, the prohibitionists of the early twentieth century encountered a more favorable political environment than their predecessors did; specifically, a greater number of state governments were responsive to citizen demands for direct legislation during the Progressive Era than during the 1880s. However, it is also obvious that the drys of the later period managed to use direct legislation more effectively. Thus, the classic version of the political process model must be supplemented by further explanation. One relatively unexplored variation of this model would look beyond the vulnerability of the movement's élite opponents and would consider the weakness of its antagonists as potential voters in the electoral system. Since the drys in both periods used direct legislation as a major vehicle[61] for achieving their goals, they frequently left the fate of their movement in the hands of the electorate rather than at the mercy of élites.

The Electoral System as an External Environment

Lloyd Sponholtz suggests one possible explanation for the success of the drys after 1900, namely that "a smaller turnout" may have enhanced "tremendously the possibility for minority rule" in referendum elections. He notes that direct legislation in the hands of well-organized groups allows them to assume a disproportionate decision-making power should their opponents fail to vote.[62] Thus, the dry victories of the early twentieth century conceivably reflected the demobilization of the American electorate that commenced after the election of 1896.

Social scientists have long underscored that a smaller proportion of the potential electorate participated in national elections after 1896, which marked the end of a period distinguished by high rates of voter turnout.[63] Scholars have offered two sets of explanations for the demobilization of the electorate in the twentieth century: one stresses the consequences of decreasing party competition, while the other stresses the establishment of legal and institutional barriers to voting.[64] Regardless of their explanation, however, most analysts agree that those segments of society lacking in wealth, education, and power became less likely to vote than social groups which possessed these attributes.[65] This shrunken, more middle-class electorate would presumably react more favorably to dry referenda than the highly mobilized electorate of the 1880s, which averaged a presidential election turnout of 78.7% nationwide.[66] After all, prohibition appealed the least to some social groups who ostensibly decreased their electoral participation after 1896, namely southern blacks, Germans, and Catholic immigrants.[67] With supporters of the saloon less prominent in the electorate, advocates of dry referenda may have encountered a more receptive voting public during the Progressive Era.

While plausible, this argument is offset by demographic changes in the U.S. population between the 1880s and the Progressive Era that hampered the prohibition cause. By the time the drys began sponsoring referenda in 1907, the number of immigrants arriving in the United States had surpassed one million for two consecutive years. In contrast, the annual number of immigrants who disembarked in the period 1880–90 averaged 518,534, or about half as many.[68] Moreover, the nation's

Table 1 Estimated Voter Turnout in Referenda Sponsored by the Prohibition Movement to Achieve State Prohibition during the 1880s and the Progressive Era

State	Year of Referendum, 1880–1890	Voter Turnout for Referendum, 1880–1890	Average Turnout, Presidential Elections, 1880–1888	Year of Referendum, 1900–1920	Voter Turnout for Referendum, 1880–1890	Average Turnout, Presidential Elections, 1900–1920
Washington[a]	1889	41.8	—	**1914**	54.3	57.1
Oregon	1883	44.5	65.2	**1914**	50.5	51.9
Michigan	1887	63.4	77.5	**1916**	71.9	73.6
Nebraska	1890	68.2	70.5	**1916**	77.6	74.2
Ohio	1883	68.6	93.2	1914	75.1	79.3
				1915	68.9	
				1917	67.3	
				1918	56.7	
West Virginia	1888	70.1	87.9	**1912**	73.6	84.1
North Carolina	1881	72.8	84.8	**1908**	37.7	51.5
Iowa	**1882**	73.7	90.5	1917	62.2	77.0
South Dakota[a]	**1889**	75.5	—	**1916**	56.1	67.9
Texas	1887	77.7	75.8	1911	48.9	35.4
				1919	26.5	

[a] Washington and South Dakota became states in 1889 and therefore did not vote in presidential elections until 1892. Turnout estimates for their 1889 referenda are based on estimates of their electorates in 1890.
All turnout figures in percent. Boldface signifies successful referendum.
Table based on turnout estimates by Walter Dean Burnham. For an explanation of his methodology, and his list of presidential turnout rates, see U.S. Bureau of the Census, *Historical Statistics of the United States: Colonial Times to 1970*, 2 vols. (Washington: U.S. Department of Commerce, Bureau of the Census, 1975), 1067–69, 1071–72.

Catholics formed 14.3% of the population in 1906, as compared to 9.9% in 1890.[69] A smaller percentage of immigrants and Catholics may have voted in the Progressive Era than in the 1880s, but this reduced participation would have occurred in populations that had increased their presence in America. Thus, the demobilization of the electorate in the early twentieth century may not have dramatically altered the composition of the American electorate to favor the drys.

Indeed, if one compares the turnout rates of the dry referenda of the 1880s with those of the Progressive Era, it becomes apparent that voter turnout has little to do with dry success in the latter period, particularly outside the South. Significantly, one cannot, according to table 1, simply infer that referenda turnout rates followed national trends toward electoral demobilization. Despite declines in presidential turnout rates between the two periods under study, this table clearly indicates that turnout rates in prohibition referenda were not very high during the 1880s, nor did they automatically become lower after 1896.

Moreover, these data fail to reveal a correlation between low voter turnout and the success of referenda. In Washington, Oregon, Michigan, Nebraska, and West Virginia, the successful referenda of the latter period actually exhibit higher turnout rates than their failed counterparts of the 1880s. In one state, South Dakota, the prohibition movement sponsored two successful referenda, one in 1889 (turnout rate: 75.5%) and the other in 1916 (56.1%). Meanwhile, in Iowa the drys proposed a successful referendum in 1882 (73.7%), and one that failed in 1917 (62.2%). Finally, three states (Ohio, North Carolina, and Texas) held successful referenda in the Progressive Era which were distinguished by lower turnout than their failed precursors of the 1880s.

Given the comprehensive nature of the South's disfranchisement efforts, one should not be surprised that North Carolina and Texas held referenda in the Progressive Era with lower rates of voter participation by adult males than their referenda in the 1880s. However, the direct impact of black disfranchisement on the success of the southern branch of the Prohibition movement during the early twentieth century is difficult to measure. First, only three southern states held referenda in the 1880s.[70] While five Southern states[71] used referenda to enact prohibition after 1900, five others relied on legislative acts to establish statewide prohibition during the Progressive Era.[72] In addition, the drys of the latter period still managed to lose four referenda that they sponsored in the South despite the diminished voting power of southern blacks.[73] In fact, the success rate of southern dry referenda during the Progressive Era (55.6%) does not differ markedly from that of the nation as a whole (55%).

If anything, the disfranchisement of blacks principally enhanced the opportunity for dry success by eliminating one of the leading rationales for Democratic unity in the South. Along with the defeat of populism and the emergence of "lily-white" Republicanism, black disfranchisement made it safe for southern state Democratic parties to tolerate competition for party nominations. Using the newly installed primary system, political entrepreneurs like Edward Carmack (Tenn.), Hoke Smith (Ga.), and B. B. Comer (Ala.) challenged party stalwarts, sought statewide office, and were ultimately responsible for helping the prohibition movement to succeed at the state level. In other words, prohibition allowed these politicians to distinguish themselves from their more traditional Democratic rivals, and these entrepreneurs in turn assisted the drys by placing prohibition on the statewide agenda. As chapter 5 argues, a similar intraparty factional warfare characterized other state party systems during the Progressive Era, and thus contributed to the drys' opportunities to succeed in those states as well.

If the turnout data suggest that the demobilization of the American electorate after 1896 does not explain the success of the Progressive Era drys, then other factors must have been involved. As indicated above, this book maintains that the prohibition movement's gains were the product of both its internal dynamics and its external environment. Within these two broader categories are three crucial factors that shaped dry success: political strategy, movement ideology, and unstable political alignments. Because of unstable political alignments, the prohibitionists had the opportunity to hold referenda during both the 1880s and the Progressive Era. However, their disparate success in using direct legislation during these two periods reflected their ideology and their political strategies. Wedded to their strategic preference for state constitutional amendments, the radical drys of the 1880s failed to secure broad-based support for their prohibition referenda and subsequently succumbed to the "iron law of involution." In contrast, their twentieth-century counterparts evaded this law by initially focusing on modest, local anti-liquor policies, a strategy which mobilized thousands of new supporters for prohibition and helped win most referenda. In short, it was the movement's shift from a radical strategy of promoting constitutional prohibition to a moderate strategy of local gradualism that allowed it to make the most of favorable political developments.

The Origins of Strategy

Assuming that the Anti-Saloon League's local gradualism spurred a more effective movement than the radicals could muster, then one must grapple with another question: Why did local gradualism catch fire as a strategy in the Progressive Era and not during the 1880s? Scholars who have studied the origins of strategies adhere to the political process school, and concentrate on the effects of state structure, élite responses to movement activity, and the movement's likelihood of success. Unfortunately, these theorists usually focus on movement "forms" or "repertoires" of collective action, as discussed above. For example, Herbert Kitschelt concludes that when "political systems are open and weak," they invite assimilative strategies by movements, and when they are closed and have considerable implementation capacities, movements "are likely to adopt confrontational, disruptive strategies outside established policy channels."[74]

A more helpful political process explanation for the origins of strategy comes from Doug McAdam's recent work. He argues that social movement forms reflect specific changes in the structure of state institutions. Thus, a movement offered a new chance to participate in a given political institution will assume a strategy tailored to take advantage of that opportunity. For example, he cites the case of Ross Perot's independent candidacy in the American presidential election of 1992 as a response to "newly liberalized procedures and guidelines structuring the mobilization and operation of third party campaigns."[75]

While concurring with McAdam's overall approach, I maintain that scholars have failed to identify the most significant innovations in state structure when accounting for the origins of the Anti-Saloon League's strategy. Among other things, they have pointed to the widespread adoption of the primary system, the initiative and referendum, and local option after 1880 as developments which aided the ASL.[76] However, the league was frequently the proponent of these reforms, as well as their beneficiary, and only a portion of its success can be directly linked to these innovations. For example, of the thirty states to adopt state prohibition during the Progressive Era, only nine "went dry" because of the initiative and referendum. In the remaining twenty-one states, the anti-liquor forces succeeded with more traditional methods. In eight states, they prevailed on state legislatures to enact statutory prohibition; in ten, they successfully exploited direct legislation procedures predating 1898;[77] and in three others, they effectively combined these two approaches.[78] Likewise, local option as a dry resource was hardly a novelty during the late nineteenth century. Indeed, as early as the 1830s some state legislatures had experimented with diverse forms of local option laws.[79]

Rather, my study will underscore the importance of other alterations in the political landscape, namely the devolution of the state legislatures' liquor licensing power to localities, and the judiciary's growing acceptance of these licensing regimes. It should be noted that these two developments, which had their greatest impact on the anti-liquor movement after 1890, advanced other causes as well. For example, they also aided proponents of stock laws, who sought to ban cattle, pigs, sheep, and other animals from grazing on local roads and uninhabited lands. Like proponents of temperance, they secured general laws which allowed communities to vote either for or against closing the open range, and typically saw those laws upheld in court as legitimate delegations of state authority.[80] While the parallels between the anti-liquor movement and other reform endeavors are often striking and warrant future study,[81] they are not surprising. After all, devolution and its legal acceptance stemmed from a fundamental shift in élite attitudes about the democratic potential of state legislatures, and in particular from the demise of legislative supremacy as a governing principle. Indeed, the anti-liquor movement's ability to use local referenda should be viewed as an integral part of this broader development, to which the movement contributed and from which it profited.

That the ASL's strategy emerged from *both* changes in state structure and collective beliefs about the appropriate distribution of power would not be surprising to some students of social movement strategy. In contrast to analysts who focus solely on political opportunities to explain the origins of strategy, other scholars maintain that collective beliefs and values may also shape the strategic choices of movements. Lee Ann Banaszak, for one, contends that the distinctive strategies pursued by the American and Swiss woman suffrage movements reflected shared beliefs about the importance of political rights, contentious politics, and local autonomy.[82] Likewise, Richard F. Hamm argues that the drys' strategic shift from a purist to a pragmatic approach grew out of the changing character of the movement's beliefs about law. According to Hamm, before the 1890s the radicals in the Prohibition party and the WCTU held that the law was a moral code that should not legitimize evils like liquor. Influenced by these ideas, the radical prohibitionists adopted an abolitionist strategy, viewing total prohibition as the only appropriate solution to the liquor problem. Once the Anti-Saloon League emerged as the dominant temperance group during the 1890s, though, it reoriented the movement's strategy to a more pragmatic approach based on the belief that all law was useful rather than moral. Hence, the drys abandoned an exclusively abolitionist strategy and instead sought to use regulation as a *means* to abolition. In the process, they came to exploit the federal system as an ally in their crusade for national prohibition, a development which led to the Eighteenth Amendment.[83]

While this book confirms federalism's significance for the success of the Progressive Era drys, it questions Hamm's claim that the ASL's legal ideas were primarily responsible for the movement's adoption of local gradualism. To be sure, the ASL and other anti-liquor moderates were less inclined than the radicals to view law as a moral code which precluded partial anti-liquor measures. However, the moderates' pragmatic view of the law does not explain why they selected general local option laws as their preferred first steps in their gradualist strategy after 1895. After all, as chapters 2 and 3 will show, the Citizens' Law and Order League (CLOL) of the 1880s also held pragmatic legal beliefs, and yet failed to pursue local option as an immediate goal that would lead to national prohibition. Instead, the CLOL focused solely on law enforcement, and its crusade proved to be transitory in its achievements.

Nonetheless, Hamm's insights are valuable because they suggest that changes in collective beliefs can alter political behavior—an approach that is gaining prominence among students of political development.[84] With respect to the shift from constitutional prohibition to local option, the ideas which supported this development involved the principle of legislative supremacy and the shared sense that the state legislatures were no longer a reliable source of democracy and should thus be weakened. While the topic of collective beliefs will be taken up in chapter 4, their strategic impact and that of devolution are briefly summarized here.

The Devolution of Licensing Power, the Courts, and Legislative Supremacy

Outside New England, most early state liquor laws failed to give the localities the power to deny liquor licenses to qualified applicants. Hence, a community's ability to limit the liquor trade often depended on its corporate charter or on special legislation. Some towns and counties successfully petitioned the state legislatures for a charter or an act which would allow them to control the Demon Rum; others failed to do so. Anti-liquor activists soon found fault with these provincial methods of shaping local liquor policy: the provisions were too narrowly drawn, and too dependent on the whims of state and local officials. General local option laws, then, promised more direct and far-reaching results for temperance advocates during the antebellum period. In its classic form, a local option law authorized the voters of the locality in question to initiate an election[85] at which the electorate would vote directly on whether liquor should be licensed. An election initiated by the local option process was also known as a "no-license" election, which meant that no liquor licenses would be issued by local authorities if the anti-liquor forces triumphed.

Early experimentation with local option statutes suggested that they were a flawed approach to addressing the liquor problem. Weak enforcement provisions often permitted an illicit liquor traffic to flourish, and state legislatures responded by quickly repealing the statutes. Meanwhile, a series of state supreme court decisions rejected the local option principle on the grounds that it unconstitutionally delegated legislative power. According to the courts, only the state legislature could enact laws, and any attempt to transfer this authority to the people violated the principle of legislative supremacy. Thus, many teetotalers continued to encounter a variety of licensing regimes at the local level, a state of affairs which reflected the piecemeal character of incorporation, the growth of special legislation, and the discretion of local officials.

As the nineteenth century progressed, however, administrative reformers wearied of the parochialism and venality of the state legislatures, which preferred special acts to general legislation. In Pennsylvania, for instance, state lawmakers enacted 1,232 special laws but only fifty-four general laws in 1872. Moreover, many of the former favored moneyed interests, such as the railroads.[86] Consequently, reformers sought to limit the rising tide of local measures, and postbellum state constitutions increasingly banned special legislation and charters. In the wake of these reforms, most state legislatures could no longer rely on special acts to delegate the liquor question to municipalities and counties for resolution. Therefore, state lawmakers who were seeking to unload the troublesome liquor issue onto the localities could only do so through general laws. When they did so, though, they enabled moderate anti-liquor activists to exploit standardized procedures for abolishing the liquor traffic in their local communities, and that step, I argue, was a prerequisite to local gradualism as a national strategy.

While the comprehensive devolution of state licensing authority to the localities provided temperance moderates with similar avenues for local activism, they also benefited from the judiciary's growing tolerance of local referenda, especially with regard to liquor licensing. Led by two prominent judges, the state courts by 1890 abandoned their efforts to prevent the state legislatures from referring the liquor question to local communities for resolution. In doing so, they often drew on the same ideas that animated the critics of special legislation. If lawmakers chose to act in a cowardly fashion and voluntarily relinquished their control over this controversial issue, the judiciary signaled that it was no longer going to defend the principle of legislative supremacy. In fact, judges suggested that the people knew more than the legislature about local liquor conditions, and were well situated to make licensing decisions.[87] Of course, once the courts interpreted local option in a manner favorable to the drys, the moderates too could employ this technique without fear of judicial objection and could challenge the radicals for leadership of the movement. Furthermore, though the anti-liquor movement faced the most resistance from the judiciary in securing approval for local referenda, its success in this endeavor reinforced the courts' increasing tolerance of laws which referred local questions to popular disposition.

In short, legislative power had grown so suspect that reformers advocated both general laws and direct legislation to reduce the discretion of state lawmakers. If the state legislatures were too easily swayed by narrow interests, then they would have to be forced to take a broader view of the public interest. Conversely, if lawmakers lacked the appropriate knowledge to govern wisely, the people would supply it. It was within this broader political climate that local gradualism flourished, and that general local option laws and related measures[88] served as initial goals on the long road to prohibition.

The Plan of the Study

The remaining chapters provide evidence and further argument to substantiate the claims made here. They do not combine to form a chronological narrative of the anti-liquor crusade; instead, each chapter (except for chapter 8) focuses on a different dimension of the movement, and traces the movement's development with respect to that dimension. Though covering some of the same historical terrain more than once, this structure is necessary to systematically isolate those aspects of the movement which may have shaped its outcome and its strategic choices.

Chapter 2 analyzes the development of the prohibition movement and its component organizations. In doing so, it sketches the formation of two parallel sets of organizations: the broadly focused radicals and the locally oriented moderates. Moreover, it contends that the movement's shift in political strategy after 1895 was not the product of organizational adaptation but rather reflected the moderates' resolve to focus on local option as their initial goal. Meanwhile, chapter 3 focuses on the origins of the movement's tactics, and seeks to explain how temperance reformers engaged in modular collective action in a federal system. In addition, it shows that the anti-liquor movement relied on a relatively stable repertoire of collective action, and demonstrates that disruptive protest tended to dissipate the movement's energies rather than to advance its goals.

Next, chapter 4 traces the development of prohibition amendments and local option as national movement goals. It shows how changes in state structure and new beliefs about the appropriate distribution of power shaped the anti-liquor movement's political strategy. While chapter 4 focuses on the origins of political strategy, chapter 5 underscores the significance of unstable political alignments in creating the opportunities for movement success. This chapter argues that the source of this instability in the 1880s was intense *inter*party competition whereas during the Progressive Era, *intra*party competition produced dry access to direct legislation and other means of influencing policy.

Chapter 6 then examines how the movement's decision to agitate at the local level enhanced prohibition's appeal. It analyzes state referendum campaigns, and demonstrates that the Progressive Era drys' local gradualism contributed to the mobilization of new adherents and to their impressive success at the polls. In a similar vein, chapter 7 surveys the careers of movement activists who were initially averse to the prohibition message, but who were drawn into the movement by their participation in modest local campaigns. These activists include Washington Gladden (a minister who advocated the Social Gospel) and Robert A. Woods (a settlement house worker).

Finally, the concluding chapter compares the prohibition movement's experience with that of other social movements. In particular, it considers American movements which effectively exploited local gradualism (the civil rights movement and the Christian Right), as well as one which has failed to make use of this strategy (the environmental movement). The chapter closes with some thoughts about the origins of movement moderation.

2 Churches, Lodges, and Dry Organizing

At the heart of this book lies the claim that a movement's choice of political strategy largely determines whether it will succeed. Moreover, strategic choices are derived from both changes in state structure and new ideas about the appropriate distribution of political power. The emergence of movement strategies, however, cannot be understood without some reference to organizational dynamics. For if "strategy" is "how a social movement defines and pursues its goals," then "organization" can be considered the arena where strategies are proposed, debated, accepted, and ultimately implemented.

Indeed, some social movement scholars have evinced a distinct appreciation for the impact of organizational factors on strategy. For example, some sociologists contend that social movement organizations shift their goals and tactics in a manner conducive to their survival.[1] Hence, the anti-liquor movement's adoption of "local gradualism" could be viewed as an act of self-preservation which allowed dry organizations to regroup after the largely disastrous 1880s. This "organizational adaptation" approach, though, fails to accurately describe either local gradualism's emergence or the behavior of the principal dry groups of the period, namely the Prohibition party and the Woman's Christian Temperance Union. Although conscious of the young Anti-Saloon League and its advocacy of local gradualism as a national strategy in the 1890s, these two organizations cleaved to a maximalist strategy until the early 1900s, a seemingly suicidal decision on their part.

More to the point, this approach presumes that a movement is governed by a centrally organized group which can alter its political strategy at will. As the account below shows, a movement's grassroots components possess discrete collective interests as social networks in their own right, interests which do not always coincide with the strategic preferences of the movement's leading organization(s). The evangelical Protestant churches, for one, rhetorically opposed the liquor traffic as resolutely as the maximalist WCTU and Prohibition party. However, their primary function as religious communities deterred them from embracing these groups' all-or-nothing radicalism, lest they alienate their heterogeneous congregations.

Significantly, "organization" refers to more than just those formal associations which seek to orchestrate social movements. Rather, these formal groups achieve their greatest potential when they can exploit the muscle of a more elemental layer of organization, namely the social networks in which people live, work, worship, and socialize. If properly meshed, these two layers of organization might form a strong web of collective action, "sufficiently robust to structure sustained relations with opponents, but flexible enough to permit the informal connections that link people and networks to one another to . . . coordinate contention."[2] Balancing organizational stability, its linkages with informal social networks, and innovation would be a challenge for the American prohibition movement and its constituent organizations. While the anti-liquor crusade enjoyed both long-lived formal associations and stable sources of grassroots support, strategic innovation often involved a complete reconfiguration of the movement's organizational structure. Ultimately, as this chapter shows, a new formal society, the ASL, had to confront existing groups to alter the anti-liquor movement's direction, and the Protestant churches only provided a stable organizational foundation for local gradualism after the League had implemented a political strategy in harmony with the churches' political and organizational inclinations.

In addition to dislodging the political strategy of long-established dry organizations, the Anti-Saloon League achieved another organizational feat, namely the creation of a truly national federation with the potential to mobilize new adherents to the dry cause. This accomplishment was particularly noteworthy, for it involved overcoming regional differences in the prohibition movement's development, which saw the North's orthodox drys struggle to gain a foothold in the South. Instead of insisting that the southern drys subscribe to radical views about prohibition, racial integration, or women's rights, the ASL sought to adapt the South's political strategy to the North, and to create an inclusive organization in line with interdenominational Protestantism that avoided the pitfalls of ideologically rigid membership associations like the WCTU and the Independent Order of Good Templars.

In the antebellum period, temperance activists pioneered two distinct solutions to the problem of coordinating collective action: working through the evangelical Protestant churches, and exploiting the tight-knit networks of the dry fraternal lodges. These two models, as well as some of their associated formal organizations, left a rich legacy for the postwar prohibition movement. Hence, the first part of this chapter reviews the prohibition movement's antebellum roots. Although political temperance activity during the years 1830–60 was less widespread and sustained than it became during the postwar period, antebellum teetotalers nonetheless set the stage for the church-based and lodge-based groups to come.

In the wake of the Civil War, the prohibition movement revived as a multilayered movement with two parallel sets of organizations: the broadly focused radicals and the locally oriented moderates. Before the national Anti-Saloon League's formation in 1895, moderates and radicals varied in strength by geographical region, and hence tended to skirmish rather than directly clash. Between 1875 and 1895, the radicals worked through a lodge-based network to assume leadership of the northern movement, and strove primarily for constitutional prohibition and prohibition through the efforts of a third party or partisan prohibition. In contrast, the moderates used church-based organizations to dominate southern temperance efforts, and urged the passage and exploitation of locally oriented laws. The second part of this chapter traces the northern radicals' development, while the third narrates the saga of the southern moderates and the rise of their northern counterparts. In the end, of course, it was the northern moderates who proposed "local gradualism" as a national—as opposed to a purely regional—movement strategy.

Anti-Liquor Organizing in Antebellum America

To say that the prohibition movement "emerged" after the Civil War would be misleading. Rather, the movement's resurgence in this period merely constituted a renaissance of the American temperance movement's political wing, which had existed for at least fifty years.[3] After 1810 a few scattered temperance groups operated in the Northeast, but as they sought to recruit a constituency of local notables, they failed to produce grassroots interest in temperance reform. In general, these organizations eschewed politics and promoted moderation in drinking rather than abstinence.[4] By the mid-1820s, however, the temperance movement had acquired a mass base and sought to galvanize support for both an increasingly alcohol-free way of life and for political action to reinforce it.

As many historians have pointed out, the antebellum temperance crusade radically challenged America's drinking practices in the early nineteenth century. In fact, Mark E. Lender and James K. Martin assert that "the period from the 1790s to the early 1830s was probably the heaviest drinking era" in American history.[5] The vast quantities of liquor consumed by Americans before 1840 only make sense in the context of early American social customs. Contemporary medical wisdom held that liquor was both a necessary part of the diet and a treatment for various ailments. As a result, Americans drank at sunrise, during the workday (instead of coffee breaks), at meals, after meals (to assist in digestion), and before retiring (to sleep). In addition, Americans considered liquor to be integral to entertaining and social gatherings, quaffing it at weddings, barn raisings, and ordinations.[6]

For many years, liberal drinking provoked only occasional reproaches from religious and political leaders, perhaps because community norms against habitual drunkenness could be upheld in the early Republic's small, stable townships. By the mid-1820s, however, activists concerned with high rates of "tippling" formed temperance groups in every state, although organizing was particularly successful in New England, New York, and Ohio's Western Reserve.[7] The initial geographical distribution of temperance activity reflected the movement's roots in two contemporary developments: the onset of the industrial revolution; and the intense evangelical revivals known as the Second Great Awakening, which climaxed during the years 1825–37 and thrived in New England, New York, and the Western Reserve.[8]

Before 1860 the Northeast in particular experienced a vast increase in the scale of industry as household production moved into factories. During this upheaval, the entrepreneurs who embraced technological and economic change often encouraged a moral transformation of society as well. As witnesses to the revivals of the Second Great Awakening (in which they often took part), these "improvers" had accepted the perfectibility of human nature, and, in their quest for progress, sought to ameliorate the impact of drinking on themselves, their employees, and their communities. In doing so, these middle-class reformers promoted sobriety as a virtue of the Protestant work ethic to ensure a harmonious and prosperous economic order.[9]

Middle-class "improvers" were joined by legions of Protestant women, "who took seriously the claims of evangelical clergy that women were morally superior" to men and who recognized that "temperance could encompass a number of issues of special concern to women." Indeed, temperance could be a weapon against the alcoholic husband, as well as a shield from the physical abuse associated with drunkenness. It could save a woman and her children from economic destitution, and rescue husbands and fathers. Moreover, their special interest in destroying the Demon Rum meant that women could agitate for temperance without offending current social sensibilities about woman's position. Though initially unrepresented in the movement's leadership, women accounted for 35–60% of the membership in temperance groups during the 1830s.[10]

As the temperance movement evolved, its followers battled over the soul of the movement. Moderate drinkers first struggled with those who abstained entirely from rum, whiskey, and other "ardent spirits."[11] Later, those who consumed less intoxicating beverages (such as wine, ale, and cider) vied with those who abstained from all alcoholic beverages, known as "teetotalers" or supporters of "total abstinence." In addition, warring Protestant ministers scoured the Bible for scriptural ammunition in their dispute over wine in communion rites. After some debate, by 1840 the teetotalers managed to impose their views on most temperance societies, and a pledge of total abstinence from all alcoholic beverages became a standard membership requirement in almost every group.[12]

The decision to enter politics would also be controversial, though many temperance activists considered enlisting the government's aid in the early years of reform. These agitators viewed temperance as a political issue partly because they regarded drinking as a social problem rather than a personal failing. While the movement did portray drunkenness as an individual tragedy, it also frequently highlighted its damage to others, their property, the family, public virtue, and the preservation of the community. However, some temperance advocates insisted that the damage caused by the Demon Rum could be corrected within the private realm, as churches and temperance societies wielded faith and reason to convince others of temperance's great benefits. In response, political activists also argued that the temperance issue was inextricably bound to the state, given the government's role in licensing and regulating the sale and manufacture of liquor.[13]

At first, temperance politics focused primarily on the local level.[14] As the 1830s progressed, however, state-level politics appeared to be the solution to the uncoordinated and sporadic temperance efforts in the local political arena. In 1838, for example, the movement's petitions flooded several state legislatures, demanding anti-liquor measures. Temperance editors, pleased that "their forces were no longer a negligible element in the body politic," noted "the unusual consideration which their cause was receiving from professional politicians."[15] In the years 1838–39 teetotalers won seven statewide victories,[16] including the enactment of the celebrated fifteen-gallon law (which banned selling liquor in amounts of less than fifteen gallons) by the Whig-dominated Massachusetts legislature.[17] Although repealed in 1840, the fifteen-gallon law taught politicians two lessons. First, as the Whig governor Edward Everett learned, partial prohibition could disrupt party unity. By the fall of 1838, the new liquor policy's unpopularity provoked dissension among the Whigs, leading to the nomination of liberal Whig tickets and to Everett's defeat in 1839. Second, the liquor question could mobilize new voters; in Massachusetts, citizens angered by the fifteen-gallon law turned out in droves to support the Democratic gubernatorial candidate, Marcus Morton.[18]

After the fifteen-gallon debacle and the failure of similar experiments elsewhere,[19] most politicians avoided statewide prohibitory legislation until the early 1850s, when the northern Whig party came unglued. In the meantime, politically

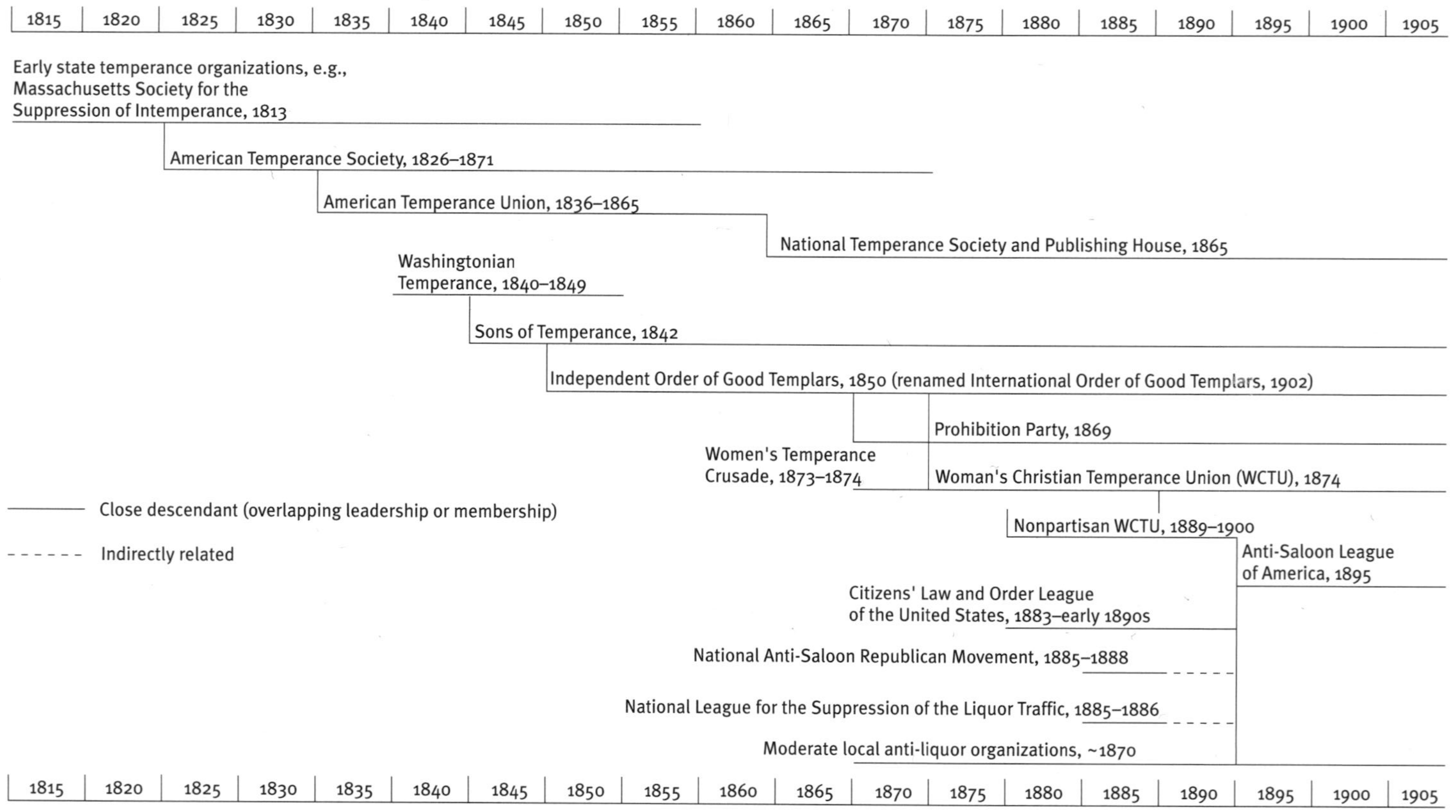

Figure 2 Development of the National Temperance Movement, 1815–1905

oriented teetotalers resumed their local efforts amid the turmoil of two new developments in the anti-drink movement: the rise of temperance revivals, and the subsequent creation of a national fraternal order, the Sons of Temperance. As a major participant in the prohibition campaigns of the 1850s, the Sons possessed several advantages over earlier national groups, the evangelical American Temperance Society (ATS) and American Temperance Union (ATU), including their capacity to closely supervise its local lodges and their broad appeal to secular as well as southern audiences. Despite such differences, though, the Sons and their forerunners would become prohibitionists by the 1850s.

Evangelical Federations and Secular Brotherhoods

All the temperance movement's internal conflicts—including that between the supporters of "moral suasion" and its more politically inclined adherents—unfolded within an organizational milieu. Temperance conventions and meetings provided public arenas for these disputes, and activists deliberated over resolutions with the seriousness of legislators considering major laws. Before 1860 four nationally based organizations sought to coordinate temperance activities in the United States: the American Temperance Society and its offshoot the American Temperance Union, and the Sons of Temperance and its offshoot the Independent Order of Good Templars (IOGT; figure 2).

Above all, the American Temperance Society and the American Temperance Union represented the evangelical Protestants' ambitions within the antebellum temperance movement. The religious character of these two groups reflected their common roots in the "benevolent empire," a loose network of Protestant voluntary associations founded during the Second Great Awakening. Primarily dedicated to missionary work, the benevolent empire countered what it saw as the domestic threats of Unitarianism, Universalism, Catholicism, irreligion, and frontier vice by systematically proselytizing for evangelical Protestantism.[20] Although temperance activity formed a semi-secular offshoot of the empire, the ATS and the ATU nonetheless inherited many of its leaders, imitated its organizations' structures, embraced its mobilization techniques, and shared its assumptions about the import of human action in achieving salvation and a better world.[21]

As one of the earliest national membership societies, the American Temperance Society was established in 1826 by sixteen prominent evangelicals, virtually all of whom had participated in the benevolent empire's reform efforts.[22] Given their background, these activists understandably fashioned an organization which mirrored the earlier reform societies' structure, a model which has been summarized as follows:

> The . . . arrangement was for the national society to have local affiliates. . . . These auxiliaries collected and spent funds, passed out propaganda, and engaged in work of their own. Connections between them and the parent society were often quite loose and disharmonious. . . . Annual conventions brought together members from throughout the union, where they proposed resolutions, listened to inspiring oratory, elected officers, and quarreled. For the rest of the year most of the national society's affairs were left to a board of managers or an executive committee. It oversaw production and distribution of printed material, tried to meet expenses, and . . . supervised paid agents who traveled about on the society's business.[23]

Organized on these principles, the ATS achieved little control over its local affiliates.[24] Indeed, the parochial political efforts of the early 1830s reflected the vagaries of individual temperance societies rather than any policy directives from the American Temperance Society.

Despite its decentralized nature, the ATS was nonetheless credited with organizing many of the 2,204 local temperance societies reported to be in existence by 1831, 70.6% of which were in New York, New England, and the Western Reserve.[25] Pioneering mobilization techniques later adopted by the Anti-Saloon League, the ATS hired itinerant agents to visit evangelical assemblies, synods, conferences, and, most importantly, church congregations, all of which were encouraged to organize temperance societies. Adopting the guise of evangelical missionaries, ATS agents delivered emotional sermons punctuated with biblical and perfectionist imagery.[26] According to these evangelists, salvation and sobriety went hand in hand, as "the Holy Spirit will not visit, much less will He dwell with him who is under the polluting, debasing effects of intoxicating drink."[27] While many communities spontaneously created unrelated temperance groups, hundreds of local churches directly responded to these agents' exhortations and founded ATS affiliates.

Early success by ATS agents in the Northeast proved especially difficult to replicate in one region: the South. Above all, this society's failure to thoroughly organize the South stemmed from the birth of radical abolitionism, which in 1830 emerged from the same evangelical network that had created the ATS. Prominent abolitionists not only participated in the ATS and its affiliates but were often their leaders, a relationship which did not go unnoticed in the South. Incidents such as the one in 1835, when Georgia subscribers to the *Temperance Recorder* were deluged with abolition literature, merely verified Southern suspicions that the temperance and antislavery movements were connected. In this case, the Georgia Temperance Society officially broke with the ATS, and advised its members to cancel their subscriptions to the *Recorder*.[28] If southerners suspected the ATS of undermining their "local institutions," many northern reformers hardly concealed their distaste for slavery when agitating below the Mason-Dixon line. One arm of the benevolent empire, the American Home Missionary Society (AHMS), often combined temperance activism with general proselytizing, and in the early 1830s it had helped found several ATS affiliates in the South. By the mid-1830s, however, as abolitionism permeated the evangelical ranks, many northern AHMS missionaries stationed in the South requested transfers to the free states, asserting that "slavery seems to paralyze Christian effort, benumb Christian feeling and prostrate . . . Christian morals."[29]

Aside from nurturing local temperance societies, the ATS could claim but one other organizational feat before it was eclipsed by the American Temperance Union: the formation of state temperance societies. While many of these state societies faded rapidly, particularly those in the South, the hardier ones would reaffiliate with the American Temperance Union and contribute to its efforts. A direct descendent of the ATS, the American Temperance Union issued from its parent in 1836, when the officers of the ATS and its affiliates fulfilled the pledge they had made in 1833 to act as a society called the American Temperance Union.[30] After this mass exodus, the ATS ceased organizing, and devoted its energies to publishing and circulating temperance literature.[31]

The American Temperance Union turned out to be little more than a contentious version of its predecessor. While intended to unify the temperance community, the ATU was instead the battleground for the clashes over total abstinence and prohibitory policies. At the convention of 1833, at which members vowed to form the ATU, activists engaged in the first national debate about using legal means to destroy the tyranny of ardent spirits; in 1836 the ATU convention was convulsed by a successful attempt to insert a ban on fermented liquors in the organization's pledge. By 1840, however, the ATU had quelled internal dissent and endorsed both prohibition and total abstinence, though its commitment to the former only extended to local prohibition after the fifteen-gallon fiasco.[32] These two positions may have alienated some affiliates,[33] and yet they mirrored the "ultraist" tendencies that drove analogous crusades (such as the abolition and peace movements) to adopt increasingly extreme and divisive policies in the 1830s.[34]

After 1840 the ATU shared leadership of the temperance movement with secular temperance advocates, such as the Washingtonians and the Sons of Temperance (described below). While the ATU initially welcomed secular activism, the erosion of its affiliates in the early 1840s prompted leaders to excoriate their rivals for their coarse entertainments, irreligiosity, resistance to political action, and, in the case of fraternal orders, affinity to other secret societies.[35] Despite the ATU's declining base, leaders remained influential advocates of political temperance, and in the late 1840s they abandoned their acrimonious attitudes to band with the Sons of Temperance as that group entered the political fray. In fact, once the political climate became more propitious, many ATU activists took the lead in mobilizing the North for stringent state prohibition laws, commonly known as "Maine Laws," which banned the manufacture and sale of alcoholic beverages and established penalties for violations.[36] Meanwhile the ATU had failed to repair its precursor's rift with the southern wing of evangelical temperance, and sustained only minimal relations with the region after the late 1830s.[37] A more systematic organization of the South for prohibition would be accomplished by a group with fewer ties to both evangelical Protestantism and abolitionism, namely the Sons of Temperance.

At first glance, the Sons of Temperance and the Good Templars could be dismissed as merely "dry Masons." Indeed, the two groups developed elaborate organizations with a myriad of offices bearing ostentatious titles, and both promoted colorful regalia, secret handshakes, passwords, and rituals. However, these organizations could also be considered the temperance equivalent of "free spaces," or "environments in which people are able to learn a new self-respect, a deeper and more assertive group identity, public skills, and values of cooperation and civic virtue."[38] Temperance revivals often inspired thousands to pledge abstinence, but it was the lodges of the Sons and Templars which became lasting sanctuaries for teetotalers seeking to solidify their dry lifestyles within a community setting.

In their early years, the Sons drew most of their supporters from temperance revivals, which borrowed from the evangelical tradition without subscribing to its religious principles. Indeed, the founders of the Sons of Temperance were all veterans of the Washingtonian revivals, so named for the nation's first president. Initiated in 1840 by six reformed drunkards, these revivals appealed to almost every segment of society: drinkers and nondrinkers, humble artisans and prominent businessmen, religious and secular audiences. As the engine that drove Washingtonian temperance, the "experience meeting" involved the emotional testimony of reformed drunkards, who relived the horrors of their rum-soaked lives in graphic detail and then affirmed the joys of their redemption. Enthralled, audience members would immediately take the pledge and presumably join the growing ranks of the abstinent.[39]

During the winter of 1842–43, however, Washingtonianism had crested. As Samuel F. Cary, a prominent Son, recounted, "There was no *organized* effort, either to reform or keep the reformed inebriate. All seemed to act from one benevolent impulse, without system, without concert, without in short, any of the elements of permanence or stability. The *pledge was all*; there were no regular meetings, no discipline, no systematic way of securing contributions to sustain the reformed, or keep up the interest."[40] In September 1842 New York participants in the Washingtonian revivals founded the Sons of Temperance, a fraternal order which sought to compensate for the defects of Washingtonian temperance by providing communal support for the newly abstinent. In general, the Sons employed two major techniques to protect its members from temptation: systematically applied peer pressure and the maintenance of alcohol-free social centers, or local "division"[41] rooms.

Peer pressure involved both the informal surveillance of fraternal brothers and the use of investigating and lookout committees. At weekly meetings, the leadership routinely asked, "Has any brother violated the Pledge?" As required by the order's constitution, members who knew of a violation reported the offending brother to an investigating committee, which then made discreet inquiries into his personal character.[42] Although the Sons sought to redeem the penitent offender, persistent violators ultimately faced expulsion, a not infrequent event. According to division reports, about 10 percent of the order's members were expelled annually during the early 1850s, the peak of the Sons' popularity.[43]

While close regulation of personal behavior constituted the stick wielded by the Sons, the local division room, with a genial atmosphere and calendar of "cold water"[44] events, was the carrot.[45] Designed to replace the barroom within the teetotaler's social life, the division room sponsored plays, debates, and musical entertainments. During the summer months, local divisions moved their social activities outdoors, sponsoring picnics, barbecues, and elaborate Fourth of July celebrations, which often included parades in regalia.[46] Beyond entertaining, the local division also sharpened its members' public skills by engaging them in the affairs of a multitiered democratic organization. The membership annually elected the division's officers, who represented them at Grand (state) Division meetings and chose the members of the National Division. Moreover, active Sons became involved in defining the order's regulations and judicial decisions. In doing so, they not only learned the rules of parliamentary order but also improved their rhetorical abilities in debates characterized by "persuasive, spirited, explanatory and judicial discussions, habitually controlled by constitutional law and . . . republican rule."[47]

The Sons' vibrant internal politics complemented their entry into the frenetic world of antebellum party politics. Although their precursors, the Washingtonians, typically avoided political action, the Sons entered politics by the mid-1840s. Initially, the extent of the Sons' political undertakings varied by locality. For instance, while state and local divisions in Ohio and Virginia actively sought the repeal of licensing laws in the period 1846–47, the Pennsylvania Sons refused to counsel any specific political action for its members at this time.[48] By 1848, though, northern divisions of the Sons began to inch toward prohibition. At a meeting of the Ohio Grand Division in July 1848, prohibitionists pushed through a resolution calling for a ban on the sale of intoxicating liquors on pain of imprisonment.[49] Later denounced by the larger community of Ohio Sons, this resolution nonetheless foreshadowed similar actions in other states.[50] As the prohibition wave accelerated in 1852, the Grand Worthy

Patriarch of the National Division, Samuel F. Cary, spoke for many Sons when he declared that "the aim is no longer to regulate or restrain the hydra-headed Liquor Traffic—but to exterminate it root and branch from the face of the earth."[51]

In contrast to both the ATS and ATU, the Sons flourished in the South. National Division statistics reveal that the southern contingent of the Sons grew from 6.3 percent of the national membership in 1847 to 35.6 percent at the group's peak in 1851.[52] Given that only 22.2 percent of the nation's white population lived in the region in 1850,[53] the South's representation in the Sons of Temperance was clearly disproportionate.[54] Lagging somewhat behind the North, the southern Sons only began advocating prohibitory policies during the early 1850s. In 1852, for example, the North Carolina Grand Division petitioned the state legislature for a prohibitory liquor law.[55] Likewise, a meeting of the Tennessee Grand Division in 1853 urged the clergy to join them in promoting a "system of measures which we hope may result in the entire suppression of Intemperance in our State."[56]

Just as the national Sons peaked with 221,187 members in 1851, a new temperance fraternal order emerged in upstate New York: the Independent Order of Good Templars.[57] While not a direct outgrowth of the Sons,[58] the IOGT ultimately recruited some of their members and resembled them in numerous ways.[59] The Templars maintained local lodges, which like the Sons' division rooms evoked "a world of commitment and fellowship, of work and good times, in which members became part of a community, enlivened by personal relationships, ennobled by a sense of purpose." Replicating the Sons' multi-tiered democracy, local Templars elected Grand (state) Lodges, which chose representatives to the national (and later international) Right Worthy Grand Lodge. Indeed, Theda Skocpol et al. view the IOGT's adoption of the Sons' three-tiered structure as evidence that nineteenth-century Americans had converged on an associational model, one that "imitated and paralleled the US constitutional order" (federal, state, local).[60] Finally, the Templars supported the Sons' contention that legal means were required to solve the "tippling problem." Early on, the Templars' political efforts varied by locality,[61] but by 1859 the Right Worthy Grand Lodge formally endorsed "the absolute Prohibition of the manufacture, importation and the sale of intoxicating liquors," a principle which animated the group's political efforts in years to come.[62]

Despite such strong similarities, the Templars diverged from the Sons in two important respects, both of which reflected the Templars' greater inclusivity. First, while both groups relied upon dues-paying members to sustain their operations, the Templars alone decided not to maintain a mutual insurance program. Their rejection of insurance enabled the Templars to keep dues low and to offer membership to those who might otherwise be excluded because of age, poor health, or inability to pay into a beneficiary scheme. Second, the IOGT sought to fully integrate families into the order,[63] and it admitted women as full members from its inception in the early 1850s. Although the Sons finally granted full membership privileges to women in 1866,[64] the Templars offered them more leadership opportunities, and, as discussed below, helped give rise to the WCTU.[65]

At mid-century the prohibition movement enjoyed an unexpected surge of support which overshadowed both the birth of the Templars and the peak of the Sons' membership. After 1850 the Free Soil party began to sponsor state prohibition laws in an attempt to revive its own sagging fortunes, and to complete the dissolution of the party system that it had begun in 1848. In doing so, the Free Soil party not only supplied northern teetotalers with increasingly fluid political conditions but also gave to prohibition a prominent place on the political agenda. Seizing on this unexpected opportunity, dry leaders set out to navigate the capricious course of a party system in flux. As a result of their skillful endeavors, thirteen state and territorial legislatures enacted statutory prohibition.[66]

After 1855, however, prohibition suffered innumerable setbacks. Despite dry efforts to reinforce the ineffectual local police, Maine Laws proved difficult to enforce, and violations were soon rampant. The state courts hardly helped; in some cases, legal challenges to prohibition laws succeeded in weakening or overturning them.[67] Meanwhile, the statutory character of prohibition prompted further legislative action, much of it sponsored by the pro-liquor forces. In some states, the wets definitively revoked prohibition once they controlled the legislature; in others, prohibition would be strengthened, diluted, repealed, or reinstated, depending on the legislature's makeup.[68] By 1875 only three Maine Laws persisted as lasting features of the political landscape—those of Maine itself, Vermont, and New Hampshire—and they were not vigorously enforced.

If the drys proved incapable of preserving many Maine Laws, they also appeared unlikely to achieve new prohibition triumphs in the near future. For one thing, with the reconstitution of the two-party system complete by 1856, prohibition became a distraction.[69] In addition, dry organizations had fallen into disarray. Wracked by prohibition's collapse as a viable issue, as well as by internal dissension,[70] most antiliquor organizations steadily lost support as the 1850s progressed. For example, after surpassing 220,000 members in 1851, the Sons suffered average net losses of 28,000 members a year until 1857, after which membership stabilized around 50,000 before briefly rising again.[71] Similarly, the ATU's decline accelerated during the 1850s, setting the stage for the organization's overhaul in 1865.[72] Even the Independent Order of Good Templars, just founded in 1851, could not fully capitalize on its competitors' waning strength. Despite its novelty and inclusivity, the IOGT signed up only 53,003 members by 1858—thus absorbing far fewer than the 174,049 members lost by the

Sons in these years.[73] Moreover, these Templar gains would be diminished in 1861 by the onset of the Civil War, which generated mass desertions in every temperance organization as teetotalers across the nation mobilized for the war effort.

The Lodge-Based Network and the Formation of the Radical Wing

The ATS, the ATU, the Sons of Temperance, and the Good Templars all weathered the Civil War in some fashion. While the ATS transferred its funds to the Massachusetts Temperance Society and vanished in 1871,[74] the ATU was reorganized in 1865 as the National Temperance Society, an association known primarily for its newspaper and publishing house. Meanwhile, the Sons would never again claim more than 100,000 members in the United States, and yet they endured as a committed force for prohibition. Of the four antebellum groups, the Good Templars would have the greatest impact on dry politics during the late nineteenth century, for several reasons. First, membership in the IOGT soared from its wartime base of 35,000 to over 300,000 toward the end of the 1860s and later stabilized at just over 200,000, a level at which it remained through 1889.[75] Moreover, the IOGT initiated the first successful state constitutional amendment campaign in Kansas, which inspired drys everywhere to adopt the same approach. Finally, as a parent organization of the Prohibition party and the Woman's Christian Temperance Union, the Templars maintained close ties with both and was a valuable ally during the prohibition campaigns of the 1880s.

Immediately after the Civil War, then, the national fraternal orders continued to supply strategy, leaders, and grassroots activists to the prohibition movement. On the other hand, the ATU's decline from a loose federation into little more than a publishing house reduced the influence of evangelical Protestant leaders in the national movement.[76] Outside the movement's distinctive southern wing, this absence of prominent evangelicals in the dry leadership made it difficult for anti-liquor organizations to systematically engage ordinary church members in their political efforts. Of course, the fraternal orders and their offspring often courted the Protestant churches, even while offering church leaders a minimal role in directing the anti-liquor crusade. In particular, the Protestant churches were desirable allies because they could provide legitimacy, an organizational base, and funds for the national movement. Hence, the national drys often prayed for the day when every cleric and every denominational assembly would oppose prohibition as fervently as they did.[77] As of 1895, however, the northern evangelical churches remained an untapped wellspring of prohibition strength, and hence a possible base for the moderate anti-liquor movement.

As the fraternal orders entered the movement's leadership in 1865, the dry lodges became influential centers of strategic innovation. Their two most significant contributions to cold water strategy—third-party prohibition and constitutional prohibition—set standards of doctrinal purity that helped define the movement's radical wing as it took shape in the years 1867–80. By proposing these strategies, fraternal entrepreneurs sought novel ways of circumventing the often unreliable Democrats and Republicans. Clearly, the formation of a new political party by the Prohibitionists[78] would directly challenge the parties in the electoral arena (see the discussion of the party below). In contrast, constitutional prohibition was designed to liberate the major parties from directly engaging the issue of prohibition at all, particularly at the state level.[79] By only requiring the parties to submit prohibition for a popular vote, state constitutional prohibition shifted responsibility for the substantive choice away from the easily swayed state legislators and into the hands of the people.[80] Naturally, if a dry referendum passed, party élites faced the disagreeable task of enacting and implementing the legislation required to activate the constitutional provision. However, if such a measure failed, party leaders could wash their hands of prohibition, for "the people had spoken."

Of these two paths to dry nirvana, constitutional prohibition had the broadest appeal, and fidelity to it tended to separate the orthodox anti-liquor activists from their more moderate counterparts during the 1880s.[81] In fact, outside their nonpartisan work for constitutional prohibition, third-party drys often occupied the movement's lunatic fringe.[82] Even Prohibitionists, though, appreciated constitutional prohibition's appeal as an immediate goal. While every dry amendment inserted in a state constitution before 1914 would be proposed by major party legislators and ratified in nonpartisan elections, Prohibitionists nonetheless argued that "constitutional amendment is the American method of revolution," by which "our Government provides for a revolution by ballots instead of a revolution of bullets."[83] The national party chairman John B. Finch may have held that constitutional prohibition could only be "made effective by a live national party pledged to carry out its provisions as a matter of policy," and yet his party toiled diligently for dry amendments during the 1880s.[84]

First promoted as a movement goal by the New York Sons in 1857,[85] constitutional prohibition resurfaced after the war at a temperance conference in Chicago in 1875. During this meeting, one delegate offered a resolution in favor of a national prohibition amendment, which sparked petition campaigns by several groups, including the Prohibition party.[86] Likewise, several Midwestern affiliates of the IOGT and the WCTU initiated state amendment campaigns during the late 1870s.[87] Hence, state constitutional prohibition would make its most stunning postwar debut in Kansas. In 1878 a Kansas Templar named J. R. Detwiler persuaded the state's Grand Lodge to support a prohibition amendment to the Kansas constitution. Along with the Kansas State Temperance Union and the WCTU, the Templars then mobilized a winning referendum campaign in 1880.[88] From then on, state constitutional prohibition galvanized the fraternal orders, the WCTU, the Prohibition party, a smattering of church leaders, and assorted other reformers. As one radical activist noted in 1881, "we are all agreed on this question of constitutional prohibition."[89]

An additional premise of the radical wing—total abstinence—also appealed to many moderates, and yet their approach to this ideal differed from that of the orthodox drys. Though typically teetotalers themselves, the moderates hesitated to impose this standard on potential political allies, whereas the radicals had no such qualms. Significantly, the radicals believed that the success of anti-liquor laws depended on the moral character of their public administrators, one vital element of which was total abstinence. In short, personal decisions about the consumption of alcohol had broader political and social consequences which the radicals refused to ignore. For example, the WCTU passed resolutions at its first convention which opposed intemperate men in office, and demanded that liquor be banished from public banquets and the tables of public officials.[90] Similarly, the Prohibition party maintained that true reform required abstinent officials who opposed the Demon Rum out of personal conviction, for "when the righteous are in authority, the people rejoice."[91]

According to Richard F. Hamm, the radicals' strong preference for such virtuous governance stemmed from their propensity to equate law and morality. Specifically, he contends that the orthodox drys inherited their legal ideals from antislavery extremists, who held that law ought to promote morality and should not legitimate evil. Hence, just as these prohibitionists rejected legal solutions to the liquor problem short of total prohibition, they could not stomach a government dominated by corrupt officials enslaved to the Demon Rum. After all, such a government could hardly foster civic morality or create a just society.[92] Though Hamm portrays the radicals' legal ideas as out of step with the dominant legal culture, their tendency to hold authorities to their own high moral standards seems only natural in light of their shared parentage: the fraternal orders, where virtuous private behavior was required. Together the WCTU, the party, and the fraternal orders would form a national lodge-based network that dominated the northern prohibition movement until 1895.

The Sons and the Templars both manifested a structure that virtually ensured exclusivity. With centrally imposed membership requirements and a close scrutiny of individual behavior, these two fraternal orders expended a great deal of energy deciding who conformed to their standards and who did not. Indeed, both groups devoted a substantial portion of their state and international lodge proceedings to the adjudication of appeals from suspended members and lodges. Above all, however, the Sons and the Templars insisted that their members strive for two unequivocal goals: total abstinence and prohibition. Pledged to uphold these imperatives, and ensconced in a group of like-minded peers, fraternal brothers and sisters were among the staunchest warriors in the cold water army.

Shortly after the Civil War, both groups were flooded with new members. At the end of 1865 the Sons had only 36,253 members in the United States; by 1871 they could claim 80,947.[93] Similarly, membership in the Templars surged from a wartime low of 34,083 members in 1863 to 367,066 in 1868.[94] Two developments spurred this growth. First, the eradication of one national evil—slavery—inspired many reformers to redouble their efforts vis-à-vis intemperance,[95] and the fraternal orders, as the most robust anti-liquor groups of the 1860s, were well situated to sustain these efforts. In fact, eminent abolitionists like Gerrit Smith and Wendell Phillips found themselves working closely, if not always smoothly, with the fraternal orders and their offspring to defeat the Demon Rum.[96] A second, more direct cause of this growth can be traced to the well-financed mobilization efforts of both Templars and Sons. Recognizing that their memberships had declined during the war, the two societies sponsored professional organizers to form new lodges and bolster old ones. In Idaho, for example, a national IOGT organizer, T. E. Bramhill, established nine new lodges by 1867.[97]

Despite their rapid postwar recovery, both the Sons and the Templars lost ground during the 1870s (see figure 3). This erosion was partly due to the orders' rancorous internal disputes over racial integration, an issue which also unsettled other northern reform organizations, including the Grange and the Knights of Labor, as they expanded in the South.[98] In the case of the Sons, the issue of "Negro membership" had smoldered since 1850, when the National Division declared "the admission of negroes into Subordinate or Grand Divisions" to be "improper and illegal." Heartily supported by southerners, this resolution irked many northern Sons, who began proposing substitute policies in 1866. In that year the National Division authorized each Grand (state) Division to devise its own plan for promoting temperance among blacks, a policy which resulted in separate black divisions. In 1871 the National Division extended an even warmer welcome to black Sons when it announced that "all are equal before the law," and banned the organization of "separate bodies in the same territory on account of any . . . [racial] distinctions."[99] Revoked abruptly in 1872, this policy nonetheless vexed many southern whites, who left the Sons to unite with the short-lived United Friends of Temperance, a southern fraternal order for "whites only."[100]

Though bitter, the Sons' dispute about integration paled in comparison to that of the IOGT. Since 1866 the Templars had supported a policy of segregated lodges, which promoted "the formation of colored Lodges and the admission of colored members on an equality with whites." By the early 1870s, however, the British Templars alleged that this policy failed to guarantee the equal treatment of blacks. They

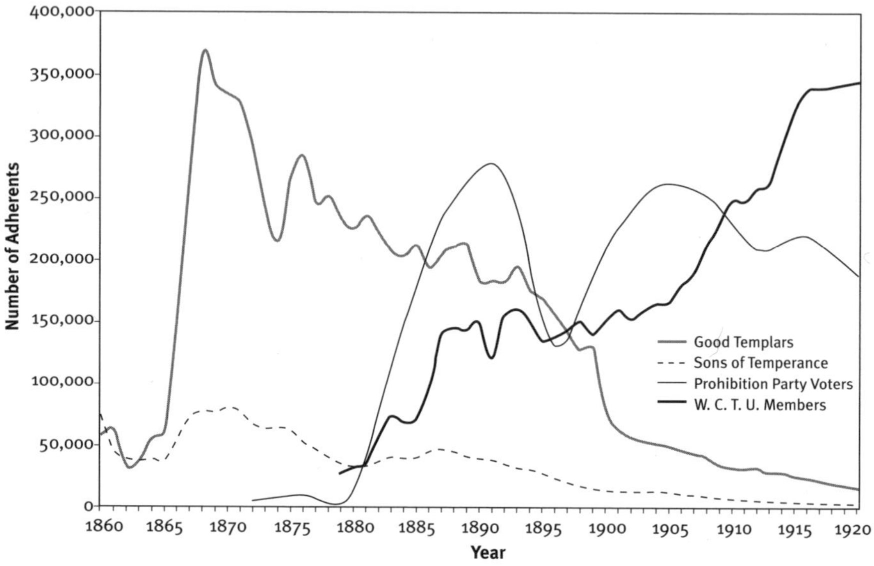

Figure 3 Number of Adherents, National Temperance Organizations, 1860–1920. Sources: *Journal of the Proceedings of the Sons of Temperance of North America* (1860–1920); *Independent Order of Good Templars, Right Worthy Grand Lodge Proceedings* (1858–94); *Independent Order of Good Templars, International Supreme Lodge Journals* (1894–1920); *Minutes of the National Woman's Christian Temperance Union* (1874–1921); Turnbull, *History of the Independent Order of Good Templars;* Petersen, *Statistical History of the American Presidential Elections,* 194–96.

argued that the South's all-white Grand (state) Lodges denied southern blacks the right to appeal the decisions of these powerful bodies, which often refused to charter black lodges and to recognize existing ones.[101] In 1875 the international Right Worthy Grand Lodge responded to these charges by adopting a "dual lodge" system, which allowed each southern state to retain two Grand Lodges—one for whites, and one for blacks. This system gave black Templars self-rule without offending their southern white counterparts, who preferred not to mingle with them in their Grand Lodges. A minority of Templars, though, insisted that "dual lodges" violated "the principle that color shall not bar those of . . . [the African race] from . . . the full privilege of membership in any jurisdiction of our order." For this reason, a small faction seceded from the IOGT in 1876 and formed the rival Right Worthy Grand Lodge of the World.[102] Despite winning approval of the "dual lodge" system, many southern Templars nonetheless reacted negatively to this dispute, and, like many southern Sons, joined "whites only" organizations.[103] By 1879 the southern presence in the IOGT dipped from 18.6 percent of total U.S. membership in 1876 to 10.6 percent.[104]

As southerners fled to all-white, regional temperance societies, the Sons and Templars also began to lose northern supporters to new temperance organizations,[105] including the IOGT's progeny the Prohibition party (formed in 1869) and the Woman's Christian Temperance Union (1874). As one Templar, Jessie Forsyth, later complained:

> Some of the things which the Order takes pride in having originated have resulted in injury to itself. This is true of the Prohibition Party which withdrew from us many of our noblest men. . . . Another Society which has grown to large proportions, often at the expense of the Order, is the Woman's Christian Temperance Union. Born in a Good Templar Lodge room, fostered and nourished by Good Templar women, it has become a great organisation. And American Good Templary is the poorer by reason of the fact that many of its ablest and most influential women have been won from its ranks to become leaders in the WCTU.[106]

Similarly, one study of the Sons argues that "the 'closed' temperance societies felt the squeeze of being replaced by the more prosperous 'open' temperance societies."[107] Though impressionistic, these charges against the Prohibition party and the WCTU can be confirmed at the leadership level. Whereas the Prohibitionists recruited more than fifty leaders and candidates from the two fraternal orders, the WCTU drew at least forty state and national leaders from the Templars.[108]

Above all, the Prohibition party appealed to many fraternal brothers because of its unwavering commitment to political action. Though pledged to total abstinence and prohibition, the fraternal orders lacked firm policies about how to achieve the latter objective in the mid-1860s. Some local lodges championed local option; others pushed for the enactment of civil damage laws, which held saloonkeepers financially responsible for selling to drunkards and minors.[109] Despite these scattered forays into politics, the two secret societies focused primarily on consciousness-raising activities, regulating membership, and resolving interminable debates about rituals and rules. For many drys, however, consciousness raising was not enough. Hence when various temperance gatherings began floating proposals for third-party action, many fraternal brothers (and a few sisters)[110] rushed to embrace this tactic as a more direct assault on the Demon Rum. For James Black, Templar and party founder, a dry party would "separate the true, sincere prohibitionists from the cowardly or hypocritical demagogues who have always proved a great hindrance to the temperance reform." Moreover, it would "put an end to all those compromise laws which have been a heavy burden to the temperance cause, . . . unify temperance effort, and make the temperance sentiment . . . successful in governing the country."[111]

Established in 1869 at the annual convention of the New York Grand Lodge of Good Templars, the Prohibition party addressed two specific obstacles to the success of the antebellum prohibition crusade: the major political parties' inconstancy as dry allies, and the state governments' failure to adequately enforce prohibition laws. Consequently, the Prohibition party nominated teetotalers for state and national offices, declaring that constitutional prohibition would only be enforced if a dry party were in power. As a party, the Prohibitionists did not recreate the structure of the national lodges, and thus lacked membership lists and annual dues for financial support. Instead, the party mobilized sporadically for campaigns, and relied heavily in the postwar period on the Sons, Templars, and WCTU activists for leadership, voluntary contributions, campaign workers, and votes.[112] For example, "one of the most earnest and devoted" financiers of the Massachusetts party was Henry D. Cushing, a veteran Son who bequeathed to it 5 percent of his property.[113] Furthermore, the party received periodic moral support from both the IOGT and the WCTU, which publicly endorsed its efforts for a time.[114]

Given its reliance on the lodge-based network, it is not surprising that the party received the most support from the North. The South never accounted for more than 13 percent of IOGT membership nationwide after 1878,[115] nor of the Prohibition party vote.[116] As for the party as a whole, like virtually every other third party in American history it barely made a dent in the vote totals of the Republican and Democratic parties during the Gilded Age. As further discussed in chapter 5, the party's political influence crested in the 1880s, and it won its largest share of the presidential vote (2.25 percent) in 1892.[117] Despite their overall lack of electoral success, the Prohibitionists generally refused to retreat from their claim to be the best hope for absolute prohibition. Indeed, this stubborn adherence to irrelevance has led many scholars to downplay the party's significance, and to name the WCTU as the most influential dry organization of the late nineteenth century.[118] However, it should be noted that the party managed to persuade over 250,000 men to vote for its national candidates at its peak (1886–92), while the WCTU could only claim about 150,000 members in this period. That was no small achievement, considering the heavy personal costs incurred by many Prohibitionists for abandoning the two major parties.[119]

Whereas many fraternal brothers enlisted in the Prohibition party because of its firm commitment to political action, their female counterparts often joined the Woman's Christian Temperance Union because of the secret societies' halfhearted promotion of woman's equality. According to Jessie Forsyth, "a little less greed for office on the part of the brothers and a little more readiness to give the sisters the equal rights promised by the [Templar] Order might have prevented the defection of some of these good women [to the WCTU]."[120] Forsyth's observation seems warranted, given the IOGT's power structure. Although women consistently formed a substantial proportion of the membership and preserved several Templar lodges during the war,[121] the IOGT continued to elect men to the most prestigious positions in the society's hierarchy after 1865. In local and state lodges, women typically served as vice Templar and headed the children's auxiliary, but rarely were they secretary, counsellor, or chief Templar, the order's most exalted offices.[122] Thus it is not surprising that it was Martha McClellan Brown, a Templar advocate of woman's rights, who first proposed the Union's formation, or that several of her IOGT colleagues participated in the WCTU's founding convention in 1874.[123]

While the WCTU may have been a refuge for many ambitious fraternal sisters, its initial purpose was to solidify the gains of a dramatic episode in the broader temperance movement: the Woman's Temperance Crusade (1873–74). Sparked by an itinerant orator's speeches, thousands of northern women marched to their local saloons, drugstores, and other purveyors of the Demon Rum, praying that the proprietors would abandon the liquor trade. Such direct action had only a limited impact on the liquor industry, and yet the crusade drew thousands of women into the temperance movement for the first time.[124] Hence the WCTU included not only disgruntled Templars but also an assortment of other women, from veterans of charitable organizations to complete novices in associational activities.

Despite its diverse membership, the WCTU nonetheless reflected its Templar origins in many ways. Like its precursor, the Union was committed to both total abstinence and prohibition.[125] Indeed, it had a pledge almost as demanding as the IOGT's and followed its lead in banning cider, a beverage which some temperance societies sanctioned.[126] If the local lodge formed the core of the Templar's social and reform life, the local union provided comparable fellowship, purpose, and cold-water activities for the average WCTU member. In addition, the union adopted the IOGT's democratic approach to selecting leaders and group policies,[127] relied on its system of dues-paying members to provide the financial backbone of its operations, and elaborated on its "system of various committees, . . . as separate from the officers proper."[128] The WCTU also mirrored the IOGT in sponsoring an international organization,[129] and in the South, many state unions ultimately resolved the racial integration issue in true Templar fashion: concerned about "racial mixing" at state meetings, these organizations created "dual" state unions, one for blacks and one for whites.[130] Finally, the union shared the Templars' interest in organizing children's temperance groups, and formed two versions of the order's juvenile temples, the Loyal Temperance Legions and the Bands of Hope.

After its formation in 1874, the WCTU grew rapidly, particularly as the drys approached the peak of constitutional prohibitionism in the years 1887–89 (see figure 3). The union added 44,423 members between 1886 and 1887 alone, a single-year record for WCTU membership growth in the nineteenth century.[131] Like the Prohibition party, however, the WCTU consistently found less support in the South than elsewhere in this period. For instance, as late as 1883 only three of the former Confederate states had a significant WCTU presence.[132] Still, of the organizations in the radical wing, the union proved most enduring in the region. Furthermore, the group would reach its fullest membership potential in the South and elsewhere only *after* it retreated from radicalism and allied with the local gradualists in the early twentieth century.

Though many fraternal members shifted their reform efforts to the Prohibitionists and the WCTU, the secret societies nonetheless worked amicably with these new groups. Significantly, the two orders combined forces with them to help coordinate the constitutional prohibition campaigns of the 1880s. To illustrate, the Nebraska affiliates of the WCTU, the Templars, and the Prohibition party created a "Triple Alliance" for that state's amendment campaign in 1890 and declared, "we are united, harmonious and deeply in earnest, standing as a triune local unit, cooperating and working for the same end."[133] In addition, the Sons and Templars continued to share key personnel with their progeny. For example, before his unexpected death in 1887 John B. Finch served as both Right Worthy Grand Templar of the United States and chairman of the National Prohibition Committee, the two highest national offices in the IOGT and the Prohibition party. Likewise, union leaders like Katherine Lent Stevenson, Eugenia F. St. John Mann, and Orpha M. Parker Stuart were simultaneously active in the Templars.

Despite the overall harmony of the national lodge-based network,[134] the major national organizations did not always profit from their proximity. First, the fraternal origins of the WCTU and the Prohibition party assuredly contributed to their initial lack of organizational bases in the South.[135] Shattered by the disputes about integration, the southern wings of the Sons and the IOGT could offer few leaders, local networks, or other resources to the national groups. Secondly, the Templars' commitment to women's equality had permeated their offspring, the Prohibition party, and had influenced party support for equal suffrage beginning in the late 1860s.[136] At a time when woman's suffrage was wildly unpopular, the party's espousal of this cause fractured its national conventions and enhanced its militant image, particularly in the conservative South.[137] Finally, both the IOGT and the WCTU engaged in divisive and counterproductive battles over their extremist ally, the Prohibition party. For instance, when third-party prohibition was endorsed by the Grand Lodge of Oregon in 1886, one observer reported that his local lodge disbanded.[138] In a similar fashion, the union leader Frances Willard provoked internecine warfare by attempting to align the WCTU with the Prohibitionists during the 1880s.[139] While both groups ultimately resolved to lend "their influence, their good will, [and their] good word" to advance the party's fortunes, they granted individual members and state branches the freedom to reject this position.[140] The compromise still rankled a tiny band of union members, however, who formed the rival Non-Partisan WCTU in 1889.

Undoubtedly, this internal strife merely reflected the lodge-based network's struggle to remain both politically relevant and ideologically pure. If so, purity triumphed. With firm positions on constitutional prohibition and total abstinence, the Sons, the IOGT, the Prohibition party, and the WCTU clearly constituted the radical wing of the anti-liquor crusade. Significantly, their common organizational heritage—the temperance lodge—had nurtured their shared tendencies toward ideological purity. Above all, this heritage required that the activists' personal and public lives serve as dry beacons to the wet world. In aspiring to such high standards of moral rectitude, however, the radicals typically found it hard to publicly compromise with the moderates and their eventual base of support: the evangelical Protestant churches. In the end, they relinquished their leadership of the movement because they succumbed to the "iron law of involution," their orthodoxy pulling them inward and away from accommodation.

The South, the Churches, and the Formation of the Moderate Wing

Though the lodge-based network easily assumed the leadership of the postbellum anti-liquor movement in the North, it struggled to maintain a southern presence. After the Civil War, both national fraternal orders were reconstructing their southern wings when their respective conflicts over racial integration erupted. Weakened by this acrimony, the southern Sons and Templars focused primarily on survival during the 1870s. In some states, these northern-based societies persisted as assets to the dry cause but faced vigorous challenges from all-white regional competitors like the United Friends of Temperance.[141] In others, their reduced numbers relegated them to a marginal role in state anti-liquor efforts. For example, the Texas Templars, who peaked in 1875 at 4,555 members, soon became secondary to the Friends, who surged to over 15,000 members in the 1880s.[142] In fact, of the southern Templars, only the Virginia IOGT remained prominent in temperance circles while escaping organizational upheaval and membership losses in the 1870s.[143]

When they could pause from the arduous task of building and rebuilding local lodges in the South, the northern-based secret societies did not automatically shift their energies to political action in the postbellum period. For instance, in 1878 the relatively robust Virginia IOGT temporarily ceded leadership of the state's dry crusade to a Christian college after hesitating to sponsor a drive for local option.[144] Moreover, while southern Templars participated in the dry referendum campaigns of North Carolina (1881) and Tennessee (1887),[145] neither order generated a militant southern network which could induce the movement to adopt constitutional prohibition as its primary goal. For one thing, most southern teetotalers had rejected the radical premise that local option was "too local and too optional." After North Carolina had enacted statewide local option in 1881, for example, both the Sons and the Templars sought to prod the state movement to follow more extreme measures (namely partisan and constitutional prohibition), but to no avail.[146] Instead, most state activists concentrated on using local option and other parochial methods to close saloons from the mid-1880s on.[147] Furthermore, their northern origins did not immunize the two orders from the moderate spirit of the South's anti-liquor crusade, and they sometimes promoted local option themselves.[148]

If the Sons and Templars were unable and often unwilling to convert the South to northern militancy, their regional competitors for dry fraternal loyalties deliberately distanced themselves from the radical wing and its political agenda. Though requiring total abstinence of its members, the United Friends of Temperance resolved in 1873 that "neither legislative prohibition, nor any other form of interposition by State or municipal government, shall be invoked as auxiliary to this Order."[149] The Friends also spurned partisan prohibition, stating that they would "repel all connection of temperance Orders with . . . political parties."[150] Likewise, the Temple of Templars, an all-white temperance order based in Alabama, claimed to be "entirely free from fanaticism and puritanical ideas."[151] Despite this disdain for radicalism, the regional orders remained neutral regarding local option. According to William E. H. Searcy, a leading Friend, "We do not oppose the enactment of prohibitory laws, or what is called local option; we leave that . . . to each citizen, as a citizen, to decide upon himself."[152]

With the fraternal orders either too weak or too moderate to sustain dry militancy, the southern anti-drink crusade maintained a small, ineffectual radical wing. In the South as in the North, radicals often joined the WCTU and the Prohibition party to better promote statutory,[153] constitutional, and partisan prohibition. Organized regionally by itinerant northerners during the 1880s, these groups periodically sought to goad southern teetotalers into vacating local option. "We do not favor local option election laws for our state," the Mississippi WCTU declared in 1889, "for the reason that through them, we obtain no permanent good."[154] This rationale informed the actions of several other southern unions, which labored for constitutional prohibition in the 1880s.[155] Meanwhile, a handful of men expressed their frustration with the complacency of local-optionists by joining the Prohibition party. In Texas and Mississippi, for instance, leading Prohibitionists only broke with their respective state Democratic party organizations after the Democrats refused to abandon local option and sponsor state prohibition.[156]

However earnest, these radical efforts did little to shape the southern prohibition movement. Three southern states managed to hold referenda on state prohibition during the 1880s, but the substantial wet majorities in these elections suggested to many that the South was "not ready" for the policy.[157] Moreover, the radicals were frequently outflanked by moderate teetotalers and their most powerful source of support: the evangelical Protestant churches. In contrast to their northern colleagues, southern church dignitaries helped direct the postbellum anti-liquor crusade. In Mississippi, for one, the chairman of the state's Prohibition Executive Committee in the 1880s was Charles B. Galloway, an eminent clergyman who became the Methodist bishop of Mississippi during the decade.[158] Likewise, the most influential Texas dry of the Gilded Age was B. H. Carroll, the pastor of the First Baptist Church in Waco and a leading Baptist spokesman.[159] With such men heading the southern movement, the evangelical influence on its direction was considerable.[160] To the radicals' chagrin, however, most church leaders shunned the Prohibition party, and many did not even share the radicals' passion for state prohibition.[161] Hence, the militant wing often found itself denouncing respected ministers for their timidity.

Both the growth in clerical anti-liquor activism and its moderate tone mirrored broader trends in the South's evangelical community. Indeed, after the mid-1870s, regional church bodies increasingly favored prohibitory policies, though not always state or constitutional prohibition.[162] "We shall take a firm and uncompromising stand in every contest against rum," avowed the Savannah Conference of the Methodist Episcopal Church in 1886, but "we affirm our faith in the local option prohibitory laws of this commonwealth as right, wise, and practicable."[163] Likewise, Christian colleges often sponsored pragmatic anti-liquor agitation. For example, in Virginia evangelicals associated with Randolph-Macon College played a crucial role in forming the state's Local Option Alliance in 1881.[164] Tennessee drys could also depend on such colleges for political initiative. Twenty-two colleges in the state, representing one hundred faculty members and fourteen hundred students, petitioned the legislature in 1881, demanding local option. Of these twenty-two institutions, the vast majority were affiliated with a Protestant denomination.[165]

To be sure, many church dignitaries united with their radical colleagues for the occasional statutory or constitutional prohibition campaign in the 1880s.[166] Otherwise, they forcefully advocated local option as a "first step" to state prohibition.[167] By 1887 dry pressure on the South's state legislatures had produced local option laws in all but two of the former Confederate states.[168] As a result, evangelical élites and their allies faced a strategic dilemma: whether to fully exploit these laws or to seek statewide prohibition. That they largely favored the former reflected the clergy's sense of what was possible in the post-Reconstruction South. Fearful that state prohibition contests might split the Democratic party and undermine white rule, many church leaders welcomed local option's provincial and nonpartisan qualities. Even so, some ministers recognized that local option could expand the prohibition crusade's mass base. In that sense, they appreciated "local gradualism" well before the Anti-Saloon League adopted this strategy in 1895.

One early local gradualist was Bishop C. B. Galloway, a future vice-president of the national ASL.[169] After the Mississippi legislature enacted local option in 1886, Galloway ignored the radicals' complaints about the legislation and instead gave advice on how best to use it in a *Handbook of Prohibition* aimed at the "Friends of Prohibition." The legislation authorized the voters to petition for "no-license" elections in the counties, at which they would decide whether to license liquor. Galloway supported the "no-license" position by addressing dozens of rallies, lobbying to strengthen local option, and publicly defending the policy as appropriate for achieving prohibition in Mississippi. Though frequently criticized by the state's radicals, Galloway and his allies persuaded most of the state's teetotalers to give the policy a "fair trial" until they could sponsor state prohibition in 1907.[170] Thus, a northern journalist would claim that Mississippi's "transition to state prohibition [in 1908] was made easy by the continual extension of 'dry' area under local option."[171]

With church dignitaries like Galloway engaged in local agitation, local clergy often answered their appeals for help. For instance, North Carolina's local option movement initially thrived in the 1880s because "the churches have taken hold of it."[172] Ministers gathered signatures for local option elections in their communities and then orchestrated "no-license" campaigns. When their enthusiasm for local option waned after 1889,[173] evangelicals increasingly used yet another provincial tactic: "local-prohibition-through-special-legislation." By this method, localities, churches, and schools petitioned state lawmakers for prohibition within a specified territory.[174] Between 1883 and 1903 the North Carolina legislature banned liquor retailing near 1,882 churches and 352 schools, and within sundry counties and towns. If these efforts fragmented the state's anti-liquor crusade and failed to eliminate many licensed saloons, they nonetheless educated their participants. As one historian notes, "The fact that thousands of voters were year after year signing petitions asking the . . . legislature for increased restrictions on liquor helped to solidify public sentiment in favor of more stringent restrictions."[175]

Despite the educational value of these alternative local techniques, it was the southerners' use of general local option laws that contributed the most to the development of the Anti-Saloon League's political strategy. Significantly, an ASL leader later credited Georgia with blazing the way "with a plan that accorded with the true American principle of local self-government" when it adopted local option in 1885.[176] Furthermore, early league officials invited southern activists to speak on "what local option has done" for Arkansas and Georgia, and closely followed the expansion of "no-license" territory under the Texas county option law.[177] At times, they also copied provisions of the South's local option laws when devising their own prohibitory schemes. For example, during the first local option crusade led by the ASL founder Howard H. Russell in 1888, he modeled the Beatty township law on "similar option measures which had been held [constitutional] in other states, especially in the South."[178] In addition, the ASL could point to the fruits of local gradualism when southern reformers later managed to translate their local victories statewide. After Georgia ultimately abandoned local option for state prohibition in 1907, the league's newspaper exulted: "We bid the weary, doubtful souls, who think that the Anti-Saloon League is going to stick forever in local option, to lift up their eyes and behold the signs of the times."[179] Finally, the South's glorious progress under evangelical leadership confirmed the ASL's belief that "the permanent success or failure" of any anti-liquor organization depended on its proximity to "the soul of the church."[180]

As southern clerics moved to the fore of the postbellum anti-liquor movement, their northern colleagues' modest efforts were eclipsed by the campaigns of the lodge-based network.[181] Meanwhile, the fraternal orders, the Prohibition party, and the WCTU failed to methodically engage the northern evangelical Protestant churches in their political endeavors. This failure to work directly through denominational assemblies and local congregations did not signify the absence of evangelical ministers or church members from the ranks of the lodge-based network. Indeed, much evidence suggests otherwise. For example, a survey by Wisconsin's IOGT concluded that 291 of the state's estimated thirteen hundred clergymen (or 22.4 percent) were Templars. Of these Templar clerics, 212 (or 72.9 percent) represented the two largest evangelical denominations, the Methodists and the Baptists.[182] Likewise, Jack Blocker shows that Prohibition party leaders were primary evangelicals, and that 19.4 percent were clergymen.[183] Lastly, the WCTU claimed several missionaries, preachers, and lay church workers within its largely Protestant membership.[184]

Despite the participation of evangelical Protestants in the postbellum national organizations, most northern church leaders refused to develop sustained political alliances with these groups to defeat the Demon Rum in this period. Church dignitaries periodically cooperated with the radical wing in nonpartisan campaigns such as those for scientific temperance instruction laws,[185] and yet they generally denied militant drys their full approbation and admittance to their pulpits, thus impeding the drys' access to potential workers and funds.[186] The churches' least favorite radical organization was assuredly the Prohibition party, which doggedly called for their endorsement. That this approval was never obtained reflected the churches' position that "every [church] member had the right to vote the ticket of any party that expresses his convictions." As the *Christian Advocate* opined: "The Church of Christ in its organic form should be kept out of the sphere of party politics. . . . If the Church were identified with . . . any political party, it would justify all honest members of other parties in withdrawing from and opposing it. . . . They who would prod us into political discussion must know not or care not that we could in a fortnight send 'firebrands, arrows, and death' into every congregation, alienating pastor from people, dividing the churches into hostile . . . factions, and making religious growth and revivals impossible."[187] Given such attitudes, it is not surprising that "Prohibition speakers were usually denied the privilege of the church in which to present their cause."[188] Moreover, even ordained party activists sometimes lacked access to individual congregations. Some churches refused to engage Prohibitionist ministers; others ousted party members from their pulpits after the presidential election of 1884, in which many Republicans angrily blamed the party for James Blaine's defeat.[189]

If northern church dignitaries maintained an icy posture toward the Prohibitionists, they were somewhat warmer toward the fraternal orders. For example, Wisconsin's two Methodist Conferences endorsed the IOGT's constitutional prohibition campaign in 1879.[190] Still, the relations between church leaders and these groups were often tense, and on occasion ordained fraternal brothers lost their pulpits. In part, this tension originated with the orders' secrecy, which included clandestine handshakes, passwords, and rituals.[191] After the Sons formed in the 1840s, church assemblies had accused this society of fostering intrigue and of uniting "together men of essentially different moral characters, who have no interest in common but that of secrecy," charges which persisted after the war.[192] The Wisconsin Baptist Convention, for one, resolved in 1871 to avoid collaboration with "secret orders" until it had weighed the effects of "secretism" on "the spirituality of the Churches, and the safety of our civil and religious institutions."[193] Along with the secrecy issue, the orders' ascendance to the leadership of the northern anti-liquor movement after 1865 led to clashes with the churches.[194] Some leading evangelicals complained that the orders had taken over the movement at the churches' expense, and fretted about their own declining influence. Finally, the orders' close ties with the Prohibition party did not go unnoticed, and gave church leaders further reason to keep their distance.[195]

In contrast to their first reactions to the Prohibitionists and the secret orders, northern church leaders initially embraced the WCTU. Church approval of the union stemmed from the group's inclusion of "Christian" in its name, as well as from its incorporation of prayer, religious themes, and liturgical music into its activities. Furthermore, the WCTU's first national president, Annie Wittenmyer, focused on temperance revivals and other forms of moral suasion which emphasized Christianity's role in saving the drunkard from the Demon Rum—an approach that pleased church officials.[196] Once Frances Willard assumed the presidency in 1879, though, the union cultivated a more visible political presence in the dry movement that did not always win church favor.[197] Indeed, many eminent clerics looked askance at Willard's attempts to unite the WCTU with the Prohibition party in the 1880s,[198] objecting not only to the goal but to the methods. For instance, in 1888 one religious journal implied that Willard and her partisan union allies had imposed a "gag law" on their nonpartisan colleagues, which allegedly enjoined them from public criticism of WCTU policies.[199] Finally, some churchmen were uncomfortable with the group's advocacy of women's rights, including suffrage and fuller participation in public and church affairs.[200] When Willard attended the General Conference of the Methodist Episcopal Church in 1888 as one of the pioneer female delegates, the conference refused to seat her. After the WCTU criticized this snub, the Methodist *Christian Advocate* retorted that no church admitted women to its legislative bodies, and that the Methodists should not be singled out for censure.[201]

While northern church leaders had specific reasons for keeping their distance from the party, from the fraternal orders, and from the WCTU, their often strained relations with these groups also reflected their relative moderation on the liquor question. In fact, what was most perplexing for the orthodox drys was the disjuncture between the churches' strong words and their moderate actions. As in the South (but with a more radical tone), the North's evangelical churches issued increasingly forceful positions that favored prohibition after the mid-1870s.[202] Still, individual ministers showed a flexibility on this issue that exasperated militant drys.[203] For example, in 1889 thirty-six eminent clerics publicly opposed constitutional prohibition in Massachusetts,[204] provoking one Templar to remark, "I think if the ministers who have opposed the amendment could have heard their names bandied about and their words quoted by those liquor men they would have felt ashamed of their position. There was no middle ground, they had to be on the side of temperance or on the side of the saloon. It was sad to know that some of the honored names of Boston pulpits were counted on the side of the traffic."[205] Similarly, Frances Willard excoriated some Michigan church leaders for their failure to support the state's failed prohibition amendment. Among other things, she accused them of assailing prohibition "with a violence that would have been virulence had they not all been 'honorable men.'"[206]

Even the Methodist press, which strongly supported constitutional prohibition, sometimes displayed a more pragmatic approach to the liquor question than that of the radicals. Whereas the radicals abhorred the use of liquor licensing to restrict liquor sales,[207] the *Christian Advocate* supported increasing the cost of retail licenses as a minor first step toward the liquor traffic's destruction. "We should work uncompromisingly for the passage of an act submitting a Prohibitory Constitutional Amendment to the vote of the people," the *Advocate* declared. "But, prior to success, if the existing license laws come under review, we should vote for every amendment which seems likely to diminish the sale of liquor, or embarrass, though in but small degree, its manufacturers and venders." Like the rejection of third-party prohibition, this willingness to work for modest anti-liquor legislation reflected the church leadership's recognition that the laity differed about political strategy, and that it was not in the churches' best interest to insist that their members subscribe to orthodox prohibitionism.[208]

Indeed, their interest in retaining diverse congregations prevented many northern clergymen from fully uniting with the prohibition movement's radical wing, a hesitancy reinforced by the radicals' periodic condemnations of church moderation. Otherwise sympathetic ministers surely shuddered when extreme drys referred to offending churchmen as "unfit to take communion at God's table," and announced that "the ungodly league between churches and saloons must be broken, if the churches have to be split from turret to foundation stone in order to do it." Meanwhile, as discussed above, church leaders were never fully comfortable with the fraternal orders, which retained their radical leanings throughout their long decline.[209] As a result, several northern church leaders sought new organizational support for their anti-liquor efforts. In general, these unaffiliated clergymen confronted several options during the 1880s. Those who favored constitutional prohibition could have joined the National League for the Suppression of the Liquor Traffic in 1885; their more moderate colleagues might have found the Citizens' Law and Order League of the United States more to their liking. At the same time, these clerics could have worked through innumerable local societies, or, all else failing, they could have founded new groups better suited to their reform interests. In any case, clergymen would be crucial to the formation of a viable moderate anti-liquor movement during the late nineteenth century.

Though they were a key component of the northern moderate wing, Protestant ministers were not the only northern anti-liquor activists to go in search of new associational ties during the Gilded Age. For example, a Chicago restaurateur named Andrew Paxton was weary of temperance groups that did little more than "pick up the refuse of saloons and try to make it over into a new man." Hoping to hold saloonkeepers financially responsible for creating drunkards, Paxton discerned that this initiative required "a new factor in the cause of temperance reform," and to this end he helped to form the Citizens' League for the Suppression of the Sale of Liquor to Minors and Drunkards in 1877, which sued liquor retailers for selling to children and inebriates.[210] Other unaffiliated activists represented a wide range of professions, reform backgrounds, and positions on the liquor question. In many cases, however, their general dissatisfaction with dry radicalism had led them away from partisan, constitutional, and statutory prohibition, and hence it is appropriate to call these reformers "moderates."

Perhaps the most novel aspect of the moderate cohort was its inclusion of a small number of Roman Catholic clerics. While some Catholics had participated in temperance revivals and total abstinence drives since the late 1840s, they had typically eschewed both political anti-liquor campaigns and the organizations that sponsored them.[211] During the 1880s, though, some Catholic teetotalers began to cross the line between moral and legal suasion.[212] Bishop John Ireland of Minnesota, for example, had been active in the Catholic Total Abstinence Union since the early 1870s, but had never identified with a specific political solution to the drink problem.[213] After witnessing open liquor sales to children, however, Ireland had concluded that "the saloonkeeper is deaf to appeals of humanity and religion." As a result, he corresponded with Andrew Paxton of the Chicago League and helped establish similar leagues in Minneapolis and St. Paul.[214]

Despite their shared abhorrence of the saloon, moderates like Paxton and Ireland often struggled to create effective movement organizations. At first, many of them had little contact with other like-minded activists, and hence operated in isolation. As Paxton recalled, "We were all in the dark. Everything was dark before us. We had no experience. We had not the experience of you in the eastern cities to carry on the work then; so we had to grow up every step that we took, and it was pretty uphill work."[215] If the northern moderates had to construct a national network, they also had to knit together the disparate elements at the base which felt excluded from the movement's radical wing. In part, this task involved pinpointing local social networks which could be woven into a more cohesive anti-liquor coalition. This daunting organizational feat would only be achieved, however, after the moderates settled on a common political strategy. Whereas the radicals had coalesced around constitutional prohibition during the 1880s, the moderates lacked such unity.[216] On the one hand, some activists still cleaved to constitutional prohibition, but were willing to try less extreme policies until this goal could be realized.[217] Meanwhile, others argued that it was more important to do "the thing that is possible to-day" than to establish an "ideal state of things beyond what is attainable with means now at command."[218] Finally, their most conservative colleagues rejected constitutional prohibition as a violation of local self-government and instead promoted local restrictions, for "there can be no question whatever as to the right of a people in any given locality to prohibit the sale of alcoholic liquors, and close absolutely the saloon."[219]

Moderate anti-liquor agitators disagreed over more than just constitutional prohibition, however. Above all, they differed in their immediate policy goals. Some moderates favored restrictive licensing laws,[220] others preferred local option,[221] and still others advocated a combination of the two.[222] Furthermore, one of this cohort's factions was so modest that it emphasized only the enforcement of existing anti-liquor laws rather than the promulgation of new ones.[223] Of course, some of this diversity reflected local variations in the liquor problem. Urban reformers, for example, were more timid than their rural counterparts because of the saloon's entrenched position in city life and politics. Nonetheless, this initial absence of a shared political aim contributed to the moderate wing's organizational woes. As early as the 1870s, a number of northern anti-liquor activists had articulated moderate views on the liquor question, and yet like-minded reformers would not build a broad-based movement organization, the Anti-Saloon League, until 1895. Still, the moderate wing's formative years proved vital to the ASL's later development, in that they incubated the group's future leaders, grassroots forces, and law enforcement techniques.

While the Anti-Saloon League was ultimately known for its nonpartisanship, it was not the first national anti-liquor organization to adopt a nonpartisan position in the late nineteenth century. Both the National League for the Suppression of the Liquor Traffic (1885) and the Citizens' Law and Order League of the United States (1883) had done so at the time of their inception. Of the two groups, though, the National League was clearly the more radical. Founded in 1885 by the noted Methodist minister Daniel Dorchester,[224] the National League was a direct response to the Prohibition party's surprise showing in the presidential election of 1884 and its alleged part in the defeat of James Blaine, the Republican candidate.[225] Like a faction within the GOP called the Anti-Saloon Republicans, Dorchester hoped to prevent the Prohibitionists from reprising their 1884 role as "spoilers"; in contrast to these partisans, he sought to unite all against the Demon Rum without "entangling this reform with partisan affiliations."[226] In addition to fostering nonpartisanship, the National League supported educational efforts and the "use of all legitimate civil legislation" to suppress the liquor traffic, including constitutional prohibition.[227] Dorchester also planned to sponsor local affiliates to coordinate local option campaigns,[228] but his inclusion of constitutional prohibition as one of the league's "Objects" persuaded less extreme reformers of the group's radical character.[229] As a result, nearly all of the group's tiny band of recruits championed national and state prohibition.[230] While the National League managed to issue over two million pages of literature and Dorchester recruited eighty-seven eminent officers, the group failed to establish either national or local organizational structures and collapsed after only a year.[231]

Unlike the National League, the Citizens' Law and Order League of the United States heartily embraced moderation. "Constitutional prohibition may be the end of the struggle," the CLOL's newspaper conceded, but "the Citizens' Law and Order League simply labors to secure complete obedience to all existing laws placing restrictions upon the liquor traffic."[232] The CLOL also underscored its conservatism by refusing to hold its members to a total abstinence pledge. As the group's national secretary explained: "The temperance societies were asking too much of their recruits at the outset. The condition of membership in most, if not all, of them being that the candidate should pledge himself to total abstinence and to prohibition before he could become a member . . . , and failing to take this extreme ground at the outset, he was not only excluded from a position where he might work in the cause, but he was denounced and placed in the same category with the law-breaking liquor dealer."[233] Apparently, the CLOL's greater inclusiveness appealed to those impatient with the militancy of the national lodge-based network.[234] Indeed, while some radicals criticized its modest aims, most reformers hailed this organization's formation in 1883, as well as its central aim, "law and order."[235]

Despite its broad appeal, the Law and Order League lacked a uniform approach to achieving "law and order" in all communities. As a loose coalition of state and municipal groups, the CLOL's capacity to enforce liquor laws depended heavily on the legal status of the liquor traffic in a given area, and on its local leaders' ingenuity. In many cases, the organization's branches were stymied by local conditions, and by the early 1890s the CLOL ceased to exist as a national group.[236] The league's decline was also undoubtedly accelerated by its high-risk methods of enforcement, which included the use of undercover agents to collect evidence on the illegal activities of saloons. After saloon keepers brutally beat several of its agents and one informer was killed, the Law and Order League found it nearly impossible to recruit men who were willing to risk their lives to achieve its modest agenda.[237] Moreover, its vigilantism struck some of the group's supporters as repugnant to its moderate purpose. As Washington Gladden, a CLOL vice-president, later maintained, "It seems to me very doubtful whether, in the long run, the cause of law and order is promoted by interventions of this sort. When volunteer agencies thus assume the prosecution of particular classes of offenders, it is a tacit notification to the police authorities that we have taken that portion of their business out of their hands, and that they need not any longer give themselves any concern about it."[238] Instead, Gladden suggested that "law and order" activists confine their efforts to encouraging public officials to perform their respective duties.

Compared to the National League, though, the Law and Order League contributed much to the moderate wing's development. For one thing, the CLOL was the first national organization to sponsor a sustained drive to enforce existing liquor laws. Secondly, through its enforcement efforts the Law and Order League bequeathed a pragmatic legal approach to the Anti-Saloon League. Instead of viewing law as a moral code that precluded the enforcement of partial measures which legitimated evil, the CLOL sought compliance with all antiliquor statutes by all available means, for it viewed all law as potentially useful. Though this legal approach did not directly lead to the movement's shift to a gradualist strategy after 1900, it did influence the ASL's litigation and enforcement campaigns.[239]

More concretely, the CLOL also passed on some practical lessons in law enforcement to its descendant. In fact, the Anti-Saloon League's leaders consciously drew on the best experiences of the Law and Order League while avoiding its worst excesses.[240] For example, Howard H. Russell, founder of the ASL, concurred with Washington Gladden's critique of the CLOL's more extreme tactics. "The law and order system of hiring detectives and lawyers and conducting prosecutions is obsolete, or ought to be," Russell wrote. "The work of our League in law enforcement will be best done, then, by the unceasing agitation for the maintenance of law in every locality, relying upon the officials to do their duty and . . . electing those who will perform these duties fearlessly."[241]

In addition to absorbing the CLOL's legal ideas and enforcement lessons, the ASL also assimilated some of its leaders, workers, and extant local branches.[242] The Connecticut Law and Order League, for instance, operated until 1898, when it began cooperating with the Connecticut Temperance Union as the dual state affiliates of the national Anti-Saloon League.[243] Finally, the CLOL's rejection of rigid membership requirements proved appealing, and the ASL adopted a similar policy. While typically led by total abstainers and prohibition advocates, the ASL placed no conditions on its friends, and accepted aid from anyone who opposed the liquor traffic's most public manifestation, "the saloon."[244] Thus, someone like Washington Gladden, who harbored misgivings about prohibition, could easily shift his support from the CLOL in the 1880s to the ASL in the 1890s.[245]

Though appealing to different sectors of the North's moderate wing,[246] both the Law and Order League and the National League shared a flawed approach to coordinating grassroots collective action. Presuming that "great men" would automatically command popular respect, these groups appointed them to national leadership positions without requiring more than the use of their names and sundry donations.[247] For example, Edwin Dudley of the CLOL had long noted the absence of business, political, and religious dignitaries in temperance organizations. Believing that such men were necessary to conquer the powerful liquor industry, Dudley began his organizing efforts with a visit to an influential Boston merchant and ex-governor, who offered the "influence of his own name" and the promise of a "liberal contribution."[248] Accordingly, the CLOL filled its national offices with famous judges, politicians, clergymen, generals, and businessmen.[249] Likewise, contemporary observers remarked that the National League had managed to recruit "many members of commanding ability," including the famed author Edward Everett Hale.[250] For all their stature, however, these men alone could not inspire local organizing, coordinate local anti-liquor campaigns, or energize the masses. Hence, the National League proved to be a shell of an organization, and the national CLOL was little more than a frail edifice imposed on disparate local units.[251]

But while the national layer of the northern moderates failed to oversee the creation of a broad-based coalition during the 1880s, its local layers demonstrated the potential for such a coalition. Along with the CLOL's local branches, several provincial organizations focused on modest goals during the decade. Of these groups, none would influence the moderate wing's future more than the Oberlin (Ohio) Temperance Alliance (OTA) and the Union Prohibitory League of Pennsylvania (UPLP). Significantly, both groups would embrace local gradualism as a movement strategy. Furthermore, they would each conclude that the expansion of their bases required the power of the evangelical Protestant churches. As it turned out, reintegrating the churches into the northern movement entailed both diplomacy and patience, and yet this organizational feat would produce the Anti-Saloon League's grassroots foundation.

The idea that the Protestant churches could work together on social reform crusades was not entirely new; after all, the American Temperance Society (and later the American Temperance Union) had united individual Protestant ministers of various denominations to lead the temperance movement in the 1820s and 1830s. However, the Second Great Awakening's theological underpinnings and antislavery agitation by many northern evangelicals had produced bitter fights within the Protestant denominations, leading to schisms within the bastions of evangelical Protestantism: the Presbyterian church (1837, 1857), the Methodist church (1844), and the Baptist church (1845). Still, the most enduring of these divisions split southerners from northerners, and it was the northerners who began a crusade for Protestant unity in the years following the Civil War. Waging a campaign to "Christianize America," in which temperance played a key role, northern Protestants increasingly promoted closer relationships among the denominations and sponsored interdenominational alliances, such as the OTA and UPLP, to achieve their goals. In forming such organizations, Protestant leaders sought to create formal structures which encouraged them to emphasize their commonalities and to achieve broadly agreed-upon goals, like reducing the number of saloons.[252]

Such processes were undoubtedly at work in the establishment of the OTA, which provided formal representation to both church pastors and church members on its executive committee. As an early forerunner of the ASL, the Oberlin Temperance Alliance is best remembered for its role in encouraging the anti-liquor activities of Howard H. Russell, the ASL's founder.[253] However, the OTA and its temporary offspring, the Local Option League, were crucial in convincing many Ohio drys that local option should be advocated as a first step to prohibition. Established in 1874 by evangelicals associated with Oberlin College, the alliance first attempted to suppress local saloons. Indeed, the group became known for its "zeal and determination" in its efforts to destroy the local liquor traffic, even when attacked with "burning red pepper."[254] By the late 1870s, though, the OTA had shifted to lobbying the state legislature for general local option laws.[255] For instance, during the years 1880–81, the Oberlin group helped the Ohio State Temperance Alliance to collect thousands of signatures in favor of statewide local option.[256] When Ohio lawmakers rejected local option in 1881 and instead placed a restrictive tax on liquor retailing, the state alliance promptly began a drive for constitutional prohibition, which the Oberlin group joined.[257] Unfortunately, that campaign's failure left the Ohio anti-liquor crusade in a shambles after 1883. The state alliance fell apart, and one of its key components, the Ohio WCTU, became enmeshed in a bitter internal battle over its relations with the Prohibition party.[258]

Of Ohio's anti-liquor organizations, then, only the Oberlin Temperance Alliance was willing to commit to local option. Indeed in 1887 the alliance hired an Oberlin seminary student, Howard H. Russell, to lead the fight for a statewide local option law. Russell gained the support of local churches, and then channeled their efforts into an interdenominational Local Option League. Together, Russell and his church allies persuaded the Ohio legislature in 1888 to pass the Beatty township local option law, which granted over thirteen hundred rural townships the privilege of holding "no-license" contests. Elated by this success, Russell was convinced "that a permanent organization of the temperance forces of the churches might make gradual and more rapid headway than hitherto in obtaining anti-saloon legislation." Pastoral duties required Russell to leave Ohio for five years, but in 1893 he rejoined the OTA and founded the Ohio Anti-Saloon League (OASL). From the start, the OASL adhered to two basic principles. First, instead of constituting a membership organization with dues, lodges, and rigid membership requirements, the league would be a federation of churches which would work through individual congregations.[259] Secondly, the group would pursue a nonpartisan political strategy which first aimed to win local bans on the saloon and then sought to expand these bans wherever possible. In short, the league advocated the following approach: "If we can keep a saloon five hundred feet from a schoolhouse, we will do that. If we can extend the exclusion to a thousand feet, we will do that; if a ward or a county, or a city, or a state, we will do that. We will take what territory we can from every saloon-cursed district everywhere until the open bar is exterminated."[260] Given the OTA's support and that of his contacts from the local option campaign of 1888, Russell had the beginnings of a broad-based state organization. However, the impetus for a national crusade along the lines of the OASL grew out of the Union Prohibitory League of Pennsylvania (UPLP).

As in Ohio, Pennsylvania's anti-liquor groups atrophied after the failure of their constitutional prohibition campaign in 1889. The Pennsylvania WCTU, for one, lost over 3,500 members between 1889 and 1890, as "the defeat of the Prohibitory

Amendment fell with a crushing blow upon scores of weak [local] unions."[261] If there was a reason for optimism in the state movement, it was embodied in the Union Prohibitory League of Pennsylvania. Although formed in 1889 by Alpha J. Kynett to help coordinate the amendment campaign, the UPLP quickly adjusted to the dry referendum's defeat. Instead of organizing a new drive for constitutional prohibition, Kynett proposed that Pennsylvania drys coalesce around a nonpartisan agenda which contained three steps of increasing radicalism. First, anti-liquor activists would focus on the stricter enforcement of existing liquor laws; second, they would seek the enactment of more stringent restrictions; and lastly, they would aspire to constitutional prohibition. As Kynett explained, a multistep plan for achieving prohibition would allow future branches of the UPLP to thrive anywhere, for not every community was ready to accept prohibition or to agitate for it.[262]

If Kynett and the UPLP were somewhat vague about their pathway to prohibition in Pennsylvania, they were far clearer about how to fully integrate the churches into the anti-liquor crusade's moderate wing. As corresponding secretary of the Methodists' Board of Church Extension for over twenty years, the Reverend Kynett had moved within the inner circles of the national Methodist Episcopal Church at a time when there was a strong movement afoot to achieve interdenominational cooperation in his area of responsibility, the development of home missions.[263] Indeed, his work for the Board of Church Extension and the UPLP had persuaded him that it was possible to link individual congregations together into an ecumenical coalition of anti-liquor leagues. Consequently, Kynett began to organize and promote interdenominational leagues in other states during the early 1890s, including Ohio, where he merged the languishing Interdenominational Christian Temperance Alliance with the Ohio Anti-Saloon League. In 1894, on a train from Chicago to Philadelphia, Kynett discussed the temperance question with a former vice-president of the Citizens' Law and Order League, Archbishop John Ireland, who suggested organizing a national anti-saloon league capable of appealing to all sympathizers, including Roman Catholics. Inspired by that conversation, Kynett called for a national convention in 1895 to establish a nationwide league of moderate, ecumenical anti-liquor groups. According to his plan, the new group would be structured according to the federal system, with the local congregation serving as its elemental organizational unit.[264]

The organization founded by that convention, the Anti-Saloon League of America, would be a true marriage of Russell's and Kynett's ideals. Following Kynett's lead, the ASL coopted state and local interdenominational temperance groups, thus giving its organizers access to individual religious bodies and allowing the league to avoid incurring heavy start-up costs. At the same time, the ASL reached out to national church assemblies, like those of the Presbyterians and Methodists, to secure their endorsements. To win over the evangelical Protestant churches, however, the league had to overcome "the divergent feelings and opinions on the part of ministers and members" regarding dry political strategy, as well as their general wariness toward a movement whose most prominent postbellum leaders had been radicals.[265] For that reason, Russell and his colleagues persistently emphasized the Anti-Saloon League's moderation, its nonpartisanship, and its distinctive solution to the liquor problem.[266] At the heart of that solution, of course, was Russell's view that local option was the first step toward prohibition: "Let us cherish the ideal of total prohibition of the liquor traffic, as Christianity and civilization cherish the ideal of a golden age of love and justice universal among men. But as Christianity plants its missions locally and makes its converts in dependence upon their own option . . . , so must prohibition do. The only real, permanent basis can only be laid through patient, loving, faithful and persistent effort upon the masses . . . by good men and women, who know and practice and commend the way of self-prohibition locally and optionally."[267]

Some scholars have suggested that the "decline of the Prohibition party" after 1890 "left a vacuum of leadership for the dry cause" to be filled by the Anti-Saloon League.[268] Given that the party achieved its peak share of the presidential vote in 1892 and only began to atrophy in 1896, it appears that such a decline occurred after rather than before the ASL's formation.[269] It is likewise difficult to claim that this vacuum appeared abruptly after 1890. While the fraternal orders lost members and influence in the 1890s, their radical allies—the Prohibitionists and the WCTU—were not irreparably harmed by either the depression of the 1890s or their internal dissension during these years.[270] Whereas the union's membership hovered at more than 130,000 in the 1890s, the party rebounded from its poor showing in 1896 to undergo a renaissance in the early years of the twentieth century, which were also marked by the Anti-Saloon League's expansion.[271] Having retained the bulk of their adherents, these two organizations did not abandon their efforts to lead the movement after 1896. More importantly, neither group was prepared to follow the ASL's strategy of local gradualism, especially if local option were its initial aim.

If anything, the national ASL's formation in 1895 signaled that relations between the northern radicals and their moderate colleagues were growing less courteous. For example, Ohio's WCTU reacted in 1896 to the national league's formation by declaring that the union "is unalterably committed to the principle of complete prohibition of the liquor traffic, and believe that any measure that compromises with this principle is not in harmony with God's law. Therefore, the WCTU of Ohio in executive session decide that to work with the Anti-Saloon League as it now stands is to defeat that for which we pray."[272] Meanwhile, as the most militant dry organization, the Prohibition party loathed the league's strategy even more than the WCTU. To third-party members, the ASL lacked a decisive plan of action for solving the liquor problem and demonstrated its inconsistency by supporting anti-liquor candidates from both major parties.[273] Worse yet, the league initially advocated local option, which the Prohibitionists continued to dismiss as "too local and too optional" for the next twenty years. "The Prohibition party must oppose local option as a policy," Alphonso A. Hopkins argued, "or lose itself in the slough of uncertain purpose, of mere opportunism. If local option is right—if it is merely good politics—there is no such basic need of a Prohibition party as we have been insisting upon."[274]

At most, the WCTU and the Prohibition party both conceded that statutory prohibition was an acceptable substitute for dry amendments during the 1890s.[275] Enacted by state legislatures, prohibition laws were easily altered by lawmakers, but at least they applied statewide. Of course, these groups preferred constitutional prohibition for its greater permanence and symbolic importance. In states like New York, where constitutional conventions were held during the decade, orthodox activists petitioned for referenda on prohibition amendments; in addition, many radicals continued to uphold constitutional prohibition as their ideal.[276] However, their numerous losses in the 1880s, the repeal of two amendments,[277] and legislative indifference to their petitions led them to question such arduous and costly campaigns. Furthermore, the Prohibitionists held that the disastrous 1880s revealed the futility of nonpartisan amendment campaigns, and that only a dry political party would consistently sustain prohibition.[278] Still, neither the party nor the union promoted legislation authorizing localities to decide the liquor question. Statutory prohibition was their limit in terms of compromise.

While many radical activists vociferously rejected the ASL's strategy of local gradualism, the league could hardly silence their objections in the early years. Money was scarce during the economically troubled 1890s, and league leaders borrowed heavily to keep the organization afloat. As a result, the ASL expanded slowly across the country without achieving a high profile outside a few northern states.[279] The group's local organizing also proved grueling, as dozens of pastors initially denied to league activists access to their pulpits, thus making it difficult for the ASL to establish its "Anti-Saloon Field Days." These events allowed league representatives to appeal directly to church members during services, to collect pledges of financial assistance from them, and to create lists of adherents who could later be mobilized to support anti-liquor candidates and policies. At first, however, even those ministers who granted them access to their pulpits were often tepid in their support, as Purley A. Baker discovered when he was introduced in this manner at one church: "Mr. Baker, the superintendent of the Ohio Anti-Saloon League, is present to present the claims of that organization to us tonight. I do not believe in his organization or in the work he is doing, but we will try to hear him patiently."[280] Suffice it to say that the early Anti-Saloon League made no great splash either in the anti-liquor movement or with its intended audience, the churches.

By 1905, though, the ASL's strategy of local gradualism had generated minor but substantive results, and the league subsequently scored two organizational coups over its most persistent radical rival, the Prohibition party.[281] First, the league had finally gained a foothold in thousands of local Protestant congregations, and could truly claim to be "the temperance arm of the church." This achievement was partly the result of grueling grassroots organizing, but it also reflected the growing sense within Protestantism that "no single denomination can expect to cope effectually with the breweries and distilleries." In fact, the ASL's ecumenical approach to temperance reform captured the spirit of American Protestantism at the turn of the century, in which regularized, official cooperation among churches was seen as necessary to building a Christian America. To achieve such cooperation, the Protestant churches advocated the establishment of federations, in which denominations were formally represented and prominent denominational leaders played key roles.[282]

As for the Anti-Saloon League, it sought to better fulfill its interdenominational mission after 1900 by authorizing the churches to elect trustees to its state and national organizations, thus institutionalizing their ability to shape the league's policies. Though the ASL was temporarily challenged for control over the churches' congressional lobbying during the years 1907–11 by the Inter-Church Temperance Committee, which was sponsored by radicals, state league reports indicate a steady growth of church support at the local level after 1905. Increasingly, local pastors agitated at the grassroots level, helped to secure lists of church voters, and staffed local league committees. At the same time, the state leagues offered advice, literature, speakers, and information about liquor politics to help these local committees conduct their local option and candidate campaigns. As partners with the league, cooperating churches allowed ASL speakers into their pulpits to raise money for their organization on annual Anti-Saloon League Field Days. The small contributions raised at these events and from special speaking tours financed the league at both the state and national levels. The money paid for the league's professional staff and operating costs and allowed the ASL to engage in lobbying, agitation, support of law enforcement and the issuance of temperance publications.[283]

Besides ending the Prohibition party's dream of working through the Protestant churches, the ASL would also seduce the party's most important ally: the Woman's Christian Temperance Union, which slowly abandoned both the Prohibition party and its anti-local option position after a new generation of union leaders assumed command. In 1898 the national WCTU appointed full delegates to the ASL's national convention for the first time; by 1906 the Union's newspaper began to publish temperance fiction extolling local option.[284] Of course, the group's transition from radicalism to moderation occasioned some awkwardness. Meeting in Omaha in 1909, for example, the national WCTU resolved that "while the WCTU stands for statewide prohibition and cannot ask for anything else, we do not wish to be understood as being opposed to the federated forces of [Nebraska] that are working for the passage of the anti-saloon league county option bill. We will be pleased to have this measure become a law and will consider its passage an advance step in the right direction, and under its operation we will most heartily cooperate to make a saloonless state."[285] Nevertheless, the WCTU enlarged the potential workforce of the Anti-Saloon League, and along with the churches contributed to its quest to win local option campaigns, then state prohibition, and finally national prohibition.

As social movement theorists often point out, the most viable social movement is "one that has several organizations that can play different roles and pursue different strategic possibilities."[286] Few movements demonstrate this insight more than the long-lived anti-liquor crusade, which included groups that were religious and secular, male- and female-dominated, lodge- and church-based, and of course radical and moderate in their strategies. At their peaks, the anti-liquor movement's radical and moderate wings each commanded vast armies of committed volunteers. For the orthodox drys, it proved fairly easy to dominate the national temperance crusade during the 1880s. The fraternal orders, the Prohibition party, and the WCTU advocated a common political goal (constitutional prohibition), emphasized total abstinence, and had some of the same leaders. Moreover, the radicals inherited the integrated networks of local lodges that served as a potent source of grassroots activists in the North.

In contrast, the 1880s found the moderates without a unifying purpose, a cadre of nationally linked leaders, or a reliable base. Hence, these reformers often toiled in the shadow of their more extreme counterparts, and only achieved influence in the South, where the radicals were weak. After 1890, however, the moderates issued fresh challenges to the orthodox leadership of the national movement and its goal of constitutional prohibition. Significantly, prominent anti-liquor activists spent the early 1890s debating "on what line may all enemies of the saloon unitedly do battle," and one oft-heard proposal was that all should coalesce around a lesser aim, such as local option. Supported strongly by the religious press, local option offered a way of uniting American Protestants and other movement sympathizers, many of whom had repudiated orthodox prohibitionism.[287]

Despite the piecemeal success of local strategies in the South and the moderates' interest in them, the existing national dry groups rejected local option as a stepping stone to state and national prohibition. Rigid in their radicalism, the Prohibition party and WCTU failed to innovate, even though a more modest approach might have allowed them to continue leading the movement. Instead, it was an upstart, the Anti-Saloon League, which recognized the potential of local gradualism. Impressed by the southern movement's achievements, the league hoped to replicate its general local option laws throughout the country and its close working relationship with the Protestant churches, a task facilitated by the broader movement for Protestant unity. Furthermore, by adopting local option as its initial goal, the ASL made it easier for "damp" individuals to join the anti-liquor crusade, thus expanding its potential base of support. But did local gradualism have the potential to be a national strategy?

3 Modular Collective Action in a Federalist System

In the preceding story, the national prohibition movement confronted a crucial strategic dilemma during the last decade of the nineteenth century. Should anti-liquor activists persist in advocating state prohibition amendments as their immediate goals and risk alienating moderate sympathizers? Or should they defy the movement's radicals, focus on local option, and thus seek a more inclusive movement? The choice of the latter strategy would hinge on several factors, including the emergence of a viable moderate wing in the North which could systematically rely on the Protestant churches for grassroots support. However, as this chapter shows, the prohibitionists also had to adopt tactics which would make grassroots activism possible while avoiding its pitfalls. In particular, anti-liquor activists could ill afford to sponsor parochial crusades which implied that the liquor question could be vanquished through local action alone. After all, local activism was not an end in itself, but rather the beginning of the end for the liquor industry.

With respect to their tactics, or "repertoire of contention," the moderate drys ultimately privileged conventional methods, including petitioning, rallies, parades, litigation, and electoral pressure, over disruptive protest. In that sense, they did not differ much from their radical colleagues, apart from relying more on litigation and nonpartisan (as opposed to partisan) electoral pressure in candidate elections (see table 2). Indeed, this chapter suggests that the anti-liquor movement made few tactical innovations after the Civil War, and retained a repertoire of collective action developed by its antebellum predecessors. This tactical consistency would be familiar to students of collective action forms. According to these scholars, social movements often revive familiar tactics as the easiest and most economical alternatives, and typically introduce tactical changes at best in a piecemeal fashion.[1] For the Pro-

Table 2 Tactics of the Anti-Liquor Movement

Tactic	Definition	Advantages	Disadvantages	National Group(s) that Frequently Used Tactic
Mass petitioning	Systematic collection of signatures on petitions to advocate anti-liquor policy; petitions are later sent to lawmakers to influence policy.	Demonstrates grassroots support for anti-liquor policy; women can participate.	Indirect method of influencing anti-liquor policy; pro-liquor forces can counter-petition.	All, but especially the WCTU
Rallies and parades	Public demonstrations of support for anti-liquor policy; often involve colorful displays of group solidarity; sometimes combined with petition efforts.	Demonstrates grassroots public support for anti-liquor policy; women can participate.	Indirect method of influencing anti-liquor policy; pro-liquor forces can counter-demonstrate.	All
Endorsing candidates (nonpartisan)	Anti-liquor forces endorse candidates for elected office who favor anti-liquor cause or specific anti-liquor policy, and then seek to secure votes for these candidates. While endorsements may go primarily to candidates from a particular party, anti-liquor forces claim that they are based on the candidates' policy positions rather than on their party identifications.	Direct method of securing political support for anti-liquor policies; demonstrates grassroots support for anti-liquor policy.	For some candidates, dry endorsement is undesirable; in office, some "anti-liquor" candidates fail to support dry cause; difficult to persuade strong partisans to engage in split-ticket voting; nonvoting women cannot participate fully.	National League for the Suppression of the Liquor Traffic; Nonpartisan WCTU; Anti-Saloon League

Table 2 Continued

Tactic	Definition	Advantages	Disadvantages	National Group(s) that Frequently Used Tactic
Endorsing candidates (partisan)	Anti-liquor forces endorse candidates who are affiliated with a party that is pledged to an anti-liquor platform, and then seek to secure votes for these candidates.	Same as with nonpartisan endorsements, but can guarantee that anti-liquor candidates are truly committed to the cause and will enforce dry laws.	Existing partisan attachments of the electorate are difficult to overcome; nonvoting women cannot participate fully.	Prohibition party; many members of the Good Templars, Sons, and WCTU
Vigilantism	Anti-liquor activists take direct action against saloon keepers, either to shut down saloons or to ensure that they are following the liquor laws. May involve occupying saloons and holding prayer meetings, violently destroying saloon contents, monitoring the activities of saloons to gather evidence, etc.	Direct method of persuading liquor dealers to abandon their trade or to comply with liquor laws; women can participate in some forms of vigilantism.	Can provoke violent response from saloonkeepers and their customers; may lack legitimacy in the eyes of other citizens, who prefer to resolve conflict through the political system.	Women's Temperance Crusade, Citizens' Law and Order League
Litigation	Appeals to the courts, either to prosecute those who violate anti-liquor laws, or to convince the courts that anti-liquor laws are legally sound.	Direct method of punishing lawless saloons; preserves anti-liquor laws from pro-liquor efforts to nullify them.	Effectiveness depends partly on juries, judges, and legal developments that anti-liquor forces cannot control.	Citizens' Law and Order League, Anti-Saloon League

Table based on various studies of the American temperance movement. See bibliography for a complete listing of studies consulted.

gressive Era drys, the push for both local option legislation and "no-license" victories required no new protest methods, for electoral pressure and mass petitioning had long belonged to the movement's repertoire.

Social movement theorists can account not only for the relative stability of the drys' tactics over time but also help explain how these reformers managed to construct national campaigns despite the obstacle of a federalist system. Specifically, analysts have sketched the process whereby repertoires of collective action become "modular," or easily "learned, adapted, routinized, and diffused from one group, one locale, or one moment to another." For protest forms to become modular, their originators and subsequent users must be able to share information about them through the press, formal associations, and social movement networks. Once established as an effective weapon, a modular form of collective action enables groups to pursue a variety of social and political conflicts across a wide range of social and territorial space with minimal effort.[2]

The first part of this chapter traces the origins of the drys' modular repertoire of collective action to two resources which allowed the anti-liquor activists to overcome the decentralizing tendencies of the American state. First, the antebellum temperance crusade, like other movements in the reform wave of the 1830s, had adapted British petitioning techniques to American conditions. By the 1850s, this variant of petitioning had given birth to a repertoire of collective action which was readily transferable from locality to locality, and flexible enough to assert claims on any layer of the American federal system. Secondly, the antebellum movement had become proficient in diffusing its tactics through its formal organizations, publications, and social networks. By 1855 teetotalers had already mobilized nationwide campaigns to wrest gains from the state legislatures. In doing so, they had developed familiar routines for influencing policy which were bequeathed to postbellum activists.

While this ability to transcend local boundaries was a clear asset, it only provided anti-liquor reformers with the means to pursue a national strategy. The sheer availability of modular protest forms, however, would hardly inoculate activists against the insularity of local activism when pursuing particularistic goals. As the second part of this chapter shows, the parochial use of direct action occasionally appealed to some anti-liquor activists, especially women and those concerned about enforcing liquor laws. In fact, this focus on enforcement frequently drew such activists into direct and sometimes violent encounters with liquor dealers. Of course, these confrontations might have been avoided if more state governments had systematically implemented their own liquor laws. Instead, enforcement fell to local authorities before 1900, and it was their dereliction that compelled bands of aggrieved and fervent reformers to rise against local saloons. As a result, such protest episodes tended to be limited in their effect and geographic reach.

Federalism and the Development of Modular Collective Action

In recent years, some scholars have sketched how long-term changes in state structure have altered the forms of collective action. In their studies, early forms of collective action, such as grain seizures, food riots, and land occupations, were typically brief, solitary, and sporadic events which directly targeted those local individuals held responsible for the injustice in question. As national states expanded their activities and intervened more directly in private life, however, they gradually became the foci of collective action, and inadvertently helped to routinize protest forms. Indeed, Sidney Tarrow asserts that "the centralization of power offers dissidents an odd sort of advantage—a unified field and a centralized target to attack once the system is weakened."[3]

While studies by these scholars offer many useful insights for the social movement analyst, they typically investigate the impact of national state expansion into policy areas that were previously free from central control or were ruled indirectly—a concern that also drives a great deal of research on American political development.[4] Moreover, those few works which consider federalism often depict it as dissipating movement energy. For example, Michael Schwartz contends that the local and state branches of the southern Farmers' Alliance possessed such divergent interests that the movement's adoption of statewide political programs later hurt its local organizations. In a similar fashion, Ira Katznelson notes that workers in the United States often organized militantly against specific industries and capitalists, and yet their loyalty to the urban machines prevented them from fully committing to a socialist agenda of systemic political change. Meanwhile, accounts of the crusade for the equal rights amendment suggest that this movement fragmented when it shifted from pressuring Congress to organizing state ratification campaigns.[5]

Given its decentralized state, one might assume that America was infertile ground for cosmopolitan movements during the nineteenth century. As innumerable observers have noted, the Constitution did not concentrate power in a core set of institutions. Instead, it provided for shared power between the national government (or the central state) and the "state" governments, which retained their own governing bodies, legal codes, and instruments of law enforcement. Although the Constitution did give national institutions like the Supreme Court some final authority over the affairs of the states, the national government itself could not reliably take coherent or decisive actions. Just as it dispersed power across a national-local continuum, the Constitution also distributed power among the three national branches of governance. Thus it is unsurprising that local and state governments acted as the primary instruments of coercion in the nineteenth century,[6] and one might well expect that the differences among these localities might have produced divergent protest forms.

Indeed, according to William J. Novak's account of nineteenth-century American life, "towns, local courts, common councils, and state legislatures were the basic institutions of governance," and they combined to produce a "local, customary, and discretionary regime" concerning regulatory policies like liquor control. Moreover, would-be regulators operated in a legal environment which gave the state wide latitude to subordinate individual rights to the broader interests of the community. Upheld by the judiciary's adherence to a philosophy of "the well-regulated society," which applied common law principles in defining government power, regulatory efforts blurred the distinction between public and private morality and relied on a bewildering array of weapons to attack moral crimes, some geared toward (public) criminal prosecution and some toward (private) civil and extralegal action.[7] Thus it might have been quite easy for advocates of stricter regulation to employ a diversity of tactics which varied from place to place, depending on local conditions.

Despite the seeming obstacles to cosmopolitan social movements in the United States, American reformers, including the pro-regulation teetotalers, constructed regional and even national crusades before the Civil War.[8] Antebellum temperance activists achieved a nationwide political presence largely because American legislatures were grounded in similar constitutions, and were developing analogous procedures and committees to cope with their constituents' demands. However, parallel legislative structures only benefited the anti-liquor crusade after teetotalers had devised a common repertoire of collective action and had disseminated it through their networks and newspapers. Ultimately, their development and the diffusion of generic protest forms helped early reformers to profit from the standardization of legislative activities even as they shaped this process.

Parochial Beginnings

When temperance advocates first entered politics, they targeted local authorities because antebellum state laws gave municipal and county officials the authority to grant liquor licenses, and at best to refuse to issue any licenses at all. For example, teetotalers encountered a favorable licensing regime in Rochester, New York. In 1834 the city's anti-liquor movement joined forces with the local Whigs, who ran a slate of radical temperance candidates for the common council and then eked out a narrow victory in each ward. Since Rochester's city charter accorded them complete jurisdiction over liquor licensing, these newly elected aldermen promptly began to satisfy their allies' demands. While the Whigs wanted to issue no liquor licenses, "their small majorities convinced them to introduce the abolition of public drinking houses by stages. During 1834 they granted only four licenses, at the prohibitive price of forty and fifty dollars each. At least two of these went to large hotels. In working-class neighborhoods, every drinking establishment had either to close its doors or operate outside the law."[9]

During the early 1830s dozens of temperance groups took the Rochester approach and looked to local politics for solutions, although their specific remedies for the "tippling problem" reflected the vagaries of state liquor laws.[10] Temperance advocates in Massachusetts, for one, found their first political efforts partly stymied by the state's tangled licensing law, which allowed town selectmen to make licensing recommendations to unelected county commissioners, who had final discretion over licensing. Though often able to elect officials who recommended no licenses, activists soon discovered that some commissioners utterly ignored this advice, and that they lacked further recourse.[11] Meanwhile in Georgia, which conferred its licensing authority on elected county courts, the teetotalers of Camden and Liberty counties mobilized in 1833 to elect sympathetic courts that would reject all license applications. After gaining the state legislature's blessing,[12] the courts obliged, and these counties became among the first to ban liquor retailing.[13]

By the late 1830s anti-liquor activists across the country had experimented with local licensing tools, and many had found them wanting. In several states teetotalers had grappled with licensing systems which gave them little direct control over the number of dramshops in their neighborhoods, towns, and counties.[14] Meanwhile, one alternative source of liquor control—using nuisance law to shut down saloons—was not readily available to social movement organizations before the Civil War. During this period legal interpretations of nuisance law held that citizens could only close saloons if they could demonstrate that they had suffered a particular harm which differed from that borne by the general public. Otherwise, it was the responsibility of government authorities to prosecute the dramshops in question as public nuisances, which again left reformers at the mercy of mayors, aldermen, selectmen, and constables.[15]

To alter such unresponsive regulatory regimes, however, reformers would have to broaden their focus to the state legislatures. Considering the great variety of state liquor laws, one might have expected equally disparate episodes of collective action to alter these laws. Furthermore, some activists might have preferred the intimacy of local activism to impersonal agitation in a distant state capital. As Neal Dow, the architect of the first state prohibition law, recalled, "Maine was behind most of her sisters in the organization of a state society." Maine's tardiness, he explained, "was due to several causes," including that "there was much work close at hand to be done in the village by the local society . . . , leaving little means, strength or time for effort beyond its immediate vicinity."[16] Nonetheless, Dow and his Maine colleagues joined thousands of other temperance advocates to inaugurate their first wave of translocal action between 1838 and 1839, when activists employed analogous tactics to win similar state laws.

The temperance press hailed 1838 as "the year of the petition" because during it anti-drink reformers deluged state legislatures with memorials. This activity persisted through 1839, after which the use of anti-liquor petitioning varied by state until the massive campaigns of the 1850s.[17] Though less extensive than these later efforts, the petition drives of the late 1830s were not unimpressive. In Massachusetts, for instance, approximately seven thousand petitioners requested harsher restrictions on the liquor traffic during the summer of 1838.[18] Likewise, in 1839, Georgia teetotalers amassed twenty thousand signatures on a single petition for a ban on the sale of spirituous liquors.[19]

That anti-liquor forces would petition seems reasonable, given petitioning's constitutional basis. First enshrined in Pennsylvania's state constitution of 1776, the "right to petition the legislature for redress of grievances" quickly spread to the national and other state constitutions.[20] Still, the antebellum reformers exercised this right in a way considerably different from their forerunners. Whereas earlier petitioners had typically prayed for legislative favors, such as a charter for a new turnpike road, a change in a county boundary, or the permission to peddle without a license, their antebellum counterparts increasingly pleaded for causes that did not directly benefit them. As in British movements, American activists had transformed a tool of private individuals and groups seeking particular benefits into a public act, seeking justice in the name of general moral claims.[21]

In fact, the parallels between British and American petitioning practices in the early nineteenth century are quite striking. Social movements in both countries habitually launched mass petitioning through their social networks, newspapers, and conventions, and several of their crusades combined this weapon with elaborate political campaigns. Credit for converting the petition into an instrument of mass protest belongs to the British antislavery movement, however. As early as 1788 British abolitionists had challenged the traditional petition and its focus on specific injuries or benefits by presenting disinterested memorials to Parliament that embodied a "humanitarian political frame of reference." By 1792 the movement produced "the largest number ever submitted to the House on a single subject or in a single session."[22] Soon, other movement activists were proffering mass petitions to Parliament, demanding the expansion of suffrage and unlimited free speech.[23]

But while British reformers like the abolitionists could petition to enlist the unlimited power of a central Parliament, their American counterparts might have felt constrained by the weakness and limitations of their political institutions. That reformers in the United States nonetheless reproduced British protest forms demonstrates the power of transnational diffusion, which saw the British impart their methods to the Americans through transatlantic news reports, correspondence, and visits. For example, in 1830 members of the London Female Anti-Slavery Society had urged petitions as "the most effective measure that women could take for the slave" in their correspondence with antislavery women in the United States. American abolitionists would later echo this advice when they mobilized their relentless petition drives of the 1830s: "Female Societies probably did more for the abolition of slavery in Great Britain than those of the other sex. They scattered anti-slavery tracts . . . they circulated petitions . . . Let the female sex, then throughout the land, emulate . . . their sisters over the ocean."[24]

Mass petitioning began tentatively in the United States during the years 1828–29, when antislavery editors sponsored a national petitioning campaign to outlaw slavery in the District of Columbia. Though their appeals incited a divisive floor debate in the House of Representatives over an appropriate response, antislavery agitators were formally rebuffed by the Committee on the District of Columbia, which published a report that detailed the inexpediency of emancipation in the District.[25] Meanwhile, a related movement, the Sabbatarians,[26] had also initiated a national petition campaign in 1829, begging Congress to rescind the Post Office Act's establishment of Sunday mail delivery. Despite receiving numerous memorials on the subject, the House of Representatives simply referred them to a select committee, "which had composed so cogent an all-purpose response as to quiet the controversy forever."[27] Chastened, the Sabbatarians shifted their focus to other activities such as molding public opinion on the virtues of Sabbath observance.[28]

Unlike the Sabbatarians, antislavery activists would support additional national petition drives, but not until after 1833, when Parliament banned slavery in the West Indies and the American Anti-Slavery Society established itself along British lines. In fact, the American organizers of the AASS waited until they had received word that Parliament had approved the Emancipation Act before assembling in Philadelphia to found their new association.[29] But the victory in England provided the Americans with more than just an example; rather, it freed up British abolitionists to personally participate in American antislavery efforts. Englishmen like George Thompson, labeled a "notorious miscreant" by hostile congressmen, embarked on speaking tours of the United States beginning in 1833.[30] Another abolitionist, Charles Stuart, came to the United States in 1834 and gave advice to his long-time friend and correspondent Theodore Weld.[31] As an AASS agent, Weld roused thousands of Americans to petition Congress for the abolition of slavery in the District of Columbia during the years 1834–36.[32]

With the aid of agents like Weld, its newspapers, and its auxiliary organizations, the AASS sponsored a massive petition campaign which garnered millions of signatures between 1834 and 1839.[33] As early as 1835, one of the petitioners' foes, Senator John C. Calhoun (D-S.C.), had remarked on the sustained, systematic, and grassroots character of this campaign. These petitions "do not come as heretofore, singly and far apart, from the quiet routine of the Society of Friends or the obscure vanity of some philanthropic club," he said, "but they are sent to us in vast numbers from soured and agitated communities."[34] Embarrassed by the avalanche of abolitionist petitions, southerners sought to ban congressional acceptance of these memorials in 1836. Although vigorously opposed by a handful of northerners, southern congressmen managed to impose a rule on the House whereby antislavery petitions were automatically tabled, without printing or referral to committee, and could not be acted upon. Known as the "gag rule," this instant rejection of abolitionist memorials lasted until 1844. For eight years, the "gag rule" was a rallying cry for both antislavery petitioners and those concerned about civil rights.[35]

It was during the national "gag rule" controversy and the antislavery movement's relentless petition drives that anti-liquor activists commenced their own mass petitioning in the late 1830s. As part of the same wave of reform, the temperance and antislavery movements shared a base in the evangelical network that emerged from the Second Great Awakening, appealed to many of the same northern constituencies, and ultimately developed similar passions for petitioning.[36] Their mobilization schemes were also broadly comparable: central societies disseminated newspaper accounts of petition drives, printed petition forms, and appointed itinerant agents to sustain their signature-gathering efforts.[37] Volunteers in both crusades carried memorials from door to door, or found names "wherever signers can be got." Indeed, the AASS advised its petitioners to "neglect no one. Follow the farmer to his field, the wood-chopper to the forest. Hail the shopkeeper behind his counter; call the clerk from his desk; stop the waggoner with his team; forget not the matron, ask for her daughter. Let no frown deter, no repulses baffle. Explain, discuss, argue, persuade."[38]

Reflecting their different institutional targets, however, the abolitionists used a national organization (the AASS) to coordinate their petitioning of Congress during the late 1830s, whereas the teetotalers first petitioned the state legislatures through the state societies formed under the auspices of the American Temperance Society and later affiliated with its offspring, the American Temperance Union. While loosely bound by the ATU, these state societies maintained distinct petitioning operations, resulting in a diversity of petition language and goals during the 1830s and 1840s. Although most anti-liquor memorials sought the legislative repeal of state licensing laws so as to delegitimize an evil trade, they failed to put forth identical plans for restricting liquor sales.[39] Despite their parochial tendencies, these petitions nonetheless converged upon two types: one advocating local option and the other proposing a statewide ban on the sale of liquor in small amounts.[40] That even this similitude was possible was because of the ATU and state temperance groups, which promoted these two policies in their publications.[41] Based on the printed accounts of these models, state and local societies simply chose the one that best fit their conditions and altered it to suit their preferences.[42]

Indeed, the content of the anti-liquor crusade's petitions would only approach uniformity after Maine adopted a state prohibition law in 1851. Heartened by this event, the movement's organizations zealously promoted this form of legislation as the prototype for future political action. For example, the ATU organized a national Maine Law convention in August 1851, and its leaders thereafter canvassed the North in favor of such laws.[43] Similarly, the Sons of Temperance enthusiastically endorsed the Maine statute at its Grand Division meetings, and its roaming lecturers peppered their usual speeches with positive references to the Maine Law.[44] Sons like Philip S. White lauded state prohibition during his organizing campaigns.[45] Meanwhile, "a large number of sermons, essays, and addresses were published, . . . especially in support of the Maine Law," and both the temperance press and the mainstream press debated its merits.[46] After 1851 the Maine Law became the sole object of memorials everywhere but in the South.[47] Fearing that their cause would suffer from its proximity to "fanatical" reforms like abolitionism, some southern teetotalers instead requested either a weak Maine Law or local option.[48]

From Mass Petitioning to a Diversified Repertoire of Collective Action

Although focused on a more local and tranquil issue than slavery, anti-liquor memorials nonetheless provoked ambivalent responses from several state legislators. Most lawmakers venerated the right to petition and were willing to introduce petitions that ran counter to their own beliefs.[49] At the same time, they often deliberately distanced themselves from anti-liquor memorials. For example, one state legislator on presenting such a petition stated "that he was not prepared to say that he would favor the enactment of a law so stringent in its character as that to which our attention is invited by the memorialists. He presented it, however, and asked that it be read and referred to the appropriate committee, that it might be respectfully and truly considered by the House. He owed that much . . . to the memorialists and the cause in which they evince so much zeal."[50] Still, some state legislators found that the admission of anti-drink petitions distracted the legislature from giving the liquor issue "the calm deliberation which its importance demands." Mr. Hill, a lawmaker from Tennessee, wondered why his colleagues introduced "the opinion of parsons and ladies," an action which forestalled "that cool and deliberative action which this house should take on the subject [of temperance]."[51]

If anything, the sheer number of signatures collected by the anti-liquor movement, particularly in the early 1850s, made its antebellum petitioning difficult to ignore. Encouraged by the enactment of Maine's pioneering prohibition law in 1851, Ohio prohibitionists reportedly presented petitions with 250,000 signatures to the legislature of 1852–53. Likewise, Maine Law petitions circulated in 1851 in Massachusetts garnered 126,000 signatures, fifty thousand of which were from legal voters, the remainder from women and minors.[52] While southern memorials contained far fewer signatures than their northern counterparts, one cannot automatically assume that southern anti-liquor sentiments were weaker. First, the region's pool of eligible voters was smaller,[53] and its rural character made it less accessible to house-to-house petitioning.[54] In addition, southern teetotalers often seemed less intent on collecting signatures from women than their colleagues in the free states.[55] For example, in Virginia the petitions submitted in 1853 advocating a referendum on a weak Maine Law contained fifteen thousand signatures, all apparently from male voters.[56] Finally, as discussed in chapter 5, the southern party system was less amenable to the dry cause than that of the North during this period, which may have discouraged extensive petitioning.

As the antebellum prohibition movement reached its climax in the 1850s, teetotalers increasingly combined mass petitioning with the collective use of public space to demonstrate the reform movement's strength. In particular, the presentation of mass memorials occurred after parades, rallies, and public assemblies. In Boston, for example, the completion of a petition drive inspired an assembly in Tremont Temple, after which the "mammoth" petition was borne in a large double sleigh to the State House, accompanied by about "five thousand persons . . . , marching four abreast . . . , with banners and music."[57] Similarly, in Albany prohibitionists made their way to the New York legislature after a parade involving an "artillery company, gorgeous sleighs filled with officers, guests, and ladies, monster rolls of petitions, with 300,000 signatures, and half a mile of teetotalers and Sons of Temperance, with splendid regalia, badges, banners, and bands of music."[58]

Eventually, such demonstrations became divorced from the petitioning process, and were held to galvanize members, pressure lawmakers, and draw public attention to the liquor menace. For instance, Nashville's dry fraternal orders rallied in 1853 for prohibition while the Tennessee legislature debated submitting a prohibition referendum to the voters. In a similar fashion, anti-liquor parades, rallies, and other public displays of dry vigor remained an integral part of the postbellum movement's arsenal. For example, drys in Massachusetts held mass meetings and sponsored a parade of children "headed by the drum corps of the English High School" during their campaign for a prohibition amendment in 1889. Their Progressive Era counterparts even held a "March on Washington" in 1913, in which three thousand drys paraded down Pennsylvania Avenue to the strains of "Onward, Christian Soldiers." At the march's conclusion, representatives from the Anti-Saloon League and the WCTU delivered their resolution for a national prohibition amendment to their congressional allies on the Capitol steps.[59]

A more crucial technique—electoral pressure—also originated as a byproduct of the early petitioning drives.[60] As Neal Dow recollected, "Again and again, . . . beginning with 1837, the more active among the temperance men of Maine had been asking for Prohibition, only to be refused by the legislators. Something more than petitioning must be done, if they were to obtain what they asked; that could only be done at the polls." Through local conventions and canvasses, teetotalers sought to promote anti-liquor candidates, as well as to defeat their opponents. In addition, if no suitable anti-liquor candidate was already in a race, the movement sometimes fielded candidates from its ranks.[61]

Of course, during the postwar period the drys would perfect the art of "single-issue" voting, which could be partisan or nonpartisan, and aimed at any elected official and any level of government. Moreover, the Progressive Era drys successfully advocated nonpartisan electoral pressure in an era when previously partisan voters were learning "to behave as voters with interests beyond party, willing to vote for whichever candidate promised more of what they wanted."[62] While the broader public may have been slow to warm to nonpartisan techniques, the drys consistently considered them part of their arsenal. In fact, contrary to many accounts of the anti-liquor crusade, the prohibitionists of the 1880s did not exclusively engage in third-party politics, nor did every Progressive Era dry embrace the nonpartisan approach advocated by the Anti-Saloon League. Instead, the movement applied both approaches throughout its long history, and often recalled its past use of these techniques when arguing for either the nonpartisan or the partisan approach.[63]

Still, as a complement to electoral pressure, mass petitioning proved the most flexible, durable, and universal instrument for advancing the prohibitionist cause. Activists could memorialize local authorities just as easily as they could plead with the state legislatures or the U.S. Congress. Furthermore petitioning, unlike voting, could be employed by women. Given the prominence of women within the temperance ranks, it would have been surprising if the anti-liquor crusade had not thoroughly exploited this tactic. Millions of women signed their names to anti-liquor petitions; thousands would also circulate them.[64] Indeed, temperance advocates developed a profound appreciation for how mass petitioning built grassroots support. As J. Ellen Foster declared in 1882, "The object of the circulation of popular petitions is not only to affect the body to whom they are addressed, but to stir the public mind to a consideration of the subject involved! Let a town be districted and a dozen women start out to get signatures . . . , and there can not fail to be a *general stirring* of dry bones, which shall cause some to rise and breathe and walk forth."[65]

Even after 1900 mass petitioning remained central to the dry repertoire, though other social movements apparently abandoned this tactic.[66] In part, this continued reliance on petitioning reflected the Progressive Era drys' heavy use of direct legislation, which usually required the movement to circulate a petition before the liquor question was placed on the ballot. For statewide initiatives, the signature requirements ranged between 5 and 15 percent of the electorate, for local option between 10 and 40 percent. In addition to petitioning for direct legislation, the prohibition movement continued to send memorials to lawmakers. However, these petitions increasingly took a modern form, and included telegrams and personal constituency letters. For instance, in 1909 the Pennsylvania WCTU sent both "petition letters and telegrams" to Harrisburg to influence state lawmakers during a local option debate.[67]

Mass Petitioning and State-Level Liquor Policy: The Case of Tennessee

Like other social movements, the anti-liquor crusade did not refine its tactics in a vacuum. Instead, teetotalers engaged in political exchanges with state lawmakers that helped to routinize protest across the nation. In the short run, prohibitory petitions formed a source of public opinion on the liquor question, and lawmakers periodically accommodated their demands. For example, seven state legislatures responded to the influx of anti-liquor petitions in 1838–39 by adopting major temperance laws during those years.[68] While most would be revoked shortly thereafter, their original enactment revealed mass petitioning's potential. Indeed, as inveterate petitioners, anti-liquor activists were responsible for a perpetual (if variable) flow of memorials which opened a continuing dialogue between them and the state legislatures. At most, this conversation helped to shape prohibitory policies; at the very least, it pressed the legislatures to create select and (later) standing committees on the liquor question. If a mixed blessing for anti-drink reformers, these bodies nonetheless amplified their state-level claims. Over time, as legislative committees became more adept at dispatching anti-liquor petitions, temperance advocates reacted by supplementing their mass petitioning with electoral pressure. As in Tennessee, however, this combination of anti-liquor memorials and single-issue voting would not in itself produce a Maine Law.

Like other southern states, Tennessee initially lodged its liquor licensing authority in the county court system.[69] At first only innkeepers could legally maintain barrooms, but after the license law took effect in 1831, any person who paid a set fee and posted bond to keep an orderly drinking establishment could be licensed by the county court. Tennessee anti-liquor activists, who had inaugurated the state's first temperance societies in the late 1820s, soon found the law to be obnoxious. According to a petition from the sundry ladies of Davidson County, the statute encouraged dramshops, "a blighting curse, withering all within their reach."[70] But neither these ladies nor their husbands could prevail in their county courts, because they were not authorized to deny licenses to qualified applicants. Hence, like other "cold water" activists across the nation, teetotalers in Tennessee began firing petitions at the legislature during the 1837–38 session, and lawmakers followed the established practice of respectfully receiving and printing them. However, given the previous lack of acrimony over liquor, the legislature lacked an appropriate committee for the referral of drink-related petitions. As a result, it established a joint select committee for that purpose.[71] Impressed by the number and tone of these memorials, the Select Committee on Tippling and Tippling Houses then recommended passage of the "quart law," which was duly enacted in 1838 and banned the sale of spirituous liquor in quantities of one quart or less.[72]

By 1846, though, the Select Committee had evolved into an increasingly permanent and independent body. The legislature's reauthorization of the Select Committee was largely a biennial ritual, and the committee's legislative proposals no longer reflected the anti-liquor position championed by most petitioners. For example, in 1846 the legislature repealed the quart law on the advice of the Select Committee, which claimed that the measure had "failed to suppress the practice of tippling" and that a "large majority of the people" preferred a licensing law.[73] While the law had inspired some backlash, repeal opponents legitimately asked whether a majority desired licensing, and pointed to a general surge in petitions in favor of the quart law during the 1845–46 session (see figure 4).[74] "If you pass this bill, you will do it in opposition to the wishes of thousands of petitioners," Senator Jones argued, piously noting: "My constituents have sent up their petitions—a long list—bearing the signatures of the most respectable citizens of both parties—of both sexes—*their voice I will heed—their wishes I will obey—their confidence I will not abuse.*"[75] Even a supporter of repeal "thought that the legislature ought not to disregard the thousand petitions that had been sent up here at this session from the various portions of the State against the repeal of the present law."[76]

The enactment of the licensing law in 1846 understandably frustrated teetotalers in Tennessee and their legislative allies. Indeed, at one point during the 1847–48 session, an unidentified "voice" rang out in the House of Representatives, moving that "a committee be appointed to keep the chairman of [the Select Committee on Tippling] sober during its examination" of legislative proposals.[77] Still, anti-liquor activists did not despair over their memorials' declining influence, and in 1851 re-

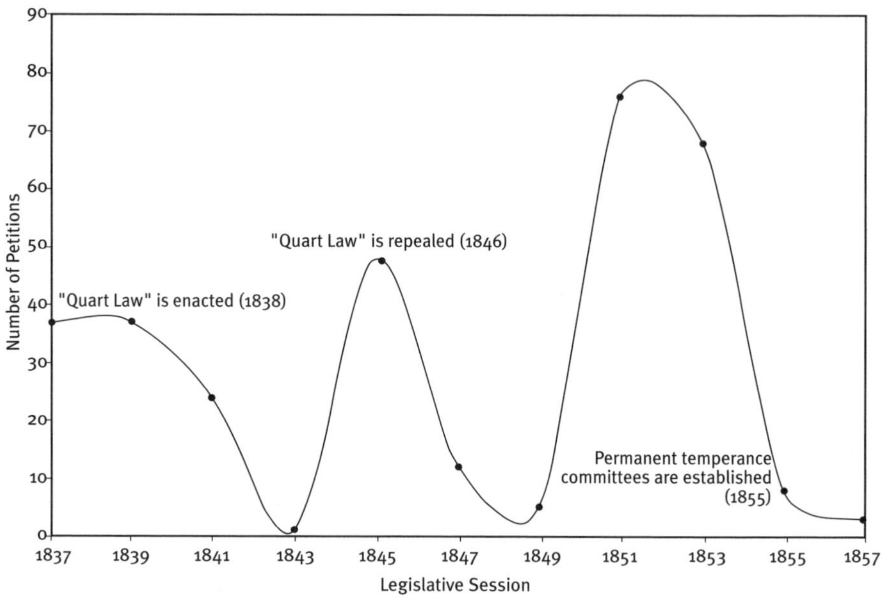

Figure 4 Total Number of Temperance-Related Petitions, by Session of the Tennessee Legislature, 1837–1857. Figure is based on the *Nashville Union's* detailed reports of legislative sessions and captures only the petitions that the paper reported. It is estimated that 75 percent of temperance-related petitions were anti-liquor, 25 percent pro-liquor. Each point represents the beginning of a legislative session, the fall of an odd-numbered year.

sumed collecting signatures at a pace that surpassed all previous efforts (figure 4). Nevertheless, when the state legislature persisted with the status quo, determined anti-drink reformers finally supplemented their petitioning with electoral pressure, beginning in 1853.

With the Tennessee state elections of 1853 looming, temperance reformers held local nonpartisan conventions to endorse legislative candidates who supported a referendum on a Maine Law.[78] While their votes may not have decided the results of the state races,[79] some observers claimed that "the election turned upon the Liquor question."[80] In any case, anti-liquor activists followed up their electoral activities with a fresh petitioning drive for a state vote on prohibition. Predictably, the Select Committee on Tippling ignored their flood of memorials and issued a report opposing a prohibition referendum.[81] The House of Representatives as a whole, however, bitterly debated a motion to "non-concur" with the Select Committee's report, and the Senate suffered from similar rancor.[82] One combatant admitted that lawmakers were under intense pressure from five thousand anti-liquor petitioners, as well as from "their constituents for the positions [on the liquor issue] assumed in the late canvass."[83] In early 1854 the Senate approved a prohibition referendum, the

House rejected it, and the teetotalers had peaked in influence without winning state prohibition.[84]

Like their colleagues in other southern states, Tennessee's antebellum reformers confronted a stable two-party system which strove mightily to prevent the liquor issue from disturbing party unity.[85] Beginning in 1845, party leaders appointed pro-licensing majorities to the Select Committee on Tippling, and in the early 1850s party organs like the *Nashville Union* "greatly" preferred "that the Maine Law should not be discussed through our columns."[86] Thus the Tennessee legislature's tepid response to the teetotalers' various petition and electoral campaigns had little to do with the tactics themselves. In the North, though, the capricious political conditions after 1848 made lawmakers vastly more responsive to identical techniques.[87] In Maine and Massachusetts, for example, both states' legislative committees on the liquor issue sustained close relationships with the prohibitionists after the late 1840s. As mass petitioning and electoral pressure escalated in this period, the select committees in question held public hearings and invited reform leaders to personally "represent the views and wishes" of the anti-liquor petitioners to the legislature.[88] On one occasion, the chair of Maine's legislative temperance committee directly negotiated with teetotalers in amending a prohibition bill, thus producing a harsher law than had been initially proposed.[89] The committees' receptivity to prohibition ultimately contributed to its enactment by both states in the 1850s.

Antebellum teetotalers in Tennessee may not have enjoyed the same political opportunities as their northern counterparts, but their persistence did force the state legislature to acknowledge the resilience of anti-liquor sentiment. In 1855 the Tennessee legislature finally converted the Select Committee on Tippling and Tippling Houses into two standing committees.[90] After the Civil War, standing committees often replaced the select committees that had dominated the antebellum response to prohibitory petitions. Anti-drink agitation was not a fad, and many state legislatures had concluded that they could not address the continuing concerns raised by anti-liquor memorials in a temporary body.[91] Whether select or standing, temperance and other relevant legislative committees habitually served as forums for public debate, vehicles for resolving the volatile liquor question, and, most importantly, points of access for the prohibition movement.

As public hearings became the norm, anti-liquor leaders testified more frequently in behalf of their cause. In addition, they increasingly engaged in informal talks with key committee members regarding the details of liquor legislation and prohibition amendments. Of course, when political conditions were inauspicious, anti-liquor activists accused these committees of "destroying every temperance bill" and of avoiding "an honest discussion of the measures advocated by the multitudes of earnest petitioners."[92] Nevertheless, these bodies and other common features of state government helped to homogenize an often-fragmented movement.

Parochial Protest and Direct Action

Anti-drink reformers would resume mass petitioning, electoral pressure, and other antebellum protest forms after the 1850s, but they failed to coordinate a significant translocal campaign until the 1870s. In the meantime, anti-liquor agitation centered on the fallout from the prohibition wave of the early 1850s, which saw thirteen state and territorial legislatures adopt prohibition laws. As state authorities began to repeal, amend, and emasculate these laws, some anti-liquor activists continued the struggle for state prohibition; others sought the enforcement of their paper Maine Laws; and still others could not be bothered with temperance so long as the war raged. Although referred to as the "years of lull and despair,"[93] the 1855–65 period witnessed the movement's first extensive use of militant direct-action tactics. As noted in chapter 1, some social movement scholars maintain that disruptive protest is more likely than conventional protest forms to secure concessions from political and social élites.[94] While perhaps true for other movements, the anti-liquor crusade discovered that direct action produced only locally uneven and transitory achievements.

That direct action periodically threatened to plunge the postbellum movement into localized mayhem followed from the state governments' diverse and weak enforcement capacities. Owing to their basic structural similarities, antebellum state governments ultimately developed analogous institutions and procedures for integrating anti-liquor agitation into the policymaking process. To execute liquor policies, however, state governments typically lacked central enforcement agencies and exerted only loose control over local criminal justice systems. This absence of state-level agencies meant that regulatory policy continued well into the late nineteenth century to be enforced by what the historian William Novak calls a "local, customary, and discretionary regime." Since the local police and courts bore the enforcement burden, anti-drink activists had to shift their gaze from the states to the localities to realize their goals. In doing so, though, these reformers could not help noticing the paucity of municipal and county efforts. Indeed, mayors, prosecutors, and constables frequently ignored unlawful liquor selling.[95] As a result, activists either sought legislative enhancement of state enforcement powers or, as was so often the case, engaged in vigilante activities themselves.

Unsurprisingly, prohibitionists first participated in widespread vigilantism after Maine Law fever had swept through the states in the early 1850s. In several

Maine Law states, teetotalers maintained Carson Leagues, Temperance Watchmen, and similar groups to preserve prohibition by electing sympathetic officials and by filing complaints against illegal liquor dealers. In this latter role, these organizations resembled private police forces, which functioned "to plug the gaps created by inefficient and unwilling local authorities." According to the Maine Law's provisions, local authorities could not search a suspect property until three complainants had testified to illicit dealing on the premises. To provide such testimony, reformers either personally collected evidence of illicit sales or paid informers to perform this unpleasant task. As might be expected, these activities directly pitted the prohibitionists against their opponents, often to violent effect.[96]

While male vigilantes usually worked within the electoral, criminal justice, and court systems, women had fewer available legal remedies and pioneered more disruptive forms of direct pressure in the 1850s. In states slow to pass Maine Laws, women sometimes organized raids against liquor dealers and destroyed their stocks.[97] Unable to rely on men to enact prohibition, "the ladies have taken the rumsellers into their own hands and enforced laws of their own making."[98] Meanwhile, in those states with stringent prohibitory laws, many women were discouraged from testifying about illicit liquor sales.[99] Rather than wait "in vain for some legal proceedings" against lawless dealers, some of these women took direct action. For example, the non-enforcement of state prohibition in Rockport, Massachusetts, gave rise to a Hatchet Gang in 1856, which raided saloons and smashed liquor casks in the streets.[100]

Whether sponsored by men or women, this early direct action had parochial qualities that resurfaced in its postwar counterparts. For one thing, successful efforts required both public support and acquiescent law enforcement, features that were absent in areas indifferent to the dry cause. For instance, the women who pursued vigilantism frequently lived in communities that shared their concerns about the saloon. As a result, they could often rely on local juries to exonerate them or, if convicted, on male sympathizers who would pay their fines.[101] In towns like Burlington, Iowa, though, the public largely tolerated violations of the state prohibition law and refused to assist both complainants and the police in their raids. Indeed, public apathy was so pronounced, a local newspaper asserted in 1856, that "not one in a hundred of our citizens will aid in" executing the state Maine Law.[102] Such lethargy undoubtedly discouraged teetotalers, but it was preferable to retaliatory violence. In Chester, Massachusetts, the local Carson League's meeting place was destroyed by a powder keg, and the perpetrators were never found.[103]

Even when it found initial public support, antebellum vigilantism generally produced only fleeting success, particularly in the face of determined liquor sellers.

Dealers often created groups and legal funds to contest the court cases instigated by the Carson League; likewise, they launched several suits against female vigilantes, seeking compensation for property damage. As local saloonkeepers mounted their counterattacks, many anti-liquor activists were discovering that direct action was both wearing and risky, and abandoned their campaigns against them. The Carson Leagues and Temperance Watchmen were therefore short-lived, and most female vigilante groups disbanded after their brief bursts of saloon violence. Thus, though their opponents periodically won in court, stubborn saloonkeepers could simply wait for the raids and the investigations to subside before resuming their trade.[104]

Overall, postbellum direct action was also sporadic, geographically dispersed, grueling for participants, and transitory in its achievements. Nevertheless, activists improved their coordination of direct action in this period, and on occasion they formed permanent movement organizations to solidify the gains of these protest episodes. For instance, the Woman's Crusade of 1873–74 used newspapers, correspondence, and roving lecturers to report on a wave of protests that originated in Fredonia, New York, but achieved its greatest notoriety in Ohio. As a result, women conducted both direct and indirect action against liquor dealers in thirty-one states and at 911 locales. While relying heavily on petitioning and other traditional protest forms in several states, the Crusaders were best known for their marches, which involved prayer and song and which culminated in saloon visits. Once there, women sought to persuade the dealer to abandon the liquor traffic and take the pledge. In some communities, the marches proceeded peacefully and induced several local saloonkeepers to close their businesses. In others, officials banned the marches, and pro-liquor crowds assaulted Crusaders with rocks, boots, eggs, and liquor.[105]

The regional variations in the Crusade's tactics, though, suggest that the translocal character of its direct action should not be overstated. As Jack Blocker has shown, saloon visitations were concentrated in the Midwest, where the saloon's social effects were the greatest[106] and where men had failed to enforce liquor restrictions.[107] If the Crusade's direct action was somewhat parochial, its effects were also temporary. For example, many local praying bands stimulated enforcement and the enactment of liquor ordinances, only to see these gains fade quickly. The Crusade's initial damage to the liquor industry proved similarly limited: after dips in the consumption of intoxicating beverages and the number of liquor dealers (aggravated by an economic depression), both indices turned upward by 1880. Still, in spite of its brief life, the Crusade taught many women a new respect for their abilities, drew thousands of women into the anti-liquor crusade for the first time, and provided the impetus for the formation of the Woman's Christian Temperance Union.[108]

By institutionalizing the Crusade, however, the WCTU diverted women's anti-liquor agitation away from marching and direct pressure, and toward more conventional protest forms such as petitioning.[109] In contrast, the founders of the national Citizens' Law and Order League hoped that a central organization would reinforce local efforts to prosecute lawless saloons. From the time of its birth in 1883, the CLOL claimed that "it is in no part of the purpose of this organization to relieve the constituted authorities of the responsibility . . . to enforce the law," and yet its attempts to "supplement" the efforts of local officials suggest otherwise.[110] Like the Carson Leagues and the Temperance Watchmen, local Law and Order Leagues usually had to gather evidence of crimes before they could compel the prosecution of saloonkeepers for violating state and local liquor laws. They therefore employed volunteers and paid detectives to pose as customers who would patronize local saloons and later testify about their illegal activities in court. While initially successful in generating convictions, such methods produced diminishing returns by the late 1880s. In particular, CLOL informers were often the victims and perpetrators of violence. Though sometimes severely beaten by their opponents, agents also engaged in their own excesses, including the demolition of saloon property. As a result, the press and the courts tired of the group's efforts, and many judges began to toss out cases that the league had sponsored.[111]

But even before the CLOL self-destructed in the early 1890s, the group had succumbed to the parochialism of the "hundreds of law and order leagues" that had "spontaneously sprung up in different parts of the country."[112] Local affiliates based their enforcement schemes on local preferences, the legal status of liquor in their communities, and the available legal remedies. In addition, the vigor of branch efforts often depended on the tenacity and creativity of their leaders. For example, the Chicago and Boston branches of the CLOL won distinction through their enforcement of the Illinois and Massachusetts civil damage acts, which banned the sale of alcohol to minors and drunkards and which held liquor sellers financially liable for damages caused by illegal customers to themselves and their dependents.[113] Moreover, the success of the local branches was partly due to the tactical innovations of men like Andrew Paxton, who not only created the first local league[114] but also pioneered ways to file suit against saloonkeepers.[115] Elsewhere, leagues in New Jersey focused on prosecuting liquor sellers for violating the state's Sunday-closing laws; in Massachusetts the Cambridge affiliate sought to shut down illicit saloons which defied the "no-license" outcomes of the city's local option elections.[116]

Unfortunately, not every community had either the legal means or the leadership to fully participate in the law-and-order movement. For instance, even though Ohio had a strong civil damage act on its books, Washington Gladden conceded: "The statutes of Ohio are not, I think, favorable to the existence of such leagues. . . . The mayors and the police authorities of our cities generally refuse to execute the laws of the State as to liquor selling, except on the complaint of the citizens; and the citizens . . . must give bonds for the payment of the costs of the suit. . . . If the case be continued from time to time, until witnesses have disappeared, the costs of the suit will . . . be borne by the complainant. Under such circumstances private citizens are loathe to engage in the prosecution of crime."[117]

Similarly, the Michigan Supreme Court's judicial activism threatened to hobble the state's affiliates. In 1887 the court had invalidated the state's new local option measure, disrupting the efforts of anti-liquor activists.[118] Hence in 1888 the court's decision to review the state's latest liquor restrictions left local Law and Order Leagues in limbo, waiting "to know what chances there are for successful work."[119] Meanwhile, the "law and order" activists of Sidney, Nebraska, found so little to do in their community that they prosecuted several men for cruelty to animals.[120] Their counterparts in Connecticut never lacked for work, but instead floundered in the late 1880s while they searched for a new state executive.[121] Finally, the weak national organization could hardly impose uniformity on its local affiliates or shore up dying branches. The CLOL almost "never had a propagandist in the field," and many league officers "learned of the existence of local leagues only from current accounts in the public press."[122]

Even after the CLOL's demise in the early 1890s, vigilantism appealed to activists who could not tolerate the lax enforcement of liquor laws. Carrie Nation, for one, led her raids on illicit liquor joints in Kansas in 1901.[123] Most direct action after 1900 involved neither women nor the use of axes but occurred under the auspices of the Anti-Saloon League, which was led by males and encouraged the limited use of professional detectives and informers to police dry localities. Because the ASL was well aware of vigilantism's pitfalls, though, it warned against "ill-advised and premature attempts at law enforcement which have only resulted in failure and the disheartenment of temperance workers."[124] Furthermore, the ASL sought to exert quality control over local enforcement efforts by compiling a list of "competent and efficient persons to do this work," who were then referred to local groups "wanting such service."[125]

Of course, not even the league could anticipate every reaction to the detectives it recommended, and their actions would periodically provoke embarrassing episodes of violence. In 1909, for instance, the Ohio League referred several private detectives to local drys in Newark, Ohio. To the ASL's chagrin, their raid on a Newark saloon stirred up a mob, which lynched one detective and only underscored the unpopularity of such tactics.[126] Nevertheless, before national prohibition the league, unlike the CLOL, managed to avoid the consequences of vigilante excess. Its ability to tolerate occasional enforcement debacles stemmed partly from its attempts to minimize the movement's reliance on detectives. Instead, the ASL focused its enforcement efforts on electing, pressuring, and assisting officials charged with this responsibility. For example, the state affiliates offered their attorneys to the states and localities as special prosecutors, as authors of *amicus curiae* briefs in court cases, and as sources of expert knowledge for officials who were preparing trial briefs.[127]

More importantly, however, the league never staked its reputation solely on law enforcement before 1920. It may have touted its enforcement victories during its lean early years to "maintain its image of progress toward prohibition," but the ASL's primary goal was to draw Americans into an escalating war against the saloon, and enforcement was only one part of this broader campaign. "Agitation has occupied and will continue to occupy, perhaps nine-tenths of the league efforts," leaders of the ASL insisted in 1900. "Attempts at Law Enforcement which are not preceded by arousing public sentiment to demand and support them are generally futile."[128]

Despite conventional wisdom, federalism need not inhibit national social movements. Beginning in the 1830s, the anti-liquor movement's access to generic protest forms and the means to diffuse those forms facilitated its quest for state liquor laws in every state of the union. Moreover, that the state legislatures were developing analogous procedures for coping with constituents' demands meant that teetotalers soon developed familiar routines for interacting with the polity. Women circulated petitions, and men voted for supporters of their cause. In response, lawmakers referred temperance memorials to the relevant committees; the committees issued reports; and legislatures and governors produced policies which best served their political interests. While these routines lacked the romance of direct action, they proved sturdy vehicles for resolving the volatile liquor question. After all, almost every legal remedy for the liquor problem required legislative action at some point, be it high license, local option, or prohibition amendments.

To be sure, federalism placed some obstacles in the path of the temperance movement. For example, Richard F. Hamm argues that two national policies impeded the drys' progress in the states after the Civil War: the federal liquor tax and the federal courts' interstate commerce rulings. Whereas the federal tax legitimated an evil trade in dry and wet states alike, the interstate commerce rulings permitted liquor retailers to introduce their products into prohibition territory, thus exacerbating the difficult problem of enforcement. Nevertheless, these barriers to anti-liquor agitation were not insurmountable; indeed, during the Progressive Era the moderates' pragmatism led them to use the federal tax as an enforcement weapon in the states and to secure federal legislation that banned liquor shipments to dry states.[129]

Meanwhile, with respect to the lower layers of government, the case of enforcement reveals that too much variation in local liquor policies and enforcement regimes produced only scattered movement activity. Instead of creating relatively homogeneous outlets for agitation, the "law and order" movement proved difficult to transmit from one community to another and remained mired in the parochialism of local politics.[130] In a larger sense, however, this account of dry vigilantism underscores the role of goal selection in shaping a movement's choice of tactics. Most anti-liquor activists were deeply troubled by the lawless acts of the liquor traffic and by the enforcement lapses of local officials. By concentrating on securing "law and order," though, many reformers found themselves entangled in personally fought local battles that generated either fleeting victories or counterproductive defeats.

Still, the parochial character of these battles might have been averted if the public and political élites had been more amenable to the creation of state police forces and other central enforcement agencies during the nineteenth century. Significantly, anti-liquor activists were well aware of the states' deficiencies in this regard and sometimes lobbied for constabularies, police boards, and other state-level enforcement mechanisms during the late nineteenth century. Alas, such enforcement regimes would only become commonplace in the twentieth century, with the rise of administrative reform movements and the ASL's crusade for these measures.[131]

In the meantime, many anti-liquor moderates were coalescing around local option as an initial goal, which they hoped would broaden the movement's appeal. Unlike enforcement, the pursuit of this goal involved the use of conventional tactics, legislative action, and interaction with state government—all of which were familiar to temperance advocates across the nation. However, the pathway to local option was not entirely clear, as the next chapter demonstrates. Indeed, given local option's spotty antebellum track record and its troubled legal history, it is not surprising that many prohibitionists should have preferred to campaign for prohibition amendments, which also relied on the movement's standard repertoire of collective action.

4 Legislative Supremacy and the Definition of Movement Goals

Not only was the anti-liquor movement's push for "law and order" influenced by the structure of the lower levels of American government, but so were its drives for constitutional prohibition, local option, and most other postwar objectives. With respect to enforcement, however, reformers struggled to translate isolated crusades into a campaign that could be pursued in every state, a problem that haunted the movement in its other efforts. The challenge for postbellum reformers was to identify initial goals that could be advocated in virtually every state and that permitted them to exploit a standard repertoire of protest. As it turned out, postbellum activists essentially found two solutions to this problem: they either exploited points of access common to most state governments, or they sought changes in government policies that would provide generic outlets for activism. The push for constitutional prohibition in the 1880s exemplifies the former approach; after all, every state had a constitution, and the procedures for altering them were fairly comparable.[1] In contrast, the Anti-Saloon League's campaign for general local options laws illustrates the latter solution. Since not every locality had the opportunity to expel the saloon, the ASL had to convince state lawmakers across the nation to grant municipalities, counties, rural districts and city wards the privilege of holding "no-license" elections.

Naturally, it proved easier to work through existing policymaking channels, but even these paths were not consistently "open" for use by anti-drink agitators. Indeed, as Lee Ann Banaszak has argued, social movements can only capitalize on political opportunities if they perceive them as such.[2] For example, as early as 1818 new state constitutions began requiring referenda to ratify constitutional revisions and amendments; such provisions became standard shortly thereafter. Nevertheless, as the first part of this chapter demonstrates, drys would not coordinate a broad-based campaign using these forms of direct democracy until the late 1870s. This delayed reaction to a new source of access reflected the slow evolution of ideas about the nature and function of state constitutions. During the antebellum period, anti-liquor activists had to justify their reliance on constitutional measures, for the question of whether temperance belonged in organic law was still murky. Moreover, their first experiments with constitutional revision suggested that constitution makers were unlikely to require positive regulatory action by state governments. By the late 1870s, though, state constitutional change had come to mirror garden-variety lawmaking, and state constitutions had evolved into more potent sources of state regulatory power. Thus drys could view constitutional reform as both vulnerable to their mass-based agitation and consonant with their cause.

Once the campaign for constitutional prohibition faltered, however, the anti-liquor movement struggled anew for a unifying purpose. While most anti-liquor activists endorsed some restrictions on the liquor traffic, they disagreed about which legal solution should be the movement's immediate focus. Ever the purists, the radicals remained strong proponents of national and state constitutional prohibition while also favoring state prohibition statutes and the repeal of all licensing laws. Meanwhile, moderate temperance advocates seemed open to any number of alternatives, including local option, civil damage laws, high license fees, and state control of liquor retailing, or the "dispensary system" (for a summary of prohibitory goals, see table 3). Undoubtedly, the moderates' strategic flexibility reflected their pragmatic legal ideas, which maintained that all law was potentially useful, even when it failed to completely eradicate evils like the liquor traffic.[3] Nevertheless, pragmatism did not preclude the moderates from privileging one goal above all others.

By the mid-1890s moderates had formed the Anti-Saloon League, steering the movement away from constitutional prohibition and toward local option as its initial goal. As the second part of this chapter will show, the shift to a provincial strategy was not the result of random dry experiments but involved a conscious adoption of a method which had produced tangible if piecemeal results in the South. Indeed, the moderates were reacting to more than just a sense that constitutional prohibition was unattainable, and there was nothing accidental about their growing interest in general local option during the 1880s. If anything, these reformers were responding to the state legislatures' devolution of liquor licensing power to the localities and their inhabitants, as well as to growing judicial acceptance of these licensing regimes, both of which reflected a decline in legislative supremacy as a fundamental principle. In short, anti-liquor activists profited from changes in the distribution of power between the states and the localities, as well as from new collective beliefs about state legislative authority—developments which aided other reform movements as well.[4]

The Origins of Constitutional Prohibition

In recent years, some scholars have portrayed national constitutional prohibition as an anomaly, the only amendment to directly address a substantive social problem. To these analysts, the Eighteenth Amendment's repeal was only just, for "a constitution ought to enable legislation and public policies to take place, . . . not determine what that legislation or those public policies ought to be."[5] However, this ideal of a constitution as a basic framework of governing principles proved far less influential at the state level. As early as the 1830s, state constitutions became so mired in political conflict that their content expanded to address issues beyond governmental structure and powers. For much of the 1800s, state constitutions "not only set out the frame of government; they also expressed the basic power structure of the state: they were pro-railroad or anti-railroad; they favored the northern part of the state or the southern part, this party or that party, this faction or that."[6] In short, an abundance of interests left their imprint on state constitutions, and the prohibitionists were but one group among many.

Though anti-liquor activists were hardly atypical, they initially had to justify their reliance on constitutional—as opposed to statutory—measures. For example, an early attempt to place a temperance provision in the Michigan Constitution of 1850 provoked one convention delegate to state that "we should only embrace general principles. We should not define the sale and use of ardent spirits to be a crime. . . . What may be considered proper now, may be deemed immoral hereafter; and what may be thought wrong in our day, may be esteemed proper in the next generation."[7] Even after the call for such provisions became commonplace, some eminent teetotalers rejected temperance as a suitable subject for state constitutions. In 1889, for example, one Harvard professor who had voted dry in local option elections nonetheless opposed constitutional prohibition. He maintained that state constitutions "were not made to be codes of law, or to embody the opinion of a momentary majority upon an entirely unsettled question, like . . . the best way to deal with the drink question."[8]

Despite such skepticism, temperance advocates first sought to use the processes of constitutional change in 1837, after public demands for greater democracy had exposed state constitutions to the designs of private interests, including evangelical reformers. Moreover, after the Panic of 1837 constitutional conventions had imposed a variety of new limits on state legislatures. Ultimately, these two trends encouraged teetotalers to petition constitutional conventions for restrictions on liquor licensing. While their efforts produced modest results before 1860, the relative permanence of these gains boded well for the future use of constitutional legislation.

Table 3 Goals of the Anti-Liquor Movement

Goal	Definition	Advantages	Disadvantages	Faction(s) That Worked to Obtain Goal
Repeal of licensing laws	By law, governments cannot issue liquor licenses, but are not required to impose penalties for selling without a license.	State symbolically divorces itself from evil trade; reduces number of saloons in some areas.	Most areas fail to ban selling without a license, allowing unlicensed liquor trade to thrive.	Antebellum activists, postwar radicals
Bans on sale of liquor in small quantities	State legislatures ban the sale of liquor in quantities less than a set amount (e.g., one quart, 15 gallons).	Bans liquor retailing in saloons, the sites of much drunkenness.	Allows wholesale liquor trade to thrive; difficult to enforce.	Antebellum activists
High-license	States and localities require liquor dealers to pay high fees for licenses; bans unlicensed sales.	Reduces number of seedy saloons; state may regulate liquor trade.	Implies state approval of evil trade and allows trade to thrive.	Moderates, especially in urban North
Sunday closing	States and localities require liquor dealers to close their saloons on Sundays.	Helps preserve Sunday as the "Lord's day" and day of rest.	Allows liquor trade to thrive on other days of the week.	Moderates, especially in urban North
Civil damage law	Private individuals who have been harmed by illicit actions of saloon may sue and collect damages.	Forces saloons to comply with restrictions on sales.	Plaintiffs and witnesses often fail to bring charges or testify.	Moderates
Law enforcement	Local police and court system combine to enforce existing anti-liquor laws.	Closes lawless bars; shows that liquor laws are effective.	Fails to impose new restrictions and bans on liquor trade.	Moderates
Local option (by special legislation)	State legislatures grant particular localities the power to choose licensing or ban on liquor sales.	Gives some localities the power to ban liquor sales.	Fails to extend dry territory to broad area; difficult to enforce.	Moderates, especially in South

Table 3 Continued

Goal	Definition	Advantages	Disadvantages	Faction(s) That Worked to Obtain Goal
General local option	State legislatures grant class(es) of localities (e.g., municipalities, counties, districts) the power to vote on whether to license the sale of liquor.	Like special legislation, but applies to class(es) of localities throughout a state.	Like special legislation, but also allows for more inconsistency in state liquor policy.	Moderates
Dispensary system	States or localities operate retail liquor stores for private consumption; bans private liquor dealing.	Closes all saloons; state may tightly regulate liquor sales.	Implies state approval of liquor; allows its producers to thrive.	Moderates, especially in South
Statutory prohibition laws (referred to as Maine Laws during the antebellum period)	State legislatures enact laws that ban sale and manufacture of liquor under threat of penalty.	Bans both sale and production of liquor; covers an extensive area; creates a consistent policy against the liquor trade.	Subject to partisan maneuvers in legislatures; can easily be repealed; courts nullify some provisions; difficult to enforce.	Radicals, moderates, (but only after state was "ready")
State constitutional prohibition	State constitutions ban sale and manufacture of liquor; states enact enabling legislation and penalties.	Like statutory prohibition, but less likely to be repealed and enshrines prohibition principle in the organic law.	More difficult to enact than statutory prohibition; difficult to enforce.	Radicals, moderates (but only after state was "ready")
National constitutional prohibition	National constitution bans sale and manufacture of liquor; Congress enacts enabling legislation and penalties.	Same as state prohibition, but covers nation and requires national enforcement effort.	More difficult to enact than state prohibition; difficult to enforce.	Radicals, moderates (but only after 1913)

Table based on various studies of the American temperance movement. See bibliography for a complete listing of studies consulted.

Like so many other aspects of American politics, state constitutions were transformed by the wave of democratic reforms that swept the United States after 1810. Among other things, Americans agitated for the direct election of governors, administrative officers, and judges, as well as for abolishing property qualifications for office holding and suffrage. In a similar fashion, this clamor for greater control by the citizenry slowly altered the procedures for state constitutional amendment and revision. Connecticut's constitution of 1818 provided for amendment by referendum; new constitutions in Maine (1819), Massachusetts (1821), New York (1821), and other states soon followed suit. Meanwhile, the practice of submitting new constitutions to a popular vote, which had originated in New England during the late eighteenth century, became customary elsewhere after 1829.[9]

Thus, as mass parties emerged on the political landscape in the 1830s, state constitutions were increasingly subject to popular pressures. Together, these two developments altered the character of constitutional change, as parties and private interests often sought to control conventions for their own aims. Whereas constitutional conventions had previously "witnessed benign factionalism and deferential politics," the conventions of the 1830s and 1840s saw the Democrats and their Whig opponents struggle "to legitimate their partisan goals through recourse to constitutional authority." In doing so, they developed the practice of constitutional legislation, or the drafting of highly specific constitutional provisions that could not be obtained through normal legislative processes.[10] As with ordinary state legislation of this period, constitutional innovations frequently concerned the states' role in economic development. For example, the ten new constitutions of the period 1836–60 included articles devoted to banks, corporations, and public finance.[11]

Relying on constitutional legislation, however, only weakened claims that the state constitutions represented forms of "higher law" which could not be tampered with lightly. Hence, the content of these documents fluctuated with changing conditions and new concerns. For instance, many state governments had borrowed heavily in the 1830s to finance internal improvements, only to default during the depression of 1837–42. Consequently, constitutional conventions in the next decade focused on curbing the power of spendthrift and venal state legislatures. The Maryland Constitution of 1851, for one, proscribed the legislature's power to appropriate money for internal improvements and to contract debts of more than $100,000.[12]

Significantly, these constitutional limits on the state legislatures contributed to the long-term erosion of legislative supremacy at the state level. First conceptualized by John Locke and his contemporaries, legislative supremacy holds that the legislature embodies the commonwealth's supreme power, to which the executive must be subordinate, for "the legislative function is prior to the executive, and the latter must be exercised according to the rules which result from the exercise of the former." Moreover, it maintains that the legislative branch cannot "transfer the power of making laws to any other hands," for lawmaking is a delegated power from the people and only the people can establish the form of their government. In short, legislative supremacy endows the legislature with a virtual monopoly on lawmaking, which in itself is "the highest act of sovereignty that can be performed in a free nation."[13]

As realized in the first state constitutions, the doctrine of legislative supremacy had ensured that the legislatures, as the most democratic of institutions, commanded great authority to determine community goals and enforce compliance. Also, given their disagreeable experience with strong colonial executives, early constitution makers rarely provided governors with more than weak veto and appointment powers, thus freeing the legislature from any meaningful interference by the executive branch. In fact, some of the first state constitutions went so far as to authorize state legislatures to select the governor, administrative officers, and judges. By the 1830s, however, constitution makers had already curtailed legislative power to select executive and judicial personnel, and they had strengthened the governors, giving them some veto power. Furthermore, the sheer fact that constitutional conventions were producing constitutional legislation on topics like banks, corporations, and public finance meant that constitution makers had come to view themselves as rival legislators, empowered to instruct state lawmakers on what they could or could not do.[14]

Fortunately for the anti-liquor cause, this attack on legislative authority also embraced issues that transcended the economic consequences of the Panic of 1837. During the 1840s and 1850s, for example, several new state constitutions contained bans on the legislature's power to sanction future lotteries.[15] In one sense, these provisions resembled other restrictions on state legislatures imposed after 1837. Like state borrowing and other methods of public finance, lotteries had funded public roads, canals, bridges, and schools; nevertheless, recurring lottery scandals only confirmed the citizenry's suspicions that these games provided tainted revenues. Therefore, when the backlash against legislative extravagance and corruption mounted after 1837, several constitutional conventions targeted lotteries in their more general assault on legislative abuses. Still, antebellum lottery bans reflected more than just a general sense that these ventures had contributed to legislative spending sprees. Indeed, evangelical reformers had denounced lotteries on moral grounds since the early 1830s, and had petitioned sundry state legislatures and constitutional conventions to outlaw them.[16]

Based in the same reform network as abolitionism and temperance, the anti-lottery movement would set a powerful precedent for its anti-liquor counterpart. Significantly, the anti-liquor forces first sought to secure constitutional legislation during Pennsylvania's constitutional convention of 1837. The Pennsylvania Society for the Suppression of Lotteries had inundated the gathering with petitions, requesting that a ban on lotteries be inserted in the Bill of Rights. Though the Pennsylvania Temperance Society's campaign was more limited, it had similarly asked that the new constitution prohibit the sale of ardent spirits, a demand more or less ignored.[17] However, this initial failure did not spell the end of such efforts, for the anti-lottery crusade's frequent successes encouraged teetotalers to view state constitutions as appropriate vehicles for their own cause. At the Ohio Constitutional Convention of 1850–51, for example, one delegate used the lottery parallel to bolster his case for a constitutional ban on the legislature's power to license liquor. Noting that the convention had recently outlawed lotteries, Mr. Lawrence easily countered the argument that teetotalers had singled out one crime for constitutional abolition. After all, "If the sale of lottery tickets is so great an evil as to demand the action of this body, is not the sale of intoxicating drinks, and the creation of a multitude of drunkards still more so? I say there are some crimes of so deep a nature, that strike so strongly at the foundations of society, as to demand the interposition of a remedy in the organic law of the State."[18]

The abolition of lotteries may have illustrated what constitutional change could accomplish, but anti-drink activists only obtained constitutional legislation in Michigan (1850) and Ohio (1850–51) during the antebellum period. While reformers worked through constitutional conventions (as opposed to the amendment process) in each state, their specific requests varied: most in Michigan desired outright prohibition, while those in Ohio only asked that the legislature be denied its power to issue liquor licenses, thus symbolically divorcing the government from an evil trade.[19] Regardless of their petitioners' preferences, both conventions responded to their requests by offering to rescind the legislature's licensing authority, a negative action that followed the trend toward more constitutional limits on legislative prerogatives. In fact, when some delegates proposed that the new constitutions require legislative action against the liquor industry, their motions were rejected in convention votes. In Ohio, delegates refused to alter the language of the constitutional provision, from "The General Assembly *may* . . . provide" to "*shall* provide" restrictions against the evils of the liquor traffic. Likewise, the Michigan convention rejected a straight prohibition article, as well as its submission to a popular referendum.[20]

The Michigan and Ohio conventions may only have eliminated the legislature's authority to license liquor, but they nonetheless produced more permanent policies than teetotalers had secured during the prohibition wave of the 1850s.[21] Because of their statutory character, many Maine Laws succumbed to either the legislative counterattack of the wets or judicial scrutiny. As a result, temperance reformers like William H. Armstrong questioned whether statutes were sufficient to cope with the liquor evil. Armstrong, a leader of the New York Sons, had fought for his state's Maine Law, which was passed in 1855 only to be struck down by the state supreme court in 1856. "It seemed to me," he wrote, that if prohibition became "solemnly incorporated into the fundamental law of the State, . . . it would be the duty of every good citizen . . . to concur in giving to it a fair opportunity for legislative, executive, and judicial enforcement." Therefore in the late 1850s Armstrong and some of his colleagues proposed using the amendment process to place this policy "beyond the power of any Court to annul it or of any legislature . . . to repeal it."[22]

As with most state constitutions, amending the New York Constitution was arduous. A proposed amendment had to be passed by two successive legislatures, and only then would it be put to a popular vote. For constitutional prohibitionists like Armstrong, though, this lengthy ordeal would allow the movement to engage in a thorough public discussion of the liquor issue, and thus rally voter support for the dry amendment should it reach that stage. Unfortunately for the reformers, their proposed amendment stalled in the Assembly in 1862 after it had won approval from state lawmakers in the 1861 session. While the amendment's demise was generally ascribed to legislative preoccupation with the Civil War, it also reflected the temperance crusade's waning political strength in those years.[23] Furthermore, the New York campaign revealed that not every supporter of statutory prohibition would advocate its constitutional variant. For instance, the Assembly speaker, Henry J. Raymond, had pledged his full support to the Maine Law in 1855, only to use legislative maneuvering to kill the amendment in 1862.[24]

Thus by the early 1860s anti-liquor activists had experimented with both constitutional amendment and revision. Amendment seemed easier, since constitutional conventions were relatively infrequent in most states. In addition, the amendment process gave activists more leverage over the political élites responsible for submitting amendments. Specifically, the teetotalers could pressure state legislatures, whereas constitutional conventions were unique, nonpartisan gatherings that never stood for reelection.[25] Despite such differences, these two techniques enabled the drys to pursue concrete, statewide goals across the nation, as every state had a constitution and initiating constitutional change was roughly comparable across the states. Nevertheless, doubts lingered as to whether prohibition was an appropriate subject for organic law, especially since it constitutionally usurped the legislature's police powers.

Constitutional change, increasingly regarded by teetotalers as a source of antiliquor policy before the Civil War, was heartily embraced after the war. National efforts to secure slavery's demise and the basic rights of the freedmen proclaimed the wisdom of harnessing constitutions to moral causes. Indeed, the ratification of the Thirteenth, Fourteenth, and Fifteenth Amendments reinforced a growing sense among radical drys that prohibition was a legitimate subject for constitutions, including that of the United States. In 1876 the Prohibition party called for a national constitutional amendment to make prohibition both "universal and permanent."[26] Often, nonpartisan drys like George Hoar also supported this aim; in 1889 Hoar asserted that prohibition "would not imperil the reverence of the Constitution," just as the "three great amendments" did not. If anything, he argued that anyone who revered the U.S. Constitution after slavery had been outlawed would likewise increase his respect for a document that abolished the liquor traffic.[27]

In addition, state constitutions evolved as new social, political, and economic forces left their imprint on them.[28] As of the 1880s, Lord Bryce found "a great deal of matter [in state constitutions] which is in no distinctive sense constitutional law, but of general law."[29] Hence, the prohibitionists could not help seeing that these documents contained numerous clauses extraneous to the government's basic framework. J. N. Stearns, for instance, noted that the New York Constitution banned "excessive bail, cruel punishment, the unreasonable detention of prisoners, the offer or promise of money to voters, the betting at elections, the leasing of the canals, the suspension of specie payment, the receiving of gifts by office-holders, and also . . . the sale of the salt springs belonging to the State." Therefore, to those arguing that prohibition did not belong in the New York constitution, Stearns could reply: "And who shall dare to say that the prohibition of the liquor traffic is of no less importance than questions like these, which from time to time have been placed into the constitution by the people . . . acting in their sovereign capacity?"[30]

Finally, as constitutions grew to resemble statutory codes, they also indirectly encouraged constitutional prohibitionism by counterbalancing powerful business interests.[31] During the 1870s agrarian reformers in the Midwest began advocating constitutional legislation to regulate railroads, warehouses, and grain elevators. For example, farmers secured a section in the Illinois Constitution of 1870 which ordered the general assembly to "correct abuses and prevent unjust discrimination . . . in the rates of freight and passenger tariffs on the different railroads in this State." Other state constitutions followed suit.[32] The Nebraska Constitution of 1875 mandated maximum railroad rates, and the California Constitution of 1879 created an independent railroad commission to regulate passenger and freight rates within the state.[33]

By adopting such provisions, state conventions sought either to prod legislatures into shielding society from the injurious consequences of property use or to seek protection through independent regulatory commissions. Either way, constitution makers had become highly involved in setting regulatory policies, a traditional prerogative of state legislatures. Of course, antebellum constitutional legislation had also reduced legislative authority, but these earlier restraints amounted to a litany of "thou-shall-nots," like the bans on liquor licensing included in the Michigan and Ohio constitutions. Postbellum organic law, on the other hand, increasingly required positive action by state governments that was justified in terms of the states' police powers.[34]

Thus, shortly after agrarian reformers had sought constitutional legislation,[35] Midwestern teetotalers initiated the first multi-state effort to win dry amendments. During the late 1870s reformers from Kansas, Iowa, Michigan, Indiana, Wisconsin, and Illinois began petitioning for constitutional prohibition, campaigns that later produced three referenda.[36] At first, however, several critics cast seeds of doubt about the legitimacy of such endeavors. In Kansas, a former governor argued that a prohibition amendment would strip the state legislature of its power to regulate the liquor traffic, rendering it unable to control liquor retailing for those purposes exempted by the amendment.[37] Thomas McDougall of Ohio also raised this issue in 1883 in a speech against the state's pending dry amendment. "Vote for no constitutional amendment depriving the Legislature of the power on which it rests," he argued. "Constitutional amendments do not enforce themselves; they are always limitations on general legislative power. No greater calamity could befall us, than the adoption of a constitutional amendment which would deprive the Legislature of the power on which [statutory law] rests."[38] Meanwhile, in Iowa, the "strongest argument used against the Amendment" alleged that "the Constitution was no place for a provision which was in nature a police regulation and, therefore should be left to legislation."[39]

By the 1880s, though, orthodox prohibitionists easily dismissed concerns about declining legislative power. John B. Finch, for one, readily admitted that a dry amendment would "define and limit" the state legislature's liquor policies. But that was only right, for the legislature "is created by the Constitution" and would still retain those prerogatives "not taken away by the amendment," such as "the power to regulate, restrain, or prohibit the manufacture and sale [of liquors] for other purposes." J. Ellen Foster was equally untroubled, for "it is an error to suppose that statutes merely voice [state] police power." In fact, "the constitutions of all the States furnish examples of police regulations embodied in organic law."[40] More importantly, like the agrarian reformers, many prohibitionists had come to view constitutional legislation as one way to force the state legislatures to restrain a powerful and corrupt industry. For instance, with respect to Michigan's amendment campaign of 1887, Finch maintained that "The proposed amendment simply operates as an indictment to bring the liquor business into the court for the people and to place it on trial for crimes against society and government. There are but two ways in our Government for trying institutions of this class—the one autocratic, by the Legislature; the other democratic, by the people."[41]

Convinced in 1882 that the people were ready for constitutional prohibition, J. Ellen Foster issued a *Constitutional Amendment Manual*, containing "argument, appeal, petitions, forms of constitution, catechism and general directions for organized work."[42] Consequently, California's teetotalers sought to emulate their Midwestern counterparts by reading and studying "Foster's Amendment Manual." The state's WCTU, which had purchased thirty copies of this book, encouraged members, "[place it] next to your Bible in these days of amendment work."[43] Indeed, between 1878 and 1886 prohibitionists in twenty-eight states petitioned their legislatures for dry amendments; by 1890 anti-liquor activists in six states had lobbied constitutional conventions to achieve the same end.[44] In contrast, only six northern and nine southern states had witnessed campaigns for general local option laws.[45] Thus, during the Gilded Age constitutional prohibition had quickly become the most popular plan for restricting the liquor traffic, particularly in the North.

Local Option, Legislative Supremacy, and the Devolution of State Power

As with constitutional prohibition, public demands for new limits on state legislatures encouraged local gradualism as a political strategy. In particular, local gradualists argued that delegating state liquor control to the localities would eliminate the legislatures' power to protect the saloon through licensing, and would turn "the whole matter over to the people" to decide in their counties, cities, townships, and wards.[46] At the same time, this focus on local agitation also dovetailed with the "home rule" movement, a diffuse crusade that gained momentum in the late nineteenth century and called on state governments to grant more governing authority to the localities. Time and time again, local gradualists would claim to be seeking "home rule" on the liquor question, even as they also asserted that such policies would completely eliminate the saloon.[47] Indeed, this apparent contradiction between local gradualism's immediate aim (local option) and its long-term goals (state and national prohibition) led radical drys to condemn this strategy as inconsistent. Furthermore, purists had long argued that such locally based strategies dissipated the movement's energies and rendered it parochial.

Thus, just as constitutional prohibitionists had to overcome the allegation that constitutions were inappropriate vehicles for their cause, local gradualists had to make a convincing case that local option would not divide "the temperance army into little detachments, to separately fight their own battles, without help or encouragement from other localities."[48] In addition, anti-liquor moderates had to demonstrate that pursuing and exploiting local option laws would not retard the progress of general prohibition, as their radical critics charged. By "scattering" temperance efforts, "Local Option . . . effectively militates against State and National Prohibition," one Prohibition party member declared. Instead of "being a stepping stone to Prohibition, it has contributed so much to thwart such legislation that State Prohibition has never followed as a result of this disunifying measure."[49] Finally, local gradualists had to dispel the radicals' claim that local option involved an unconstitutional delegation of legislative authority to the people. In adopting local option, "the government shifts its own responsibility to the shoulders of the people," the WCTU's *Union Signal* opined in 1894. It "transfers the lawmaking power to them (contrary to the letter and spirit of the constitution) and makes them bear the expense of doing what they have already elected and paid legislators to do."[50]

While driven in part by the internal rivalries of the temperance crusade, many radical critiques of local option also cited its history, which began in the 1830s. Since local option had such an extensive track record, its opponents often assumed that they could predict its future operation by analyzing its past performance. For example, in his historical overview of local option laws in 1891, H. A. Scomp emphasized their brief lives and their failure to produce lasting results. He concluded that similar statutes would also be "subject to change and repeal," and that any gains achieved under their provisions would surely be temporary.[51] In a similar fashion, the orthodox critique of local option as an unconstitutional delegation of legislative power was derived from a series of state and territorial supreme court decisions which nullified several local option laws during the years 1847–88 for violating legislative supremacy. In short, early local gradualists faced not only opposition from the radicals in the 1870s and 1880s, but also a set of historical and legal precedents which suggested that their initial aim—local option—would not meet their expectations. It would simply be too parochial, short-lived, and illicit to serve as an initial goal that could be advocated in virtually every state, lest the ultimate objective of prohibition be harmed.

As discussed in chapter 3, anti-liquor activists first engaged in mass petitioning for statewide local option in the 1830s after their fights against local dramshops had been stymied by unresponsive licensing systems. Above all, local option would remedy the inadequacies of existing general license laws and counter the parochialism of special charters and legislation. Outside New England, most early state laws gave localities the power to approve or disapprove license applicants but not the authority to refuse all applicants.[52] Instead, a community's ability to limit the liquor trade often depended on its corporate charter or on special legislation. Of these two factors, charters initially had the most impact on municipal liquor policies. Through their incorporation powers, state legislatures awarded charters to cities and towns as they reached the appropriate size.[53] While charters outlined many of the same rights, duties, and powers, their differences resulted in a variety of licensing regimes.

To illustrate, the Arkansas legislature passed general laws in 1838 and 1855 empowering its county courts to license liquor establishments and to impose some restrictions on retailers and would-be retailers. So long as license applicants met the conditions of these two state laws, the county courts had to supply them with licenses. For those towns which desired more local control over the barrooms within their boundaries, however, the legislature first addressed their concerns through incorporation. For instance, according to Dover's charter of 1852, the town council could issue its own licenses, separate from those of the county court. In the following year, Fort Smith obtained a charter which allowed its town council to license, regulate, and revoke permits at will. Still, the "most comprehensive regulation" of the liquor traffic in antebellum Arkansas could be found in Greenwood, incorporated in 1858. This town's council had the exclusive power to license; it could suppress immorality and vice in tippling houses; it could impose strict requirements on license applicants; and it could set the price of a license. Furthermore, the Greenwood charter authorized the council to impose substantial fines for violations of its liquor ordinances.[54]

Meanwhile, in 1857 the Arkansas legislature used its incorporation powers to create a six-mile prohibition zone around the newly established Female Collegiate Institute and the Arkansas Military Institute, both in Tulip. Later the Crooked Creek Male Academy, the Pleasant Hill Church, and several other religious and educational institutions secured similar anti-liquor zones through their charters. Of course, incorporation provided a rather limited means for addressing local concerns about liquor retailing; after all, towns, academies, and churches did not replace their basic charters very often. Nonetheless, the Arkansas legislature's power to enact special legislation—or acts which only applied to particular regions and localities—allowed it to amend charters ad hoc. Thus when dissatisfied localities requested new powers to regulate the liquor traffic, legislators could respond by revising their charters. In 1838, for instance, Little Rock won an amendment to its city charter (1835), which granted sole licensing authority to city officials. Finally, special legislation offered counties some autonomy in designing their own liquor policies. Unlike towns, counties were not corporate entities but instead existed to maintain local courts and collect state taxes. As a result, counties desiring more control over the liquor traffic than was sanctioned by state law depended solely on local legislation. In 1855, for example, Ouachita and Phillips Counties both gained the power to prohibit liquor sales in small quantities through a special act of the Arkansas legislature.[55]

The Arkansas case was far from unusual; with respect to Indiana, for instance, one historian records that "the period of [liquor] legislation between 1830 and 1850 may be characterized as the period of local legislation." In Indiana alone, state lawmakers passed 126 different liquor measures, most of which applied only to counties and municipalities.[56] For anti-liquor activists, the legislatures' willingness to restrict licensing through incorporation and special legislation was a promising, if limited, development. As a teetotaler in North Carolina wrote in 1840: "The legislature seems to have indicated a consciousness, that the [license] system was iniquitous and mischievous in forbidding the sale of ardent spirits around the University of N. Carolina within the limits of five miles, and in enacting the same prohibition in relation to Davidson College within two miles. We greatly rejoice that the legislature has been so careful to protect the young men of those institutions from the blighting influence of the spirit-seller, and can only regret that the youth of the whole State are not equally protected by the general extension of such wholesome laws."[57] Similarly, the Pennsylvania legislature's decision to limit its local option law (1846) to eighteen counties and two boroughs angered teetotalers in Philadelphia. Their county had been excluded from the law's operation despite their numerous petitions, and they were reduced to condemning the state legislature's actions.[58]

To be sure, some anti-liquor activists enjoyed more favorable state liquor policies than others. In New England, where many towns had long operated as miniature commonwealths, state liquor laws gave local officials a great deal of licensing discretion. That discretion, along with the region's distinctive town-meeting system of local government, meant that many New Englanders "did not even wait for the local-option law before they began to vote out saloons."[59] Occasionally, though, even temperance advocates in these states encountered recalcitrant or indifferent officials. For instance, in 1842 the teetotalers of Portland, Maine, managed to persuade the board of aldermen to refuse to issue any liquor licenses, but these officials "took no steps to impose the penalties provided for those who should sell without license." Instead, the aldermen claimed that "the people did not wish the law enforced," and liquor sales flourished.[60]

Unlike such roundabout methods, general local option laws promised more direct and far-reaching results for temperance advocates. Of course, Maine Laws and state bans on the sale of liquor in small quantities had even more sweeping effects, but enacting such measures was not always possible. By 1860 teetotalers had gained general local option measures from fourteen state legislatures, along with several other acts which embraced the essential elements of the same policy.[61] Like their postwar counterparts, antebellum local option laws authorized the electorate to vote directly on whether liquor should be licensed in a given locality. Early variants of this procedure also resembled later ones in that they allowed fresh "no-license" elections to be held from time to time. Before the war, however, new elections were usually possible annually, whereas postbellum citizens had to wait an average of two years before they could reverse the outcomes of their previous elections.[62] In either case, a local community could easily experience volatile shifts in its liquor policy, as voters repeatedly changed their minds about the virtues of licensing.[63]

Despite these basic similarities, early local option statutes were never as complex, effective, or long-lived as many of those enacted after the Civil War. For example, most antebellum laws directly mandated that "no-license" contests be held concurrently with annual elections and town meetings,[64] while postbellum drys generally had to initiate such votes through an intricate petitioning process. On the other hand, the modesty of early local option measures ensured that they lacked strong enforcement provisions, a defect that later local-optionists would seek to correct. For instance, the laws typically failed to authorize enforcement by state and county officials,[65] and they imposed relatively minor penalties on liquor dealers who operated in "no-license" territory.[66] Hence, these statutes granted local officials substantial discretion in interpreting the meaning of "no-license" outcomes.

To some local authorities, "no-license" only meant that they lacked power to issue liquor licenses. This policy may have pleased many teetotalers on a symbolic level by removing the government's blessing from an evil trade, but it also tolerated retailers who were willing to operate without a license. Conversely, other officials understood a vote for "no-license" to mean that their constituents favored abolishing public drinking houses, and prosecuted illicit dealers more vigorously. Still, since early local option laws specified only small fines for violations, enforcement campaigns often had a minimal impact on illegal retailing. As a result, the liquor traffic could escape serious damage in "no-license" communities, and many anti-drink reformers concluded that local option was inadequate to suppress it.[67]

Given its reputation as ineffectual, local option legislation was frequently repealed. For example, New York and Iowa both repealed local-option measures that they had enacted in 1845 (Iowa in 1847, New York in 1849). In fact, only a few states sustained this policy for more than five years during the antebellum period.[68] Meanwhile, a series of state supreme court decisions rejected the local option principle on the grounds that it unconstitutionally delegated legislative power. To illustrate, the Pennsylvania Supreme Court held in 1847 that the state's 1846 local option law possessed "no innate force" and "remains a dead letter, until breathed upon by the people and called into activity by an exertion of their voices" through annual elections. "Until then," the court continued, "it prohibits no act, creates no offence, points out no mode of trial, fixes no penalty." In other words, state lawmakers had created a statute that was "imperfect and unfinished; for it lacked the qualities of command and prohibition absolutely essential to every law." Consequently, this law was "nothing other than a delegation of the legislative franchise by an act of the

General Assembly" that illegally invited "the people to exercise a function which the constitution makes the peculiar business of selected bodies of persons."[69]

The Pennsylvania judiciary's emphasis on legislative supremacy was not uncommon before the Civil War; in fact, the high courts of Delaware (1847), Indiana (1853), Texas (1856), and Iowa (1857) all used similar reasoning to support their decisions against local option.[70] On one level, these courts curbed legislative authority. Though "judicial review of state statutes was a rare, extraordinary event in 1850," four state court decisions negated legislative acts.[71] The courts in question, however, felt that only drastic measures would preserve the power of representative bodies. "The judiciary looks to the acts of the legislature with great respect, and reconcile and sustain them if possible," the Indiana Supreme Court declared in 1853. But "if one enactment may be submitted to [a popular] vote, so may another, so might all: thus would the representative system be wholly subverted."[72]

In effect, these courts saw themselves as shielding the legislatures from recent political developments, and their concerns were understandable. For one thing, as discussed above, the principle of legislative supremacy was already waning in antebellum America, as the public demanded new constitutional limits on legislative power after the Panic of 1837 and various scandals. In addition, the expanded use of referenda during this period—be it through local option or a statewide vote—also symbolized legislative decay, as lawmakers increasingly "declined the responsibility which it was their duty to assume."[73]

Indeed, the state legislatures did little to reverse their fading fortunes. Instead, as James Bryce argued, the "legislatures fell in with the tendency, and promoted their own supersession." If constitution makers increasingly placed limits on their authority to enact legislation which favored narrow interests, that was largely because "the chief interest of [state legislators] is in the passing of special, or local Acts," as opposed to "general public legislation." State lawmakers also proved to be "extremely timid," and "afraid to stir when placed between the opposite fires of two such sections, as for instance, between the Prohibitionists and the liquor-sellers." Thus "they welcomed the direct intervention of the people as relieving them of embarrassing problems," and began referring matters to popular votes which were "clearly within their own proper competence, such as the question of the liquor traffic."[74]

Antebellum state judges concurred when they depicted local option as the product of legislative abdication. Chief Justice Booth of Delaware, for one, accused the state legislature of "purposely" avoiding its constitutional duty when it adopted a variant of this policy in 1847.[75] Likewise, the local option law enacted in Indiana in 1853 worried Judge Stuart, for he recalled that the "practice of submitting enactments on vexed questions to the popular vote had obtained to some extent under the old constitution [of 1815]. . . . Such was the school law approved January 1849. Such also, were several license laws embracing more or less territory. The legislature had thus, in some measure, ceased to be a representative body, and was gradually becoming a mere proposer of laws for the consideration and final action of the people."[76] In sum, if local option signaled a return to the "old days," Stuart was willing to force the legislature to resume its responsibility as sole lawmaker.

Along with its reputation for ineffectiveness, then, the state courts' reluctance to embrace local option did not bode well for its future as an initial movement goal during the postbellum years. Focusing on local option was costly enough to begin with, as it channeled the movement's energies away from advocating statewide prohibition and other possible ends. However, many postwar teetotalers found this policy even less appealing because it promised little in permanent results. Moderates and southerners might agitate for local option, but the radicals refused to push such measures. John B. Finch, for example, maintained that "Local option delegates power to a municipality to prohibit the traffic, but does not give the municipality the power to fix an adequate penalty for violations." Convinced of its inadequacy, Finch concluded that "where a State has not local option, the worker is foolish indeed who will petition or work for it."[77]

Although beset with legal and enforcement complications, local option persisted as an anti-liquor goal after the Civil War, even in the North where constitutional prohibition became the preferred option. First, this plan was nonpartisan, which appealed to reformers who were dismayed by the Prohibition party's formation in 1869.[78] Second, many teetotalers viewed general local option laws as a logical "next step" in those states where the legislatures had long granted individual counties, towns, and institutions the power to ban liquor sales through special legislation.[79] Finally, some anti-drink activists saw local option as the first skirmish in a total war against liquor. As one local gradualist put it in 1872: "When a mouse is brought forth, and the effect properly observed, let us follow it with a cat, then a dog and then a lion. Let us approximate gradually if we cannot accomplish the end in any other way."[80]

Despite their optimism, moderate reformers were periodically stymied in their efforts to exploit local option during the 1870s. For example, activists in Iowa had participated in thirty "no-license" elections under the state's county option law of 1870, only to see the act struck down by the state supreme court for illicitly conferring legislative power on the people.[81] Meanwhile, teetotalers in Tennessee failed to acquire local option from either the Constitutional Convention of 1870 or the General Assembly in 1870 and 1871. They came closer in 1873, when the legislature approved a local option bill, but Governor John C. Brown vetoed it. While Brown cited technical reasons for his veto, he also claimed that the bill involved an unconstitutional delegation of legislative authority, a rationale that reinforced the Tennessee movement's doubts about the legitimacy of local option measures.[82] In 1874 California's temperance advocates suffered a comparable defeat. In March the state legislature had enacted a local option law and sparked a wave of local agitation to use it. As feared by many, the state's high court nullified this statute in August as an illegal transfer of lawmaking power to the people.[83]

In contrast to Iowa, Tennessee, and California, local option won greater legal acceptance in other states during the 1870s. The high courts of Massachusetts (1871), New Jersey (1872), Maryland (1874), Kentucky (1874), Connecticut (1875), and Minnesota (1877) all sanctioned local option measures by denying that they involved a delegation of legislative power.[84] This new legal trend was most visible in Pennsylvania, where the state supreme court revisited the local option question in the early 1870s. In 1872 approximately half a million people petitioned the Pennsylvania state legislature, requesting a general local option law. The legislature acceded to their wishes, even though a cloud of uncertainty hung over the new statute. Indeed, wet lawmakers had questioned its constitutionality during legislative debates, and had alluded to the state supreme court's nullification of local option in 1847, discussed above. Hence, when a test case arose in 1873,[85] the state's temperance forces waited anxiously to see whether the Court would act in their favor. Four days before Pennsylvania voters were to participate in statewide "no-license" elections, the high court won the gratitude of teetotalers by reversing its 1847 decision and declaring the principle of local option to be valid in *Locke's Appeal*.[86]

Written by a nonpartisan prohibitionist, Chief Justice Daniel Agnew, *Locke's Appeal* sustained local option by declaring it to be conditional legislation. For years, state and federal courts had readily acknowledged the legislature's authority to pass an act that would take effect upon a contingency. In 1813, for example, the U.S. Supreme Court had upheld a federal statute that imposed or revoked economic sanctions against England and France, depending on the subsequent actions of the two nations.[87] In *Locke's Appeal*, Agnew contended that the character of a local option law "is precisely that of hundreds of others" because its operation hinges on a future fact, namely the public's desire or need for licensing in their communities. As a conditional measure, local option is not "an imperfect and unfinished act" and thus does not rely on the people "to breathe into it all its vitality." Instead, it is "a mandatory law in all its parts, and the only thing committed to the people was to vote for or against the issuing of licenses, and thereby supply evidence of expediency." Consequently, the legislature remains "within the sphere of its just powers" when it enacts local option, for this legislation "only calls to its aid the means of ascertaining the expediency . . . of a measure, and does not delegate the power to make law itself."[88]

Agnew's logic in *Locke's Appeal* was hardly original; in fact, some antebellum district attorneys had sought to characterize local option and similarly structured measures as conditional acts.[89] Still, postbellum state courts proved increasingly receptive to Agnew's rationale for local option, even though its impetus may have been his own anti-liquor views. Whereas only one antebellum high court had vindicated this policy as conditional legislation, several state supreme courts relied on this argument to bolster their own decisions upholding local option during the postwar period.[90] In short, Agnew's redefinition of local option as a conditional act buttressed its legal basis and encouraged judicial tolerance of legislative cowardice on the liquor question.

In addition to the "conditional legislation" argument, postbellum anti-liquor activists also profited from another developing line of legal reasoning that enhanced local option's legitimacy. First articulated by Horace Gray of the Massachusetts high court in *Commonwealth v. Bennett* (1871), this position upheld local option because state legislatures had traditionally been free to delegate power to the localities when they were best situated to decide and administer a public policy. Gray, an eminent proponent of considering historical practice as well as legal precedent for the purposes of adjudication, posited that liquor licensing had long involved a purely local interest and therefore fell "within the class of police regulations, which may be intrusted by the legislature" to towns and counties by an express enactment. On similar grounds, the court had previously ruled that the legislature could give local officials the power over liquor licensing. If these officials could lawfully exercise this prerogative, Gray saw no reason why the voters, acting as a local unit, could not do the same.[91]

Commonwealth v. Bennett, like *Locke's Appeal*, buoyed moderate anti-liquor activists. For one thing, Thomas M. Cooley, the celebrated jurist and legal scholar, declared its logic to be an "impregnable ground" for sustaining local option in his highly influential treatise on constitutional limitations.[92] Moreover, state courts increasingly cited this case as a major precedent or relied on similar reasoning in upholding local option.[93] In a closely watched case in New Jersey, for example, the state's highest court asserted that the validity of a county option law enacted in 1888 "may be rested securely upon the right of the legislature to delegate the powers of local government to political subdivisions of the state."[94]

Along with the "conditional legislation" rationale, the "local interest" argument contributed to the courts' willingness to abandon legislative supremacy, a willingness which reflected their view that the people were in a better position than the legislature to decide the volatile liquor question. As Chief Justice Champlin of

Michigan wrote of his state's county option law of 1889, "The law, very wisely, in my judgment, provided for ascertaining the will of the qualified electors of the county upon the subject; for experience has demonstrated that a prohibitory law cannot be enforced unless the law itself has the moral support of the majority of the electors. If public sentiment is not in favor of such law, it ought not to be forced on the public."[95]

Furthermore, both the conditional-legislation and local-interest arguments improved the prospects of local referenda as policy goals, both for anti-liquor agitators and for other reformers. If activists could be sure that local referenda would be upheld in the courtroom, they might be more willing to fight for them in the first place. Temperance advocates could not know it at the time, but the Supreme Court of Washington Territory would be the last (in 1888) to rule that local option involved an unlawful delegation of legislative authority.[96] Significantly, the state courts' shift toward upholding the local option principle had occurred piecemeal. As a result, the trend was not always clear, and some reformers remained skeptical that local option's legal status had improved.

In 1884, for instance, Helen M. Gougar, a WCTU activist and lawyer, researched the constitutionality of local option in Indiana, only to conclude that it violated the state's organic law and was not a worthy goal for Indiana's drys.[97] Though probably influenced by her radical leanings, Gougar's conclusion was not unreasonable. After all, in *Maize v. State* (1853) the Indiana Supreme Court had nullified a local option law, and it had not explicitly reversed *Maize* as of 1884.[98] On the other hand, the Court had used a variant of the "local interest" argument to sustain a law enacted in 1873 requiring each license applicant to secure the signatures of a majority of his locality's voters before obtaining a liquor license.[99] Indeed, Judge Cooley had interpreted this decision to mean that *Maize* had been overruled.[100] Clearly, the Indiana record's ambiguity raised questions about local option's legitimacy in the state.

In part, the ambiguity surrounding local option's legality was fostered by those judges who did not share their colleagues' willingness to abandon legislative supremacy. Through their spirited dissents to decisions upholding local option, several justices expressed grave reservations about the continued health of state legislatures. As late as 1890, for example, Justice Morse of Michigan responded to the courts' increased tolerance of local option with concern. He argued, "This would [be] a convenient thing for a legislature wishing to shirk their responsibility—to submit all their laws to the vote of the people—for if they can submit one, they may submit all; but it is not the way provided by our constitution for the enactment of our laws.[101] Similarly, Justice Kinne of Iowa in 1895 denounced his court's decision in favor of local option as "full of peril." It "invites members of the legislature to put aside the discharge of the duties properly devolving on them," Kinne wrote. Furthermore, such a decision "removes the personal responsibility which, under our form of government, must ever rest upon the lawmaking power, and takes away the constitutional safeguards against unwise, ill-considered, and hasty legislation." In doing so, it may "encourage the very evils in legislation which our representative form of government was created to correct."[102]

After 1895, when court support for local option had solidified, dissents like those of Morse and Kinne disappeared. Nevertheless, their logic and that of the various decisions against local option bolstered the radicals' arguments against the policy. Such support became crucial between 1885 and 1905, when orthodox drys increasingly faced moderate proposals which advanced local option as the anti-liquor movement's primary goal. In response, the radicals leveled a number of charges against local option, including that it was unconstitutional. Their arguments sometimes focused on its unlawful delegation of lawmaking authority to the people;[103] at other times, they insisted that local option violated a common state constitutional provision which required laws of a general nature to have uniform operation.[104] But neither position was legally tenable by the 1890s, and the extremists were unable to get much mileage out of them.

As discussed above, legislative delegation had slowly faded as a legal issue after the 1870s. Meanwhile, the second charge—that local option failed to have a uniform impact on all portions of the state—had received some attention from dissenting judges in postbellum cases,[105] but had only contributed to two decisions against local option, both of which dated back to the 1850s.[106] Radical drys thus often fell back on abstract claims about local option's illegitimacy. In a restatement of the "uniform operation" argument, for example, the *Union Signal* asserted that "the state is the smallest unit of territory that, consistently with domestic quiet and uniformity in government, is entitled to enact laws affecting the welfare of the people of the whole state. Hence, [local option] laws seem to us, if not literally, yet in a larger, higher sense, to be unconstitutional."[107]

In rejecting local option, the orthodox drys demonstrated their ambivalence toward the emasculation of state legislatures during the nineteenth century. On the one hand, they often castigated state lawmakers for representing the liquor interests at the expense of their temperance constituencies. John B. Finch, for one, blamed the repeal in 1875 of Massachusetts's prohibition law on state lawmakers who had been elected by the liquor traffic's "fraud, trickery, and political combinations," and claimed that the measure would not "have been repealed if it had been necessary to refer it to the people." Given the Demon Rum's influence over state legislatures, the radicals preferred to bypass them and to subject constitutional prohibition to a popular vote. On the other hand, when confronted with local option, the radicals firmly supported legislative authority. As Wilfred M. Kellogg insisted, "Local option has no place in the genius of our institutions. No provision was made for it by our forefathers, and we have not revolutionized our system. We have not abandoned representative for local option government."[108]

Meanwhile, the moderates welcomed the vindication of local option by the courts. The Methodist *Christian Advocate*, for one, considered the New Jersey Supreme Court's upholding of local option in 1888 to be an "important . . . and far-reaching" decision that afforded the state's reformers "a great opportunity."[109] Likewise, Ohio moderates like John B. Russell could address the constitutionality issue by preparing "a legal brief upon similar measures which had been held good in other states" for sympathetic lawmakers when fighting for the Beatty township local option law in 1888. Later, Russell presumed that the Ohio Court's decision in favor of local option, *Gordon v. State* (1889), gave Ohio drys wide latitude to pursue local option measures to supplement the 1888 law. After forming the OASL in 1893, then, Russell and his colleagues campaigned for a more comprehensive local option law, which they achieved in 1902. Predictably, the liquor interests challenged this statute as unconstitutional on the basis of legislative delegation and uniform operation. The ASL, however, was hardly ruffled. League leaders cited *Gordon v. State*, noted that other high courts had sustained similar laws, and urged their followers to exploit the law "with more vigor than ever."[110] When the Ohio high court later upheld the 1902 act, the league's optimism seemed well founded. Indeed, no local option law sponsored by the ASL was ever declared unconstitutional, in Ohio or elsewhere.[111]

While justified by legal precedents, the courts' growing acceptance of local option after the war coincided with a legislative willingness to grant more local autonomy on a range of issues, including drink. Daniel Agnew's comment in *Locke's Appeal*—that local option laws were like "hundreds of others"—referred to conditional acts in general, but it applied just as well to the myriad state acts authorizing communities to assume greater control over their own affairs. By century's end, more state legislatures gave cities the power to frame their own charters, a development that fostered the "home rule" movement and its quest for municipal powers independent of legislative sanction. Furthermore, lawmakers often allowed municipalities to vote on new charters, to alter their boundaries, to establish local schools, to invest in railroad stocks, to issue bonds, and to regulate cattle that ran free in their highways. Many county voters could exercise similar prerogatives, and they could also establish and change their county seats.

Local option on the liquor question was therefore part of a larger legislative trend that referred local questions to popular disposition. Indeed, its role in this broader trend can be seen in the litigation surrounding the question of legislative delegation to the localities. On the one hand, local option benefited from some legal rulings which sanctioned voter approval of other more mundane issues. On the other hand, its legal victories encouraged further delegation, as judges cited court cases supporting local option to bolster local referenda on other issues as well.[112] Hence, local option both profited from and contributed to the increased legitimacy of legislative delegation after 1860.

Moreover, local option was part of a widespread abdication of state liquor control through general (as opposed to special) laws, a legislative development that accelerated after the war. As noted previously, antebellum teetotalers had frequently encountered a variety of licensing regimes at the local level, which reflected the piecemeal character of incorporation, the proliferation of special legislation, and the discretion of local officials. Beginning in the 1850s, though, state legislatures gradually abandoned parochial laws when transferring liquor control to the localities, an important step for prohibitionists who were hoping to use a locally based but cosmopolitan political strategy. While lawmakers did not always strip licensing discretion from local authorities, they ultimately opted for a more comprehensive devolution of state licensing power than was possible through local acts. This shift away from narrow legislation came about through the efforts of political reformers, who wanted to reduce the appalling legislative burden of granting and revising special acts and charters.

For many administrative reformers, the proliferation of local measures after 1830 threatened to fragment the legal system into "something like the Holy Roman Empire," whereby "every town and village would have its own rules." More importantly, the multiplication of such legislation absorbed the state legislatures' time and energy, and was viewed by many as a major source of corruption. As a result, state constitutions after the Civil War increasingly contained clauses which banned special legislation and charters. In a related development, the heavy demand for purely local restrictions on the liquor traffic sometimes propelled lawmakers to support general laws delegating the liquor question to the localities. Therefore, most antiliquor activists could expect to secure fewer acts which granted localities and corporations their own unique liquor policies, and had to look to favorable statewide laws instead.[113]

With few exceptions, narrow temperance laws had ceased to be a source of new local licensing regimes in the North by 1880. In Pennsylvania, for example, the state legislature had approved dozens of these statutes for the benefit of schools, boroughs, townships, counties, and coal mines during the mid-nineteenth century.[114] In 1871, however, Governor James Geary called for a constitutional convention, charging that the legislature had abused special legislation to the extent that people moving from one county to another "frequently found themselves under entirely different laws." In addition, he claimed that "special legislation is the great and impure fountain of corruption, private speculation and public wrong." The *Pittsburgh Gazette* agreed that special laws were often venal and noted that the legislature preferred drafting them over general statutes. These critiques of the legislature's practices were so widespread that the Constitutional Convention of 1872–73 easily approved provisions which severely restricted the General Assembly's power to enact special laws, including grants of municipal charters.[115] After the constitution of 1874, Pennsylvanians could only abolish local saloons through general acts, and they were not alone. Among others, the constitutions of Indiana (1851), Ohio (1851), Iowa (1857), Kansas (1859), Illinois (1870), Nebraska (1875), New Jersey (1875 amendments), and Missouri (1876) included similar limitations on the legislature's capacity to pass local laws and issue special charters.[116]

On the other hand, the decline of special liquor legislation was less dramatic in the South, where antebellum lawmakers had enacted the greatest number of purely local measures to satisfy the towns, counties, schools, and churches seeking additional liquor control. After the Civil War, southern anti-liquor activists had resumed their special pleading with their respective state legislatures, and in some states they would be rewarded with such parochial acts until the early 1900s.[117] Even in this region, though, local legislation became less common. Tennessee's constitution of 1870 forbade most special acts;[118] and in states like Arkansas, Georgia, and Virginia, both anti-liquor activists and legislators recognized that general local option laws "would save communities the burden of having to ask the legislature" for local liquor control while also sparing "legislators the distraction and sometimes the embarrassment which petitions for special treatment were apt to entail." During Virginia's legislative session of 1881–82, for example, Representative Stubbs proposed that the assembly enact a general local option law. To justify his support for this measure, he pointed to the flood of petitions for special local option elections that poured into the assembly.[119] Indeed, by 1887 ten of the eleven former Confederate states had passed general acts which afforded identical reform opportunities to all of these states' localities (see table 4).[120]

Of course, the decrease in special legislation did not automatically generate statewide measures that delegated the liquor question to the localities, particularly in the North. For instance, after the Pennsylvania Constitution of 1873 banned local acts, some teetotalers fought unsuccessfully for a state policy to authorize local liquor control. In 1875 they failed to prevent the legislature from repealing the state's general local option law of 1872, and they could not secure its replacement in the years 1876–79. Nevertheless, in this latter crusade, members of the state local option committee were obliged to mount a statewide effort. Based in the western cities of Pittsburgh and Allegheny, these activists concluded that their campaign would fail without the support of their eastern colleagues. Hence, they invited more eastern members to serve on their executive committee, and became better integrated in the state's anti-liquor movement as a result.[121]

Table 4 General Liquor Laws Enacted in the South during the Postbellum Period

State	Years of General Law's Operation	Type of General Restrictive Law	Requested by a Substantial Number of the State's Anti-Liquor Activists?	Preferred Policy of the State's Most Prominent Drys, When Enacted
Arkansas	1879–1915	Local option in towns and counties	Yes	General local option law
Georgia	1885–1907	Local option in counties, cities, towns, and districts	Yes	General local option law
Florida	1885–1918	County local option	Yes	General local option law
Louisiana	1881–1920	Local option in parishes, cities, and towns	Yes	General local option law
Mississippi	1886–1908	County local option, indirect popular control in municipalities	Yes	General local option law
North Carolina	1883–1908	Local option in counties, cities, towns, and police wards	No	Statutory prohibition
South Carolina	1882–1893	Local option in cities, towns, and villages	Yes	General local option law
Tennessee	1877–1909	Indirect popular control through Four Mile Law	No	General local option law
Texas	1876–1918	Local option in counties, towns, and districts	Yes	General local option law
Virginia	1886–1914	Local option in counties, magisterial districts, and cities	Yes	General local option law

Sources: Annual Reports of the National Temperance Society, 1875–90; Cherrington, *Standard Encyclopedia of the Alcohol Problem*.

As in Pennsylvania, other northern campaigns for general local option strengthened state temperance networks but produced few lasting results during the postwar period. In the 1870s and 1880s, for example, centralized anti-liquor committees formed by teetotalers to coordinate their drives for statewide local option secured only a short-lived county option law (1888–89) in New Jersey and a civil damage act (1881) in Delaware.[122] Still, it is difficult to generalize about the effectiveness of such efforts, given that most northern teetotalers did not zealously campaign for local option before 1900. Having embraced constitutional prohibition in the 1880s, their major organizations (the fraternal orders, the WCTU, and the Prohibition party) slighted lesser aims. Northern political élites, rather than temperance advocates, were largely responsible for enacting and sustaining the most durable general laws which transferred liquor control to the localities during the Gilded Age. As politicians, major party leaders and state lawmakers had their own reasons for delegating the liquor question to local communities, and often proposed such policies in spite of dry preferences.

To illustrate, orthodox prohibitionists blanketed the Nebraska state legislature with petitions for constitutional prohibition in 1881. Many attended legislative sessions by day; in the evening, "they held rallies, meetings in the streets, and parades around the state capitol, all in full view of the legislature, which could not ignore them because of their large numbers." While the state's Templars and WCTU activists brought visibility to their cause, state lawmakers quietly introduced seven bills that were designed to reinforce Nebraska's licensing laws. Indeed, the legislature had no intention of submitting an amendment to the people, preferring a "high license" policy that would remove the volatile liquor question permanently from state politics. To its supporters, a stringent license law that imposed high fees on liquor dealers would reduce the number of saloons, raise money for local school funds, and serve as a compromise between the wets and the drys. Consequently, in a closed session the Nebraska House of Representatives killed the prohibition amendment and began debating "high license" bills, one of which had the blessing of two prominent teetotalers.[123]

The statute that ultimately emerged from the 1881 session—the Slocumb Law—contained several provisions which favored Nebraska's anti-liquor forces. This act banned concealed bars, held saloonkeepers financially responsible for the damages caused by their activities, and encouraged citizens to report violations of the law. Most importantly, though, section 25 of the Slocumb Law gave all cities and villages the power to license, regulate, and prohibit liquor retailing within their boundaries. As early as April 1881, some local temperance groups sought to exploit section 25 by sponsoring dry candidates for municipal office. While aware of its anti-liquor features, extreme drys nonetheless excoriated lawmakers for approving the Slocumb Law, asserting that it "had the effect of giving a legal status to vice, corruption, and murder." Thus Nebraska's radical drys spent the next nine years denouncing this measure and seeking to replace it with a state prohibition amendment.[124]

Elsewhere, northern radicals reacted similarly to other comparable acts passed during the postbellum period. As table 5 illustrates, many northern anti-liquor policies were not the direct result of petition campaigns by prohibition groups, which were typically clamoring for constitutional prohibition when the policies were enacted. Rather, most general prohibitory laws were offered as moderate alternatives to prohibition amendments, and orthodox drys were largely unimpressed with the powers that these laws gave to local communities to decide the liquor question. For example, Mary T. Lathrap of the Michigan Union rejected local option in 1887, as-

Table 5 Major State Liquor Laws Enacted in the North during the Postbellum Period

State	Years of General Law's Operation	Type of General Restrictive Law	Requested by a Substantial Number of the State's Anti-Liquor Activists?	Preferred Policy of the State's Most Prominent Drys, When Enacted
Connecticut	1881–1920	Municipal local option and license	No	Constitutional prohibition
Illinois	1883–1907	Indirect popular control and high license	No	Constitutional prohibition
Indiana	1895–1908	Indirect popular control and high license	Yes	Divided
Massachusetts	1881–1920	Municipal local option and high license	No	Constitutional prohibition
Michigan	1889–1916	County local option and high license	No	Constitutional prohibition
Minnesota	1887–1913	Township local option, indirect local control, and high license	No	Constitutional prohibition
Missouri	1887–1920	City and county local option and high license	No	Constitutional prohibition
Nebraska	1881–1916	Indirect popular control and high license (Slocumb Law)	No	Constitutional prohibition
Ohio	1886–1902[a]	Rural township local option, indirect popular control, and taxation	No	Constitutional prohibition
New York	1896–1917	Rural township local option and high license (Raines Law)[b]	Yes[c]	Divided
Pennsylvania	1887–1920	Indirect popular control and high license (Brooks Law)	No	Constitutional prohibition
Rhode Island	1889–1920	Municipal local option and high license	No	Constitutional prohibition
Wisconsin	1889–1920	Municipal local option and high license	No	Constitutional prohibition

[a] Enacted indirect popular control and taxation in 1886, rural township local option in 1888.
[b] Though the Raines Law provided for township local option, it also centralized liquor control elsewhere in New York under the control of a state commission.
[c] For township option.
Sources: Annual Reports of the National Temperance Society, 1875–90; Cherrington, *Standard Encyclopedia of the Alcohol Problem*.

serting that it "does not settle the attitude of the State, but turns over a great moral and political question over to . . . bitter local contests. . . . Local option is therefore no substitute for constitutional prohibition."[125] Likewise, the Massachusetts WCTU complained about the local option law of 1881, which required every community to vote directly on the liquor issue during annual municipal elections. "The law of the Bay State is Local Option," the union declared in 1881, "but when the Woman's Christian Temperance Union flung its banner to the breeze, upon its folds was inscribed 'Prohibition.' " In other words, the WCTU had asked lawmakers for an amendment, only to be rewarded with a partial measure. Undaunted, the group announced that "at the coming session of the Legislature another petition for constitutional amendment will be presented."[126]

Given their commitment to constitutional prohibition, the northern radicals understandably lacked the resources and motivation to systematically orchestrate "no-license" campaigns, or to effectively use the indirect local methods authorized by statutes like the Slocumb Law. Before the Anti-Saloon League's formation, local groups unaffiliated with the national organizations tended to make the most of the state legislatures' gradual devolution of liquor control. For instance, C. C. M'Cabe of Athens, Ohio, could hardly contain his enthusiasm for the Dow Law, a measure enacted in 1886 which granted municipal councils the power to prohibit liquor retailing. "All hail, Athens, Ohio!" exulted M'Cabe, after his fellow citizens elected a dry town council in 1886. He saw prohibition in his birthplace as a sign "that the great revolution goes steadily onward," and urged other towns "to go to the polls and choose between darkness and light, poverty and wealth, crime and security."[127]

To be sure, orthodox prohibitionists did participate in grassroots temperance crusades like that in Athens. In fact, the Prohibition party's literature insisted that its members worked devotedly for village, city, and county prohibition.[128] In a similar fashion, WCTU and IOGT activists toiled in a variety of local campaigns against the saloon during the late nineteenth century.[129] Despite their participation in such campaigns, however, leading radicals clearly did not believe that locally based activism would advance the cause of prohibition. Moreover, they considered campaigns to secure general local option and related policies to be naive at best. The union, for one, reacted in this fashion to the drive in 1894 by the Ohio ASL for the Haskell Bill, a comprehensive local option law: "The Haskell bill . . . has been defeated by the Ohio legislature. . . . Ohio has already tried five different local option bills only to have each pronounced a failure as far as . . . dealing with the drink evil is concerned. All measures looking toward compromise must from their very nature, result in disappointment to the enemies of the liquor traffic, their only value being as object-lessons. We prophesy that the experiences of the past will induce temperance people of Ohio ere long to concentrate their forces upon securing . . . state prohibition pure and simple."[130]

Obviously, the Ohio local gradualists who formed the ASL viewed the matter quite differently. Contrary to the WCTU's assumptions, league founders were not overly discouraged by their own attempts to exploit the state's general provisions for local liquor control. If anything, Howard Russell and his colleagues in the Oberlin Temperance Alliance had found measures like the Dow Law (1886) to be small but positive steps toward prohibition. In 1887 Russell himself had exploited the Dow Law to close saloons in Berea, Ohio; in 1888 the Oberlin Temperance Alliance had sponsored a campaign for township local option in order to reinforce that act's prohibitory provisions.[131] In short, the young Ohio ASL's willingness to work for a comprehensive local option bill in 1894 was as much a tribute to the fruitfulness of earlier restrictive laws as it was a critique of their inadequacies. Furthermore, until a measure like the Haskell Bill became law, league leaders recognized that their cause would stagnate if they could not demonstrate the benefits of locally based agitation to potential adherents. Therefore, they promoted the use of existing policies like the Dow Law and township option by grassroots activists across Ohio, and celebrated every local victory as a sign of progress.[132]

As discussed in chapter 2, the southern states were the first to methodically employ local methods to address the liquor question, and the ASL hoped to import their techniques to the North. Until that happened, however, local gradualism seemed to be little more than a regional strategy suitable to a distinctive setting. "Local option has made a great success at the South," conceded the WCTU's Mary T. Lathrap in 1887, "but the conditions are very different from ours" in the North. "Their population is almost purely American, while ours is largely foreign; their negro element is docile, our foreign element is turbulent."[133] Meanwhile, the Prohibitionist A. A. Hopkins claimed that local option had "made singular headway in the Southern States" because the policy "was clearly akin to the Democratic doctrine of States' Rights."[134] Conversely, the ASL's leaders expected local option and related methods to thrive in the North, for they held that the principle underlying such policies was universal, not regional, in origin. "It is one of the dearest rights of the people to determine for themselves what they want done with one of the most prolific sources of poverty, crime, insanity, and social misery known to civil society," insisted the *American Issue*, organ of the ASL. "The local option principle is right in moral principle, right in the Constitution, and right in law."[135]

Furthermore, the league was undoubtedly aware that many anti-liquor moderates supported local option as an acceptable approach to the liquor problem. As one prominent moderate put it, "At the present stage of progress and of public opinion no Temperance movement, union or other, can in my judgement afford to dispense with the feature of Local Option. . . . With all its drawbacks, it is capable of producing the best results, and, supplemented by the new spirit of law enforcement, it can work marvels of reform."[136] Such support was particularly significant to the ASL, which had high hopes of enlisting moderate clergymen, businessmen, reformers, and other opinion leaders in the ranks of its crusade.

Still, a locally based strategy would have been difficult to pursue across the North if a general devolution of state liquor control had not occurred after the Civil War. In Maryland, for example, the legislature's unimpaired power to grant special acts meant that the state lacked a uniform liquor policy, and that "each community worked to secure legislation for its own peculiar needs, without regard for the needs of its neighbors." As a result, the Maryland ASL confronted a "peculiar situation" during the early 1900s, in which "each county had seemingly built up a Chinese wall of exclusion around itself." Much of the league's initial work in Maryland involved persuading local dry groups to combine into a central organization and to work for a general local option law. Without such unity, the ASL argued, they would fail to rouse the entire state for prohibition.[137]

Fortunately for the league, Maryland was an exception. In other states, local gradualists could immediately seize upon existing general laws as outlets for local activism. For instance, the Michigan ASL's early leaders were pleased to discover that "there was a splendid county local option law that had existed for ten years." Likewise, their Nebraska counterparts boasted in 1901 of having a strong law, "known as the Slocumb Law, which makes it difficult for the saloon-keeper to do business without a constant violation of its provisions."[138] Indeed, such legislation was especially valuable to the state leagues during their infancy, for until 1905, they were often still constructing their bases in local churches, and were in no position to sponsor major campaigns for new state laws. Paradoxically, therefore, anti-liquor moderates sought to advance the cause of prohibition through general laws which had been designed to keep prohibition off the political agenda.

While the delegation of state liquor control to the localities had provided northern moderates with numerous avenues for local activism, the judiciary's tolerance of local option allowed them to exploit several of those policies without fear of reprisal. For instance, drys in Montana first made use of their state's county option law, passed in 1895, during the early years of the twentieth century. After Ravalli County voted "no-license" in 1903 and violators faced prosecution, the wets sued, charging that the measure involved an unlawful delegation of legislative power and failed to have a uniform impact across the state. Given the previous trend in state cases, though, it was no surprise when Montana's high court upheld county option.[139]

In addition, state judiciaries did not hinder the ASL's efforts to supplement and improve the existing methods of local liquor control in the North. Compared to the situation in the South, northern activists had fewer and less direct local tools at their disposal. The Texas local option law of 1876, for one, authorized the voters of counties, cities, towns, and precincts to petition for elections on liquor sales. In contrast, the local option provisions of Minnesota's law (1887) only applied to villages and rural townships, so town and city residents had to appeal to municipal authorities for bans on local liquor sales. Thus for years, the Anti-Saloon League sought more comprehensive local option in the North, a crusade that went unimpeded by the courts. In Ohio, for example, the state ASL supplemented its township option law (1888) with municipal option (1902), ward option (1905), and county option (1908), all of which survived the "threadbare arguments" of the wets about their unconstitutional character.[140]

Unfettered by judicial activism, the ASL could concentrate on perfecting its locally based methods. League leaders selected their local battles carefully, and they advised their grassroots adherents to do the same. The saloon "is not going to go out as the result of a few superficial, hasty, ill prepared efforts," the *American Issue* declared.[141] Furthermore, the organization sought strict statewide enforcement laws so as to preserve its local gains from erosion. The Idaho ASL, for instance, could report in 1911 that it had secured a strong "search and seizure" law, which had materially improved the conditions of its dry counties.[142] Such "search and seizure" measures provided for searches of buildings where citizens believed the law was being violated, and allowed the complaining citizen to accompany the officer on his search to guarantee honest enforcement efforts. The ASL also sought to counter the lax enforcement efforts of municipal officials by winning the right to appeal to county officers as well.[143]

After 1905 most northern temperance activists were thus committed to using and extending local methods of eradicating the saloon. Instead of focusing on the distinctiveness of the South's anti-liquor efforts, they hoped to replicate the region's gradual shift toward state prohibition. As one northern reformer wrote in 1908, the stunning progress of prohibition in the South "is not the result of any sudden or unaccountable transition of public opinion; it is not due to any hidden causes; they are easily visible. . . . It is not the result of an earthquake, nor the eruption of a volcano; it is a ripening process like the blooming of a rose." The reformer concluded that "local option has proved to be the most effective legislative or elective measure," while "state-wide prohibition is a dangerous experiment until the way for it has been paved by local option."[144]

During the postbellum period, the actions of constitutional conventions, state courts, and state legislatures enabled anti-liquor activists across the nation to coalesce around common goals and generic campaigns. Whereas the drive for prohibition amendments reflected the changing character of state constitutions, local gradualism owed more to the general devolution of state licensing power to localities and to the judiciary's acceptance of this process. Significantly, though, constitutional prohibition and local gradualism both reflected an abiding mistrust of state legislatures, and the decline of legislative supremacy as a governing principle.

In other words, once collective beliefs about state legislative power had changed, the drys found it easier to secure constitutional amendments and general local option laws. As the nineteenth century progressed, a variety of reformers came to criticize the state legislatures for their unwillingness to enact universal laws for the public good. In seeking to restore legislative power to its rightful purpose, these reformers often pressed constitutional change to curb the legislatures' power to serve special interests. Such practices, however, inadvertently encouraged many drys to push for their own constitutional legislation and to advocate prohibition amendments. Moreover, successful efforts to enact constitutional bans on special acts meant that temperance advocates could no longer secure liquor policies that favored their own particular localities. Thus, general legislation became the source of most local liquor control, and moderate anti-liquor activists quickly capitalized on its potential.

In fact, a locally based strategy might have produced only parochial activism if a *comprehensive* devolution of state liquor control had not occurred. In chapter 3, the case of enforcement suggested that too much variation in local policies produced only scattered activity in the prohibition movement. Hence, it is not surprising that local gradualists sought to apply the same methods to as many localities as they could. After all, a local option election in one part of the country was very much like a local option election anywhere. In short, the Anti-Saloon League understood that a locally based strategy required a certain amount of homogeneity if the antiliquor movement hoped to transcend local boundaries.[145] Ultimately, it was statewide legislation that channeled the energy of the grassroots temperance forces into a nationwide crusade. Gaining further statewide legislation, however, required focusing on the party system and the character of party competition, as the next chapter will show.

5 Political Alignments, Party Systems, and Prohibition

The previous chapters portray the postbellum anti-liquor movement as essentially divided between the nationally prominent radicals, who favored constitutional prohibition, and their more provincial, moderate counterparts, who preferred local gradualism as a political strategy and who had their greatest impact on the South's anti-liquor policies. After several state courts and legislatures sanctioned the local control of liquor licensing, however, the moderates were free to promote local gradualism as a national political strategy and to challenge the radicals for leadership of the movement. Moreover, they were in a strong position to advocate this political strategy because they had adopted an organizational form which gave them access to the North's Protestant churches, and they could rely on a repertoire of collective action that was both modular and familiar to their adherents.

While the movement's adoption of local gradualism would prove vital to its remarkable success during the Progressive Era, this political strategy could only work because the political system was conducive to dry policy innovations in this period. Likewise, the movement's access to direct legislation in the 1880s stemmed largely from the vulnerability of political élites to its demands during the decade. But why did the 1880s and the Progressive Era generate so many reform opportunities for the anti-liquor crusade? In short, why were the referenda sponsored by the movement so closely grouped together in time (figure 1)?

According to political process theorists, social movements are most likely to receive some response from the political system when they have eluded state repression, won partial access to the polity, received support from influential allies, exploited divisions within élites, or otherwise gained leverage over unstable political alignments.[1] While all five dimensions of this "political opportunity structure" have yielded insights about the development of various movements, some analysts consider the last of these dimensions to be crucial in shaping movement outcomes in liberal democracies.[2] Indeed, Frances Fox Piven and Richard A. Cloward unequivocally declare that it is the movement's capacity "to galvanize and polarize voters, with the result that electoral coalitions fragment or threaten to fragment," which elicits gains from representative electoral systems.[3] Within the context of American politics, this focus on the interaction between challenging groups and unstable political alignments seems warranted, given that a movement's demands are often translated into reforms by the actions of elected officials.[4] Unfortunately, the current literature on American social movements has failed to outline the basic conditions under which challenging groups may best exploit shifting political alliances to achieve their goals.

This chapter proposes that two factors shape a movement's path to effecting policy change within the American two-party system: (1) the movement's situation vis-à-vis the party system and (2) the character of party competition. As elaborated below, the first of these factors considers whether a movement is excluded or included by the dominant party coalitions. The second factor refers to the source of alignment instability, and whether a movement's reform opportunities flow from an increase in interparty competition, intraparty competition, or both.

Beginning in the 1960s, American historians rediscovered political parties and produced several studies that vividly chart the dynamics of the American two-party system over time.[5] In particular, a number of works recount the parties' efforts to reconstitute winning coalitions in the wake of electoral defeats, economic crises, demographic shifts, and, depending on the author, disruptive social movements.[6] For the movement scholar, the "party systems" literature casts welcome light upon the interaction between movement and party. Since they commonly seek to explain major transformations in electoral behavior, these studies typically focus on movements which have provoked such change. These challenging groups can be considered "coalitional outsiders," in that their leaders and their demands have been effectively excluded from existing party coalitions and thus raise issues which may threaten the customary stability of the party system.[7] If successful in shattering this stability, these "outsiders" precipitate a severe political crisis marked by ideological polarization, coalitional disarray, and finally a widespread partisan shift in the electorate's voting behavior, a process known as "critical realignment."[8]

While students of political change dwell on "outsiders," other social scientists often depict movements as "coalitional insiders." As such, the leaders of challenging groups link their participation in party coalitions with the (often unwarranted) expectation that such alliances will provide the political bases for achieving their goals.[9] "Outsiders" and "insiders" may both upset existing party coalitions, and yet their respective routes to winning leverage over these coalitions diverge. For the outsiders, reform opportunities stem largely from their own capacity to either provoke a major realignment or to directly participate in the realigning process. To illustrate, one outsider—the antebellum nativist movement—managed to secure stricter state naturalization laws during the 1850s because of its crucial role in the early stages of the decade's realignment.[10] On the other hand, since much of their political clout derives from their party alliances, insiders prefer to exploit coalitional fissures rather than disrupt the party system. In contemporary politics, for instance, the leaders of the Christian Right in the Republican party have challenged secular Republican activists in their crusade to dominate local party committees, and yet their movement nonetheless unites with the party's secular wing during state and national campaigns.[11]

After exploring how a coalitional outsider becomes an insider, this chapter will focus on two sets of political conditions which enhance the reform prospects of coalitional insiders. In the first scenario, such prospects improve dramatically when fierce interparty competition coincides with the possibility of the insider's defection, thus magnifying the movement's value to its party coalition. For example, Republican progressives in New York won modest concessions from the party machine at the turn of the century because the party needed their support in the era's tight gubernatorial contests. In this case, "good government" reformers had underscored their willingness to defect from the Republicans when they voted for independents and Democrats in the municipal elections of 1897, a tactic which cost the GOP several mayoralties.[12]

Coalitional insiders may also benefit from increased competition within a party. While parties commonly experience internal rivalries over power, position, and patronage, such conflict often intensifies during periods of one-party rule. One-party regimes may be particularly vulnerable to factionalism because the ruling party can no longer silence internal dissent by appealing to party unity as a key to electoral success. Within the dominant party, entrepreneurship thrives, loose blocs congeal into factions, and insider movements may gain support for their goals from sympathetic factions. For instance, after the election of 1896 crippled the Democratic party in California,[13] the state's Republicans gradually split between the party regulars, who tolerated the Southern Pacific Railroad's control of the GOP, and the anti-railroad entrepreneurs, who formed the "Lincoln-Roosevelt League" in 1907.[14] As the two factions vied for control of the state legislature in 1909, anti-vice activists in the party won a narrow victory, the Anti-Race Track Gambling Act, largely through the efforts of upstart Lincoln-Roosevelt legislators.[15]

In short, while outsiders profit from coalitional earthquakes of their own making, insiders gain reform opportunities when they can successfully exploit a party system rife with competition within and between parties. As a long-lived social movement, the prohibition crusade garnered reform opportunities as a coalitional outsider, insider, and, in the 1880s, both. In its first empirical section, this chapter portrays the antebellum prohibitionists as classic outsiders, who secured only fleeting benefits from the Jacksonian party system. With the realignment of the 1850s, however, the northern branch of the movement won the chance to achieve its goals within the nascent Republican coalition.

Henceforth, most northern teetotalers remained within the Republican coalition and labored for their cause as coalitional insiders, while southerners generally became Democrats after the Civil War. While their presence in the Democratic coalition had more to do with the war than with the party's affection for prohibition, southern drys nonetheless relied on the Democratic party as their reform vehicle. At the same time, though, a minority of anti-liquor activists opted to become coalitional outsiders when they formed the Prohibition party in 1869 and sought to transform the two-party system. Thus, the postbellum prohibitionists staked out three main positions with respect to the parties: Republican insiders in the North, Democratic insiders in the South, and a small band of third-party outsiders.

The second part of this chapter contends that the prohibitionists obtained reform opportunities during the 1880s by finessing the decade's tight interparty competition. The razor-thin electoral margins of the 1880s coincided with the possibility that some anti-liquor insiders would defect to the Prohibition party. As a result, nineteen state legislatures submitted state prohibition referenda to the voters, and dozens of others sought to placate the teetotalers by enacting general prohibitory measures, such as local option.

Whereas the drys of the 1880s capitalized on intense interparty competition, intraparty strife offers advantages to the coalitional insider, as discussed in the third part of this chapter. During the Progressive Era, the prohibition crusade confronted several one-party regimes, some in the Republican North, and others in the Democratic South.[16] Since most dry leaders remained insiders within these party systems, they could exploit the factionalism induced by progressive politicians to secure several anti-liquor statutes, forty referenda on state prohibition, and the chance to parlay their state-level victories into a serious campaign for a national amendment.

Coalitional Outsiders and the Fruits of Realignment, 1835–1855

James L. Sundquist has argued that an issue may undermine a party system's stability if the issue arises from a grievance that is both broad and deep, is intrinsically moral, and has the capacity to polarize the electorate.[17] Beginning in the late 1830s, temperance would haunt the party system as just such an issue, and yet party leaders avoided its destabilizing effects until the 1850s. In their communities, teetotalers consistently received their greatest support from the statist Whigs, who "found it just as logical to attack local saloons as to defend the Bank of the United States." After all, the Whigs saw themselves as the party of improvement, a vision that embraced both government-sponsored economic activity and the advocacy of personal discipline, reason, and progress—all of which could be degraded by drink.[18] In the state legislatures, though, the Whigs resembled the Democrats in their refusal to agree to a party position on temperance legislation, despite the issue's potential to disrupt a party system dominated by their opponents.[19] As a result, roll-call votes on anti-drink laws rarely split along party lines, and they were passed by legislatures controlled by Whigs as well as those controlled by Democrats.[20] That is not to say that these liquor control efforts were uncontroversial; if anything, the frequent repeal of state liquor laws occasioned contentious debates.[21] Rather, party élites sensibly preferred more predictable electoral contests based on Jacksonian economic issues (such as banking, the tariff, and internal improvements) rather than the more uncertain liquor question. Clearly, they were loath to risk party unity and electoral success over an issue that might alienate key constituencies, be they prosperous Whig merchants or lower-class Democrats.[22]

As long as Jacksonian economic issues dominated antebellum party politics, party leaders evinced little interest in the most stringent variety of temperance legislation, namely state prohibition.[23] While this policy appealed to increasing numbers of teetotalers as the 1840s progressed, the political obstacles to prohibition discouraged it as a goal.[24] As a result, petitioning for state prohibition remained limited during the decade, and only Maine's legislature passed a statute resembling prohibition before 1851.[25] In the early 1850s, however, two new developments galvanized the anti-liquor radicals. First, anti-liquor forces in Maine persuaded the state legislature to upgrade the state's liquor policy from partial prohibition to total prohibition in 1851.[26] Heartened by the passage of this pioneering prohibition law, northern branches of the ATU and the Sons launched "Maine Law" campaigns in their states on an unprecedented scale. In addition, these northern activists had found a willing ally: the Free Soil party. A hodgepodge of antislavery activists from the Whig, Democratic, and Liberty parties, the Free Soil party sought to use prohibition in the 1850s to restore its own fading fortunes and to complete the dissolution of the party system that it had begun in 1848.

After a respectable showing in the presidential election of 1848,[27] the Free Soil party faced the task of building an organization capable of competing at every level of government. In the absence of a national plan, state Free Soilers pursued a mélange of strategies in nominating candidates, writing party platforms, and plotting campaigns. Despite such eclecticism, Free Soilers everywhere sought coalitions with the major parties with the aim of backing, whenever possible, major party candidates who shared their opposition to extending slavery to the territories.[28] Unfortunately, this approach rested on two optimistic assumptions: that the Free Soilers owned the moral high ground on slavery, and that the issue would remain salient. By 1850, though, any hopes that the slavery dispute would be advantageous to the party had been dashed by its lackluster performance in state elections, the co-opting of the free soil issue by unallied Democrats and Whigs in the years 1849–50,[29] and the Compromise of 1850.[30] Indeed, this last development temporarily dispelled northern concern about the "slave power" and lulled the antislavery men "into a drowsy indifference to the portents of the future."[31]

That the Free Soilers would turn to the prohibition issue in the early 1850s is hardly surprising. As previously noted, the antislavery and temperance crusades both emerged from the same evangelical Protestant network, and they overlapped to a considerable extent in the North. In addition, Free Soil workers reported that "nearly every Free Soiler is a Maine Law man"; hence, the endorsement of prohibition seemed a logical instrument for shoring up support among the party faithful.[32] Finally, a dry Free Soil party could draw support from the Whigs, whose leaders remained wary of prohibition despite its considerable appeal to their constituents. As the weaker of the two major parties, and thus the most strongly harmed by the Free Soil insurgency, the Whigs could scarcely afford further defections in the early 1850s. Yet the Whigs' muted enthusiasm for the Maine Law allowed the Free Soilers to outbid them for the support of the most ardent prohibitionists, and to fracture Whig unity in several northern states by 1854.[33]

While fatal to the Whig party, the Free Soilers' embrace of prohibition ultimately failed to establish the party as a serious contender or successor to the Whigs. For northern anti-liquor forces, though, the Free Soilers' failure to achieve major party status did foreclose their chances of enacting Maine Laws, given the altered state of the political system.[34] As insurgents, the Free Soilers had furnished the northern prohibition cause with both an increasingly volatile party system and a prominent place on the political agenda.

Once on the agenda, however, prohibition's fate rested chiefly in the hands of state dry leaders and their ability to exploit the dramatic fluctuations in state-level political conditions. No single factor—whether common partisan allies, fissures in the party system, or dry endorsement strategies—can explain prohibition's triumph in twelve northern states and territories or its failure in others.[35] Adopting a posture of nonpartisan pragmatism, the prohibitionists usually endorsed candidates who advocated the Maine Law regardless of their party affiliation, and only proffered separate nominations when the existing field lacked a satisfactory candi-

Table 6 Partisan Control of Government in States and Territories Adopting Prohibition Laws, 1851–1855

State or Territory	Date When Prohibition Law Adopted	Party Affiliation of Governor	Dominant Party or Coalition in Legislature
Maine	June 2, 1851	Democratic	Democratic
Minnesota	March, 1852	Democratic	Democratic
Rhode Island	March 7, 1852	Democratic	Democratic
Massachusetts	May 27, 1852	Democratic	Democratic–Free Soil
Vermont	November 23, 1852	Whig	Whig
Michigan	February 12, 1853	Democratic	Democratic
Connecticut	June 16, 1854	Whig	Whig-Temperance–Free Soil
Iowa	January 22, 1855	Whig–Free Soil	Whig–Free Soil
Indiana	February 8, 1855	Democratic	People's[a]
Delaware	February 27, 1855	American[b]	American[b]
Nebraska	April, 1855	Democratic	Democratic
New York	April 19, 1855	Whig-Free Soil	Whig
New Hampshire	July 14, 1855	American[b]	American[b]-Republican

[a] Fusion of American and Anti-Nebraska

[b] Also known as the "Know Nothings"

Table based on various state studies. See bibliography for a complete listing of state studies consulted.

date. Teetotalers in Indiana, for example, campaigned in 1854 for the People's party ticket (which supported the temperance, nativist and antislavery causes), but only after they had grown dissatisfied with the Democrats and Whigs. Their prohibition statute was thus secured from a legislature dominated by People's party adherents. Conversely, anti-liquor activists in Massachusetts endeavored "to elect true temperance men to the Legislature" in the early 1850s, without reference to party. Thus the state's Maine Law was enacted by a coalition of Free Soilers, Whigs, and a bare majority of Democrats. In short, as table 6 shows, the teetotalers' success stories varied considerably by state.[36]

Beginning in 1854, organized nativism in the form of the American (or Know Nothing) party amplified the chaos in the party system, and played a crucial role in establishing prohibition in four states.[37] As exploiters of both anti-Catholic and anti-foreign sentiment, the Know Nothings shared with the prohibitionists an abiding uneasiness about immigrant drinking customs.[38] However, the party vividly displayed its limitations as a potential dry ally in one region of the country: the South.[39] In contrast to their northern colleagues, southern teetotalers generally confronted a fairly stable two-party system in the early 1850s. Although somewhat disturbed by the Compromise of 1850, this system featured two polar blocs of voters—the Democrats and the Whigs or ex-Whigs—until 1856.[40] In fact, even as the name of the primary opposition to the Democrats changed from "Whig" to "American" in

1854, the South's two-party structure persisted, a development which reflected the new party's strong appeal among former Whigs.[41] As a result, most southern states never experienced a three-way race during the realignment of the 1850s (see table 7.)

Like their Whig predecessors,[42] the southern Know Nothings were consistently loath to champion Maine Laws. Though more sympathetic to temperance than many Democrats, they clearly recognized the divisiveness of prohibition, and at best they occasionally endorsed modest anti-drink measures.[43] In addition, some of the southern Know Nothings' disdain for prohibition reflected their fear of being further tarred with the brush of abolitionism. Broad Free Soil support for the Maine Law, as well as its stringent provisions, allowed southern prohibition opponents to link "Maine Lawism" with the other seemingly eccentric "isms" emanating from the North, including mesmerism, spiritualism, nativism, and worst of all, abolitionism.[44] Faced with the sudden emergence of the Know Nothings in 1854, the southern Democrats pounced on the support expressed by many American party candidates in the North for the antislavery and anti-liquor causes in the fall campaigns of that year, and declared that the "isms" were on the march. "We shall next have a candidate for the Presidency, who will represent . . . the Whigs, the anti-Catholics, the Native Americans, the Abolitionists, the Freesoilers, the Maine Law folks, and perhaps the Spirit-rappers, Mormons and Millerites," complained the *Nashville Union*, which was aligned with the Democrats.[45] Eager to distinguish themselves from their northern counterparts and to refute the Democrats, the southern Know Nothings understandably avoided a strong association with the Maine Law and its dubious allies. Thus the South lacked an insurgent party that deliberately championed prohibition, and the Know Nothings directly generated but one Maine Law victory below the Mason-Dixon line: that of Delaware.

Between 1851 and 1856 state legislatures in the North were therefore vastly more receptive to prohibition than in the South. This sectional disparity partly reflected the utter disarray of the northern party system. Characterized by fusion parties, multiparty state races, and unexpected alliances, the North was a fluid environment that promised greater chances for temperance success than the South's relatively stable two party alignment. In Connecticut's gubernatorial contests, for example, the electorate voted for Democrats, Whigs, *and* third party candidates representing the Free Soilers (1853), the Temperance party (1854), the American-Temperance fusion ticket (1855), the Republican party (1856) and the American party (1856).[46] In contrast, North Carolina voters consistently confronted two basic electoral choices in this same period: the Democrats and the Whigs (1853–54), and then the Democrats and the ex-Whigs who became Know Nothings (1855–56).[47]

Still, the weakness of prohibition in the South also stemmed from the perceived link between "Maine Lawism" and abolitionism. As it turned out, this perception

Table 7 Contours of the State Party System in the South: The Gubernatorial Vote, 1848–1856

State	Year	Democratic Party Vote	Whig Party Vote	American Party Vote	Other Party Vote
Alabama	1849	98.1			
	1851	85.5[a]			12.8[b]
	1853	65.0[a]	20.0		15.0[b]
	1855	57.2	1.4	41.4	
Arkansas	1849	50.5	49.5		
		55.0			45.0[c]
		64.6		35.4	
Florida	1848	46.9	53.1		
	1852	51.6	48.4		
		51.3		48.7	
Georgia	1849	51.8	48.2		
	1851	40.3[a]			59.7[d]
	1853	50.3[a]			49.7[d]
	1855	51.2		41.9	
Louisiana	1849	51.5	48.5		
	1852	53.0	47.0		
	1855			46.4	
Mississippi	1849	59.0	41.0		
	1851	49.1[a]			50.9[b]
	1853	54.1	45.9		
	1855	54.2		45.8	
North Carolina	1848	49.5	50.5		
	1850	51.6	48.4		
	1852	53.0	47.0		
	1854	51.1	48.9		
	1856	56.2		43.8	
Tennessee	1849	50.6	49.4		
	1851	49.3	50.7		
	1853	50.9	49.1		
	1855	50.8	49.2		
Virginia	1851	53.0	47.0		
	1855	53.2		46.8	

[a] State's Rights Democratic Party (opposed Compromise of 1850).
[b] Union Democratic Party (favored Compromise of 1850).
[c] Independent Democratic and Whig Party (favored Compromise of 1850).
[d] Constitutional Union Party (or Union Democratic and Whig Party; favored Compromise of 1850).
All party vote figures in percent. Table omits data on Texas (where Democratic dominance made interparty votes insignificant) and South Carolina (where governors were not popularly elected until 1865).
Source: Roy R. Glashan, *American Governors and Gubernatorial Elections*, 1775–1978 (Westport, Conn.: Meckler, 1979).

was well founded, and many northern anti-liquor activists favored creating a new antislavery party as sectional tensions intensified during the 1850s. For instance, the author of the Maine Law, Neal Dow, was a charter member of Maine's Republican party in 1856.[48] Not surprisingly, many northern teetotalers affiliated with the Republican party in the mid-1850s.[49] Thus, the realignment of the 1850s not only created reform opportunities for the North's prohibitionists, but also drew them into the GOP.

Insurgents, Loyalists, and Interparty Competition, 1865–1890

From its birth in the mid-1850s, the unruly Republican coalition required deft management. Like other participants in this coalition, the party's temperance contingent received its share of blandishments from a Republican élite seeking party unity and electoral victories. Indeed, early Republican leaders fretted that a dry party would alienate antislavery Germans,[50] and they sought to minimize the prohibition crusade's impact on party platforms by convincing their anti-liquor allies that slavery —not prohibition—was the pressing issue of the day.[51] For example, in 1856 Republican party chiefs in New York skillfully rebuffed the teetotalers' demand for a prohibition plank in the state party platform. As John Marsh of the American Temperance Union later recalled, "Thousands of men, we were told, there were in the state who would vote for an anti-slavery Governor who would not vote for prohibition. Now you must stand aside; give us your vote or New York goes for slavery."[52] In the end, the party's task was aided by prohibition's failure. Instead of reducing crime, many Maine Laws had produced social disorder, as rigid enforcement efforts provoked brawls and other mob violence. In other states, these laws had barely taken effect before they were nullified by pro-liquor court decisions and legislative actions. By 1856 the party system had re-formed around the issue of slavery, and prohibition had been relegated to the Republican party's back burner.[53]

In describing the period 1856–65, one prominent teetotaler recorded that "temperance was sacrificed to politics and party, and the standard which had been carried so high trailed in the dust."[54] In fact, several Republican-led state governments either toned down existing anti-liquor policies or failed to enact restrictions on the liquor industry.[55] Worse yet, in 1862 the Lincoln Administration established a national liquor tax, which seemingly legitimized the liquor traffic and gave the national government a stake in its continuation.[56] While some of their neglect of the anti-liquor cause was due to the war,[57] the Republicans also periodically disassociated themselves from temperance to cultivate German voters, who opposed prohibitory laws.[58] Finally, Republican politicians could not help noticing the decline of the anti-liquor organizations in the wake of prohibition's failure. As the American Temperance Union, the Sons of Temperance, and Good Templars shed hundreds of members and affiliates during this period,[59] the movement's legislative campaigns lacked their previous zeal.[60]

Even after the dry fraternal orders revived in the late 1860s, Republican state lawmakers often temporized and compromised on the liquor issue.[61] As a result, a small band of frustrated anti-liquor Republicans decided to establish the Prohibition party in 1869.[62] In later years, this party attracted Labor Reformers, Greenbackers, southern Democrats, and other restless agitators,[63] and yet its core was consistently dominated by ex-Republicans like James Black.[64] Black, a founder of the party, spoke for many of these rebels when he voiced these complaints about the Pennsylvania GOP: "Here is a party . . . I helped to place in power. It is in power in my city today. It has been in power in Pennsylvania for a long time past. I ask, has there been any material effort on the part of this party having the law-making power; have they endeavored at any time to use their power for the promotion of prohibition of the [liquor] traffic in any degree? No. We have met now for three years and resolved and besought, but to no purpose."[65]

Though incensed by Republican apathy, Black and his colleagues nonetheless situated their party within the Republican reform tradition. As Gerrit Smith, an architect of the New York Prohibition party, declared, "Right was it [for] Americans to form an anti-slavery party, and right is it now for them to pass on from the overthrow of slavery to an anti-dramshop party." Likewise, the gubernatorial candidate of the Massachusetts Prohibition party in 1870, Wendell Phillips, allowed that "the Republican party deserves our gratitude" for "it has achieved great results." However, he also accused the GOP of resting on its laurels, and declared that any prohibitionist who clung to this party "proclaims beforehand his willingness to be cheated."[66]

Steeped in the Republican tradition, the Prohibitionists often described their party's formation as analogous to that of the antebellum antislavery parties, including the GOP.[67] In 1876, for example, Black asserted:

> Our political history clearly shows that every new great issue called forth a new great political party for its support. The old Whig and Democratic parties . . . being unable to satisfactorily deal with the slave system, because divided upon it, the issue of freedom against slavery gave birth to the Republican party. So now the Democratic and Republican parties, having members holding diverse views on the liquor question are impotent for its solution; and the demand for protection from the evils of the drink-trade has called into being the Prohibition Reform party.[68]

The "antislavery parallel," as this analysis came to be known, undoubtedly encouraged the Prohibitionists' conviction that they would follow the lead of the abolitionists and provoke a realignment of the party system.[69] Insignificant vote totals for their party were initially tolerable, for "the vote of the Anti-Slavery men" was also "at first discouragingly small."[70] Even after decades of agitation had failed to spark a realignment, party activists still fell back on the antislavery analogy. "The slave block existed as long as it was . . . upheld by political parties," Helen M. Gougar wrote in 1895. It vanished through the work of a third party; "so it has been and so it will be with the liquor saloon."[71]

Despite its resonance with many party activists, the antislavery parallel was assuredly downplayed in the South. By the early 1880s some Prohibitionists touted the region as fertile soil for their message. Moreover, in 1885 the party resolved to build a truly national organization, including the white-led South. Several of the party's best speakers went on a southern tour in the winter of 1885–86, and its Memorial Day gathering in 1887 included veterans of both the Blue and the Gray.[72] To enhance their appeal, Prohibitionists stressed that their party raised "an issue that is in no sense sectional" and would help "remove sectional differences, promote national unity, and insure the best welfare of our entire land."[73]

Nevertheless, the Prohibition party's southern wing was much weaker than its northern one.[74] Undoubtedly, this frailty was shaped by the South's insular anti-liquor movement, as well as by its distinctive postwar political development. In contrast to their northern counterparts, southern temperance advocates generally rejected the party of Lincoln as a potential reform vehicle in the aftermath of the Civil War.[75] Of course, their rejection of the GOP was largely a response to its wartime and Reconstruction policies, but it also reflected their sense that the South's anti-liquor efforts would be more effective if separate from northern reform elements. By distancing themselves from both the Republicans and the northern wings of anti-liquor groups like the Good Templars, though, most dry southern activists also withdrew from the reform network which formed the Prohibition party.[76]

The Republicans may have been unacceptable to southern teetotalers, but the region's Democrats hardly raised dry hopes after the war. Indeed, the Democrats had seldom supported reform efforts, and had forged strong links with local liquor interests. Furthermore, the party was consumed with "redeeming" the South from Republican rule throughout Reconstruction. After the Democrats gained control of the region's state governments in the late 1870s, however, temperance advocates secured several local option laws from Democratic state legislatures.[77] Apparently, Democratic lawmakers believed that provincial, nonpartisan anti-liquor measures would prevent the prohibition issue from undermining party unity and white Democratic rule.[78]

The success of this strategy, combined with the isolated nature of the southern temperance movement, accounted for much of the South's muted response to the Prohibitionist insurgency. Like their party's élite, temperance Democrats desired party unity, and rejected accusations that they were a disruptive force.[79] For instance, in 1881 drys in Mississippi disclaimed any intention "to interfere with political parties or their management." Furthermore, once the state's Democratic legislature enacted local option in 1886, most anti-liquor agitators welcomed the law as a step forward, and used its provisions to ban liquor in dozens of counties. Beginning in the late 1880s, most of Mississippi's teetotalers adhered to a nonpartisan local option policy and considered the Democratic party an adequate source of support.[80] On the other hand, some southern Democrats were "learning that new occasions need new parties."[81] Just as sundry northern teetotalers had bolted from the GOP after being snubbed, so a handful of dry southern Democrats joined the Prohibitionists after failing to win radical concessions from the Democratic party.[82] Thus, the third-party insurgents could claim a tiny wing beneath the Mason-Dixon line.

Unlike their antislavery precursors, the Prohibitionists failed to instigate a realignment or to replace one of the major parties. Their national vote totals, while rising steadily from a baseline of 5,588 votes in 1872, never surpassed the 2.25 percent of the popular vote achieved in 1892. At the state level, the party peaked in 1886, when it captured almost 300,000 votes nationwide and won over 3.5 percent of the popular vote in eleven gubernatorial elections.[83] Like other minor parties in American history, the Prohibitionists attracted few votes but would achieve power by altering "the content and range of political discourse" and by affecting public policy.[84] Their influence depended on two crucial factors: anti-liquor coalitional insiders and close interparty competition after 1876.

When the dry GOP insurgents had called for an anti-liquor party in 1869, most of their temperance colleagues reacted with hostility.[85] As one party activist recalled, "good temperance men . . . felt that the Republican Party held a mortgage on their vote" and considered the Prohibition party's formation to be "treachery, base ingratitude and detrimental to the cause, for nearly all the [third party's] votes would be drawn from the Republican Party."[86] In the South, many temperance activists showed even less respect. After ridiculing the Prohibitionists for including "*woman suffrage* and other *silly things*" in their platform, the anti-liquor *Alabama Christian Advocate* opined, "We think it mighty proper for the real temperance workers of this state to come together at an early day and organize as temperance workers under our local option laws, ignoring politics and political parties and presenting to the public the temperance cause on its own merits."[87]

Beyond such anecdotes, more systematic evidence points to the existence of a substantial contingent of dry coalitional insiders. That a significant proportion of the prohibitionists remained within the two major parties can be inferred from the vote totals of nonpartisan state prohibition elections. In the 1880s nineteen state

Table 8 Partisan and Nonpartisan Support for Prohibition, 1869–1896

	Highest Number of Votes Received by the Prohibition Party from Statewide Electorates, 1869–1896		Highest Number of Votes Favoring State Prohibition in Nonpartisan Referenda, 1880–1890	
Connecticut	4,960	1874, gubernatorial	22,379	1889
Iowa	10,545	1877, gubernatorial	155,436	1882
Kansas	8,094	1886, gubernatorial	91,874	1880
Maine	3,873	1886, gubernatorial	70,783	1884
Massachusetts	16,354	1877, gubernatorial	85,242	1889
Michigan	28,681	1890, gubernatorial	178,636	1887
Nebraska	9,511	1888, gubernatorial	82,296	1890
New Hampshire	2,137	1886, gubernatorial	25,786	1889
North Carolina	2,789	1888, presidential	48,370	1881
North Dakota	899	1892, presidential	18,552	1889
Ohio	29,700	1887, gubernatorial	323,189	1883
Oregon	2,727	1886, gubernatorial	19,973	1887
Pennsylvania	32,458	1886, gubernatorial	296,617	1889
Rhode Island	2,585	1886, gubernatorial	15,113	1886
South Dakota	683	1896, presidential	39,509	1889
Tennessee	11,082	1890, gubernatorial	117,504	1887
Texas	19,186	1886, gubernatorial	129,270	1887
Washington	3,587	1892, gubernatorial	19,546	1889
West Virginia	2,145	1892, gubernatorial	41,668	1888

Sources: Roy R. Glashan, *American Governors and Gubernatorial Elections, 1775–1978* (Westport, Conn.: Meckler, 1979); *Cyclopedia of Temperance and Prohibition*; Svend Petersen, *A Statistical History of the American Presidential Elections.*

governments submitted nonpartisan referenda on state prohibition to their respective electorates. As table 8 demonstrates, prohibition supporters vastly outnumbered the Prohibition party's adherents. Unless a considerable number of dry referenda voters abstained from candidate contests (which seems unlikely, given the decade's high turnout rates),[88] a majority of temperance advocates never abandoned the major parties.

Relations between these party insiders and third-party members were not particularly warm. The Prohibitionists considered the major parties "irresponsible and irregular," and were in turn derided by them as "a combination of misguided enthusiasts, moral peacocks, disgruntled politicians, mercenaries and cranks operating in the sacred name of temperance."[89] Despite such mutual antagonism, these coalitional outsiders and insiders combined to gain dry leverage over the party system in the 1880s. By the late 1870s the Prohibition party presented a credible alternative to the major parties in Connecticut, Massachusetts, New Hampshire, Pennsylvania, New York, Michigan, Iowa, Rhode Island, and Minnesota, and major party élites feared defections by their anti-liquor constituents. This concern only increased as interparty competition heightened between 1876 and 1892 in several states. In fact, Paul Kleppner has characterized this period as "a protracted political stalemate," in which neither major party proved able to dominate the party system.[90]

Faced with continued electoral uncertainty in the Gilded Age, party managers resorted to a variety of remedies. At their worst, they periodically engaged in fraud, bribery, and coercion at the polls, although it remains difficult to assess the extent of corruption.[91] While corrupt electoral practices represented a hidden and unsavory path to power, an attack on the sordid liquor industry could burnish a party's image and prevent dry defections to the Prohibitionists.[92] For Republicans, their party's advocacy of prohibitory legislation during the late 1870s and 1880s served to reaffirm a reform tradition rooted in evangelical Protestantism and the forces that gave rise to it. Though a bane to the GOP's wet constituencies, anti-liquor legislation could be touted as a return to the party's "first principles."[93] In summoning his fellow Republicans to a new moral crusade, the national party activist William Windom declared that "the Republican party is the great party of moral ideas now as well as in the past. And I have no doubt that to its already splendid record, it will add this last achievement—the destruction of the liquor power here in America."[94] In contrast, the South's Democratic party leadership deftly retained both dry and damp Democrats by depicting local option as a reform measure which also ensured local control. As an extension of their party's "states' rights" principle, this policy appealed to many Democrats because it secured "the right of each locality to administer its own affairs with full freedom."[95]

As in the antebellum period, party leaders first confronted the full force of the anti-liquor crusade after a successful state prohibition campaign. Like Maine's prohibition statute of 1851, the ratification by Kansas in 1880 of constitutional prohibition electrified the drys, encouraging other state prohibition referenda.[96] Almost every state legislature received a flurry of petitions, calling for constitutional amendments which mandated prohibition upon voter approval.[97] WCTU activists in Iowa, who had pioneered the amendment approach in tandem with sundry Midwestern Templars, would be the second group of state drys to secure a referendum, thanks to the Iowa GOP's fear of the Prohibitionists. In 1877 Iowa's Prohibitionist gubernatorial candidate had received 4.3 percent of the popular vote, which helped reduce the GOP's share of the vote from 57 percent in 1875 to 49.4 percent.[98] With the third party threatening to nominate another gubernatorial candidate in 1879, the Republicans yielded to dry demands for a prohibition referendum by declaring their support for submission in their state platform. As a result, the GOP gubernatorial candidate won with 54 percent of the popular vote, whereas the Prohibitionist share shrank to 1.1 percent. Following their party platform, Iowa's Republican lawmakers duly authorized submission in both 1880 and 1882, as stipulated by the state constitution.

In 1882 Iowans went to the polls and embraced prohibition by a vote of 155,436 to 125,677.[99]

After the votes in Kansas and Iowa, seventeen additional states held referenda on state prohibition between 1880 and 1890. Thirteen elections occurred after 1886, which marked the peak of both the Prohibition party and the Anti-Saloon Republicans at the state level. Launched in 1885 by drys in Kansas, the Anti-Saloon Republican movement sought to induce the GOP everywhere to adopt "a platform of uncompromising hostility to the saloon."[100] The liquor question's urgency had become clear to many Republican leaders after their party's defeat in the presidential election of 1884: in that year James Blaine's loss of the presidency was attributable to his having lost New York by 1,149 votes while the Prohibitionist candidate polled 25,006.[101] With the Prohibitionists crowing about holding the "balance of power" in national elections, the Anti-Saloon Republicans held several state conventions in 1886 to ensure that their party "should never again be embarrassed by the temperance issue."[102] Although the precise role of the group in drafting many state party platforms remains uncertain,[103] it is nonetheless true that ten state Republican platforms, an unprecedented number, favored submitting prohibition to a popular vote in 1886.[104] The Anti-Saloon Republicans were less successful at the national level, however, merely persuading the 1888 convention to resolve that "the Republican party cordially sympathizes with all wise and well-directed efforts for the promotion of temperance and morality."[105]

While the Anti-Saloon Republicans challenged the GOP's northern wing to promote new anti-liquor efforts, their less-organized southern counterparts also increased their demands on the Democratic party during the 1880s. For example, in North Carolina over 100,000 voters in 1880 petitioned the General Assembly, controlled by Democrats, requesting a state prohibition law. Similarly, in other southern states "the friends of temperance were launching a new phase of their campaign which, for determination and aggressiveness, was not to be matched" until the Progressive Era. In some cases, this dry assertiveness generated local option legislation; in others, temperance and church leaders insisted that the Democrats go beyond local option and support referenda on prohibition.[106]

Given the strong presence of prohibitionists within many northern Republican and southern Democratic state parties, one would expect these parties to have been responsible for submitting the referenda. As table 9 shows, such an assumption would be generally correct: all three southern prohibition referenda were put forth by Democratic state legislatures; fourteen of seventeen in the North were put forth by Republican legislatures or constitutional conventions.

The political conditions surrounding submission become even clearer if one focuses on the referenda held in states which had entered the Union before 1889

Table 9 Partisan Control of State Government in States Holding Prohibition Referenda, 1880–1890

State	Year of Vote	Body Submitting Referendum	Party Affiliation of Governor	Dominant Party in State Legislature or Constitutional Convention
Kansas	1880	Legislature	Republican	Republican
North Carolina	1881	Legislature	Democratic	Democratic
Iowa	1882	Legislature	Republican	Republican
Ohio	1883	Legislature	Republican	Republican
Maine	1884	Legislature	Republican	Republican
Rhode Island	1886	Legislature	Republican	Republican
Michigan	1887	Legislature	Republican	Republican
Texas	1887	Legislature	Democratic	Democratic
Tennessee	1887	Legislature	Democratic	Democratic
Oregon	1887	Legislature	Republican	Republican (upper house), Democratic (lower house)
West Virginia	1888	Legislature	Democratic	Democratic (upper house), Republican (lower house)
New Hampshire	1889	Convention	Republican	Republican
Massachusetts	1889	Legislature	Republican	Republican
Pennsylvania	1889	Legislature	Republican	Republican
South Dakota	1889	Convention	Republican	Republican
North Dakota	1889	Convention	Republican	Republican
Washington	1889	Convention	Republican	Republican
Connecticut	1889	Legislature	Republican	Republican (upper house), Democratic (lower house)
Nebraska	1890	Legislature	Republican	Republican

Sources: Roy R. Glashan, *American Governors and Gubernatorial Elections, 1775–1978* (Westport, Conn.: Meckler, 1979); *Cyclopedia of Temperance and Prohibition*, 102–28.

and thus had an established record of electing governors (as opposed to being subject to appointed territorial governors).[107] In fifteen of these states, lawmakers (as opposed to nonpartisan conventions) proposed dry constitutional amendments and one statutory referendum, that of North Carolina (see the top two rows of table 10). All these states were characterized by state party systems that manifested more interparty competition in gubernatorial elections than states which did not hold referenda. Furthermore, the fourteen states that sanctioned constitutional prohibition contained, on average, stronger and more established Prohibition parties than elsewhere. Ten of the fourteen states had witnessed Prohibitionist votes of 2.7 percent or more in gubernatorial elections closely preceding the legislature's decision to submit a referendum.[108]

In the years 1880–90, then, the Prohibitionist party and the dry coalitional insiders had inadvertently collaborated to secure access to direct legislation from a number of competitive state party systems. In that they gained such access in nineteen states, it can be said that the prohibitionists acquired major reform opportunities. The disappointing referenda results, however, only revealed their failure to mobilize popular support for state constitutional prohibition. During the decade, the voters of twelve states immediately rejected prohibition; in four others, the cause of constitutional prohibition won but short-lived victories. As the dry losses mounted, major party leaders cooled on the liquor issue during the 1890s.[109] In the Midwest, for example, the unpopularity of prohibition and Sunday closing laws "led to a reorientation of the [Republican] party" after 1889. Instead of supporting prohibitory measures and losing wet votes in the process, Midwestern Republicans authorized modest anti-liquor policies in the hopes of muting more radical appeals.[110]

Finally, in its frustration, the radical wing of the prohibition movement insinuated that the liquor interests had thwarted its referendum campaigns, and concluded that "non-partisan or petitioning methods are now effectually blocked by the liquor traffic in most of the states."[111] Frances Willard, for one, described how the drys had learned "by bitter experience" that their amendment efforts could be defeated through intentional miscounts and other wet tricks. She compared the amendment process to the labors of Sisyphus, one of "wearily rolling a heavy stone to the top of the hill, only to see it swiftly finding its way to its first position." Other lead-

Table 10 Electoral Competitiveness and Prohibition Party Strength in States Holding Dry Referenda, 1880–1890

Form of Referendum Sanctioned by States	Number of States Holding Dry Referenda, 1880–1890	Electoral Competitiveness, as Measured by Average Margin of Victory in Gubernatorial Elections, 1880–1890 (in Percent)[a]	Average Support Received by State Prohibition Party at Its Peak, 1880–1890 (in Percent)[a]	Average Number of Prohibition Party Candidates Nominated for Governor, 1880–1890
Submitted by legislature, statutory	1	5.1	0.0	0.0
Submitted by legislature, amendment	14	10.5	4.6	4.0
Submitted by constitutional convention	4	17.1	0.9	2.0
Totals	19	11.6	3.6	3.4

Average Margin of Victory in Gubernatorial Elections, All States (1880–1890): 17.1%
Average Support Received by Prohibition Party at Its Peak, All States (1880–1890): 2.6%
Average Number of Prohibition Candidates for Governor, All States (1880–1890): 2.3

[a] Mean difference between percentages received by winning candidates and percentage received by candidate who placed second in the gubernatorial elections during the years 1880–1890.

[b] Percentages reflect Prohibition party's peak performance in gubernatorial elections during the years 1880–1890. They do not include races in which the Prohibition party formed a fusion ticket (e.g., with the Labor Reform party in Massachusetts in 1870).

Table based on data contained in Roy R. Glashan, *American Governors and Gubernatorial Elections, 1775–1978* (Westport, Conn.: Meckler, 1979).

ing Prohibitionists wondered whether the party's funds might be better spent on party-building activities, a particularly pressing need after the group split in 1896 over whether to pursue a broad array of reforms or merely focus on prohibition.[112] During the 1890s the orthodox drys thus campaigned for only a handful of constitutional amendments, all of which were rejected by the legislatures and constitutional conventions involved. Consequently, no additional prohibition referenda would be submitted for popular vote during the years 1891–1906.

Coalitional Insiders and Intraparty Competition, 1900–1920

The prohibitionists of the 1880s and those of the Progressive Era confronted two distinct sets of political conditions. While the earlier prohibitionists had faced an intensely competitive party system characterized by fierce party loyalty and high voter turnout, the later ones encountered a seemingly more tranquil political terrain. To begin with, the election of 1896 had sapped the strength of the northern Democrats and largely annihilated the southern wing of the Republican party, thus decreasing electoral competition between the two parties. This decline in interparty competition, along with new legal and institutional barriers to voting, depressed voter participation, principally among lower-class groups.[113] At the same time, party élites found it increasingly difficult to command intense party loyalty from the electorate, as numerous reforms reduced their influence.[114] In sum, turn-of-the-century politics combined a minimum of interparty strife with the emergence of a more exclusive and less partisan electorate.

The new political environment had a variable impact on the anti-liquor crusade. First, the decrease in interparty strife after 1896 meant that the prohibitionists had to wrest reform opportunities from several uncompetitive state party systems. That they managed this feat is reflected in the first two rows of table 11. Second, as noted previously, a shrunken, more middle-class electorate may have reduced the costs of factionalism, especially in the South where it was feared that a split in the Democratic vote would permit black rule. Among other things, the southern Democrats' increased reliance on the direct primary in statewide elections after 1900 demonstrated greater tolerance for intraparty conflict.[115] Finally, the rise of nonpartisanship may have disrupted the drys' party alliances. Indeed, at first glance this hypothesis seems quite plausible, particularly with respect to the North.

To begin with, after the nonpartisan Anti-Saloon League assumed leadership of the prohibition forces, it periodically induced its followers to engage in split-ticket voting to reward or punish political leaders for their position on the liquor question. In 1905, for example, the Ohio ASL sponsored a successful campaign to oust the state's Republican governor, Myron T. Herrick, who had prevailed on the legislature

Table 11 Electoral Competitiveness in States Holding Dry Referenda during the 1880s and the Progressive Era

Form of Referendum Sanctioned by States	Number of States Holding Dry Referenda, 1880–1890	Electoral Competitiveness, as Measured by Average Margin of Victory in Gubernatorial Elections, 1880–1890 (in Percent)[a]	Number of States Holding Dry Referenda, 1900–1920	Electoral Competitiveness as Measured by Average Margin of Victory in Gubernatorial Elections, 1900–1920 (in Percent)[a]
Submitted by legislature, statutory	1	5.1	4	49.3
Submitted by legislature, amendment	14	10.5	13	20.9
Submitted by constitutional convention	4	17.1	1	8.0
Proposed by initiative, statutory[b]			1	11.3
Proposed by initiative, amendment[b]			11	13.0
Totals	19	11.6	29[c]	21.6

Average Margin of Victory in Gubernatorial Elections, All States (1880–1890): 17.1%

Average Margin of Victory in Gubernatorial Elections, All States (1900–1920): 22.1%

[a] Mean difference between percentage received by the winning candidates and percentage received by the candidate who placed second in the gubernatorial elections during the years 1880–1890.

[b] The initiative and referendum became a statewide form of direct legislation in 1898, through the amendment by South Dakota of its constitution.

[c] Subtotals do not sum to total because Missouri, where the state legislature submitted one constitutional amendment to the electorate (1918) and the drys used the initiative and referendum process twice (1910, 1916), is counted only once.

Table based on data contained in Roy R. Glashan, *American Governors and Gubernatorial Elections*, 1775–1978 (Westport, Conn.: Meckler, 1979).

to dilute the provisions of the ASL's local option bill. While electing an anti-liquor Democrat by a margin of 42,000 votes, the Ohio electorate simultaneously elected Republicans to every other state office that year. Similarly, drys in Tennessee distrusted the Democratic party's promise to enforce the state's prohibition law of 1909 and they persuaded a small band of independent Democrats to endorse the GOP's nominee for governor, Ben Hooper, in the election of 1910. In response to this party split, Tennessee voters elected the first Republican governor in the state since 1880, even while returning a Democratic legislature.[116]

As dry voters became more willing to put cause over party, the prohibition issue lost much of its partisan overtones within the northern electorate. During the 1880s northerners who voted Republican also tended to support prohibition referenda; meanwhile, the vast majority of the voters who preferred Democratic candidates opposed such measures (see the first column of table 12). As table 12 demonstrates, though, the sharp partisan divisions that had characterized nineteenth-century voting behavior in the North became blurred in the region's dry referenda after 1900. To account for this shift, Paul Kleppner speculates that William Jennings Bryan's leader-

Table 12 Percentage of Party Electorates Supporting Prohibition Referenda during the 1880s and the Progressive Era

	1880–1890		1900–1920	
	Democrat	Republican	Democrat	Republican
Iowa	0.0	75.2	40.4	48.6
Ohio[a]	18.0	100.0	31.0	70.0
Michigan	0.0	67.0	60.5	49.3
Nebraska	0.0	75.4	52.0	46.1
South Dakota	0.0	76.0	60.0	28.0
West Virginia	11.0	39.0	69.0	35.0
Pooled data	9.0	60.0	54.0	47.0

[a] Data for Ohio taken from Kleppner (1987), which is based on a pooled data set for the twentieth century, rather than Kleppner (1982), which is based on only one referendum in the period 1900–1920.

Sources: Kleppner, *Who Voted?* (1982), table 4.8, 78; Kleppner, *Continuity and Change in Electoral Politics* (1987), table 41, 210. Kleppner's data are regression estimates of the proportions of the Democratic or Republican electorates at the nearest state or federal election. His pooled data combine the data for eight states for nineteenth-century referenda and seven states for twentieth-century referenda.

ship of the Democratic party in 1896 drew more rural and native-born voters, and hence more prohibitionists, into the party. Meanwhile, Bryan's coup d'état alienated some wet conservative Democrats, who fled to the Republicans.[117]

Despite their followers' party affiliations, though, northern dry leaders remained close to the GOP during the Progressive Era, thus qualifying them as coalitional insiders.[118] In part, this alliance was the product of habit. Many of the ASL's northern leaders were Republicans, and they gravitated toward their party's nominees.[119] In addition, the pooled data in table 12 suggest that a substantial proportion of the Republican electorate was still willing to vote for prohibition. Hence, league leaders were presumably not the only northern drys who placed their hopes in the Republican party after 1900. Most importantly, however, the Anti-Saloon League often had little choice but to cultivate close relations with northern GOP organizations. Immediately after the election of 1896, the Republicans strengthened their position in several northern states, thus contributing to at least eighteen one-party regimes at the state level.[120] Although the Progressive party split the Republicans in 1912, most of the Progressive defectors reunited with their state Republican parties after the elections of 1914.[121] As a result, the anti-liquor forces again confronted the prospects of working solely through the GOP in many states, regardless of the many Democratic voters now supporting prohibition.

Of course, the situation in the South allowed for even less discretion by the drys. By 1900 the Republican party had become negligible in all but two states,[122] and southern anti-liquor activists faced entrenched Democratic regimes. Therefore, while drys in the North frequently won their greatest legislative victories through the Republican party, in the South they relied upon the Democrats. To illustrate, table 13 lists the most significant state anti-liquor measures of the Progressive Era. The movement prevailed in twenty-three northern states where the Republican party dominated both the executive and at least one branch of the legislature, in eleven southern states, all controlled by Democrats, in seven northern states controlled by Democrats, and in six states where party control was divided.

How did the prohibition movement obtain reform opportunities and other benefits from so many one-party regimes? Above all, the Anti-Saloon League's leadership of the Progressive Era drys altered the character of the movement's legislative campaigns. Not only were the league's campaigns ostensibly nonpartisan, but they frequently sought only modest prohibitory laws. Indeed, as table 13 shows, some of the league's most important state-level achievements included local option statutes, licensing limits, and enforcement laws. Naturally, ASL leaders considered such measures major victories that would lead to still greater triumphs, but it is undoubtedly true that their minor gains reflected the moderation of their demands.

More to the point, the dry crusade clearly profited from the wave of reform movements in the Midwest, the West, and the South during the first decade of the twentieth century.[123] After 1904 "a remarkable number of cities and states experienced wrenching moments of discovery that led directly to significant political changes. Usually, a scandal, an investigation, an intraparty battle, or a particularly divisive election campaign exposed an illicit alliance of politics and business and made corruption apparent to the community."[124] This discovery that "business corrupts politics" prompted political entrepreneurs to challenge existing party leaders for control of the party apparatus by raising the issue of political corruption. In doing so, they typically created their own reform wings in the parties, the most famous being the "Lincoln-Roosevelt League" within the California GOP. Significantly, the development of Progressive politics affected each party differently. In the North, Progressivism operated mainly within the Republican party; in the South, Progressive factions formed within the dominant Democratic party.[125] Hence, dry leaders were often coalitional insiders in those regional parties that experienced the most intraparty competition during the Progressive Era.

This internecine warfare benefited the prohibitionists in two ways. First, the drys achieved substantial gains from fractured parties that more unified organizations would have withheld. For instance, as coalitional insiders in the Illinois GOP, the ASL's leaders were able to play off the downstate Republicans against their wet party colleagues from Cook County to push their local option measure through the state legislature in 1907.[126] In similar fashion, the Wisconsin Anti-Saloon League secured its resident district option law in 1907 through an alliance with the rural

Table 13 Partisan Control of State Governments during the Prohibition Movement's Greatest Legislative Victories, 1900–1920

State	Most Significant General Anti-Liquor Measures Secured by the Prohibition Movement from State Legislature, 1900–1920	Party of Governor	Control of Legislature
Alabama	Statutory prohibition 1907, submission of amendment 1909, statutory prohibition 1915	Democratic	Democratic
Arizona	Local option in cities and counties (outside cities) by majority vote 1909	Republican (territorial governor)	Democratic
Arkansas	Statutory prohibition 1915	Democratic	Democratic
California	Local option for towns and supervisorial districts 1911	Republican	Republican
Colorado	Local option in municipalities, wards, and precincts 1907	Republican	Republican
Connecticut	Establishment of state police 1903	Republican	Republican
Delaware	Statewide district local option election held 1907	Republican	Republican
Florida	Submission of constitutional prohibition 1909, 1918	Democratic (1909), Democratic-Prohibition fusion (1918)	Democratic
Georgia	Statutory prohibition 1907	Democratic	Democratic
Idaho	Statutory prohibition 1915, submission of constitutional prohibition 1916	Democratic	Republican
Illinois	Local option in townships, municipalities, and precincts 1907	Republican	Republican
Indiana	Statutory prohibition 1917	Republican	Democratic (upper house), Republican (lower house)
Iowa	Statutory prohibition 1916, submission of constitutional prohibition 1917	Republican	Republican
Kansas	Enactment of Bone Dry Liquor law outlawing possession of liquor 1917	Republican	Republican
Kentucky	Submission of constitutional prohibition 1919	Democratic	Democratic
Louisiana	Enactment of Gay-Shattuck law banning saloons within 300 feet of school or church 1908	Democratic	Democratic
Maine	Enactment of Sturgis (enforcement) law 1905	Republican	Republican
Maryland	Submission of statutory prohibition with wet regions voting as separate units 1916	Democratic	Democratic
Massachusetts	Bar and Bottle bill limiting number of liquor licenses 1910	Republican	Republican
Michigan	Search and seizure law, Warner Cramton law limiting number of licenses 1909	Republican	Republican
Minnesota	Submission of constitutional prohibition 1917	Republican	Republican
Mississippi	Statutory prohibition 1908	Democratic	Democratic
Missouri	Submission of constitutional prohibition 1918	Democratic	Democratic

Table 13 Continued

State	Most Significant General Anti-Liquor Measures Secured by the Prohibition Movement from State Legislature, 1900–1920	Party of Governor	Control of Legislature
Montana	Submission of constitutional prohibition 1915	Democratic	Democratic
Nebraska	Enactment of the Eight o'clock Closing law limiting saloon operating hours 1909	Democratic	Democratic
Nevada	District local option 1911	Republican	Democratic
New Hampshire	Statutory prohibition 1917	Republican	Republican
New Jersey	Municipal local option 1918	Republican	Republican
New Mexico	Submission of constitutional prohibition 1917	Republican	Republican
New York	Municipal local option (except New York City) 1917	Republican	Republican
North Carolina	Submission of statutory prohibition 1908	Democratic	Democratic
North Dakota	Enactment of the Bootlegging (enforcement) law 1909	Democratic	Republican
Ohio	County option 1908	Republican	Democratic (upper house), Republican (lower house)
Oklahoma	Enactment of Bone Dry Liquor law outlawing possession of liquor 1917	Democratic	Democratic
Oregon	Enactment of Anderson (enforcement) law 1915	Republican	Republican
Rhode Island	Tightening of liquor policy, limits on number of licenses, ban on saloons near schools 1908	Democratic	Republican
South Carolina	Submission of statutory prohibition 1915	Democratic	Democratic
South Dakota	Submission of constitutional prohibition 1916	Republican	Republican
Tennessee	Statutory prohibition 1909	Democratic	Democratic
Texas	Statutory prohibition 1918, submission of constitutional prohibition 1911, 1918	Democratic	Democratic
Utah	Statutory prohibition 1917, submission of constitutional prohibition 1917	Democratic	Democratic
Vermont	Submission of statutory prohibition 1916	Republican	Republican
Virginia	Submission of statutory prohibition 1914	Democratic	Democratic
Washington	Local option in cities and counties (outside cities) 1909	Republican	Republican
West Virginia	Submission of constitutional prohibition 1911	Republican	Republican (upper house), Democratic (lower house)[a]
Wisconsin	Residence district option 1907	Republican	Republican
Wyoming	Submission of constitutional prohibition 1917	Democratic-Progressive fusion	Republican

[a]The West Virginia State Senate was evenly divided between Republicans and Democrats in 1911; Republicans were eventually allowed to organize the chamber.

Table based on various state studies and the Anti-Saloon League's yearbooks and national proceedings. See bibliography for a complete listing of state studies consulted. Table does not include data about states (e.g., Pennsylvania) that failed to pass significant liquor laws during the Progressive Era.

faction of the progressive Republicans in the state legislature, which was ascendant at that time over both the Milwaukee progressives and the stalwarts in the Republican party.[127] In fact, Wisconsin drys had high hopes of winning county option until 1910, when a wet Milwaukee progressive, Frank McGovern, became governor and the legislature cooled to the anti-liquor cause.[128]

A second advantage of intraparty competition was that some reform candidates promised to support the dry cause as a means of differentiating themselves from their competitors. This strategic embrace of prohibition was particularly prominent in the South, where reform candidates like Braxton B. Comer (Ala.), Edward W. Carmack (Tenn.), George M. Donaghey (Ark.), and Thomas M. Campbell (Texas) all endorsed either state prohibition or the submission of dry referenda in their gubernatorial primary bids.[129] Meanwhile, in Georgia the Democratic party was torn by an intense rivalry between the progressives, led by Hoke Smith, and conservatives, led by Clark Howell and Joseph E. Brown.[130] When Smith and Howell battled one another for the Democratic gubernatorial nomination in 1906, Smith indicated his willingness to support the Anti-Jug Bill, sponsored by the ASL, and thus encouraged the drys to push for his election and that of his followers in the legislature, who were quietly interviewed about their positions on the liquor question. Their faith was not misplaced, for after Smith won the primary, he announced that he would sign a prohibition bill if the legislature passed it. As a result, Georgia's anti-liquor activists mobilized a massive campaign to petition state lawmakers. Apparently their efforts paid off, for on July 30, 1907, the Georgia state legislature enacted a state prohibition law which Smith approved.[131]

Notably, the drys obtained most of their initial legislative victories during the administrations of reform governors like Smith (see table 14). Some of these governors, such as Hiram Johnson (Calif.) and James Brady (Idaho), promised to support local option legislation in exchange for the anti-liquor movement's electoral support.[132] Others, like J. Frank Hanly (Ind.) and Henry A. Buchtel (Colo.), were true believers in the prohibition cause.[133] In either case, the Anti-Saloon League appears to have made the most of the intraparty competition of the period 1900–1912.

While many reform politicians looked favorably upon anti-liquor legislation, the drys also profited from the progressives' support for statewide direct legislation. Between 1898 and 1912 eighteen states adopted the initiative and referendum, reforms that many prohibitionists had viewed as beneficial to their cause since the late nineteenth century.[134] As one WCTU activist claimed in 1897, "By the use of the initiative and referendum . . . the citizens of this country could soon be living under laws of their own enactment. . . . A great and well-organized society like the WCTU, which possesses the power to educate rapidly through its organization, would find [direct legislation's] usefulness in hastening all the reforms it advocated doubled, perhaps

Table 14 Factionalism and the Enactment of the Prohibition Movement's Most Significant Legislation, 1900–1912

State	Most Significant General Anti-Liquor Measure(s) Secured by the Prohibition Movement from State Legislature, 1900–1912	Governor in Power	Party Wing Represented Governor
Alabama	Statutory prohibition 1907, submission of constitutional prohibition 1909	Braxton B. Comer (D)	Reform
Arkansas	Tightened enforcement, new bans on public drunkenness and licenses in rural areas 1907	John I. Moore (D)	Reform
California	Local option for towns and supervisorial districts 1911	Hiram Johnson (R)	Reform
Colorado	Local option in municipalities, wards, and precincts 1907	Henry A. Buchtel (R)	Reform
Connecticut	Establishment of state police 1907	Abiram Chamberlain (R)	Conservative
Delaware	Statewide district local option election held 1907	Preston Lea (R)	Conservative
Florida	Submission of constitutional prohibition 1909	Albert W. Gilchrist (R)	Reform
Georgia	Statutory prohibition 1907	M. Hoke Smith (D)	Reform
Idaho	County option 1909	James H. Brady (R)	Reform
Illinois	Local option in townships, municipalities, and precincts 1907	Charles S. Deneen (R)	Reform
Indiana	County option 1908	J. Franklin Hanly (R)	Reform
Iowa	Enactment of Moon law limiting number of liquor licenses 1909	Beryl F. Carroll (R)	Reform
Kansas	State prohibition law amended to include ban on the sale of liquor as medicine 1909	Edward W. Hoch (R)	Reform
Kentucky	County option 1912	James B. McCreary (D)	Reform
Louisiana	Enactment of Gay-Shattuck law banning saloons within 300 feet of school or church 1908	Jared Y. Sanders (D)	Conservative-Moderate
Maine	Enactment of Sturgis (enforcement) law 1905	William T. Cobb (R)	Conservative
Massachusetts	Bar and Bottle bill limiting number of liquor licenses 1910	Ebenezer S. Draper (R)	Conservative
Michigan	Search and seizure law, Warner-Cramton law limiting number of licenses 1909	Fred M. Warner (R)	Reform
Mississippi	Statutory prohibition 1908	Edmund F. Noel (D)	Reform
Nebraska	Enactment of the Eight o'clock Closing law limiting saloon operating hours 1909	A. C. Shallenberger (D)	Reform

Table 14 Continued

State	Most Significant General Anti-Liquor Measure(s) Secured by the Prohibition Movement from State Legislature, 1900–1912	Governor in Power	Party Wing Represented Governor
New Hampshire	Enactment of Preston Amendment banning liquor shipments to dry towns 1909	Henry B. Quinby (R)	Reform-Moderate
New Jersey	Enactment of the Bishops' law to help enforce Sunday Closing law 1906	Edward C. Stokes (R)	Conservative
Nevada	District local option 1911	Tasker L. Oddie (R)	Reform
North Carolina	Submission of statutory prohibition 1908	Robert B. Glenn (D)	Reform
North Dakota	Enactment of stringent law enforcement measures 1909	John Burke (D)	Reform
Ohio	County option 1908	Andrew L. Harris (R)	Conservative-Moderate
Oklahoma	Enactment of the Billups bill enhancing enforcement powers of the state 1908	Charles N. Haskell (D)	Reform
Rhode Island	Tightened liquor policy, limits on number of licenses, bans on saloons near schools 1908	James H. Higgins (D)	Reform
South Carolina	County option 1907	Martin F. Ansel (D)	Conservative
South Dakota	Governor empowered to oust lax enforcers, ban on saloons near dry areas 1909	Robert S. Vessey (R)	Reform
Tennessee	Statutory prohibition 1909	Malcolm R. Patterson (D)	Reform
Texas	Submission of constitutional prohibition 1909	Oscar B. Colquitt (D)	Conservative
Utah	Local option in counties, towns, and cities 1911	William Spry (R)	Conservative
Vermont	New limits on saloon locales, ban on municipal use of license revenue 1908–9	George H. Prouty (R)	Reform
Virginia	Enactment of Mann Law prohibiting manufacture and sale of liquor in rural areas 1903	Andrew J. Montague (D)	Reform
Washington	Local option in cities and counties (outside cities) 1909	Marion E. Hay (R)	Reform
West Virginia	Submission of constitutional prohibition 1911	William E. Glasscock (R)	Reform
Wisconsin	Residence district option 1907	James O. Davidson (R)	Reform
Wyoming	Prohibition of liquor sales in unincorporated territory 1909	Bryant B. Brooks (R)	Reform

Table based on state studies and the ASL's yearbooks and proceedings; see bibliography. States that failed to pass major dry laws before 1912 are omitted.

trebled and quadrupled, under this form of government. Reforms could move as fast as the people were ready for them."[135] In the twentieth century the Anti-Saloon League also supported direct legislation. By fighting for the initiative and referendum, one ASL official argued in 1906, "the League would be aiding itself to secure by far the most powerful weapon that it has ever had to smite the liquor traffic."[136]

Not surprisingly, anti-liquor organizations were key players in several state campaigns for direct legislation. In Arizona, for instance, the ASL, along with the state's suffragists, labor movement, and progressive Democrats, helped ensure that the Arizona Constitution of 1910 provided for the initiative and referendum.[137] Similar dry alliances with reformers and progressive politicians contributed to the adoption of these procedures in other states, including Washington, Nebraska, California, Missouri, and Colorado. Although anti-liquor activists opposed the enactment of direct legislation in states like North Dakota (where they feared that it would be used to reverse dry gains), they ultimately used this method to initiate prohibition referenda in twelve states, beginning in 1910 (see table 15).[138]

In short, the Anti-Saloon League managed to secure reform opportunities and tangible gains from several one-party regimes because it capitalized on the internal strife that plagued dozens of ruling parties during the Progressive Era. Of course, the Prohibition party—that quintessential "coalitional outsider"—was not completely irrelevant in state politics after 1900. For example, the Illinois party savored the election of its national chairman, Oliver Stewart, to the state legislature in 1902. Since Prohibition party candidates usually ran the strongest in states dominated by the GOP, however, they rarely threatened the domination of the ruling party, and thus had little leverage over it. In Iowa, for instance, the Prohibitionist candidate, A. U. Coates, may have won 4 percent of the vote in the gubernatorial election of 1901, but that relatively impressive showing did not thwart a Republican victory. If anything, the Republican winner in the 1901 contest, Albert B. Cummins, increased his party's share of the vote to 58.1 percent from 55.3 percent in 1899.[139]

Thus it was the Anti-Saloon League and its allies—acting as "coalitional insiders" within the state party systems—that obtained most of the prohibition movement's reform opportunities and gains during the early twentieth century. To be sure, they achieved some tangible benefits directly from the state legislatures, including statutory prohibition laws, that were produced solely by the deft application of dry electoral pressure on vulnerable lawmakers. Nevertheless, most of their important legislative triumphs involved securing reform opportunities, such as local option laws and state prohibition referenda, that required further anti-liquor agitation.

As was true when it developed its national organizations, the prohibition movement encountered a fragmented, regionally divided landscape when it sought to exert its political influence in the United States. Navigating the complexities of the American party system would prove challenging, and yet the anti-liquor movement succeeded in forcing prohibition onto the political agenda during three periods: the 1850s, the 1880s, and the Progressive Era. During the first of these periods teetotalers were able to capitalize on the political disarray of a realigning party system; in the latter two, the drys operated primarily from within party coalitions, which presented them with far less fluid conditions in which to operate.

If anything, the prohibition movement's experience in these periods demonstrates that coalitional insiders can periodically overcome the limits of working from within. This chapter suggests that once a movement becomes enmeshed in a party coalition, its opportunities to effect change depend on a variety of factors related to the character of party competition. These factors may include the existence of a

Table 15 Use of the Initiative and Referendum by the Prohibition Movement to Achieve Statewide Prohibition, 1898–1919

	Year				
State	Statutory Initiative and Referendum Adopted	Constitutional Initiative and Referendum Adopted	Number of Initiatives and Referenda on State Prohibition, Statutory	Number of Initiatives and Referenda on State Prohibition, Constitutional	Number of Successful Initiatives and Referenda on Prohibition
Arizona	1910	1910	0	1 (1914)	1
Arkansas	1909	1909	0	1 (1912)	0
California	1911	1911	1 (1918)	2 (1914, 1916)	0
Colorado	1910	1910	0	2 (1912, 1914)	1
Michigan	1908	1908	0	1 (1916)	1
Missouri	1908	1908	0	2 (1910, 1916)	0
Nebraska	1912	1912	0	1 (1916)	1
Nevada	1904/1912[a]	1904/1912[a]	0	1 (1918)	1
Ohio	1912	1912	0	4 (1914, 1915, 1917, 1918)	1
Oregon	1902	1902	0	2 (1910, 1914)	1
South Dakota	1898	1898	0	1 (1916)	1
Washington	1912	No constitutional initiative and referendum	1 (1914)	0	1
Totals			2	18	9 (45% of total)

[a] Nevada adopted constitutional provisions that legalized the referendum in 1904 and added provisions for the initiative in 1912.

Sources: Thomas E. Cronin, *Direct Democracy*, 51; David Magleby, *Direct Legislation*, 38–40; Ernest H. Cherrington, *The Evolution of Prohibition in the United States of America*; and various state studies. See bibliography for a complete listing of state studies consulted.

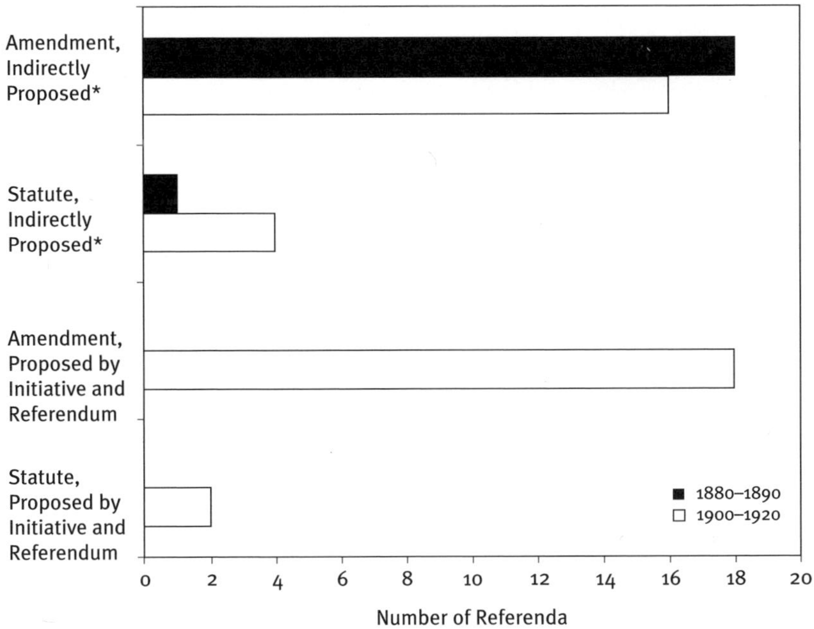

Figure 5 Use of Different Forms of Direct Legislation by the Prohibition Movement during the 1880s and the Progessive Era. Sources: Cherrington, *The Evolution of Prohibition in the United States of America*; Colvin, *Prohibition in the United States*, 435. * "Indirectly proposed amendments" were proposed by state legislatures and constitutional conventions; "indirectly proposed statutes" were proposed by state legislatures.

credible alternative to the movement's party base, as well as increases in competition between and within parties. That said, the character of party competition does not seem to determine whether a group can make effective use of its opportunities, as discussed below.

In general, the prohibitionists of the early twentieth century encountered a more favorable political environment than their Gilded Age predecessors did. Because party unity was no longer at a premium, anti-liquor activists were able to persuade a greater number of state legislatures to accede to their demands. True, dry demands had moderated after 1900, thus making it difficult to be certain how much of their success stemmed from political acumen and how much from more achievable goals. In any event, the twentieth-century drys managed to secure forty referenda on statewide prohibition (compared to nineteen referenda for their forerunners). These analogous cases[140] allow the most effective comparison between the two generations of prohibitionists.

If one just focuses on statewide referenda, the Progressive Era drys were clearly more effective in using direct legislation. As noted previously, 55 percent of their ref-

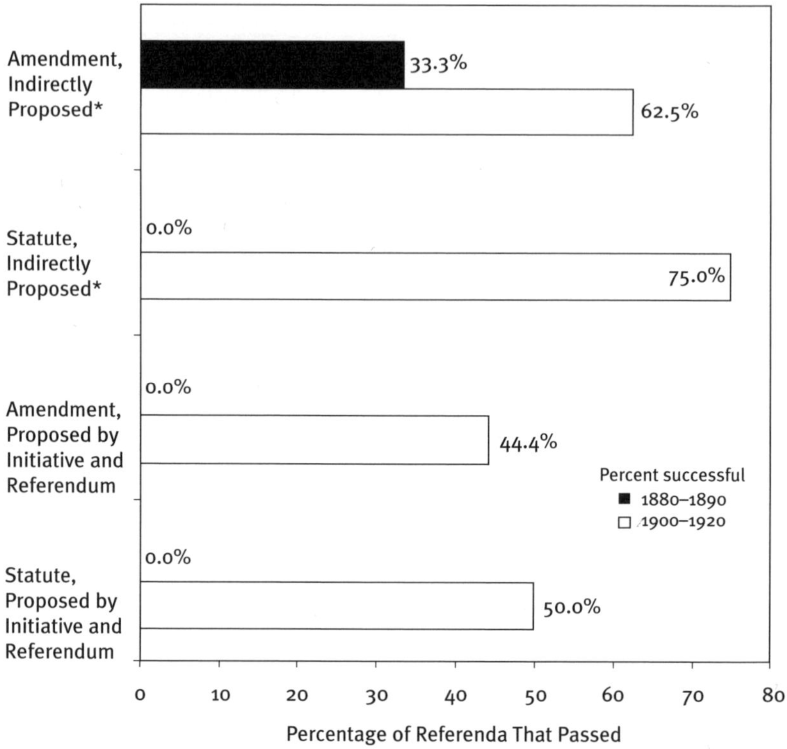

Figure 6 Prohibition Movement's Success in Using Different Forms of Referendum during the 1880s and the Progressive Era. Sources: Cherrington, *The Evolution of Prohibition in the United States of America;* Colvin, *Prohibition in the United States*, 435. *"Indirectly proposed amendments" were proposed by state legislatures and constitutional conventions; "indirectly proposed statutes" were proposed by state legislatures.

erenda passed, whereas only 31.6 percent of the nineteenth-century referenda did. Interestingly, the advent of the initiative and referendum had little to do with the Progressives' superior use of direct legislation. As figures 5 and 6 demonstrate, the prohibition movement won a greater proportion of the referenda that were proposed indirectly by state legislatures and constitutional conventions than of referenda initiated directly by the citizenry.[141] In other words, the initiative and referendum undoubtedly helped the drys to bypass twelve state legislatures, but these procedures alone could not guarantee the necessary electoral support. In sum, once movements have gained the opportunity to influence policy, their fate often rests in their own hands, with political strategy—not structural conditions—serving as the deciding factor.

6 The Dynamics of Local Gradualism in the States

Chapter 5 demonstrated that both the "maximalist" radicals of the 1880s and the "gradualist" moderates of the Progressive Era managed to wrest reform opportunities from their respective party systems. By exploiting the competition between and within the major political parties, the prohibition movement became one of the leading initiators of statewide referenda in the years leading up to the First World War.[1] Ultimately, however, many of these reform opportunities proved to be just that: opportunities. For its adherents, its opponents, and other observers, the prohibition movement achieved its greatest state-level triumphs when it won state prohibition referenda and laws, not merely when it contributed to their origins. In order to accomplish this task, then, anti-liquor activists organized elaborate campaigns designed to mobilize public support. It was through these campaigns for dry amendments and laws that the movement sought to translate public support into concrete gains.

Though drys in both the 1880s and the Progressive Era orchestrated several statewide prohibition campaigns, those in the later period achieved five times as many statewide victories, including over three times as many in state referenda. These impressive achievements have been explained variously, but as discussed in chapter 1, these accounts often ignore the parallel case of the 1880s. Rather than revisit these alternative explanations, this narrative provides evidence for my claim that a social movement's choice of political strategy explains a significant share of its success. Moreover, it suggests that political strategy may interact with ideology to either discourage or encourage the mobilization of social movements. Finally, it contends that dry success in the twentieth century reflected long-term political strategy rather than short-term campaign tactics on the part of the prohibitionists.

To illustrate how strategy affected the prohibition movement in both periods, this chapter will emphasize the drys' use of direct legislation to achieve state prohibition. Of course, anti-liquor activists also secured tangible gains when they obtained statutory prohibition, local option, and other restrictive measures from state lawmakers and Congress. However, state prohibition referenda provide the best basis for comparison. In both the 1880s and the Progressive Era, the drys viewed state prohibition referenda as crucial, for winning these contests would bolster their claims to broad public support and for a national constitutional amendment. Concerning referenda campaign tactics, then, the first part of this chapter will conclude that they had a marginal impact on the movement's divergent referenda outcomes in the two periods. Meanwhile, the second part contends that the movement's shift from promoting state and national prohibition to a strategy of local gradualism led to its greater popularity and success in the Progressive Era.

Short-term Political Tactics

Clearly, drys in both the 1880s and the Progressive Era believed that state prohibition referenda required their finest efforts if they hoped to defeat the Demon Rum. In 1883, for example, the submission of constitutional prohibition in Ohio was such a galvanizing event that the state WCTU's president left "all personal cares and interests aside" to devote herself full-time to coordinating the campaign.[2] Anti-liquor activists in the early twentieth century were no different: in 1907 North Carolina drys "eagerly and enthusiastically" planned for their state prohibition referendum.[3] Consumed by organizational logistics, the drys often spoke in terms of short-term factors when explaining their referendum successes and failures. In particular, they believed that referendum outcomes depended on the effectiveness of their campaigns and on their ability to neutralize their opponents' tactics.

For instance, one activist explained the failure of Tennessee's prohibition vote in 1887 in this way: "When the question [of prohibition] was submitted, there is not a doubt that there was prohibition sentiment enough in the state to carry by a large majority. Soon the liquor dealers of the North and elsewhere began to send money into the state 'by the barrel.' Speakers were sent everywhere over the state to fill the minds of credulous people with misrepresentations."[4] Similarly, the Oregon Anti-Saloon League rationalized its referendum defeat in 1910 thus: "We had good reasons for hoping our effort to carry the whole State would succeed. But the election of the fall of 1910 was a surprise to many people. . . . The liquor men traversed the State with many speakers of nationwide notoriety. Money by the hundreds of thousands was expended. Blunt falsehood was yoked with sly deception, and as a result, our reform received a check."[5] Conversely, successful referenda reflected their opponents' failure to counter their own effective campaigns. After Rhode Island voted dry in 1886, for example, the prohibitionists congratulated themselves on a canvass that was "very dexterously managed," and noted that the overconfident wets had flexed their political muscle in the state's GOP convention rather than in the referendum campaign.[6] Likewise, the leader of Oregon's successful prohibition campaign of 1914 claimed that his able organization had mobilized "drys who usually loaf at home election day, and kick the next."[7]

One might argue that the prohibition movement's better track record in the Progressive Era was due to more sophisticated campaign tactics after 1900. However, the following analysis of the Progressive Era and the 1880s suggests that campaign efforts during both periods were remarkably similar. Twentieth-century prohibitionists usually organized their prohibition drives through state federations of anti-liquor organizations; their predecessors deployed a comparable array of state alliances, unions, and associations to coordinate major state campaigns. In both periods, prohibitionists constructed organizations in imitation of the party machine down to the local level. Furthermore, they consistently exploited national movement networks to secure speakers, organizers, and campaign funds. Finally, in both periods they confronted a well-financed opposition that could afford full-scale media campaigns to advocate wet outcomes.

In her study of popularly initiated referendum campaigns, Betty H. Zisk suggests that both "careful organization" and "an army of volunteers" can "make a major difference" in campaign outcomes.[8] Given their considerable grassroots support, though, dry organizations were typically more concerned with coordinating their volunteers than with recruiting them. Indeed, since anti-liquor activists frequently belonged to competing movement organizations, this coordination sometimes proved problematic. In particular, drys who were Republicans and Democrats had rocky relations with Prohibition party affiliates, who often criticized them for failing to support dry candidates and who regularly endorsed controversial positions (such as woman suffrage) which marked them as politically extreme. Hence, movement leaders usually mounted referendum campaigns through nonpartisan, single-issue state alliances. In Michigan, for example, the State Amendment Committee in 1887, composed of ten Republicans, ten Democrats, and ten Prohibition party members, combined the Prohibitionists with the WCTU, the dry fraternal orders, and other groups. Moreover, the prohibitionists were careful to hold "non-partisan meetings—no politics in them; they were genuine temperance meetings, held to muster the entire temperance vote for the prohibitory amendment."[9] Likewise, in 1915 activists in Michigan created the United Dry Federation for its referendum campaign and thus united, among others, the ASL, the WCTU, the Prohibition party, and the Detroit Pastors' Union.[10]

Of course, the Anti-Saloon League typically dominated the anti-drink federations of the Progressive Era, whereas the Prohibition party, the WCTU, and the dry fraternal orders dominated the coalitions of the 1880s. Several authors have argued for the organizational superiority of the ASL, given its hierarchical structure, professional staff, and close ties to the evangelical Protestant churches. At its peak in the Progressive Era, they note, hundreds of thousands of church members were pledging donations to the ASL; in addition, these supporters often petitioned, registered sympathetic voters, and distributed campaign literature on the league's behalf.[11] However, such accounts often ignore the effectiveness of the earlier organizations in developing reliable sources of campaign volunteers and funds. During the referendum campaigns of the 1880s, for instance, the Good Templars had 200,000 members, the Sons of Temperance about 40,000, and the WCTU 150,000 (up from 75,000). In addition, all these groups maintained permanent federations of state and local branches, thus providing a stable source of workers and donations for referendum campaigns. At the same time, the Prohibition party increased its national vote from 10,000 to over 250,000.[12]

Regardless of who led them, state prohibition alliances in both periods attempted to unify the anti-liquor forces around campaign efforts that would rally confirmed and potential drys. As demonstrated below, prohibition associations from both periods managed to effectively combine the resources of their various constituent groups to create elaborate referendum campaigns. Hence, the greater success of the Progressive Era campaigns compared to those of the 1880s cannot be due to the development of innovative organizing techniques after 1900.

From the beginning, anti-liquor leaders saw organization as a key to winning dry referenda. Consequently, even before the Kansas legislature had submitted the first prohibition amendment in 1880, the state's temperance groups had already sought to establish "prohibition clubs" in hundreds of cities, towns, and villages. Technically, no alliance existed among the three major state organizations (the Kansas State Temperance Union [KSTU], the WCTU, and the IOGT), and yet all recognized that the KSTU would be the "nerve center" of the referendum campaign. As a result, the KSTU was responsible for circulating campaign literature, distributing the movement's meager funds, and directing the activities of about twenty lecturers. In addition to this local organizing, the national dry groups dispatched many of their most prominent speakers to Kansas to assist in the campaign.[13]

The Kansas drys' victory in 1882, with 52.3 percent of the vote, encouraged similar state drives. In the eighteen referenda campaigns that followed, anti-liquor activists refined and expanded on the grassroots approach used in Kansas. Before Iowa's successful effort, for instance, the state's Prohibitory Amendment Association had developed branches in the state's legislative districts, thus allowing it to apply direct pressure on legislators who were wavering about a dry referendum.[14] By the time anti-drink activists mounted their campaign in Ohio in 1883, they had instituted the first statewide umbrella group, the Constitutional Amendment Association, to coordinate its constituent organizations at the county level. While dominated by the Ohio WCTU, the association also included the Good Templars, the Ohio Temperance Alliance, and local groups like the Oberlin Temperance Alliance.[15]

Although Ohio's campaign ultimately failed, almost every campaign thereafter involved a statewide federation of major anti-liquor organizations.[16] Furthermore, many of these federations copied their mobilization techniques from the political machines, widely regarded as the most effective electoral organizations in late-nineteenth-century America. In the Texas campaign of 1887, for example, the state's anti-liquor forces attempted to organize counties for their amendment as well as senatorial districts, where they would also hold periodic conventions. Below the county and district levels, activists were supposed to work through their town Prohibition Clubs, engage local speakers, hold weekly meetings, distribute literature, and stage entertainments. Finally, on election day the drys worked at the polls, dispensing refreshments, last-minute appeals, and encouragement to voters.[17] In more urban states, such as Pennsylvania, Massachusetts, and New Hampshire, anti-drink reformers organized down to election districts, precincts, and wards. Campaigns canvassed door to door and used "watchers" and their own system of ballot distribution to guard against fraud at the polls.[18]

As local campaign organizations grew more complex, the national prohibition groups nevertheless maintained a strong presence in the amendment drives. Whereas the Kansas campaign of 1880 involved the exertions of twelve out-of-state speakers, that in Rhode Island in 1886 included at least sixteen.[19] Likewise, nineteen eminent prohibitionists from the WCTU, the Prohibition party, and the IOGT trekked to South Dakota for its contest in 1889.[20] National networks also paid for a greater proportion of campaign expenses as the 1880s progressed. Less than $500 of the Kansas State Temperance Union's campaign funds came from out of state in 1880; by the time of the Nebraska campaign of 1890, the national WCTU alone contributed $3,684.68.[21] Furthermore, the national organizations contributed in kind by shipping vast quantities of literature to local campaign workers. One activist in South Dakota felt so overwhelmed by these deliveries that he requested only "a small package, neatly sealed, each week." While grateful for the assistance, he noted that "a busy person can find time to dispose of only a few hundred papers and tracts," whereas "thousands" only "overtax his possibilities."[22]

Despite their increasing sophistication, the movement's campaigns failed in all but two states after 1886. In most instances, the anti-liquor activists could find no fault with their campaign organizations and laid the blame elsewhere. After their loss in New Hampshire in 1889, one reformer noted that "the temperance people of the state did grand work during the campaign. Speakers and literature were sent over the state, and the WCTU made a personal canvass, urging the voters to vote for the home. The defeat cannot be laid at the doors of the women of New Hampshire. They have worked loyally, faithfully, and in some instances, heroically."[23] In fact, their faith in their campaign organizations was often so strong that many drys were completely staggered by their losses. As another teetotaler from New Hampshire confessed, "The defeat is a terrible shock. It is like an abyss suddenly opening before our feet where we looked for solid ground."[24] Instead of faulting their organization, the prohibitionists largely attributed their defeats to the liquor industry's huge war chest.

A generation later, the Progressive Era drys had only disdain for their precursors' campaigns. "The [Pennsylvania amendment] defeat of 1889 proved beyond question that prohibition would never be won until there could be raised up an organization of specially trained leaders, abundantly financed and always at their task," sniffed Harry Malcolm Chalfant, a leader of the Pennsylvania Anti-Saloon League.[25] Still, the dry referendum campaigns of the twentieth century followed the basic pattern established in the 1880s. Confronted with the opportunity to use direct legislation, activists generally formed state anti-liquor federations and sought to organize down to the lowest units of political geography. Meanwhile, national prohibition groups sent orators, funds, and propaganda to supplement local efforts. As election day approached, anti-liquor forces sponsored dozens of meetings, parades, and entertainments, flooding the state with tracts, posters, and special editions of their newspapers. Finally, on election day itself legions of volunteers manned the polls, providing sandwiches, ice water, and a barrier against the allegedly corrupt voting practices of their opponents.

During the West Virginia campaign of 1912, for example, the West Virginia Ratification Federation consisted of the ASL, the WCTU, the Prohibition party, the Church Temperance Society, the IOGT, and assorted others. Its numerous volunteers distributed thousands of pages of literature, and it employed hundreds of clergymen and lay workers at the county, town, and precinct levels. Moreover, the federation could rely on William E. "Pussyfoot" Johnson, famous for his stealthy work in enforcing federal liquor laws in Indian Territory. Johnson, who had recently joined the national ASL, went undercover in West Virginia to expose the links between the state's newspaper editors and the liquor interests.[26] The national ASL also chartered a special train for the celebrated evangelist Billy Sunday for a statewide speaking tour.[27] Aroused by the "aggressive and fearless" tactics of their leaders, anti-liquor activists concluded their campaign by working at the polls on election day.[28]

While the West Virginia campaign succeeded, the Progressive Era drys nonetheless lost 45 percent of the state prohibition referenda that they sponsored. In Missouri, for instance, they lost referenda in 1910, 1916, and 1918, despite their best efforts to "tighten up" their organization.[29] Even if Missouri's defeats could be ascribed to the political and economic clout of the state's breweries,[30] not every failure could be similarly explained away. In the Alabama campaign of 1909, for one, the prohibitionists were "stunned and deeply disappointed" at the failure of a campaign organized down to the precinct level.[31] Like their nineteenth-century forerunners, the Progressive Era drys often blamed defeats on the ability of their wet opponents to outspend them in campaigns.

In recent years, many social scientists have claimed that a ballot proposition faces almost certain defeat if opposition groups significantly outspend its proponents during the campaign. In fact, several studies have suggested that approximately 90 percent of ballot propositions fail when referenda proponents are considerably outspent by their opponents.[32] Conversely, John R. Owens and Larry L. Wade argue that the role of negative campaign spending has been greatly exaggerated. When they tested the one-sided negative spending hypothesis, their regression analysis "yielded no statistically significant results." Owens and Wade insist that "there is at best only a modest connection between campaign spending and the vote," and that "other undefined, unspecified factors are much more important than money in shaping electoral outcomes in direct legislation campaigns."[33]

Although the evidence is sketchy, the prohibition movement's referendum experiences seem to support Owens and Wade, because the liquor industry outspent the drys in virtually all their state referenda campaigns, regardless of period. In other words, for the one-sided negative spending hypothesis to hold true, the prohibition movement should have won very few referenda in both periods. Clearly, this model would not have predicted the relatively high success rate of dry referenda after 1900, as ultimately turned out to be the case.

To account for dry failures in the 1880s, analysts often asserted that the prohibition movement was crushed by the liquor industry's vast wealth and power. One prohibitionist, D. Leigh Colvin, declared that the wets had directly blocked prohibition's advance during this decade in three ways, each of which involved the liquor industry's strategic use of its riches. First, he noted that the liquor interests systematically concentrated their resources in those states where referendum campaigns were being conducted. Second, Colvin accused the industry of employing unfair campaign tactics, "such as subsidizing the press, manufacturing news dispatches, disseminating fake statistics and systematically deceiving the people." Lastly, he charged that the liquor industry had purchased politicians and the services of political machines, both of which helped the wet cause by engaging in corrupt acts.[34]

In making these claims, Colvin provided some specific allegations about wet campaign spending (alleging, for example, that "in the amendment campaign in Pennsylvania in 1889 over $200,000 was raised in the city of Philadelphia alone").[35] Since campaign finance reporting was not legally required at the time, the accuracy of these assertions cannot be assessed.[36] However, Colvin's broader contention—that the wets skillfully wielded large sums in the 1880s—was considered a truism by many late-nineteenth-century observers, dry or not. For example, one prominent moderate on the liquor question acknowledged in 1888 that "the business of the liquor dealers is lucrative; they have plenty of money to spend, and they are shrewd enough to spend it freely; they will not allow any legal burdens or restrictions to be placed upon their business, if they can help it."[37] Likewise, a study by moderate reformers concluded that "the liquor traffic, being very profitable, has been able, when attacked by prohibitory legislation, to pay fines, bribes, hush money, and assessments for political purposes to large amounts."[38] Finally, Ernest H. Crosby, who believed prohibition to be unenforceable, nonetheless maintained that the brewers raised "enormous funds for use in all canvasses in which the temperance issue is raised."[39]

Although proficient in fund raising, the prohibition movement could not exploit the financial self-interest of its supporters, nor did it ever appear to equal the liquor industry's spending. For example, the Prohibition party "raised a fund of $34,000" for the Nebraska referendum campaign of 1890, "which was a larger amount than the Prohibition National Committee had received in any national campaign year up until that time." However impressive, this was still less than the estimated $50,000 spent by the liquor interests, half of which was apparently from a few brewers.[40] In similar fashion, South Dakota's drys had budgeted $15,000 for their successful campaign in 1889. For a sparsely settled state $15,000 was a tidy sum, and yet it hardly approached the estimated $80,000 spent by the liquor forces on media and other propaganda efforts.[41]

Like many of today's citizen activists, the drys often felt that their lack of funds stymied their ability to communicate with voters through the mass media. J. R. Wolf, an organizer of the Texas referendum campaign of 1887, complained that "the *Dallas Morning News*, one of the most widely circulated papers in the State, charges $36 a column for all manuscript matter on either side [of the prohibition issue]. The Whiskeyites use this by the half-sheet, and more, because they have plenty of Northern money to pay for it; but we have to use it sparingly for lack of Northern money to pay for it."[42] And, like today's activists in the wake of a referendum defeat, the drys found their opponents a convenient scapegoat for their rejection at the polls. Clinton B. Fisk, when confronted with dry losses in Michigan, Texas, Tennessee, and Oregon, blamed the liquor industry, "with its controlling interest in politics, supplemented by its lavish expenditure in money in paying for talent and purchaseable votes."[43]

Compared to their predecessors, the Progressive Era drys clearly conducted more systematic and lucrative fund raising activities. Between 1912 and 1918 the national Anti-Saloon League alone raised $2,383,310 in subscriptions. However, the prohibitionists of the early twentieth century needed every penny, given the continued growth and prosperity of the liquor industry. During the period 1913–18 (exclusive of 1916), the U.S. Brewers' Association (USBA) by itself accumulated $4,457,941 in its central treasury. The money was easily raised; the USBA simply imposed a three-cent barrelage tax on members for its war chest.[44] Whereas the highest estimates of campaign spending by the wets tended to be in the hundreds of thousands of dollars during the 1880s, observers calculated that the liquor industry spent more than $1 million to defeat dry referenda in key states like Ohio, Michigan, and California.

On the other hand, historians have frequently emphasized the internal disarray of the liquor industry during the Progressive Era, and in particular have focused on the persistent hostility between the U.S. Brewers Association and the distilling interests, represented by the National Wholesale Liquor Dealers' Association.[45] Despite their frequent disunity, the liquor groups promptly joined forces and raised vast quantities of money when confronted with the possibility of annihilation.[46] As in the 1880s, though, the wets never publicized their total expenditures on referendum campaigns. Instead, contemporary observers approximated wet disbursements by analyzing the liquor industry's capacity to pay for office space, workers, and publicity efforts such as newspaper advertising, speakers, and campaign literature.[47]

According to available sources, these estimated campaign expenditures consistently dwarfed those of the drys. For example, the dry leader James Cannon recalled the liquor industry's outlays in the Virginia prohibition campaign of 1914 as follows:

> The enemy was there in force. The smallest estimate of the amount expended in Virginia by the liquor traffic during the six months of the campaign is $850,000. By some the estimate is $1,150,000. The National Liquor Dealer's Association, the Brewers and the Distillers joined hands with the State Liquor Dealers' Association, established headquarters in Richmond with an entire floor of one of the largest office buildings in the city with a great force of employees under the direction of their trained National workers brought in from other states. . . .

> They literally flooded every corner of the state with slanders and falsehoods, hoping that they would be able to overwhelm the Prohibition workers by their tremendous output.[48]

In contrast, the Virginia Anti-Saloon League directly dispensed about $80,000 in 1914 (chiefly for campaign literature) and authorized a three-month contract with the Richmond *Virginian* for $25,000, an agreement which ultimately drove the organization into debt. Although the drys appear to have disbursed about $130,000 all told to win the Virginia referendum, they were nonetheless outspent by over six to one (assuming that Cannon's lower estimate of the liquor industry's expenditures was more accurate).[49]

In similar referendum campaigns, dry leaders acknowledged their comparative financial weakness and tried to compensate for it. As they embarked on their initiative campaign in March 1916, drys in Michigan estimated that the wet campaign fund totaled $1.5 million, while their own fund amounted to $300,000. While this differential forced the drys to conduct a stingy, volunteer-based campaign,[50] it did not prevent them from winning 55.4 percent of the votes in November. Meanwhile, in North Carolina prohibition activists overcame their opponents' "barrels of money" by sponsoring rallies and parades that galvanized their supporters and garnered free media coverage for their cause.[51] Finally, in Ohio "the drys' funds were too limited to purchase as much advertising as the liquor and brewing trades could afford, but they did allow the placement of posters in streetcars and billboards in prominent locations, each carrying a pithy prohibition message designed by a professional advertising agency." Such inexpensive publicity efforts helped the Ohio drys win their referendum in 1918.[52]

Local Gradualism, Mobilization, and Movement Outcomes

Since the prohibitionists in both the 1880s and the Progressive Era used similar campaign strategies and tactics, then these alone cannot account for the disparate outcomes of their state prohibition drives. Instead, one must look to the movement's shift away from a maximalist strategy at the turn of the century. By adopting local gradualism instead of pursuing state-based prohibition, the dry movement charted a new course for itself, one which was slow, piecemeal, and extremely labor intensive. However, this new political strategy vastly expanded the movement's base, increasing the number of people willing to agitate for prohibition, vote for anti-liquor candidates, and approve dry referenda. The capacity of local gradualism to mobilize new movement adherents can be demonstrated in a number of ways. This empirical section will illustrate local gradualism's impact on the WCTU's patterns of member-

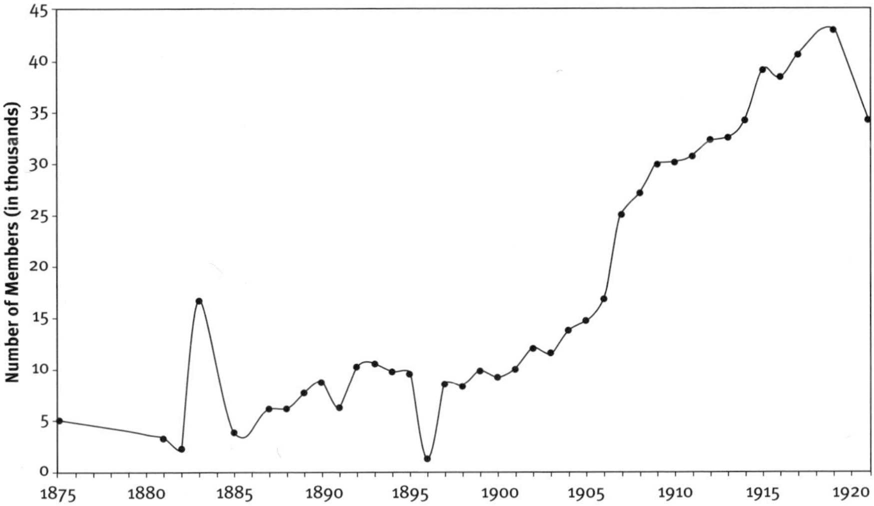

Figure 7 Pattern of Membership Growth, Ohio WCTU, 1875–1920. Source: *Minutes of the National Woman's Christian Temperance Union* (1874–1921).

ship growth, as well as its role in channeling new movement support into positive outcomes.

As discussed in chapter 2, the Woman's Christian Temperance Union staunchly supported state and constitutional prohibition during the last twenty years of the nineteenth century and rejected local option as "too local and too optional." By the first decade of the twentieth century, though, most state unions had relinquished their objections to local option and had joined the Anti-Saloon League in agitating for this tool and using it to further the dry cause. For example, in 1894 the Ohio WCTU's president had expressed grave reservations about the Ohio ASL and blasted local option as a compromise measure that violated the state constitution's spirit. As the league gained more influence with the legislature and won some minor local option victories, however, the union slowly warmed to both the ASL and its goals. In 1898 the Ohio union granted its members the freedom to work with the league; and in 1902 it rejoiced at the enactment of a municipal option bill sponsored by the ASL, the Beal Law. Impressed by the ASL's vigorous use of the Beal Law, the Union then offered its first official expression of support for the league in 1904. In 1906 the Ohio WCTU first formally endorsed a local option law (the ASL's county option bill); and finally, in 1907, it endorsed the league itself.[53]

The Ohio Union's embrace of local gradualism after 1906 coincided with the onset of a spectacular growth in its membership (see figure 7). Between 1900 and 1919 the group increased its absolute membership by 367.7 percent, and its per capita membership by 345.5 percent.[54] Of course, the Ohio WCTU's expansion during these years may have resulted from any number of factors. For instance, some social scientists maintain that the upsurge of the prohibition movement during the Progressive Era was generated by other broad-based changes. Joseph Gusfield, for one, argues that "the rise of Prohibition strength owed a great deal to the sense of cultural change and prestige loss which accompanied both the defeat of the Populist movement and the increased urbanization and immigration of the early twentieth century."[55] Humiliated by the decisive defeat of the Populist agrarian vision in 1896, the rural, native-born Protestant "felt that he was threatened by the increasing strength of institutions and groups whose interests and ideals differed from his." Thus, "he took a radical stand toward his society when he began to feel that he was no longer as dominant, as culturally prestigeful as he had been in an earlier period," and sought to impose a legal norm of sobriety on the secular, urban, and non-Protestant population.[56] Gusfield contends that increased rates of industrialization, urbanization, and immigration frightened the rural states, solidified wet strongholds within the urban states, and encouraged movement activity in the former rather than in the latter.[57]

Although influential, Gusfield's account of the prohibition movement may be irrelevant in explaining the divergent mobilization patterns of the Woman's Christian Temperance Union. Instead, as the following paired comparison suggests, state unions which consistently adhered to local gradualism enjoyed steady and often dramatic growth, while those which remained faithful to a maximalist strategy (or which later reverted to this strategy) experienced slower membership growth and even losses. Furthermore, the relationship between rapid WCTU growth and local gradualism often surfaced in urban states with substantial immigrant populations, as well as in more rural states, with fewer wet citizens.[58]

Pennsylvania and Illinois: The WCTU in the Industrialized North

After 1903 the Pennsylvania and Illinois branches of the WCTU experienced starkly different patterns of development. While the Illinois WCTU's membership stagnated in the range of twelve to fourteen thousand between 1900 and 1919, in Pennsylvania membership exploded from 13,741 to 46,632 over the same period (see figure 8). Measured per capita, membership declined by over 50 percent in Illinois and increased by 145 percent in Pennsylvania (see table 16).

Does Gusfield's theory account for this divergence? As table 17 shows, Pennsylvania and Illinois had nearly the same proportion of urban, Catholic, and foreign-born citizens during the Progressive Era, as well as approximately the same net industrial output in 1909 (about $135 per person), a number significantly above the national average for that year ($92.73 per person). Illinois may have urbanized faster

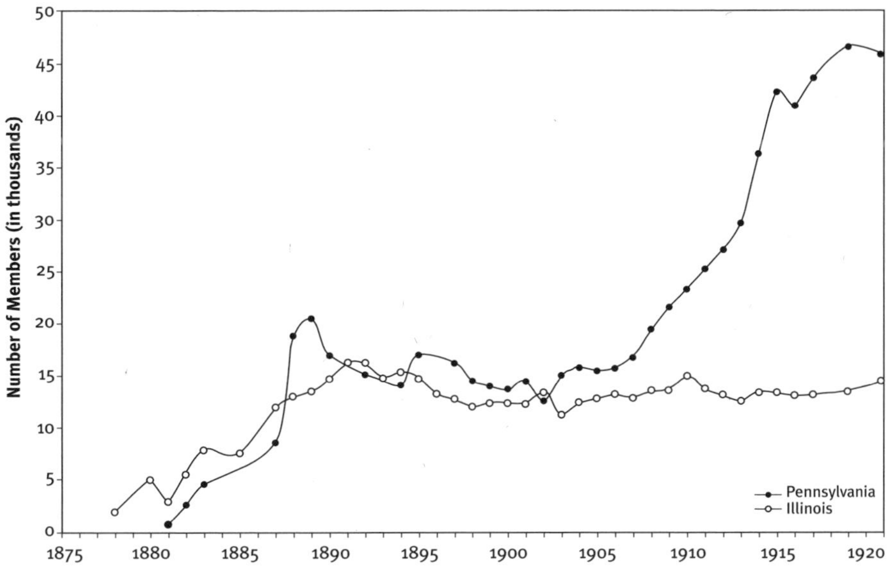

Figure 8 Patterns of Membership Growth in the Illinois WCTU and Pennsylvania WCTU, 1880–1920. Source: *Minutes of the National Woman's Christian Temperance Union* (1874–1921).

than Pennsylvania in the period 1880–1920, but the Catholic and foreign populations grew more rapidly in Pennsylvania. In other words, neither state was significantly more urban, Catholic, foreign, or industrialized than the other in 1910, and both had witnessed the growth of wet social groups in the decades just preceding the Progressive Era.

But although Gusfield's theory cannot account for the distinctive growth patterns of the Pennsylvania and Illinois unions, political strategy can. While the WCTU of Illinois generally sustained its preference for a state prohibition amendment during the early twentieth century, in Pennsylvania it combined forces with the ASL to fight for statewide local option and to use extant local methods for outlawing the saloon. As discussed below, the divergent paths of the two unions stemmed largely from their leaders' strategic preferences.

From the first, the WCTU consistently adopted more radical positions in Illinois than in Pennsylvania, for several reasons. Most notably, the Illinois affiliate counted Frances Willard, the second president of the national Union, as both a member and former president until her death in 1898.[59] Throughout her career, Willard pressed the WCTU to embrace several progressive and controversial political causes—from woman's suffrage to Christian socialism. Likewise, Willard endorsed both constitutional prohibition and the ultra-dry Prohibition party during the 1880s. While many state and local unions failed to follow her lead on every issue, the Illinois

Table 16 Patterns of WCTU Membership Growth in Pennsylvania and Illinois

	Peak Year of WCTU Membership 1900–1919	Absolute Membership Growth, 1900–Peak Year	Absolute Membership Growth, 1900–1919	Per Capita Membership Growth, 1900–Peak	Per Capita Membership, Growth, 1900–1919
Pennsylvania	1919	239.4	239.4	145.5	145.5
Illinois	1910	21.4	9.2	−44.9	−51.0

All growth rates in percent.
Source: Minutes of the National Woman's Christian Temperance Union, 1874–1920.

WCTU usually indulged Willard's enthusiasms. In 1876, for instance, Willard delivered an impassioned plea for woman's suffrage at the Illinois Union's convention, which ratified her position.[60] Willard's influence was also evident in the Illinois group's decision to provide official support for the Prohibition party.[61] After expressing interest in third-party action at a summer gathering in 1881, Willard next raised the issue at the Illinois Union's fall convention. Again, the Illinois WCTU adopted Willard's views, becoming the first state affiliate to endorse partisan prohibition.[62] Though the Prohibitionists never became a major political force, the Illinois WCTU remained a faithful ally. In 1889 the Union's president could refer to the group as "radical."[63]

In Pennsylvania, by contrast, the key figure was Annie Wittenmyer, a Philadelphian and the national Union's first president (1874–79). Ousted by Willard in 1879, Wittenmyer had opposed her successor's drive to include woman's suffrage in the national organization's program, among other things.[64] After relinquishing the national presidency, Wittenmyer served as superintendent of the Pennsylvania Union's Committee on Legislation and continued to resist Willard's ongoing efforts to radicalize the WCTU.[65] Above all, Wittenmyer challenged her rival's attempt to align the Union with the Prohibition party and promoted nonpartisanship, an approach supported by many in her state union, including its president, Frances L. Swift.[66] By the late 1880s Wittenmyer and her allies had sparked an intense debate within the Pennsylvania WCTU about the dry third party. Acrimony in the Pennsylvania group peaked during the state convention of 1889,[67] shortly before the national union endured its own divisive gathering.[68] Objecting to the national group's increasingly rigid position on the Prohibition party, the corresponding secretary, Ellen M. Watson, sought to convert the Pennsylvania affiliate into a "non-sectarian and non-partisan" society.[69] After this effort failed, Watson, Wittenmyer, Swift, and other sympathizers abandoned the WCTU to join nonpartisan versions of the union.[70] Still, they left a relatively conservative organization in their wake. Though unwilling to explicitly declare its nonpartisanship, the Pennsylvania WCTU also refused to support the Pro-

Table 17 Barriers to Dry Mobilization during the Progressive Era in Pennsylvania and Illinois

	Urban Population in Percent, 1910	Percentage Change in Urban Population, 1880–1910	Catholic Population in Percent, 1916	Percentage Change in Catholic Population, 1890–1916	Foreign-Born Population in Percent, 1910	Percentage Change in Foreign-Born Population, 1880–1910	Value Added by Manufacture per Capita, 1909
Pennsylvania	60.4	18.8	22.1	9.6	18.8	5.1	$134.50
Illinois	61.7	31.1	19.1	4.5	21.4	2.4	$136.23

Source: U.S. Bureau of the Census.

hibition party. In fact, "it was the policy of the [state WCTU] to have no part in [partisan] politics or the franchise" before 1900.[71]

Willard and Wittenmyer set the tones for their state unions, as history bore out. After Willard's death in 1898 the leaders of the Illinois WCTU developed an amicable (if distant) relationship with the Anti-Saloon League but continued to prefer the state Prohibition party, a strident opponent of local option.[72] Moreover, the Illinois group's official position on local option never changed: local unions and individual members were encouraged to participate in local campaigns, but in principle local option was a poor substitute for state prohibition.[73] Consequently, no WCTU representative endorsed local option at the legislative hearings and public demonstrations on the subject.[74] Finally, after municipal local option was passed in 1907, several union leaders joined the chorus of dry radicals who denounced the law and its county variant as compromise measures.[75]

At best, leaders of the Illinois WCTU granted that local option had produced some "splendid victories," while insisting that their group press on to win "a state prohibitory law that will banish the saloon not only from towns and counties, but from the entire state."[76] In 1910, for example, the WCTU helped organize a conference to inaugurate a new state prohibition crusade. Though seeking harmony between dry radicals and "those working for [county] local option," the gathering nonetheless endorsed "state wide prohibition as the only means of solving the liquor problem in Illinois, condemned county option, and administered a slap at the Anti-Saloon league in deciding that it would recognize no solution to the liquor question not based on state wide prohibition."[77] Similarly, when the ASL merely sought to protect its recent gains from wet retaliation in 1915,[78] the union planned "special agitation" toward the state's upcoming constitutional convention in the hopes of initiating a dry amendment.[79]

Neither moderate nor radical Illinois teetotalers poured resources into a state prohibition campaign after 1907, however. If the state ASL aimed to win county option and use the municipal option law,[80] radical prohibitionists like J. H. Hoffstitler maintained that "there is no use in the party indorsing state wide prohibition unless the party in power is in sympathy with the cause."[81] Lacking allies, the Illinois union confined itself to reiterating its preference for state prohibition. In terms of actual agitation, the WCTU became best known for its antivice campaigns and its educational efforts against drink and Mormonism.[82] Meanwhile, though union members both worked and (after 1913) voted[83] in the state's local option drives, they often did not direct them.[84] As a result, the Illinois WCTU suffered from a low profile in the state's dry politics, and found its membership stalled at thirteen thousand while the Illinois ASL was flourishing.[85]

The Illinois Union's ambivalence toward local gradualism undoubtedly reflected the generational radicalism of its leaders. For example, two of its state presidents Marie C. Brehm (1901–6) and Helen L. Hood (1913–20s), had both been active in the Illinois Union during Willard's lifetime.[86] In contrast, the Pennsylvania WCTU profited from its more moderate history during the Progressive Era. Unburdened by a prior association with the Prohibition party, the Pennsylvania Union had only to jettison state-based prohibition and accept local option as a major goal.

Initially, it appeared as though the Pennsylvania Union would match the radicalism of the Illinois WCTU. Concerning the Pennsylvania ASL's local option bill of 1905, the WCTU state president, Rebecca Chambers, declared that her group's attitude was "generally friendly," but that the bill was not acceptable "as the policy of our organization or as a substitute for prohibition." Indeed, she went so far as to say that constitutional prohibition was "the only real remedy and regulation."[87] Nevertheless, the union sent its state legislative superintendent, Marjorie M. Steese, to Harrisburg to testify on behalf of the ASL's legislative proposal. In an even more promising development, the group publicly reversed itself on local option in 1908. At its state convention that year, the Pennsylvania WCTU strongly endorsed local option as the "magic weapon against our enemy, the liquor traffic," and distributed 1,343,000 leaflets in support. In 1909 the union's president, Ella M. George, testified before the House Law and Order Committee in favor of the Fair Local Option Bill, sponsored by the ASL, and Steese coordinated a petition and telegram campaign to support the measure. Though never able to achieve this aim, the Pennsylvania women continued to cooperate with the league's local option drives until 1918, when national prohibition became the top priority.[88]

Given its lack of legislative success, the Pennsylvania union might have been expected to hemorrhage members, not gain them. However, the organization made the most of the state's meager opportunities for dry activism, and leveraged that activism into increased support. One such opportunity surfaced in 1908, when the state ASL proposed that dry groups unite to systematically exploit the provisions of the Brooks

Law (1887). According to that law, the judges of the local Courts of Quarter Sessions had sole authority to determine how many applicants, if any, should be granted retail liquor licenses. Before deciding, the judges were required to examine all remonstrances for and against license applications. Consequently, the drys decided to make a statewide effort to elect sympathetic judges and circulate remonstrances against license applicants. The WCTU, which had sporadically worked through the Brooks Law on its own since 1888, reacted to the ASL's plan with enthusiasm and masterminded several county and local campaigns. Between 1909 and 1919 seventeen counties went dry, and various other counties experienced partial success.[89] For the union and its allies, these "no-license" campaigns also produced less obvious benefits. As one league activist recalled, "They put the conduct of the saloonmen in the limelight. Many facts were brought out which compelled local communities to recognize the real character of the traffic which they were tolerating in their midst. . . . Workers were discovered and developed who became valuable assets in the political fights being waged by the Anti-Saloon League in its efforts to achieve national prohibition." In a similar fashion, a union worker reported that "the educational value of individual remonstrance, with the thorough airing given the liquor traffic in our courts, is bearing a rich harvest of prohibition."[90]

In fact, these remonstrance campaigns fostered the creation of new local unions after 1908. For example, the York Springs Union was organized in 1909 and shortly thereafter embarked on its "most dramatic project": using remonstrances to shut down local saloons.[91] While new affiliates were formed to exploit the Brooks Law, established unions were often reinvigorated by remonstrance campaigns. Several branches reported that their memberships had expanded during these efforts; for instance, the Northampton County Union claimed that "a new day had dawned" after it had asked the License Court to issue no licenses. The "hearts of [Northampton] mothers spoke," and "nothing could silence them." More importantly, "the [Northampton County] WCTU was put on the map as a force henceforth to be reckoned with."[92]

In short, the Pennsylvania WCTU's embrace of local gradualism had sparked its growth in the years after 1900. Unlike its Illinois counterpart, its willingness to work with the state ASL meant that it basked in the league's glory and received public credit for several political efforts.[93] In contrast, the press rarely mentioned the Illinois WCTU in connection with the ASL before 1916, thus affirming its marginal position with respect to the leading dry organization in Illinois.[94] Instead, news reports often linked the Illinois women with the extremist Prohibition party.[95] As a result, moderate anti-liquor women may have preferred to work directly through the state ASL's Woman's Department, or through groups with only loose ties to the Union, such as the Woman's Church Federation.[96]

Table 18 Barriers to Dry Mobilization during the Progressive Era in Michigan and the United States

	Urban Population in Percent, 1910	Percentage Change in Urban Population, 1880–1910	Catholic Population in Percent, 1916	Percentage Change in Catholic Population, 1890–1916	Foreign-Born Population in Percent, 1910	Percentage Change in Foreign-Born Population, 1880–1910	Value Added by Manufacture per Capita, 1909
Michigan	47.2	12.3	17.2	4.7	21.3	−2.4	$112.62
United States	46.3	16.8	15.7	1.1	14.7	1.4	$92.73

Source: U.S. Bureau of the Census.

From Mobilization to Referendum Victory

Of course, neither the Pennsylvania union nor the Illinois union ever had the opportunity to mobilize for a state prohibition referendum after 1900. In both states, powerful urban interests were staunchly opposed to prohibition, and their representatives in the state legislatures dutifully squashed most of the ASL's proposed restrictions on the liquor industry.[97] In contrast, Michigan's drys had access to the initiative and referendum after 1908, and they could bypass the state's wet majorities in the legislature. Furthermore, the Michigan case warrants attention because the state's referendum in 1916 was of particular importance to the prohibitionists, who had yet to achieve a statewide triumph in a major manufacturing state.[98] Michigan was not only more industrialized than the United States as a whole but also included a more urban, Catholic, and foreign population (see table 18). Hence, when the Michigan prohibitionists triumphed in 1916, they demonstrated that their cause had broad support outside the sparsely settled southern and western states. At the same time, the campaign displayed the power of the movement's locally based mobilization efforts, which can best be seen by comparing them with Michigan's prohibition campaign of 1887.

Michigan's drive for a prohibition amendment began in 1878, when the state temperance alliance hired Captain Van Etten, an itinerant orator, to sustain a recent wave of temperance revivals that had swept through the state.[99] During his speaking tour, he besought his audiences to petition the Michigan legislature to submit a prohibitory amendment to the electorate for a vote.[100] By 1880 the WCTU, Prohibition party, and assorted local groups had taken up Van Etten's cause; in 1881 state lawmakers received between 100,000 and 200,000 petitions in favor of constitutional prohibition.[101] That the Michigan drys were unyielding on this issue surfaced early. In January 1881, a state prohibition convention resolved that the proposed amendment should not even exempt sacramental wine, a position bound to offend voters whose churches used it.[102]

Despite their rigid approach, anti-liquor activists nevertheless won a pledge of submission from the Republican State Convention in February 1881.[103] Unfortunately, the three subsequent Republican legislatures failed to carry out their party's repeated pledges in favor of submission. As a result, a small but growing number of anti-liquor Republicans shifted their support to the Michigan Prohibition party, whose share of the gubernatorial vote leapt from 1.9 percent in 1882 to 6.6 percent in 1886.[104] Given the highly competitive party system of the 1880s,[105] the Republican state legislature of 1887 reasonably feared that further defections might produce Democratic victories. Consequently, Michigan lawmakers approved a prohibition amendment in January 1887, to be submitted to the voters in April.[106]

Because the Prohibitionists were instrumental in placing the amendment on the ballot, the state's nonpartisan drys were somewhat wary of the party's efforts to lead the referendum campaign. Still, partisans and nonpartisans papered over their differences in their common pursuit of state prohibition.[107] They combined into a nonpartisan State Amendment Committee and organized down to the township. The whirl of the campaign began; routes for speakers and singers were laid out, and literature "was scattered all over the State like autumn leaves." Some "liberal contributions of money were made," and seventeen prominent speakers from around the country offered their services. According to one participant, "no political party was ever thoroughly enough organized to accomplish as much in the same time as was done in those short weeks."[108]

On April 4, 1887, however, Michigan voters rejected the prohibition amendment by a vote of 184,305 to 178,470. Although the voters were "more enlightened on the important questions at issue than they ever were before," the wets had triumphed with 50.8 percent of the vote.[109] After their loss, many prohibitionists blamed the liquor interest, which it accused of ballot abuses and misleading propaganda.[110] But observers also suggested that the movement had failed to win over the moderate anti-liquor forces in the state. Significantly, even the drys had noticed that only about eighty of the state's five hundred newspapers endorsed constitutional prohibition.[111]

Analysts explained the results in two ways. First, they suggested that the amendment's extreme language alienated many otherwise sympathetic voters. W. W. Washburne, for one, pointed to the amendment's failure to exempt sacramental wine, and to its wording, which "seemed to make an attack on personal rights."[112] Secondly, some commentators contended that the Michigan drys had antagonized potential supporters by fulminating against supporters of "high license."[113] During the referendum campaign, the state legislature was considering a "high license" bill, which imposed substantial annual fees for the privilege of selling liquor. When several respected anti-liquor moderates endorsed this restrictive policy over the pending amendment, dry activists lashed out at them. For example, Frances Willard referred to clergymen who supported "high license" as "hypocrites, Scribes and Pharisees."[114] Such disdain for "high license" comported with radical prohibitionist doctrine; licensing laws not only sanctioned an evil trade, but also ostensibly failed to reduce the crimes of the liquor traffic.[115] However, the drys' assaults on the moderate temperance men undoubtedly hurt their cause. As the *Christian Advocate* commented,

> A great many persons do not believe in Prohibition. . . . Yet many of these are total abstinence men in their practice and in favor of restricting saloons and even of closing them. But they and all who are disposed to favor High-License were in some cases roundly denounced as bad or worse than rumsellers—as in league with hell. The resources of the English language were exhausted in holding them up as criminals of the deepest dye. This extravagance of denunciation . . . caused a current which ran against the movement. Such heat and rancor were unfavorable to conviction, and still more to persuasion.[116]

Estranged by the prohibitionists' "apparent vindictiveness," several "great friends of Prohibition," such as the former governor Cyrus G. Luce, also remained aloof from the referendum campaign. To them, support for the amendment implied support for the condemnation of prominent citizens, "personal friends, and brethren in the Church."[117]

The anti-liquor movement sustained a new fissure, between constitutional prohibitionists and local-optionists, after the amendment was defeated in April. Even as lawmakers in Michigan debated local option, constitutional prohibition retained much dry support. In May 1887 a state convention of nonpartisan drys affirmed its commitment to constitutional prohibition and sought to organize every county in Michigan for a new amendment campaign.[118] Similarly, the president of the Michigan WCTU, Mary T. Lathrap, declared in June 1887 that the union was "fully committed to constitutional prohibition," and that "local option is . . . no substitute."[119] In the following year, the state Prohibition party voted to condemn local option over the protests of a minority, and instead "heartily" endorsed the national platform, which asserted that "Prohibition must be secured through Amendments to our National and State Constitutions."[120] Conversely, A. D. P. Van Buren, a moderate Michigan dry, bitterly complained in 1888 that there were too many people "with too much prohibition to be of any practical use." These people, he continued, "cannot begin with prohibition in a town or county; they must start with an entire state, or do nothing."[121] As an early local gradualist, Van Buren maintained that local option "is the first step in the right direction, and will lead on, not only to carrying the town, but the county, and finally the state, for prohibition."[122]

Unfortunately, his preferred strategy was ahead of its time. To be sure, the county option law of 1889 authorized 25 percent (and later 33 percent)[123] of qualified voters to petition for "no-license" elections in their counties. But local gradualists like Van Buren were a minority in the state branches of the WCTU and the Prohibition party, whose disdain for a locally based strategy persisted throughout the 1890s. Just as no organization appears to have pressured the state legislature for local option,[124] no group made systematic use of the 1889 law as a prelude to prohibition during the decade.[125] For local gradualists, then, the challenge lay in tapping into the vast array of local churches, temperance groups, good government associations, and antivice leagues which shared their moderation on the liquor question.

By 1896 local gradualists in Michigan could claim an organizational home. In that year, several clergymen established the Michigan affiliate of the Anti-Saloon League. Like other league branches, the Michigan ASL had inauspicious beginnings. In fact, despite its relentlessly upbeat reports to the national league,[126] the group had only organized six counties for local option elections by 1900.[127] Early league leaders also encountered difficulties in exploiting the county option law of 1889, given their limited funds and manpower, as well as the expanse of the state's counties.[128] These difficulties were aggravated by the high rate of turnover in state ASL superintendents: during its first ten years, the Michigan league was led by four clergymen.[129] Meanwhile, the group's cultivation of local evangelical churches lagged behind its initial expectations.[130]

By 1907 the ASL's strategy of local gradualism had abolished few saloons, though it had aided the group in its pursuit of allies and a mass base. Frustrated in its use of county option, the Michigan league shifted its sights even lower. Beginning in 1904 the ASL lobbied the state legislature for a local option law that would apply to smaller geographical units—townships, villages, wards, and districts. According to the organization's leaders, their "township and ward" measure would prepare the way for county option. "As fast as counties are ready," the ASL asserted, "they can be added to the dry column. And when sentiment is developed and resolute, . . . a state campaign for prohibition will be in order." Such a law was also practical, for "the average legislature would much more readily grant township option than a state plebiscite in the face of liquor opposition."[131] In the end, the Michigan league only achieved an indirect means of banning the saloon in towns, villages, and cities, through the rejection of bonds by majority petition.[132] Nevertheless, its persistence cemented its base in the Protestant churches, which had been wary of prohibitory policies because of their tendency to divide the laity. Specifically, the ASL carefully consulted with church bodies and held denominational meetings about its local option proposals so as to maximize clerical support. Hence, it could report in 1907 that seven or eight league men were speaking in churches each Sunday to seek volunteers, donations, and electoral support for its various endeavors.[133]

Furthermore, its modest aims strengthened the league's growing alliance with secular moderates, such as businessmen and the state Grange. By 1906 the group reported that "the business men and interests are giving the League an increasing moral and financial backing."[134] Finally, this relatively unsuccessful effort to extend local option also brought the state's ASL and WCTU closer together. Like its Illinois counterpart, the Michigan Union had been wedded to the Prohibition party during the 1880s and 1890s and had retained its radical tendencies after 1900.[135] While still primarily interested in a state prohibition amendment, the Michigan women ultimately proved more amenable to local gradualism than their Illinois sisters. For example, their group was a key ally of the league during its early efforts to exploit the county option law.[136] By 1905 the union declared that "there is greater and more united effort among temperance workers than at any previous time since the [1887] amendment was submitted," and in 1907 its members petitioned the state legislature for the ASL's local option proposal.[137] Consequently, when the WCTU and the Prohibition party (unsuccessfully) sought a prohibition amendment from the state constitutional convention in 1907, the ASL temporarily abandoned its opposition to the policy to provide a united front.[138]

In 1908 the union would return the favor. When the ASL initiated a massive county option campaign, the WCTU's "local unions entered heartily into [no-license] elections in several counties." Union members "circulated literature, paid for speakers, had rallies and parades, interviewed voters, published posters with telling temperance truths, gave freely from their treasuries and from their individual pocketbooks."[139] Significantly, this wave of local option elections coincided with the rapid expansion of the Michigan union's membership (see figure 9). As the local option drives multiplied between 1907 and 1910, the WCTU added 3,845 new members. Likewise, the state ASL reported that its annual income rose from $16,309 in 1906 to $41,000 in 1911, which reflected its increasing capacity to tap small donors for contributions.[140]

After 1907 anti-liquor activists not only gained new supporters and held more "no-license" elections; they also won 64.9 percent of the time.[141] By the time of the vote on constitutional prohibition in 1916, forty-five of the state's eighty-three counties, including over fifty cities, had banned the saloon through county option.[142] Indeed, WCTU leaders saw a connection between the expansion of dry territory and their upsurge in membership during the local option agitation (see figure 10). "For years we have had only one prohibition county; now we have eleven," Julia R. Parish wrote in 1908. "We have reached and passed the 10,000 membership (10,855) for the first time in our history." In similar fashion, the Michigan union reported that the drys' county option victories in 1909 produced "an unusually large attendance of

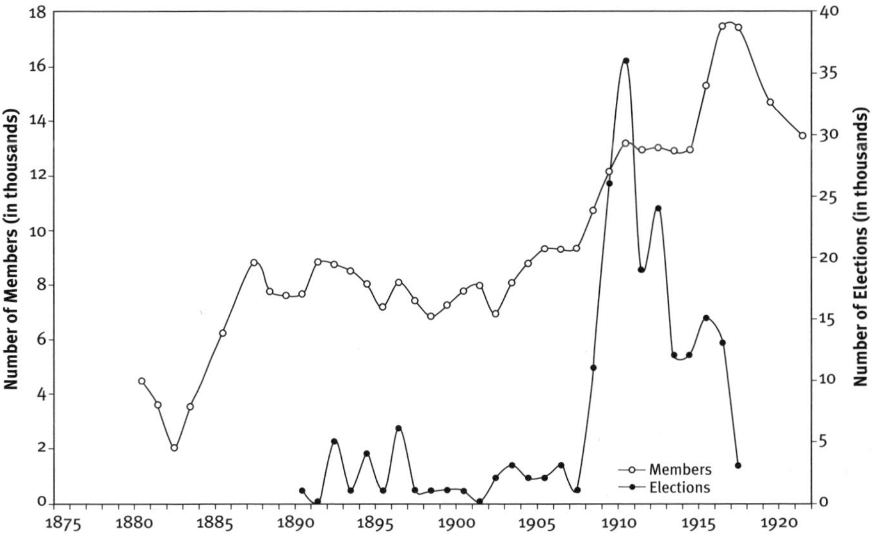

Figure 9 Pattern of Membership Growth, Michigan WCTU, as Compared to the Frequency of County Option Elections, 1875–1920. Sources: *Minutes of the National Woman's Christian Temperance Union* (1874–1921); Larry D. Engelmann, "O Whiskey: The History of Prohibition in Michigan" (Ph.D. diss., University of Michigan, 1971), 100.

delegates and citizens at the annual WCTU convention" as well as "the largest gain in membership ever recorded—1,463."[143]

Just as union growth after 1907 suggested that Michigan residents increasingly favored prohibitory policies, the anti-liquor movement gained more support from opinion leaders as well. In 1910 the Anti-Saloon League sponsored the formation of a Local Option Press Association, which embraced over one hundred state newspapers. These newspapers agreed to disseminate local option news across the state, and issued weekly news bulletins. Although countered by the brewers' Michigan Central Press Service, anti-liquor forces won over a majority of the state's newspapers by 1916. Even some traditionally wet Detroit papers went dry; for example, the *Detroit News* supported the drys in their amendment campaign in 1916 by publishing front-page cartoons which vividly illustrated the dangers of the saloon.[144]

Still, anti-liquor activists in Michigan hardly made a smooth transition from advocating local option to demanding statewide prohibition in the aftermath of its substantial local victories. For one thing, the transition required that the movement shift resources from the county to the state level at the expense of locally oriented activism. While counties continued to vote on whether to license liquor until state prohibition became effective in 1918, much of the county option activity after 1910

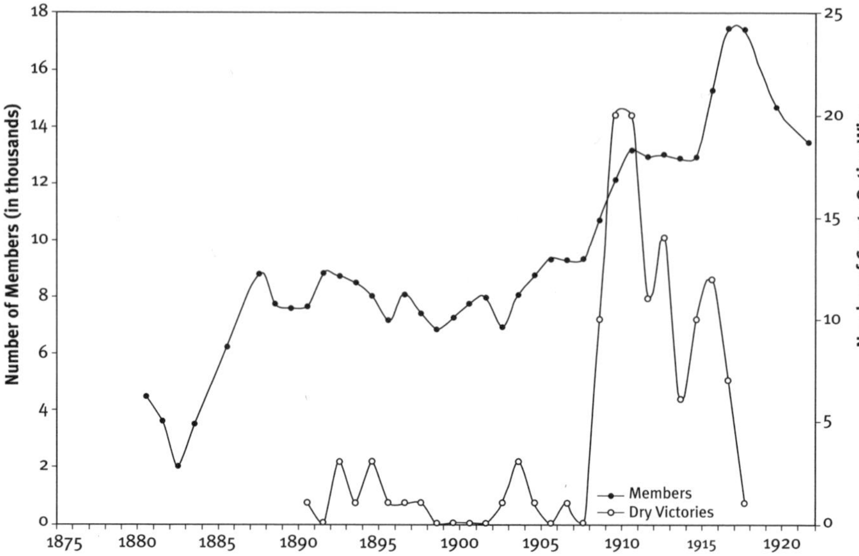

Figure 10 Pattern of Membership Growth, Michigan WCTU, as Compared to the Pattern of County Option Victories, 1875–1920. Sources: *Minutes of the National Woman's Christian Temperance Union* (1874–1921); Engelmann, "O Whiskey," 100.

reflected requests for fresh elections by citizens disappointed with the outcome of the previous election. (According to the local option law of 1889, "no-license" elections could be held once every two years.) In other words, the drys refought many old battles after 1910, but gained little additional territory in new contests.[145] Hence, as figures 9 and 10 show, local option activity ebbed and flowed in two- to three-year intervals, even as the number of county option elections and dry "no-license" victories declined after 1910, the year the Michigan Union began to work "with heroic effort for state-wide prohibition."[146]

At the time, abandoning county option for state prohibition seemed a logical "next step" for many Michigan drys. The state WCTU, for one, had been so encouraged by the development of anti-liquor sentiment that it had formally settled on the policy at its state convention in 1910. For the Anti-Saloon League, though, the decision to adopt a more radical posture was never taken lightly. Fearful about getting too far ahead of public opinion, ASL leaders wanted to be reasonably sure of success before risking a costly and embarrassing defeat. Hence, the League's challenge lay in gauging when it had enough public support to gain a statewide dry law or referendum victory. In Michigan, some ASL activists had advocated a move to the state level as early as 1910 and 1911, after the movement had won an impressive number of county option victories. League leaders disagreed, however, and focused on preserving the county option law and its local gains from a wet counterattack, launched in 1911.[147]

By December 1912, the ASL leadership felt confident enough to unite with the WCTU for a state prohibition campaign. The drys had retained most of their "no-license" territory, and they had secured both continued support for county option and additional anti-liquor measures from state lawmakers.[148] Unfortunately, the two groups misjudged the strength of their cause, for neither the electorate nor their grassroots workforce was ready for a statewide campaign in 1913. According to the state's initiative and referendum law of 1908, the prohibitionists needed to collect about fifty thousand signatures from voters to place their amendment on the ballot, and they hoped to exceed that number. By the fall of 1913, though, they had failed to collect even the minimum, an unremarkable outcome since few local unions were focused on the effort.[149]

This temporary setback convinced the Anti-Saloon League that it had to lower its sights and to stake out a more moderate position. The ASL's most radical move in the next two years was to advocate a weak state prohibition statute, the Straight Bill (1915), that would be subject to voter approval and could be resubmitted every two years if a certain percentage of the electorate petitioned for a new election. Indeed, this measure was so modest that it would have authorized individuals to order shipments of alcoholic beverages from out of state for consumption in their homes. While it fell to defeat, the Straight Bill gained the support of the state's "damp" governor, as well as that of many moderate state legislators. Moreover, its rejection by the wets allowed anti-liquor activists to assert that "it was useless to try to get a fair liquor bill from the wet state legislature."[150]

In other words, the Straight Bill's defeat meant that the ASL and its allies could portray the liquor traffic as uncompromising. They themselves had been willing to accept half a loaf, only to see it snatched away by their entrenched foe. It was in 1915, then, that the league decided to sponsor its second referendum on constitutional prohibition. Uniting again with the WCTU, the ASL constructed an effective umbrella organization (the United Michigan Dry Federation), collected the requisite signatures, and initiated an all-out campaign which galvanized more local unions than in 1913. More importantly, their short-term campaign tactics promoted their long-term political strategy of mobilizing the state's anti-liquor moderates. For example, instead of allowing old radicals like Samuel Dickie of the Prohibition party to capture the campaign spotlight, the federation used middle-class businessmen as its spokesmen. In addition, activists even avoided using the word "prohibition" as much as they could in the campaign, for it resonated in the public's mind with "long haired men, short haired women, or bald headed deacons."[151]

That is not to say that the referendum campaign lacked excitement. In the fall

Table 19 Patterns of Membership Growth in the Michigan WCTU during the 1880s and the Progressive Era

	1880–1890	1900–1920
Peak Year of WCTU Membership	1887	1917
Number of Members, Peak Year	8,790	17,451
Absolute Membership Growth, First Year to Peak Year	96.7	125.5
Absolute Membership Growth, Entire Period	71.2	89.7
Members per Thousand Residents, First Year	2.73	3.20
Members per Thousand Residents, Peak Year	4.49	5.35
Per Capita Membership Growth, First Year to Peak Year	64.5	67.2
Per Capita Membership Growth, Entire Period	33.7	28.1

All growth rates in percent.
Source: Minutes of the National Woman's Christian Temperance Union, 1874–1920.

of 1916 the famed temperance evangelist Billy Sunday stormed through Michigan, whipping up fervor for the dry amendment. In Detroit, "when Sunday asked who was going to vote for prohibition, ten thousand men rose to their feet with a mighty shout." In Grand Rapids, he received a similar response. "Standing on the pulpit, waving an American flag, he heard seven thousand men shout that they would vote for prohibition the next day." On November 7, 1916, voters in Michigan embraced prohibition by a vote of 353,378 to 284,754.[152]

When their referendum received 55.4 percent of the vote, the drys were naturally elated. The victory in Michigan, along with those elsewhere, allowed national ASL leaders to claim that over 60 percent of the country's population would soon be living in dry territory. Furthermore, they asserted that the Michigan victory demonstrated the feasibility of uniting urban workers with their employers in destroying the liquor menace. Such developments encouraged the league leadership to increase the pressure for a national prohibition amendment.[153] But did local gradualism itself expand the base of the Michigan movement, thus contributing to its referendum triumph?

Two pieces of evidence suggest that the prohibitionists had succeeded in broadening their base of support as of 1916. For one thing, by 1916 the union had achieved its highest per capita membership ever, 5.2 members per 1,000 state residents. In contrast, their nineteenth-century forebears had mobilized but 4.5 members per 1,000 state residents by 1887 (see table 19).[154] Secondly, one historian's statistical study of the election data suggests that Michigan's drys had convinced significant minorities of the urban and foreign-born electorates to vote "dry" in 1916, even though these groups had traditionally voted "wet." His county-by-county analysis shows that the size of urban populations and the percentage of foreign-born inhabitants are only modestly correlated with opposition to prohibition. He concludes that "prohibition had triumphed because of the votes of the moderates in the state." These moderates "probably drank but voted dry in the expectation that the state would be a better place without the saloons and the producers of alcoholic beverages."[155]

In Michigan, local gradualism paved the way for "damp" voters to enter the prohibition movement. The years of local agitation, the halting shift to more radical aims, the reasonable tone of the state drys, and the timing of their amendment campaign in 1916 had allowed the movement to appeal to unlikely prohibition voters, such as the foreign-born and urban residents. Instead of "turning inward" and appealing only to committed prohibitionists, the movement was able to unite with businessmen, farmers, churches, and other groups in the larger community. By consciously "turning outward," they were able to temporarily evade the "iron law of involution," which holds that ideologically based social movements are ultimately rendered ineffectual by their exclusivity.[156]

Of course, Michigan was but one of twenty-nine states to hold at least one referendum on statewide prohibition during the Progressive Era. However, once the league became firmly established in any state, its strategy generally conformed to Michigan's pattern. First, the ASL hoped to supplement the state's existing prohibitory measures with modest laws that advanced the drys' position vis-à-vis the wets. In northern states like Michigan, where the extant local option system was often limited, the league sought to extend and improve on that system, so as to facilitate more effective local activism. Meanwhile, in the South, with well-developed local option laws, the ASL often focused on winning statewide measures that established prohibition in rural areas. If successful, such state legislative campaigns helped the league to consolidate and add to the amount of dry territory in the nation as a whole. However, even if their legislative proposals faltered—as the "township and ward" bill did in Michigan and as county option did in Pennsylvania—league leaders recognized that these campaigns would be beneficial to the prohibition movement in other ways. In 1903, for example, William H. Anderson made the following arguments in favor of a crusade for local option in Illinois:

> The indirect benefits of the passage of the bill will be greater than the direct ones. . . . The important thing will be the aroused, organized public sentiment that will make it possible. It affords a tangible concrete rallying-point. It will impress men with the practicability of temperance work, and prepare them to follow intelligent leadership in the next step. But best of all, it will allow us to

force upon the liquor men an issue of our own choosing, whether majority rule shall be perpetuated in this state or go down in shame before an oligarchy of brewers.[157]

In either case, the ASL invariably exploited each state's unique legal situation with the tools available to press its cause at the local level. As in Michigan, most state leagues relied on some variant of local option; in others, the group had to make do with more indirect methods. In Pennsylvania, for example, the prohibitionists had no choice but to revert to the Brooks Law (1887) and its byzantine procedures for abolishing local saloons. Nonetheless, as the Pennsylvania WCTU discovered, this measure allowed them to dry up seventeen counties while engaging new followers in the process.

Like the campaigns for modest state prohibitory laws, locally based efforts proved invaluable to the prohibition movement. Obviously, the Anti-Saloon League sponsored local campaigns to drive the liquor traffic out of as many villages, towns, and counties as it could, but that was hardly its only purpose. For league leaders, the outcomes of these local crusades gave them rough indications of the strength and weakness of anti-liquor sentiment at the state and local level. Furthermore, "no-license" contests demonstrated the extent of the ASL's influence, and informed public officials of their constituents' preferences on the liquor issue. Finally, as the league itself argued, "the greatest service of [a locally based] system consists in its creation of public sentiment in the various communities of the state by bringing the question directly before the people and compelling its thoughtful consideration at the hands of the citizens engaged in all pursuits."[158]

Indeed, ASL leaders only sponsored state prohibition campaigns after they sensed that public opinion ran in their favor. Sometimes, as in Michigan, they miscalculated and had to retreat to a less advanced position. In other states, the league knew that a state prohibition campaign would be futile and refused to sponsor one. For instance, when the Illinois Prohibition party declared for state prohibition in 1910, the state ASL, well aware of the movement's weakness in Chicago, opposed the plan. "We believe it would be a foolish blunder to bring on a statewide vote," one league leader declared, "and we are hoping the friends of local option will see the wisdom of striving for something that is possible instead of something that is impossible."[159] But once the ASL thought that state prohibition was possible, it drew upon its carefully cultivated base of mass support to fight for the policy.

In part, the drys won more state prohibition referenda in the Progressive Era than in the nineteenth century because they chose their battles more carefully. Instead of expending scarce resources on securing referenda in states that were unlikely to vote dry, movement leaders limited themselves to building up as much support for prohibition as they could in "hopelessly wet" states. In New York and New Jersey, for example, the league struggled for years before municipalities were authorized to hold referenda on local prohibition. In other states, like Massachusetts and Wisconsin, the ASL remained stalled at the municipal level for the entire Progressive Era. For the league, though, its apparent lack of progress in these states was beside the point. After all, local gradualism involved more than simply acquiring dry territory; it was also a device for educating and radicalizing those who sympathized with the anti-liquor cause, as the next chapter will show.

7 Turning Moderates into Radicals

As shown in chapter 6, the Progressive Era drys combined their moderate stance on the liquor question with an emphasis on grassroots agitation, thus creating the necessary momentum for state prohibition measures. Across the United States, the Anti-Saloon League sought both modest state limits on the liquor traffic and the abolition of local saloons. While not always successful, these endeavors nevertheless galvanized anti-liquor moderates and their WCTU allies into action. Moreover, as the Michigan case showed, these campaigns often demonstrated the intransigence of the liquor interests, which often fought back with an uncompromising zeal. After a legislative battle over local option, for example, one dry activist declared that "the opposition has fought every inch of the way" and probably resorted to "undue influence."[1] Though often effective in thwarting the anti-liquor cause, their opponents' hardball tactics only convinced many temperance advocates that modest anti-liquor policies were not enough. As a result, many reformers who began the Progressive Era with "damp" proclivities later became ardent prohibitionists, and the number of prohibition states increased from three to thirty-three by 1919.

Of course, the Anti-Saloon League would later claim that its work at the state and local levels lay the foundation for its greatest achievement, the Eighteenth Amendment to the U.S. Constitution:

> When Congress voted to submit to the states a constitutional amendment providing for National Prohibition . . . , the liquor traffic as a legalized institution was doomed. No one knew this fact better than those who had closely followed the progress of the Prohibition movement and who . . . understood something of the overwhelming sentiment for Prohibition which existed in most sections

> of the nation outside the great cities. More than 65 per cent of the population of the United States was under Prohibition either by virtue of the operation of local option or state-wide Prohibition laws.

Not surprisingly, the orthodox prohibitionists rejected this explanation for the Eighteenth Amendment. The "step theory," as they called it, was flawed for several reasons. First and foremost, they accurately pointed out that not every state which adopted prohibition after 1900 advanced smoothly from "wet" to "dry." Towns and counties would adopt "no-license" policies one year, only to reverse themselves later on. As a result, the amount of dry territory in a state often fluctuated, and the drys periodically lost ground to their opponents in these contests. In similar fashion, some states passed dry referenda without having accumulated much dry territory, or having endured years of local agitation. If anything, the radicals argued, "local option hindered and delayed national prohibition," which only came about because the dry movement embraced national prohibition as a major goal after 1913.[2]

Despite this skepticism, no one had more confidence in local gradualism than the ASL's leaders. To them, the "step theory" was not just about amassing dry territory or subjecting the states to local agitation for set time periods. Instead, the league's political strategy from the beginning was aimed at developing public support for prohibition. First, their program's moderation would unify the temperance forces and secure "the active support of men and women who were not and could not be enlisted by any agency then in the field." The league's plan also appealed to common sense, "in that it proposed to attack the liquor traffic first at the points of least resistance, namely, the country cross-roads, the townships, the villages, and the rural counties." Finally, ASL leaders hoped "to use [anti-liquor] sentiment already in existence, crystallizing it for immediate use while at the same time by that very process creating more sentiment for the larger conflicts ahead." Intuitively, they knew that "nothing succeeds like success and that nothing makes more sentiment than the proper utilization of the sentiment which already exists."[3]

Ultimately, the actual workings of local option also created new prohibition sentiment. For instance, Wellington R. Burt, a businessman from Michigan, explained in 1916 that he had changed his views about statewide prohibition after his state's experiments with county option. Though long a temperance advocate, he had opposed inserting a prohibition clause in Michigan's constitution of 1907 because he doubted that "sentiment was strong enough to enforce it" at that time. Since 1907, however, "the sentiment of the people of the state has become stronger for the enforcement of Prohibition." He continued: "I believe now such a law could be enforced. We have demonstrated that it can be enforced in small units in the counties until the larger portion of the state is now enjoying Prohibition, and I believe the sentiment is now strong enough to carry this movement."[4] Likewise, Fred M. Jackson of Birmingham, Alabama, reported that public support for prohibition grew while his city was dry under county option. In his view, the citizens of Birmingham were more likely to support prohibition after county option had decreased both liquor consumption and liquor-related crimes.[5]

While local option changed some minds about state and national prohibition, its positive effects were probably limited to those who already disliked the saloon. Indeed, while the press published many testimonials that celebrated the efficacy of local option, the media also printed critiques of the policy, pointing out its failure to reduce liquor sales, crime, poverty, insanity, and public spending on social problems. Stephen P. Monahan, for example, asserted that "there is more liquor sold in the local option territory of Illinois than ever before," and that the speakeasy produced drunkenness and disorder. Undoubtedly, there was a grain of truth in the claims of both sides. Most communities that voted "no-license" saw some decrease in liquor retailing, but its extent and permanence varied widely across localities.[6]

Overall, though, local option's flaws were not fatal to the prohibition cause. After all, the Anti-Saloon League never offered local option as a panacea to the liquor problem but merely as the first step in the slow path toward national prohibition.[7] To achieve this end, the ASL recognized that it had to mobilize beyond the movement's core constituency to include additional supporters. For decades, evangelicals from the Methodist, Baptist, Presbyterian, and Congregational churches had been most sympathetic to the temperance cause, regardless of region or theological differences over issues like biblical literalism, which later produced the fundamentalist schism of the 1920s. Though middle-class, native-born evangelical Protestants still composed the dry crusade's base after 1900, the league needed nontraditional activists to win state and national victories.[8] Significantly, evangelical Protestants constituted a minority of the population in many states. For instance, Richard Jensen estimates that evangelicals accounted for only 41 percent of the Midwest's population in 1890.[9] Thus it was in the prohibitionists' interest to obtain the support of anti-liquor moderates like Washington Gladden, Robert A. Woods, and Chester Rowell, discussed below. While all middle class and native born, they hardly conformed to the evangelical Protestant stereotype.

The importance of winning over anti-liquor moderates was confirmed by the efforts of the liquor interests, who assiduously courted them after 1907. Convinced that the distribution system was responsible for much of the public's animus toward the liquor industry, the distillers mounted a campaign for the creation of model license laws and model saloons, which would shut down retailers who accommodated prostitution and gambling and refused to limit their hours of operation. Meanwhile, the brewers tried to convince anti-liquor moderates that beer, because of its low alcohol content, was a temperance drink, and sought to gain exemptions for beer in state prohibition measures.[10] Of these two approaches, moderates found the "model saloon" campaign more appealing, though as the stories of Robert A. Woods and Chester A. Rowell will demonstrate, they felt no qualms about working with the ASL and for saloon regulation. Hence, once the saloon appeared impossible to reform, anti-liquor moderates were already enmeshed in the prohibition movement and could easily engage in more radical agitation.

But were anti-liquor moderates really radicalized by their participation in campaigns initiated by the Anti-Saloon League? Or, did the drive after 1913 for national prohibition "bring the whole nation to that standard," as the radicals alleged? Surely D. Leigh Colvin is correct to note that "the purest effect of the local option step process was in the period preceding 1914," for in November 1913 the league formally united with other anti-liquor groups to advocate national prohibition.[11] Nonetheless, as the following case studies suggest, the ASL's local gradualism drew some atypical activists into the prohibition movement. Though latecomers to supporting national prohibition, these activists developed more positive views of the anti-liquor movement before 1913 by observing and taking part in league efforts.

Washington Gladden: The Crusading Minister

As the self-styled "church in action against the saloon," the Anti-Saloon League clearly hoped to convert the ministry to its cause. But not every cleric wished to join a "fanatical" reform like prohibition at the turn of the century. Washington Gladden (1836–1918), for one, remained moderate on the liquor question in 1900, despite his lifelong interest in the liquor question. While growing up in central New York, Gladden had first become interested in temperance after attending a "rousing" speech by Neal Dow, the father of the Maine Law, in 1852. In 1854 Gladden joined a local lodge of the Independent Order of Good Templars and helped to elect a pro–Maine Law candidate to the New York state legislature. It is unclear how long he supported state prohibition, but he did remain a teetotaler for the rest of his life.[12]

Like many others inspired by the reform movements of the 1850s, Gladden found himself called "to realize the Kingdom of God in this world." Churches were moving beyond concerns with personal sin and salvation to serve the broader interests of humanity. "The interest which the churches were taking in the temperance reform and the anti-slavery reform was an indication of a new spirit," Gladden later remarked, and "my mind was turned to the Christian ministry." Nevertheless, he can hardly be classified an "evangelical Protestant," in the sense of emphasizing salvation through the "conversion experience," or a direct, personal confrontation with Christ wherein an individual suddenly acquires faith. Indeed, Gladden had waited in vain for this mystical experience in his youth, and was most attracted to Protestantism as a force for social—rather than individual—regeneration. Hence, after he was ordained a Congregational minister in 1860, he began to break away from traditional dogmas that focused on individualistic pietism.[13]

As the pastor of an influential parish in Columbus, Ohio, Gladden emerged by the 1880s as a central figure in a new movement for progressive social Christianity which would later be termed the Social Gospel. In particular, this approach to faith advocated the church's active involvement in the search for a better society, and its adherents fought, however unsuccessfully, for concrete measures of improvement. Over his lifetime, Gladden advocated several political causes, including "home rule" for the cities, municipal ownership of utilities, and the regulation of trusts. Often, his reform endeavors grew out of his pastoral work. For example, after witnessing labor struggles in Massachusetts and Ohio during the 1870s and 1880s, Gladden increasingly denounced laissez-faire capitalism and the harsh economic conditions of the Gilded Age. To ameliorate these conditions, he proposed that Christian principles be applied to the conflict between labor and capital to produce a more cooperative social order.[14]

While he developed a reputation as a labor reformer, Gladden also joined the "law and order" movement of the 1880s. As described above, this crusade sought total compliance with state and local liquor laws and appealed to anti-liquor moderates. Along with his other reform efforts, Gladden saw his participation in the national Citizens' Law and Order League as part of his Christian civic duty. "Citizenship brings with it duties that cannot be shirked with impunity," he declared, and it is both "idle and disgusting" for the people "to rail at anarchy, while they themselves are suffering the plainest laws to be trampled under foot without protest."[15]

But Gladden's affiliation with the CLOL also reflected his belief that the saloon was corrupting state and local government. He insisted that "the rumseller rules us, year after year, and we bow to the yoke, and smile serenely as they heap on our shoulders the burdens of taxation and the loads of degradation."[16] Moreover, he pointed out that the liquor traffic "flagrantly violated" existing laws, such as the statute which prohibited the sale of liquor to minors.[17] Finally, he maintained that excessive drinking contributed to "offenses against the public peace and welfare," such as crime, poverty, insanity, indebtedness, disadvantaged children, and the high costs of public almshouses, hospitals, and other institutions.[18]

Still, Gladden's general distaste for the saloon and its social effects did not automatically translate into support for constitutional prohibition. During Ohio's amendment campaign of 1883 he opposed this goal, and he publicly clashed with the Reverend James Brand about the policy after its defeat at the polls. Among other things, he charged that constitutional prohibition was unenforceable in Ohio's cities, did not compensate retailers and manufacturers for their property losses, and stripped state lawmakers of their power to otherwise regulate the liquor traffic. At best, Gladden advocated "taxation, combined with local option" as the most practical solution to the drink problem. Meanwhile, Brand, a leader of the Oberlin Temperance Alliance and a future founder of the Ohio ASL, politely challenged his views, and regretted that he "who is so forward in all good works in other directions, should take a position twenty-five years behind the wave of Christian progress in this."[19]

Gladden replied in a courteous fashion, for it was the first response he had received from a prohibitionist that did not contain "personal abuse or mean insinuation." Consequently, when Brand and other members of the Oberlin Temperance Alliance formed the Ohio ASL in 1893,[20] they found him a reliable supporter. As early as 1893 he lent moral support to the league, even while distancing himself from its long-term goals of state and national prohibition. At an Anti-Saloon Congress in 1894, for example, Gladden declared for the local option bill sponsored by the Ohio ASL, even while warning against the enactment of laws which would not be rigidly enforced by the authorities.[21] Likewise in 1897, when Purley A. Baker of the state ASL sought to expand the league's activities into Columbus, Gladden generously offered the use of his pulpit, even though leading members of his parish would be displeased with his decision. He said, "If I have not sense enough to know what cause I should introduce into my pulpit, I have not sense to be pastor of the church."[22]

Undoubtedly, Gladden's willingness to aid the ASL from its inception stemmed from both its moderation and its advocacy one of his pet causes: law enforcement. "This Anti-Saloon League commends itself to our support because it does not attempt the impossible," he informed his congregation. "It asks only for such improvements in our laws as can easily be enforced," and "it insists first of all that existing laws should be obeyed." Furthermore, the ASL's campaign to ban saloons near the Ohio State Fair grounds in Gladden's home city, Columbus, appeared to be "very successful." He noted that "there were fourteen arrests and fourteen convictions for a violation of this law forbidding liquor sales near the grounds."[23] The league also retained Gladden's support because its leaders refused to condemn him for his reluctance to support prohibition, unlike other anti-liquor groups. To illustrate, Gladden belonged to a self-constituted "Committee of Fifty" during the late 1890s which investigated sociological questions such as the liquor question.[24] When this committee of eminent men issued a report critical of prohibition, the WCTU immediately pounced on the fact that its authors held unsatisfactory positions on the drink problem, and insinuated that their personal beliefs may have influenced their findings.[25]

By the turn of the century, Gladden and the ASL had seemingly developed a friendly if somewhat distant relationship. The league claimed that it had "no more generous supporter and contributor in Ohio than Dr. Gladden and his church,"[26] while in 1902 he remained publicly committed to local option "as the method which is now most promising." Nevertheless, he continued to oppose state prohibition as "a complete failure in the cities," and he became a strong proponent of "substitutes for the saloons," a favorite panacea of moderates. This reform required those who favored abolishing the saloon "to see that something better takes its place," such as coffeehouses and other social clubs for workingmen.[27]

While the ASL did not oppose "substitutes for the saloon," it did not work for them either. Instead, the Ohio ASL spent the first decade of the twentieth century lobbying state lawmakers for more comprehensive local option legislation. It was during these efforts that Gladden and the league found new common ground. In 1904–5 the Ohio ASL waged a tremendous war to extend local option to city residence districts, a policy that Gladden also favored.[28] To obtain their preferred bill, though, league leaders first had to take on Governor Myron T. Herrick and his allies in the wet Republican machine, led by Boss George B. Cox of Cincinnati. Of course, the attack on "bossism" provoked criticism from the wet GOP press, which charged the league with benefiting financially from its anti-liquor activities.[29] Fortunately for the ASL, its crusade against government corruption struck a chord with reformers like Gladden, who had seen their own legislative proposals thwarted by the state's political machine. In fact, they supported the League vigorously in its campaign against Herrick's reelection.[30]

Between 1906 and 1914 Gladden apparently resolved his doubts about prohibition in the cities. While he never fully explained his change of mind, he was undoubtedly influenced by the ASL's increasing success. For example, in 1906–7 the league held mass rallies in his home city, Columbus, which persuaded the city council to pass an ordinance that aided the police in their enforcement of the Sunday saloon closing law. Shortly afterward, Gladden publicly endorsed E. L. McCune, an anti-liquor Republican and the ASL's favorite, for mayor of Columbus.[31] Similarly, Gladden agreed to serve as a national vice-president of the ASL in 1908–9 in the wake of a "temperance tidal wave."[32] Just before accepting this honorary position, several southern states had adopted prohibition, and the Ohio ASL had made use of the state's new county option law—which Gladden had favored—to outlaw the saloon in fifty-seven counties.[33]

Gladden may have been impressed by the league's interdenominational approach to temperance reform. As an early proponent of closer cooperation among the churches, he had written two books in the late nineteenth century which had argued that associations of churches could be highly effective in dealing with missionary, social, and urban problems. In any case, when Gladden retired from the pulpit in 1914, he also relinquished his position as an ASL national vice-president.[34] By that time, however, he had already embraced constitutional prohibition. For example, he supported the Ohio Progressive party when it stood for state and national prohibition in 1914.[35] Moreover, he refused to allow his anti-prohibition articles from the 1880s to be reprinted in 1917, explaining that "he has changed his views and says he has voted for state-wide prohibition in 1914 and 1915."[36]

This faith in prohibition was further buoyed by Gladden's sense that World War I would encourage new advances in education and domestic life, thus making prohibition "practicable."[37] Quietly and without much fanfare, Gladden had followed the ASL's gradual shift to more radical goals as the twentieth century wore on. Though he was hardly the most active dry, Gladden was nonetheless a good example of how urban Protestantism ultimately warmed to prohibition. Along with Josiah Strong, Walter Rauschenbusch, Charles Stelzle, and other advocates of the Social Gospel, he believed that the "liquor problem was inextricably bound up with the general problem of establishing the Kingdom of God on earth," and added prohibition to his program for social reform.[38]

Robert A. Woods: The Settlement House Worker

Like Gladden, Robert A. Woods (1865–1925), of Boston, was not the typical anti-liquor activist. For one thing, he too lacked an evangelical background. Baptized an Episcopalian, Woods had studied as a young man at the Andover Theological Seminary (1886–90), an interdenominational Protestant institution. Despite completing his course of study, he decided against a career in the ministry and became an irregular churchgoer. When Woods did attend services, he went to an Episcopalian church, though "it was the ritual and not the creed" that attracted him. "Dogmatic tenets had no place" in his personal religious life, and his approach to Christianity focused on the Social Gospel's practical social reforms.[39]

He also differed from many drys in his basic understanding of the liquor question. Like many settlement house workers, Woods appreciated the saloon's social function, and tended to view its position in the urban environment from the vantage point of his clientele, the Irish of South Boston. According to Woods, "the appetite for alcohol is but a blind outreaching for exaltation, for the fulfillment of life," and this appetite would only be redirected when "all the avenues to more abundant life" were opened up to the people.[40] The complete suppression of drink would deprive the poor man of "his easiest and most direct way over the restraints of his narrow and hard lot," as one of his collaborators put it.[41] Unlike Gladden, who viewed coffeehouses and clubrooms as replacements for barrooms, Woods wrote that "it was a mistake . . . to think there can be any substitute for the saloon so far as those who frequent it are concerned." Likewise, to drys who sought legal bans on the liquor traffic, he retorted in 1898 that "only a doctrinaire would ask for no-license" in South Boston.[42]

Of course, Woods was not entirely unsympathetic to temperance. He was personally a teetotaler and held that the saloon contributed to crime, insanity, poverty, political corruption, and family ruin.[43] His antipathy toward the saloon grew from his personal experiences as the head of the South End House (1891–1925), a trustee for the State Hospital for Inebriates (1907–19), and a long-time member of the anti-vice group the Watch and Ward Society. His intimate knowledge of the licensing system led him to join other anti-liquor moderates in 1909 to sponsor the Bar and Bottle Bill, a measure which forbade saloonkeepers to engage in both retail and wholesale liquor business from a single location. Carefully portraying himself as an expert, Woods defended the legislation in front of the Massachusetts legislature's liquor law committee in 1909, 1910, and 1911.[44] Among other things, he claimed that the law would limit the overall number of licenses, "prevent the influence of the saloon [from] being carried into the home," and "reduce some of the dangers of a hazardous business."[45]

Although a modest effort, the Bar and Bottle Bill nonetheless provoked the unrestrained hostility of the liquor interests, and it was rumored that liquor men engaged in bribery to ensure its defeat and repeal.[46] This determined resistance only aggravated Woods's suspicions of the liquor industry. He believed that the bill was largely "promoted by patient, practical people who are prepared to take one step at a time and who have a habit of being quite certain of that step before they take it." To Woods, the liquor interests demonstrated an "inept fixity of mind" by insisting that "amiable theorists and fanatics" were using the bill to seek "wholesale prohibition." Furthermore, he chided the brewers for not recognizing that "the safety of their business lies in the model saloon." Instead of striving to place the liquor trade "under decent and sanitary conditions," the brewers were only concerned with bigger profits and bigger markets.[47]

As his doubts about the liquor trade deepened, Woods was also impressed with the Anti-Saloon League, which had been a major sponsor of the Bar and Bottle Bill. In steering the measure through the state legislature, Woods had worked amicably with Arthur J. Davis, the ASL field secretary who later assumed the state league's highest position, state superintendent, in 1913. This "happy partnership" would resume a few years later, but only after Woods had become further embroiled in liquor politics.[48] He entered this political quagmire in 1913, when Governor Eugene Foss appointed him to the Boston License Board. To his dismay, his appointment was criticized by the city's liquor dealers and the "extreme wing" of the prohibition movement. To the dealers, Woods's goal in accepting the position—to ensure that city saloons were responsible and lawful businesses—threatened illegal, unsavory, and profitable practices such as Sunday sales and the provision of "rounds" of drinks[49] to customers. Meanwhile, radical drys had little patience for Woods's indecisiveness on the drink question, fearing that by making the liquor industry respectable, Woods would blur their portrayal of the saloon as a den of vice and iniquity.[50]

Caught in the middle, Woods might have simply hewed to his moderate efforts at liquor reform. In fact, his actions as a board member suggested that he had every intention of pursuing an independent course. Undoubtedly, Woods irked saloon-keepers with his drive for stricter law enforcement, punitive measures to ensure compliance, and anti-vice plan of segregating men and women in the saloons. At the same time, he angered middle-class Bostonians with his proposal to issue more licenses in their neighborhoods, so as to lessen the number of barrooms that infected poorer neighborhoods. He reasoned that if middle-class citizens were willing to patronize saloons, they could also bear to have some of these nuisances located in their districts.[51]

Though under fire from many Bostonians, Woods believed that he was making progress until 1916, when Governor Samuel McCall replaced him on the license board with a lawyer whose firm had represented liquor retailers. In retrospect, his dismissal should have come as no surprise; city and state officials had found his dominant presence on the board an irritant to both their wet constituencies and like-minded political allies. For example, during Woods's tenure in office, Mayor James M. Curley of Boston, a wet, had employed several tactics to undermine the license board's authority and pressured Governor David Walsh to appoint a more lenient board member to counter Woods's stringent approach to licensing.[52] Still, to Woods and other observers, his replacement by a man with ties to the saloon hinted at a political deal between McCall's campaign manager and the liquor dealers.[53] Given his success in shutting down the worst dealers, Woods concluded, "The upshot was a formidable combination of saloon-keepers, headed by brewers, . . . decided that the base old order of things must be restored. By means of that network of political power by which the liquor interests have so long corrupted the politics of the State, . . . the Licensing Board was radically reorganized and its policy tacitly made conformable to the interests of those who procured the change."[54]

At last, "this conclusive evidence of the nefarious power in politics of the liquor interests" persuaded Woods that local liquor control efforts were futile. It was at this point that he began to consider the feasibility of national prohibition, and in late 1916 he embraced it wholeheartedly. "To-day the majority of the States in the Union are committed against the sale of liquor within their bounds," he wrote. "It looks as if the question of the next few years will be—shall our State share in this great moral revolution or shall we be written down in history among the baser sort who had to be coerced into submission?" Renewing his former alliance with Arthur J. Davis of the state ASL, Woods agreed to lead the Massachusetts committee working toward ratification of the Eighteenth Amendment in 1917. He "poured an enormous amount of personal work" into the ratification campaign and came to appreciate Davis's ability to keep the "endless complications inherent in this plan strongly and steadily in hand." Against the expectations of national dry leaders, Massachusetts became the eleventh state to approve the amendment on April 2, 1918. Subsequently, Woods joined the Massachusetts ASL's headquarters and executive committees, and served on the Committee of Sixty on National Prohibition (1919) and its Subcommittee on Wartime Prohibition (1918–19). When national prohibition became a reality in 1920, Woods, like many drys, shifted his efforts toward securing strong enforcement.[55]

Until his death in 1925 Woods remained a loyal prohibitionist, a conviction born of his own gradual realization that anti-liquor activists were right about the saloon. "As a settlement worker and hospital trustee," he recalled, "I followed hundreds of alcoholic tragedies; and never found liquor dealers facing their own share of the trouble. The saloon, I learned from authority, was a democratic necessity. Beer was perishable. The rich man had his refrigerator. The poor man hadn't and must be supplied by the glass. But my dream of a beer saloon was shattered by the brewers!" While for most of his life a "curious spectator" of the prohibition movement, he threw in his lot with "the plain church-going people of the towns and country who by their inherent moral force" were bringing about a "stupendous achievement." Impressed by the anti-liquor movement's leadership, its organization, and its support from physicians, businessmen, and politicians, Woods found it relatively easy to shift from "damp" to "dry."[56]

Chester H. Rowell: The Progressive Editor

Of the three activists analyzed here, Chester H. Rowell (1867–1948), a newspaperman and political leader from California, was perhaps the most unlikely prohibitionist. Though a professed Christian, he remained unchurched. Furthermore, he periodically expressed a gentle impatience with preachers who lectured on the wickedness of card playing and other social vices. However, one of Rowell's most glaring sins in the eyes of radical drys was his rejection of the total abstinence principle. As a young man-about-town in Washington, Rowell had befriended "drunkards and libertines," an experience that taught him charity for human frailties. In addition, his years of study in Berlin during the early 1890s had exposed him to a society which celebrated "food, drink, nature, companionship and sex."[57]

Consequently, Rowell saw nothing wrong with moderate drinking. "I am not a total abstainer," he wrote in 1907, "either by precept or example. I drink wine on my own table, and have no rule against drinking beer in saloons, though I do not do it much." Meanwhile, Rowell also rejected prohibition as an appropriate policy for a diverse nation like the United States. It was undemocratic, impossible to enforce, and would deprive many people of a pleasure they had long enjoyed without serious harm. For example, he predicted that "we shall be obliged to accept the Continental Sunday and Continental drinking" in the cities, as they were largely populated by Europeans.[58] Nevertheless, despite Rowell's personal habits and his tolerance for the insobriety of others, he did not oppose all restrictions on the saloon. For one thing, he could not ignore how the saloons in his adopted home city, Fresno, California, harbored crime and vice. They frequently operated slot machines, lewd peep shows, card games, and brothels, while the local authorities looked the other way. In fact, Fresno's reputation was that of "the hottest and the wickedest spot in the state." Shortly after becoming editor of the *Fresno Morning Republican* in 1898, Rowell campaigned through his paper's columns for enforcement of the state's liquor license law and its ban on gambling. He applauded when the city trustees outlawed bawdy entertainment in the saloons (1901), as well as when they limited the operating hours of drinking establishments (1904). In the early years of the twentieth century Rowell supported an unsuccessful campaign to apply the local option principle to Fresno County's districts.[59]

Rowell hoped that these modest regulations would make saloons into more respectable gathering places for those who wished to drink. Like Woods, he initially held that if the liquor retailers would only correct their worst abuses, they would retain public support. After all, the saloon was legitimate as long as it shunned less savory activities such as prostitution, gambling, and the bribery of public officials. Pimps and professional gamblers lurked about the saloon, targeting drinkers with their "persuasive blend of dares and lurid promises." At the same time, Fresno's "tenderloin" (or vice) district corrupted city government and undermined the public's respect for the law. Once the saloon was divorced from such evil behavior, however, it could resume its legitimate function as a place where men went for a drink and conversation.[60]

At the same time, Rowell was not blind to the toll of excessive drinking on the drinker and society as a whole. For example, Rowell thought that the demands of modern business and professional life would overwhelm the man "whose brain is muddled by drink or whose nerves are shaken and conscience dulled by gambling." He also believed intoxicated automobile drivers to be major threats to themselves and to public safety, and he advocated their arrest. For radical drys, though, Rowell hardly qualified as a true friend of temperance. Significantly, in 1899 Fresno's Ministerial Union advised its member congregations to accept no advice about the drink question "from compromising newspapers or politicians." When the editor replied that the majority of Fresno's population wanted saloons (albeit cleaner ones), the prohibitionists condemned his position and challenged him "to stand with them on the side of the good and the righteous."[61]

Thus it is not surprising that Rowell drew closer to the moderate Anti-Saloon League than to other anti-liquor groups during the Progressive Era. Indeed, he felt particularly comfortable with the state League's advocacy of local option after 1908. This policy's deference to majority vote fit well with his belief that successful social reforms required the majority's support. "The right to run a saloon," Rowell declared in 1911, "is a public right, not a private right. Any community that wants them ought to be permitted to have them; and any community that does not want them should have the right not to have them."[62] Moreover, as a key leader of the state GOP's reform wing, Rowell found the ASL a useful ally in his crusade against the Southern Pacific Railroad in California politics. For instance, the league agreed to support anti-railroad Republicans in the state elections of 1910, especially after the gubernatorial candidate Hiram Johnson promised to recommend a local option measure upon election.[63] But even after the progressive Republicans controlled state government, Rowell continued to cooperate with the Anti-Saloon League. In 1911 he testified in favor of the league's local option bill before state lawmakers, offering "sane arguments" which "took the opponents of the bill off their feet."[64] Likewise, in 1912 he pushed the "Red-Light Abatement and Injunction Bill," an anti-prostitution measure that the ASL also supported.[65]

It was during these years that Rowell's views about the liquor traffic began to change. Although he once considered drinking establishments to be legitimate settings for conviviality, he became increasingly convinced that the saloon served no productive economic purpose. In 1913, for example, he wrote, "Financially the saloon is 100% loss to everybody and everything concerned." He also paid close attention to the reports from California towns that had adopted "no-license" policies to see whether they were "good for the people." Still, he had not abandoned his faith that restrictive measures could control the worst aspects of the liquor traffic. In his home city of Fresno, for example, he noted that the mayor's decision in 1909 to limit the number of saloons had produced some progress by 1913, though he hoped that "conditions would be still further improved." In short, one might have expected Rowell to remain a stalwart in the ASL's crusade to win further modest limits on the saloons.[66]

As it turned out, neither the ASL nor Rowell found it easy to rein in the demands of the orthodox drys after 1913. Instead exploiting the state's local option law of 1911, the California affiliates of the Prohibition party and the WCTU sponsored a constitutional prohibition amendment in 1914 which was so radical that it would have become effective five days after the election, giving the liquor interests no time to arrange their affairs. League leaders were aghast; they advised against a statewide campaign, "for their strategy required that the local option law be given more time to do its work," and prohibition was sure to lose. Rowell was similarly perturbed; he was running for the U.S. Senate in 1914, and the extremists insisted that he endorse the dry amendment. Even as the ASL reluctantly joined the campaign after the referendum qualified for the state ballot, Rowell ignored the extremists' demands and only restated his preference for local option. Perhaps he would come to support state prohibition if California's dry territory was so extensive that the remaining wet spots were "practically intrusive foreign bodies, inconsistent with the general make-up of the state." In the meantime, the referendum of 1914 appeared premature.[67]

Rowell lost in the senatorial primaries, and yet both he and the league knew better than the orthodox drys how California voters would respond to prohibition. Shortly after 59.6 percent of the electorate rejected the policy, however, the ASL and Rowell temporarily parted company. Fearful of yet another extreme referendum campaign, league leaders sought to regain control of the state movement by offering to lead a statewide prohibition campaign of their own in 1916. Meanwhile, Rowell clung to local option and only seriously began to consider more radical goals in 1917. In that year the league shifted its focus from state prohibition to a moderate statewide anti-saloon law. The Rominger law, as it was called, abolished the saloon and the sale of distilled liquors but permitted the limited sale of beer and wine in hotels, restaurants, and clubs. Though killed in the state legislature by the distilling interests, several cities—including Los Angeles and San José—adopted the provisions of the bill through municipal referenda. Still, cities like San Francisco and San Diego remained adamantly wet, as did Fresno, even though much of Fresno County had banned the saloon as early as 1913. As a result, Rowell hinted in 1917 that state prohibition might be necessary to protect the rights of localities which had outlawed the saloon. "Good roads and automobiles have extended the contamination of a wet city to the dry country," he opined. In addition, with most Americans living in dry territory at the time, his major condition for a reform's success—that it have majority approval—had seemingly been met at the national level. Hence, he was already considering the advisability of national prohibition in 1917, "though he stipulated that the larger the unit covered, the more carefully the law must be applied and the more limited must be its functions."[68]

In the spring of 1918 Rowell finally committed to national prohibition, and he joined the National Campaign Committee for the Ratification of the National Prohibition Amendment. Mere restrictions had been unable to control a "reckless and regenerate liquor traffic," and he had often been disappointed by the intransigence of the wets. For instance, as a supporter of the state's wine industry, he had been irked by the refusal of the State Viticultural Commission to make any concessions to temperance sentiments. Furthermore, Rowell had developed a close working relationship with the ASL state superintendent Daniel Gandier, who was skilled "in drawing about him a number of men not theretofore particularly interested in the Prohibition movement, but who, as journalists, political managers, and interested citizens, had a wide knowledge of State history and political methods." Along with Gandier, Rowell cheered when California became the twenty-fourth state to ratify the Eighteenth Amendment.[69]

Gandier died of cancer in 1920, but by then Rowell was already a committed propagandist for prohibition, which he supported, along with the Anti-Saloon League, until repeal in 1933. There had once been "two honest sides to the [liquor] question," he asserted in 1920, but "there is only one honest side now." Moreover, since a decisive majority of Americans had supported national prohibition, he argued that they were bound to obey the law lest they undermine the democratic system. The issue, he declared in 1922, "is not wet or dry, but law and lawlessness." Nonetheless, all his concern for the social effects of alcohol had failed to convert Rowell to total abstinence. Significantly, he "entered the prohibition era with a private supply of wine until a gardener broke into the wine cellar and with his friends drank up the entire contents." Like so many other middle-class drinkers of the Progressive Era, Rowell demonstrated that an anti-liquor reformer could be opposed to public but not to private tippling, especially if he was personally well supplied.[70]

Clearly, the radical drys were correct to argue that national developments contributed to some of the prohibition movement's momentum after 1913. For example, many scholars have persuasively argued that "the prohibition movement took on a renewed vigor" after Congress enacted the Webb-Kenyon Act in 1913. By prohibiting the interstate transportation of liquor into dry territory, this law enhanced the states' power to enforce state prohibition and local option and thus encouraged "an all-out-drive to win new dry territory in the states."[71] However, it was the ASL's locally based activism that led to positive congressional action on both the Webb-Kenyon Act and the Eighteenth Amendment. After all, local option and referendum outcomes were yardsticks of dry sentiment, and few elected officials could ignore the messages sent by such elections. Indeed, the league's strongest congressional support came from states which had either adopted state prohibition or had come close to that goal, whereas its weakest support came from the wet Northeast, California, and Midwestern states like Missouri and Illinois. In addition, the Anti-Saloon League excelled at applying nonpartisan electoral pressure. As K. Austin Kerr put it, "the decision for [national] prohibition was not made in Washington; it was made on election days in the precincts and townships across America."[72]

Furthermore, local gradualism had already begun to broaden the anti-liquor movement's support during the first decade of the twentieth century. Bruised by the radical drys, anti-liquor moderates like Gladden, Woods, and Rowell found refuge in the ASL. Led by ecumenically inclined Protestants, this group proposed modest legislation, tolerated unorthodox views on the liquor question, and sought common ground with any number of reformers. Finally, by initially focusing on local restrictions to the liquor traffic, the league appealed to the moderates' personal experiences with the saloon and its immediate social effects. Gladden worried about drinking near the Ohio State Fair, Woods about liquor being carried into South Boston homes. By addressing these issues, the ASL seemed to be taking practical steps to make their communities better places to live.

Conversely, the extreme drys persisted in doubting the sincerity of the moderates after the turn of the century, just as they had in the 1880s. It is little wonder that the Michigan ASL sought to exclude some of these "cranks" from its referendum campaign in 1916. At times, the radicals even disrupted the moderates' efforts to apply local gradualism thoroughly. In California, for example, they had forced the ASL to campaign for a prohibition amendment long before the league felt that it had fully exploited the state's local option law. The failure of that initiative, and others like it,[73] suggests that an orthodox dry strategy would not have been particularly fruitful in the Progressive Era. As a result, it is difficult to see how this alternative approach would have hastened the enactment of the Eighteenth Amendment, as its proponents later claimed.[74]

8 Local Gradualism and American Social Movements

This study has maintained that long-term political strategy helps explain the divergent fortunes of the prohibition movement in two distinct periods of American history. Simply put, it was the shift in the movement's strategy from demanding state constitutional amendments to promoting local gradualism that led to success in the Progressive Era. By initially advocating locally based anti-liquor battles, the twentieth-century drys could unite with moderate opponents of the liquor traffic, such as Robert A. Woods and Chester H. Rowell. Later, as local efforts proved futile against an entrenched foe, movement leaders found it relatively easy to engage their moderate adherents in more radical state and national campaigns.

Undoubtedly, this strategy was very much shaped by the decline of legislative supremacy as a governing principle, the South's effective use of local option, and the Anti-Saloon League's quest for a goal which could unite church leaders and other moderates. Clearly, it would have been much more difficult to apply local gradualism if the courts had not been amenable to the states' comprehensive devolution of licensing authority toward localities and if the Protestant churches and "damp" individuals had not witnessed the South's local option successes. However, even after the state judiciary had abandoned legislative supremacy and leading moderates had embraced local option as an initial goal, many radical prohibitionists remained wedded to statewide prohibition as their initial aim. Significantly, it was only after the ASL recognized the potential for a locally based strategy that the movement began to shift in this direction. Paradoxically, the drys who expected the least from their followers would win the biggest prize: a national constitutional amendment.

Of course, once prohibition was placed in the U.S. Constitution in early 1919, the movement had realized its primary long-term goal. After 1919 dry leaders struggled with the problem of "goal succession," whereby the "attainment of organizational objectives generates a strain toward finding new objectives."[1] Torn between two aims—education and enhancing law enforcement—the league ultimately chose enforcement. Enforcement was intrinsically problematic, for it shifted the ASL's focus away from the destruction of a sordid industry and toward the regulation of personal behavior, an aspect of prohibition that it had downplayed in its quest for moderate support. Moreover, as chapter 3 demonstrated, anti-liquor activists had historically found enforcement to be a troublesome objective which involved them in personally fought local battles that generated short-lived victories or counterproductive defeats. Instead of demanding centralized enforcement by the national government, the ASL included a "concurrent powers enforcement" clause in the Eighteenth Amendment to placate its southern congressional allies. This clause divided enforcement responsibility between the state and national governments, as did the amendment's enabling legislation, the Volstead Act. Under this measure, the states would bear the brunt of enforcement while federal agents would only intervene in areas that refused to enforce prohibition. In the end, this enforcement regime gave little coherence to an already challenging goal.[2]

The ASL was aware of the need for more centralized enforcement efforts than had been pursued during the nineteenth century. After 1910 it had increasingly advocated state-level enforcement regimes. In some states, league affiliates demanded "ouster" laws, which granted state officials the power to discharge negligent police officers. In others, the Progressive Era drys either obtained new state offices designed to address their concerns, or co-opted existing agencies such as state food and drug departments. Lastly, the ASL sometimes fought for state constabularies that would both investigate general criminal matters and enforce liquor laws. All told, these campaigns resulted in at least thirty state-level enforcement mechanisms in nineteen states before 1919, and to several more after national prohibition was enacted.[3]

Throughout the 1920s, however, the federal Prohibition Bureau and most of its state-level counterparts remained underfunded. Unwilling to acknowledge the extent of illicit liquor sales, dry leaders and legislators generally failed to secure the resources these agencies needed. As in the nineteenth century, enforcement remained largely a local affair, and violations were soon rampant in big cities. In addition, periodic crackdowns sparked violence, and despite their pressure the drys often found that the local police avoided the crossfire between those who favored prohibition and those who did not. Not surprisingly, grassroots public support for the ASL eroded as the group could not neutralize the growing backlash against the Eighteenth Amendment. Naturally, the Great Depression and the wholesale triumph of a wet Democratic party in 1932 accelerated repeal, but most scholars agree that the drys were mortally wounded by their close association with unpopular enforcement drives.[4]

In a way, then, the adoption of the Twenty-First Amendment underscored the fragility of local gradualism. The strategy had helped the league to identify prohibition with the advance of civilization, as local anti-liquor victories led to greater triumphs and eventually to a dry nation. As success produced further success, activists predicted that prohibition would generate an "amazing economic and moral transformation" in the nation. Moreover, this piecemeal approach meant that prohibition was a "work in progress" for many years, thus allowing the ASL to evade difficult questions about enforcement. Once national prohibition became a reality, however, the league could hardly claim that it had reduced urban crime and disorder, issues of concern to its middle-class sympathizers. Furthermore, prohibition relinquished its progressive image after the middle class developed a new appreciation for social drinking and the ASL's efforts were increasingly linked to the Ku Klux Klan and its bigotry. Perceived as narrow-minded and passé, prohibitionists lost the support of many middle-class women, some of whom joined the Women's Organization for National Prohibition Reform, and businessmen, some of whom joined the Association against the Prohibition Amendment. Confronted with declining support and organizations representing respectable opponents for the first time, the league was in no position to stop the repeal juggernaut after the Great Depression struck.[5]

Nevertheless, the enactment of the Twenty-First Amendment should not obscure the extraordinary achievements of the prohibitionists during the Progressive Era. In terms of tangible benefits, they secured a national constitutional amendment, as well as state prohibition in thirty states. In the process, they destroyed a powerful and wealthy cluster of industries, an unusual feat in a nation that has long valued free enterprise and property rights. But the Anti-Saloon League also proved that locally based efforts do not always fragment a movement, and that federalism need not dissipate the potential for protest. Instead, anti-liquor activists exploited this feature of the American state to construct a truly nationwide movement. No city or state escaped their agitation, and reformers even ventured into wet strongholds like New York and Chicago. Furthermore, the ASL succeeded in transforming a radical, exclusive crusade into a more moderate, inclusive social movement. Indeed, this group seemed to temporarily reverse Jane Mansbridge's "iron law of involution," which holds that movements organized according to ideological incentives tend to turn "inward," rather than "outward" toward accommodation and reform.

While the drys' accomplishments were surely impressive, it should be pointed out that the key to their success—local gradualism—has also been used, albeit less thoroughly, by other American social movements. Though it might make more sense to compare the prohibitionists with other Progressive Era reformers, to do so would imply that local gradualism is an antiquated strategy which could only be pursued in a particular historical epoch. One could make that case. A recent book by Nina Eliasoph, for example, suggests that locally oriented voluntary societies in the late twentieth century are often so parochial that they fail to connect their efforts with broader political concerns. Indeed, the notion that local agitation could produce the necessary momentum for a national movement seems incongruous in her version of contemporary America, where community-spirited citizens often avoid politics and "big" problems, thus limiting their contributions to the common good.[6] While Eliasoph's observations are perceptive, she presents no evidence that there has been a recent historical shift in the political inclinations of American voluntary groups, which have always included organizations that eschewed politics.

In any case, as a consciously political strategy local gradualism has only prospered in social movements which already possess an ambitious agenda for the nation as a whole, and those have appeared in every American epoch. To illustrate, the first part of this chapter will assess the use of this political strategy by the civil rights movement and the Christian Right. The second part considers how local gradualism might be applied by one movement that has not used this strategy, namely the environmental movement. Finally, the chapter speculates about the origins of movement moderation.

The Use of Local Gradualism by Contemporary Social Movements

As discussed in chapters 2–4, locally based agitation only escapes parochialism after grassroots activists have (1) developed a translocal mass organization to sustain and diffuse their efforts; (2) adopted modular forms of collective action; and (3) cultivated generic local outlets for activist energy. In addition, chapters 6 and 7 imply that locally based activism will only mobilize new support for its cause if it is framed as a moderate endeavor. Finally, chapter 5 indicates that the ability to leverage public support into tangible benefits from the state and national governments may depend on the movement's situation vis-à-vis the party system, and the character of party competition. Under favorable political circumstances a challenging group may then parlay its initial accomplishments into further ones.

The Anti-Saloon League had inherited some of the requisites for local gradualism. For example, the league's petitioning and other pressure tactics had been developed by earlier temperance advocates. Likewise, the Progressive Era drys typically retained their predecessors' alliances with the northern Republicans and southern Democrats to good effect, given the prevalence of intraparty competition during the period. Most importantly, the ASL profited greatly from both the comprehensive devolution of state liquor licensing power to the localities and the judiciary's acceptance of this process. These long-term developments provided the movement with a set of relatively homogeneous outlets for local activism, enabling the ASL to conduct analogous grassroots campaigns across the nation without fear of judicial reprisal.

Still, the initial application of local gradualism was hardly trouble free. For one thing, the league first had to build a translocal network of individual Protestant congregations that would supply the organization with steady grassroots support. In addition, the ASL had to wrest leadership control from the radical drys before it could reframe the anti-liquor movement as a moderate one acceptable to a variety of sympathizers. As local campaigns bore fruit, the league also had to finesse the transition from local activism to efforts at the state and national levels. Otherwise, the group might have alienated its moderate adherents and slowed the momentum toward national prohibition.

Like the anti-drink reformers, the civil rights movement and the Christian Right were both blessed with advantages and burdened with disadvantages in their uses of local activism. In analyzing these two challenging groups, the following sections will discuss how they managed to build broad-based, powerful movements on the foundation of parochial efforts.

The Southern Phase of the Civil Rights Movement (1955–1965)

Whereas the twentieth-century drys had envisioned their local campaigns as stepping-stones to the state and national levels, civil rights activists eschewed negotiations with the segregationist state legislatures and instead focused on the national government during the years 1955–65. Whether initiating bus boycotts, sit-ins, jail-ins, Freedom Rides, voter registration drives, or community-led protests, black insurgents used local and regional action to secure favorable responses from the federal courts, the executive branch, and Congress that would dismantle racial apartheid in the South. Nonetheless, most of these campaigns also sought modest, parochial goals, whose achievement would allow the movement to claim some progress toward racial equality. Moreover, the civil rights movement's reliance on locally based activism broadened its base of support and won over racial moderates to its long-term objectives.

Until it sponsored its first locally based campaigns in 1955–56, the civil rights movement was narrowly grounded in the black middle class and could not secure significant tangible benefits from the executive branch and Congress.[7] While the legal arm of the National Association for the Advancement of Colored People (NAACP) could justly celebrate the Supreme Court's landmark decision in *Brown v. Board of Education* (1954), Gerald Rosenberg has convincingly shown that before 1964, the federal courts had a minimal independent effect on both the desegregation of southern public schools and the mass mobilization of the civil rights movement.[8] Instead, scholars have traced the most visible campaigns of the black insurgency's early years—the bus boycotts in Montgomery and other southern cities—to a local boycott in Baton Rouge, Louisiana, in 1953.[9]

Like the Progressive Era drys, the organizers of the Baton Rouge and Montgomery boycotts initially had a very modest aim. Rather than demand the repeal of bus segregation laws, local activists merely requested that white officials establish the principle of "first come, first served" segregated seating. Under this arrangement, "white passengers took seats from the front of the bus towards the rear, while blacks seated themselves from the back towards the front. It eliminated the more objectionable features of bus segregation: the need for blacks having to surrender their places to whites, or being compelled to stand while reserved 'white' seats remained empty."[10]

This limited objective was especially appealing at the outset, for many black southerners "harbored reservations, ranging from mild uneasiness to outright opposition, about the use of direct action to change the law." It also seemed more practical; after all, other city governments had already authorized "first come, first served" bus policies. As it turned out, such calculations proved accurate in Baton Rouge, where city authorities surrendered to this reasonable demand in seven days. In Montgomery, however, local officials stonewalled, and boycott leaders like Martin Luther King Jr. experienced intimidation and bombings. As they fought to keep the boycott afloat during 1956, the Montgomery protesters therefore upped their demand to outright bus desegregation, an objective that would ultimately be secured later that year by a federal court decision, *Browder v. Gayle*.[11]

For many participants, the victory in Montgomery transformed the struggle. King, for one, was struck by how the campaign had united the city's black community—regardless of class—in a common mission.[12] In addition, he saw it as the beginning of a large-scale crusade in which the everyday action of black people could be a powerful tool for social change. For example, he spoke of integrating all the southern buses before 1960, and hoped that similar local changes could be won through interracial negotiations rather than court cases.[13] Finally, the Montgomery boycott increased the political saliency of the civil rights issue,[14] and even the lethargic Eisenhower administration began to take note, as electoral considerations prompted "scattered voices within the administration" to push for legislation in 1956 which would allow Eisenhower to assume "a stronger official identification with the integration cause." Eisenhower captured an estimated 40 percent of the black vote in 1956, which suggested that the black vote was "a more volatile political commodity than it had heretofore been."[15]

In short, the Montgomery campaign had demonstrated the potential of a locally based political strategy. Like the prohibitionists who exploited local option, advocates of the boycott had initially embraced a modest goal, which had allowed them to create an inclusive movement. Furthermore, the protest had contributed to a "revolutionary change in the Negro's evaluation of himself," as southern blacks acquired greater political confidence. More importantly, the boycott's impact on the Eisenhower administration had underscored the role of a competitive party system in converting local gains into policy initiatives at a higher level of the federal structure. Significantly, the veterans of this effort recognized that the time was ripe for mass action "to maintain the psychological momentum Montgomery had generated." Bayard Rustin, for instance, argued that "the movement needed a sustaining mechanism that could translate what we had learned during the bus boycott into a broad strategy for protest in the South."[16]

Despite the Montgomery boycott's success, though, civil rights activists generally struggled to broaden their crusade during the late 1950s. This effort was not purely parochial; as Doug McAdam's research shows, the early civil rights movement grew out of indigenous organizations that supported three distinct communication networks: one that connected individual black churches, a second that united local NAACP affiliates, and a third that linked campus activists in various locales. In this particular case, black ministers used a church-based network to diffuse the Montgomery boycott strategy to colleagues in Tallahassee, Atlanta, New Orleans, Birmingham, Mobile, Chattanooga, Memphis, Savannah, and Rock Hill, South Carolina, among others.[17]

In most of these cities, however, activists did not sustain boycotts on the same scale as in Montgomery. For one thing, in the wake of Montgomery other local black leaders could rely on *Browder v. Gayle*. There was no need to construct a long, arduous boycott if black groups could desegregate the buses by suing in court. Hence, many of the "boycotts" that followed Montgomery "were little more than one-day protests designed to provoke the necessary arrests on which to base a legal challenge after the precedent of *Browder v. Gale*." Elsewhere, in cities which ignored the decision, other boycotts fizzled because the climate was too repressive, or because local civil rights crusades lacked strong leadership and effective coordination. As one activist in Birmingham recalled, "We tried . . . to take Montgomery to Birmingham and fell flat on our faces because Montgomery was not exportable."[18]

In the long run, *Browder v. Gale* may have helped the civil rights movement to secure the desegregation of public transportation. On the other hand, the federal courts may have deprived the movement of a generic local outlet for activism in cities where collective action was sustainable. In either case, the organization that emerged from the Montgomery campaign—the Southern Christian Leadership Conference

(SCLC)—was hard pressed to find a new goal as galvanizing as bus desegregation, and its voter registration drives of the late 1950s did not stimulate the grassroots interest in the movement that was intended by King.[19] Consequently, the SCLC failed to initiate any new direct action campaigns, and the number of civil rights demonstrations reported by the *New York Times* plummeted from 173 in 1956 to 10 in 1959.[20]

Conversely, the civil rights movement only reignited in 1960, when activists located new local targets for desegregation protests. Its successive waves of sit-ins, jail-ins, Freedom Rides, and community-led campaigns in the years 1960–65 exploited the movement's discovery that lunch counters, railroad stations, bus terminals, courthouses, and assorted local businesses were vulnerable to its protests. Though varied, such segregated facilities provided the black insurgency with relatively homogeneous outlets for local agitation. Moreover, their prevalence across the South allowed activists to use similar nonviolent protest techniques to advocate the same moderate initial goal (racial integration). During the early 1960s several locally based protests obtained minor concessions from municipal authorities and businessmen which first cracked the walls of local segregation. In Savannah, for instance, activists secured a desegregation plan covering hotels, motels, theaters, and bowling alleys after a series of protests in July 1963.[21]

Of course, many of these local campaigns were also designed to provoke repressive responses that dramatized the white South's intransigence to a broader national audience, including federal officials. In Birmingham (1963) and Selma (1965), for example, the civil rights movement successfully exploited supremacist actions to secure the intervention of the Kennedy and Johnson administrations in support of black interests.[22] However, most local protests did not involve federal intervention, nor did they play to a mass audience. Instead, they helped to expand the movement's base, and convinced federal authorities that civil rights activism was a large-scale phenomenon. For instance, after the relatively parochial Montgomery boycott, the movement's Washington Pilgrimage attracted only 27,000 protesters in 1957.[23] In contrast, the successful Birmingham campaign was followed by more than one thousand local protests that generated more than twenty thousand arrests during the summer of 1963 alone, when organizers of the March on Washington in August amassed over 300,000 participants. The Kennedy administration regarded this growth of widespread direct action as a "dangerous and disturbing development," and its civil rights bill in 1963 was partly intended to get blacks off the streets.[24]

In short, challenging segregated facilities at the local level enabled the civil rights movement to sustain a vibrant grassroots component. At their best, as in Birmingham and Selma, local campaigns not only made parochial gains but also played upon the tight interparty competition for black votes to secure such federal initiatives as the Civil Rights Act of 1964 and the Voting Rights Act of 1965. But even when the black insurgency failed to translate its locally based campaigns directly into nationally significant results, these actions helped to build a broad-based movement that spanned the South. By shifting its activities to the North after 1965, though, the movement lost its opportunities for local agitation, as well as its organizational base in the South's black churches and colleges. Thus, it fragmented just when it was deprived of a shared moderate goal, desegregation, that had involved homogeneous outlets for local activism. In the end, "insurgents found it increasingly difficult to organize strong, focused campaigns," and the civil rights movement divided into "a veritable profusion of small groups addressing a wide range of issues by means of an equally wide range of tactics."[25]

The Christian Right: A New Case of Local Gradualism

While the civil rights movement grew out of locally based protests like the Montgomery bus boycott, the early Christian Right emerged in the late 1970s as a coalition of Washington-based groups whose primary mission was to lobby Congress on behalf of "traditional values." At the time, Congress seemed to be the appropriate arena for action because it was the most permeable national institution, and because the groups viewed the federal level as the best place to resolve issues like abortion, school prayer, and tuition tax credits.[26] Some locally based activism by conservative Christians did occur; for instance, ad hoc Christian Right groups sponsored campaigns against gay rights and ratification of the Equal Rights Amendment during the 1970s.[27] However, the temporary character of their sponsoring organizations allowed the national groups—the Moral Majority, the National Christian Action Coalition, the Religious Roundtable, and Christian Voice—to take center stage.

During the early 1980s these groups "quickly and effectively placed their concerns on the public and congressional agendas, obtaining action on issues that had laid dormant for years." By the late 1980s, though, all four major Christian Right organizations had either closed up shop or become moribund. Narrowly rooted in the fundamentalist camp, these groups had failed to reach out to other conservative Protestants from the evangelical and Pentecostal traditions. Likewise, the Christian Right's first direct foray into presidential politics—Pat Robertson's campaign for the Republican nomination in 1988—ultimately demonstrated the limited appeal of a candidacy based in the Pentecostal churches. While it "raised $41 million for the campaign, won victories in a number of caucus states . . . , and galvanized a new corps of evangelical activists," Robertson's effort never united the greater evangelical community in his behalf.[28]

Furthermore, such nationally oriented activism had done little to draw the American public at large into the early Christian Right. Survey research showed that the movement's flagship organization, the Moral Majority, appealed to only a small and unrepresentative segment of the population, and that even sympathetic citizens tended to disagree with this group's stances on many issues. Meanwhile, Robertson's campaign sputtered as the action shifted from caucuses to primaries. His well-organized network of conservative Christians might have challenged party regulars in the relatively intimate caucus rooms, but Robertson fared poorly in primary elections, which involve a larger share of the electorate. Regardless of whether it was responding to the Moral Majority's agitation or to Robertson's campaign, the general public viewed the early Christian Right negatively as a band of conformist zealots at odds with a diverse citizenry.[29]

Finally, the early Christian Right's problems stemmed from its attempt to build a social movement through direct-mail solicitations on nationally prominent issues, like abortion and aid to the "contras" in Nicaragua. "Members" of the Moral Majority and other conservative Christian organizations were often one-time contributors rather than committed activists, and movement leaders found it difficult to sustain their long-term interest in the national movement. As one activist recalled, "One of our weaknesses has been that it was hard to sustain grassroots coalitions around national issues. In other words, we suffered from trying to keep local people focused on national issues. . . . What the movement had to do, it has begun to do: build local coalitions around local issues."[30]

Ultimately, Pat Robertson's failed presidential bid in 1988 stimulated the development of a locally based Christian Right movement. After his failure to secure the Republican nomination, Robertson used his huge mailing lists to form the Christian Coalition and turned its operations over to Ralph Reed, a former director of a national GOP student committee. Reed and his leadership team rebuilt the organization from the bottom up, with activists much more involved in local issues. In doing so, the coalition's leaders identified several generic local outlets for activism: elections for local school boards and city councils, campaigns against pornography and gay rights, and contests for control of local GOP committees. Through such activities, the Christian Coalition hoped to develop grassroots leaders and build local bases. At the same time, the organization sought to soften the Christian Right's extremist image by championing mainstream issues like deregulation and welfare reform. Finally, movement leaders reached out to traditionalist Catholics, orthodox Jews, and black churches in an effort to expand the movement's base.[31]

In the short run, the Christian Right's use of local gradualism produced a robust grassroots sector which contributed to some initial successes. At its peak in 1995, the Christian Coalition alone[32] claimed forty-eight state units, fourteen hundred local chapters, 1.5 million active supporters, and an annual budget of $25 million. In addition, the group's infiltration of local GOP committees apparently paid off. One-fourth of the delegates at the Republican National Convention in 1992 described themselves as "members" or "supporters" of the Christian Right; and the magazine *Campaigns and Elections* reported in 1994 that the movement completely dominated eighteen state Republican parties and considerably influenced thirteen others. More importantly, the movement's ability to mobilize its followers through its voter guides has led some scholars to describe it as an "electoral powerhouse." In fact, its significant role in the GOP's takeover of Congress in 1994 encouraged some to declare that the elections in that year "marked evangelical Protestantism's arrival as a force in national politics."[33]

Nevertheless, the Christian Right's long-term prospects do not look as rosy. In particular, its capacity to win tangible benefits from the national government may be limited by its position as a coalitional insider within the Republican party that is most unlikely to defect. In a way, the movement's situation mirrors that of the northern drys just before the Prohibition party's emergence as a credible electoral alternative in the late 1870s. During those years, GOP élites neglected their dry constituents for the sake of party unity and electoral victory, and movement leaders could hardly affiliate with the hopelessly wet Democrats. In the case of the Christian Right, the GOP's leaders have similarly sought to prevent the movement from dictating the party's legislative agenda and thus alienating mainstream American voters. As a result, radical Christian Right activists have already lashed out against party leaders for their compromises with the "anti-family" elements in the party. It is unlikely, however, that conservative Protestants will desert the GOP for a Democratic party that has embraced feminist, gay, and civil libertarian constituencies.[34]

Still, with the decline of political parties and the rise of candidate-centered politics in the twentieth century, the Christian Right has been able to profoundly alter the Republican party's character by "recruiting candidates, providing campaign resources to them, and directly mobilizing voters on their behalf." GOP candidates for state and national office often cannot avoid addressing the movement's agenda, and many accommodate its demands in some fashion. At this point, though, the Christian Right's internal candidate recruitment efforts have been far from successful. Its preferred candidates "are usually energetic proponents of the movement's core agenda and are often more conservative than other movement activists. In addition, they frequently lack other credentials, such as previous government service and a well-developed agenda on the full range of issues of concern to voters. . . . These are also the candidates that give the movement's opponents the best targets for criticism. . . . The stereotype of the 'extremist' religious candidate has some factual basis."[35] This quote underscores yet another danger: if the Christian Right proves unable to moderate its image, it will fail to broaden its core base of support.

Even so, the Christian Right's local gradualism has produced a much stronger movement than its earlier "inside-the-Beltway" strategy. Significantly, the movement's focus on local issues has allowed it to survive an unsympathetic White House, as well as the national media's premature forecasts of its decline. For instance, some analysts blamed the Christian Right for George Bush's defeat in 1992 and predicted the movement's subsequent eclipse, only to be confounded by its major role in the GOP's unexpected congressional triumph two years later.[36] Moreover, some local movement trends may address the chronic problem of inclusivity. By pursuing "biblical racial reconciliation," for example, local evangelical churches may develop a new reputation for racial justice. Among other things, white evangelicals have participated in multiracial pulpit exchanges, church socials, religious conferences, and revivals to overcome race problems.[37] Such attempts to address racial divisions at the local level may increase the movement's support among black evangelicals. Regardless of whether they succeed in that monumental task, though, conservative Christians will surely remain a considerable force in the state and national political arenas for the foreseeable future.

The Environmental Movement: A Candidate for Local Gradualism?

Unlike the other movements discussed in this chapter, the national environmental movement has failed to systematically harness the energy of grassroots activists. Instead, its structure is bifurcated: national organizations such as the Sierra Club, the National Wildlife Federation, and Friends of the Earth lobby Congress in Washington and rely largely on passive financial contributors to sustain their efforts,[38] while at the grassroots level thousands of committed local activists generally work through state and local government. Significantly, cooperation between the movement's two layers is minimal, and local greens fault their national colleagues on a number of grounds. Some castigate the national environmentalists for being professional Washington insiders; as one local activist has said, "[National] environmentalists have found themselves in the position of knowing how bad things are" but "are only capable of making a deal." Meanwhile, local greens often complain that the mainstream movement is "almost obsessively oriented toward wilderness, public land, and natural resources management" to the neglect of environmental justice and other community-based health concerns. Lastly, grassroots activists characterize the national movement as an elitist "white men's club" which often fails to share power, credit, and resources.[39]

Despite their criticism of the mainstream, local activists appreciate the national groups' history of legislative success and their impressive capacity to lobby Congress for new federal initiatives during the years 1970–80. Among other things, these organizations contributed to the enactment of the Clean Air Act of 1970, the Marine

Protection Act (1972), the Endangered Species Act (1973), the Toxic Substances Control Act (1976), the Clean Water Act (1977), and the Comprehensive Environmental Response Compensation and Liability Act, or "Superfund" (1980). In the process, the national greens earned the respect of the Washington community for their ability to counter business interests with their legal and technical expertise on behalf of complex environmental policies.[40] Since 1980, however, these groups have generally been on the defensive and have only participated in one major advance in federal environmental legislation: the 1990 amendments to the Clean Air Act.[41]

Frustrated by recent developments, some greens have declared that American environmentalism is a "movement courting irrelevance." Though tinged by their own disdain for the national groups, these activists are partly correct in their assessment of mainstream environmentalism.[42] Beginning in 1990, several national environmental groups began to run deficits, and organizations like the Sierra Club, the Wilderness Society, Greenpeace USA, and the Audubon Society lost paid memberships.[43] While these declines partly reversed with the congressional Republicans' assault on environmental programs, the public remains deeply pessimistic about the government's capacity to solve rather than create social problems. Furthermore, environmental advocates face recurrent challenges from those concerned about the economic costs of environmental policies.[44] In particular, businesses, loggers, ranchers, and farmers have thwarted many environmental initiatives during the past decade and recently gained an ally in Gale Norton, interior secretary in George W. Bush's administration.[45]

More optimistically, many observers predict that the environmental movement's future lies at the grassroots, the level where thousands of community groups formed after 1970; this sort of activism exploded after the Love Canal Homeowners Association's successful campaign in 1978–80 to secure compensation for a contaminated neighborhood in Niagara Falls, New York. About ten thousand local groups participate in national networks like the Citizens' Clearinghouse for Hazardous Wastes, and some greens have suggested that the environmental movement should cultivate "direct action at the local level" so as to reverse its declining fortunes.[46] Could an emphasis on local gradualism reinvigorate the environmental movement?

It is true that local environmental conflicts have succeeded in galvanizing constituencies that rarely engaged in green politics before 1980, such as African Americans, Native Americans, Latinos, and working-class women. Demanding "environmental justice," these newly mobilized activists seek to organize poor and vulnerable communities that bear a disproportionate share of the country's environmental problems.[47] If their locally based groups could work with the national organizations, perhaps American environmentalism could become a unified, broad-based crusade that blends passion with expertise, agitation with lobbying, and justice claims with concerns in such traditional environmental areas as the wilderness and wildlife.

At this point, though, it seems rather unlikely that the movement's grassroots sector will adopt local gradualism as a long-term strategy. To begin with, local greens have shown little interest in large-scale collective action. Instead of identifying generic local outlets for activist energy, the movement has engaged in particularistic conflicts concerning hazardous waste incinerators, economic development projects, specific wetlands, mountains, forests, reservations, and so forth.[48] One scholar's attempt to analyze such conflicts was thwarted because the groups involved are "so ephemeral and so informally organized that it was almost impossible to find contact people or to study them over time."[49]

Moreover, even environmental networks which seek to disseminate locally based methods have failed to systematically cultivate targets that can be pursued in most localities. For example, environmentalists often point to organizations like the Citizens' Clearinghouse for Hazardous Wastes (CCHW) and the National Coalition Against Misuse of Pesticides (NCAMP), which aid local greens in their fights with polluters. Such groups offer advice, leadership training, and technical assistance to grassroots activists, while also advocating legislation to enhance local influence over policymaking. However, these loose networks do not provoke environmental conflicts in communities where local agitation does not already exist. Rather, such conflicts typically surface first locally and only later percolate up to groups like CCHW and NCAMP. Consequently, "not every community confronting an environmental threat engages in conflict," and citizens may tolerate long-standing environmental problems for years without engaging in collective action. People living near Yellow Creek, Kentucky, for instance, had endured decades of visible, nauseating pollution before mobilizing against it in the early 1980s. Likewise, communities without significant environmental threats may never develop a viable grassroots movement, given the greens' general failure to export environmental conflicts.[50]

At best, locally based greens have managed to construct regional networks to battle regional foes, even while failing to establish a truly national movement on the same basis. For instance, to stem the tide of nuclear power, local environmental and public interest groups with access to the initiative and referendum formed the Western Bloc in 1974. Together, this loose coalition of organizations based in the western United States[51] coordinated signature collection efforts, shared expertise, and managed to place antinuclear initiatives on the ballot in eight states during 1976. Elsewhere, however, local opposition to nuclear energy remained primarily plant specific. In New Hampshire, for instance, after antinuclear activists exhausted all possible legal channels to halt construction on the Seabrook Nuclear Power Plant, they formed the Clamshell Alliance in 1976 to use nonviolent civil disobedience as their primary tactic. As the Northeast's version of the Western Bloc, the alliance "was to function as a facilitator to bring grassroots groups in the region together and pool their information, resources, and energies in halting Seabrook."[52] But the Clamshell Alliance remained a fairly parochial affair, and the only assistance that the members of the short-lived Western Bloc offered to their eastern colleagues was advice about how to acquire the initiative for their own use.[53]

But even if the greens tried to unite their fragmented grassroots, the movement's very understanding of "local activism" would probably not lead to true local gradualism. For other movements, this phrase has suggested piecemeal actions more modest than the sweeping initial goals advocated by purists. The Anti-Saloon League, for example, held that one virtue of local activism was its moderate character, which would increase the appeal of the prohibition movement among "damp" reformers. Even southern civil rights activists' use of dramatic direct action focused on minor targets (segregated local facilities) and was consciously nonviolent, testimony to its moderation. Martin Luther King Jr., for one, periodically contrasted the Southern Christian Leadership Conference's "reasonable demands" with those of the Black Muslims, whose extremism threatened a "frightening racial nightmare."[54]

Furthermore, local gradualists have generally acknowledged that their locally based actions would only produce minor tangible benefits. A "no-license" outcome to a local option contest was undoubtedly a victory for the prohibitionists, as was the desegregation of a local business for the civil rights movement and the capture of a local GOP committee for the Christian Right. Nevertheless, their leaders clearly recognized that over time, such small triumphs had to translate into more substantial gains at the state and national levels of government for them to have much impact. For instance, the ASL initially advocated local option "to secure as large a prohibition zone as possible," only to later insist that it be "relegated to the rear" to make way for state and national prohibition.[55] Similarly, the Christian Right's efforts to dominate local GOP organizations are attempts to give it leverage over the party's committees, nominations, and platforms at the state and national levels.[56]

In contrast, grassroots environmentalists often claim that local activism, in and of itself, can fundamentally transform existing political, economic, and social relations. As two greens have argued, "grassroots environmental organizations constitute a social force with the potential to alter significantly the structures of our basic social institutions. For the greater the public participation in decisions that have environmental consequences, the closer we move to the ideal of democracy but the further we move from the dictates of private ownership. And private ownership is the foundation of the capitalistic economic institution."[57] Partly informed by the ideals of the New Left, this emphasis on local activism as a vehicle for radical transformation may simply marginalize this sector of the movement. The dangers of such an approach become apparent when one takes a closer look at grassroots environmentalism.

Like radical feminists, peace activists, and others steeped in the philosophy of the American New Left of the 1960s, many local greens privilege egalitarian organizational structures over hierarchy, consensual decision making over majority rule, and direct action over lobbying. In their view, a tame, bureaucratic movement is less desirable than a confrontational, participatory one that will (theoretically) empower individuals and build a strong movement base. While not every grassroots environmental organization embodies these values,[58] a substantial number of local greens practice as much internal democracy as is practicable in their groups, and initiate disruptive protest far more than their national colleagues.[59] Likewise, even local environmental groups that rely little on New Left principles have sometimes demonstrated strong preferences for decentralization. In a study by Paul Lichterman, for example, two local groups opposed to toxic pollution proved willing to affiliate with a regional organization, but preferred that the organization function merely as a "resource center" which disseminated information.

By advocating specific organizational arrangements and tactics as integral to local environmentalism, though, some activists may only isolate themselves from others who do not share their enthusiasm for decentralized structures or direct action. In the Boston area, for instance, little cooperation occurs between traditional environmental groups and their New Left–inspired counterparts, a division that reflects tensions over tactics and organizational methods. Meanwhile, though the two organizations in Lichterman's study accepted technical, logistical, and monetary support from Greenpeace and the Sierra Club, they were uncomfortable with the national groups' operating styles and never forged true partnerships with them. In one case, the group maintained its distance out of fear that its "affinity-group feeling and highly participatory format" would be replaced with a "more bureaucratic organization of officers and standing committees."[60]

In similar fashion, local greens may exacerbate tensions within the broader movement by embracing "identity politics." Most prevalent within groups consciously committed to multiculturalism, this approach rests on the premise that racism, sexism, poverty, and environmental degradation are inseparable issues. Hence, greens must avoid reproducing social hierarchies in their organizations, and they should be responsive to the unique position of minorities, women, and the poor in both the movement and the world. At first glance, such an argument would seem uncontroversial within the environmental movement, which possesses solid progressive credentials. In reality, though, greens operating under the mantle of "identity politics" have not flinched from publicly charging their white, middle-class colleagues with elitism and a failure to address the concerns of "people of color."

In 1990, for example, two local green groups sent letters to the Wilderness Society, Friends of the Earth, the Sierra Club, and other mainstream organizations, accusing them of "racist hiring practices." Meanwhile, at a gathering of environmentalists in 1993, one Native American activist addressed her mostly white audience in this manner:

> You can't imagine the pain your society creates by breaking up our connections to our land and our community. Grand Coulee Dam flooded the land of our ancestors, and we were "relocated." Our children were taken away to be educated at residential schools, and they returned without any sense of community. They didn't know how to relate to each other, or to plants and animals in a loving way. *Your* disconnections with *your* community ruins ours. I'm happy to be here with you, but mostly I feel grief for you.[61]

Such criticisms of the national environmental organizations are not entirely unfounded; after all, studies have long shown that these groups are typically led by white males, and that their memberships are "drawn disproportionately from the college-educated, higher-income segments of society."[62] However, as local greens themselves admit, "few people enjoy being labeled racists," and some of their mainstream colleagues took umbrage at their accusations. Worse yet, those national groups which responded constructively to such complaints seem unable to please their grassroots critics, who believe that the nationals' efforts to diversify their staffs are proceeding too slowly, smack of tokenism, and too often involve raiding talent from the local movement. Grassroots environmentalists likewise grumble when their national counterparts circulate grant proposals to foundations seeking funds for diversity initiatives and "environmental justice" projects. Such resources, they argue, would be better spent locally, where "organizations continue to struggle over every penny and every dollar."[63]

Along with the local movement's advocacy of participatory democracy and direct action, its focus on "identity politics" has created high, even unrealistic, standards for activism. As a result, grassroots environmentalism may never be as inclusive as its adherents hope. The most common form of movement purity found among the local greens, though, involves their unwillingness to compromise, which most see as a virtue. Significantly, their criticism of national environmentalists often reflects their militancy. For example, Mark Dowie offers the following assessment of the national greens' effectiveness:

> During [the 1980s], when environmental conditions and political circumstances called for tougher, more confrontational tactics, most of the mainstream organizations lost the momentum they had developed in previous de-

> cades. In a desperate drive to win respectability and access in Washington, mainstream leaders politely pursued a course of accommodation and capitulation with elected officials, regulators, and polluters. Compromise, which had produced some limited gains for the movement in the 1970s, in the 1980s became the habitual response of the environmental establishment.[64]

In contrast, observers often depict grassroots environmentalists as tough negotiators who refuse to barter away the public good.[65] Unfortunately, by adopting an anti-compromise approach to environmental issues, local greens have simply erected yet another barrier to participation in their activities.

Ultimately, the grassroots sector appears to devote more energy to distinguishing itself from the "corrupt" national organizations than it does to building bridges to them. That is too bad, for a recent analysis of local environmental conflicts suggests that local efforts "are most enduring and effective when there are powerful alliances between local grassroots groups and regional or national organizations." This study also argues that autonomous local greens are "fighting a battle that is becoming less relevant to the very outcomes [they] desire" and should abandon the idea that "they can act locally in sustainable ways" to defeat "extralocal powers and interests." If anything, this analysis concludes that "doing good is more important over the short and long run than feeling good," a piece of advice that local greens might well take to heart.[66]

Unfortunately, local environmentalists do not seem to have a long-term strategy that allows them to build on their parochial victories. While one can fault the grassroots greens for their principled rigidity, one can hardly blame them for their interest in local agitation. The American prohibition movement, the civil rights movement, and the Christian Right all profited from the energy of their mass bases by transforming it into tangible results. By adopting a strategy of local gradualism, they could exploit opportunities within the political system and win concessions from political élites.

Sources of Moderation?

That groups like those consisting of local greens often suffer from ideological exclusivity is not surprising; surely, that is so with many social movements. Perhaps what was more striking about the Anti-Saloon League was its ability to remain inclusive and moderate for over two decades, thus allowing it to lead a movement which temporarily evaded the "iron law of involution." But what was the source of the ASL's moderation? Jack Blocker contends that the prohibition movement's moderation after 1900 reflected a broader social trend, whereby the middle class abandoned revolutionary possibilities during the economic crisis of the 1890s. However, his explanation is premised on the notion that Prohibition party leaders, who flirted with radical challenges to capitalism before 1896, were representative of the postbellum movement.[67] As chapter 5 demonstrates, though, most postbellum drys never deserted the two major political parties, thus suggesting that the movement never truly embraced revolutionary aims.

Instead, I would argue that the ASL's moderation reflected its leaders' experience as members of the church establishment. Unlike the orthodox drys, who were drawn into politics from exclusive lodges, league leaders were typically clergymen and Protestant lay leaders who shared their churches' uneasiness with the radicals' leadership of the postbellum movement. Having witnessed the radicals' counterproductive efforts to demand ideological purity from the churches, league leaders sought to pursue a more inclusive tack, one which allowed the churches to simultaneously work for prohibition and secure salvation for its members. "If we were proposing a church league for temperance which . . . would lend its aid to some political party, or oppose some other party or parties," Howard H. Russell declared, "we should soon have confusion worse confounded, and the spirit of God would be driven out of our churches." Likewise, league founders drew upon their own knowledge of church preferences when they created a group that was an "open society without grip or password" which refused to impose a total abstinence pledge on its constituency.[68]

However, the ASL leadership's most instructive experience in the Protestant churches had to do with the growth of interdenominational cooperation during the late nineteenth century. As Russell recalled in 1913, "Forty years ago the churches were widely divided upon questions of doctrine and methods of work. . . . Twenty-five years ago the Evangelical Alliance called delegates of the churches together at Washington for a council upon co-operation in Christian work. A Pentecost was begun there which spread throughout the country, and the new God-sent spirit of toleration made possible our League for sobriety and against saloons." While greater interdenominational cooperation gave the ASL new opportunities to create an inclusive movement, it also served to reinforce its moderation. After all, if ASL leaders hoped to appeal to a broad range of religious groups (including Roman Catholics), they would have to seek goals—like local option—on which their allies could agree.[69]

Indeed, other social movements would do well to consider how inclusiveness and moderation can go hand in hand, a phenomenon that may be especially prevalent in movements which rely on diverse organizations accustomed to seeking common ground. In particular, the ecumenical movement, which institutionalized the endeavors of religious denominations to maximize their similarities, may be an especially fertile source of ideas. For example, during the civil rights movement's quest to forge strong ties with white mainline churches and their ecumenical groups, it emphasized moderate goals (integration and voting rights) and hence received their support. Meanwhile, Clyde Wilcox argues that the Christian Right "can attract its largest possible constituency by staking moderate positions on most issues." Significantly, he suggests that the movement's pragmatists, who emphasize interdenominational cooperation, are the most likely to win a large audience.[70]

In the end, though, most social movements cannot sustain moderation indefinitely. The ASL found no middle-of-the-road solution to the problem of enforcement; the civil rights movement splintered when the radical refrain of "Black Power" became common. More recently, the moderate Christian Coalition shed members and key leaders when its founder, Pat Robertson, proposed that conservative Christians abandon their extremist demands for Bill Clinton's impeachment and a total ban on abortions.[71] Mobilized by ideology, "true believers" are unlikely to sacrifice their beliefs for their movement's well-being. Finding the correct balance between compromise and orthodoxy will continue to haunt movements for years to come.

Notes

1 Political Strategy and Social Movement Outcomes

1 Mark Dowie, *Losing Ground: American Environmentalism at the Close of the Twentieth Century* (Cambridge: MIT Press, 1995), 76; Betty Zisk, *The Politics of Transformation: Local Activism in the Peace and Environmental Movements* (Westport, Conn.: Praeger, 1992), 44–45; Aileen S. Kraditor, *Means and Ends in American Abolitionism: Garrison and His Critics on Strategy and Tactics, 1834–1850* (New York: Vintage, 1970), 164.

2 John B. Finch, "What, Why, and How," in *The People versus the Liquor Traffic*, ed. Charles A. McNully (Milwaukee: Literature Committee, IOGT, 1887), 207; Daniel Dorchester, "An Argument for Constitutional Prohibition," in *The Constitutional Prohibitionist*, ed. J. N. Stearns (New York: National Temperance Society and Publishing House, 1889), 9; D. Leigh Colvin, *Prohibition in the United States* (New York: George H. Doran, 1926), 360–61.

3 See, e.g., Alphonso A. Hopkins in *Wealth and Waste: The Principles of Political Economy in their Application to the Present Problems of Labor, Law, and the Liquor Traffic* (New York: Funk and Wagnalls, 1895), 181–82.

4 F. A. Noble, "Waiting for Public Sentiment," *Union Signal*, 15 March 1883, 3.

5 The eighteen states that held constitutional prohibition referenda during the 1880s were Kansas, Iowa, Ohio, Maine, Rhode Island, Michigan, Texas, Tennessee, Oregon, West Virginia, New Hampshire, Massachusetts, Pennsylvania, South Dakota, North Dakota, Washington, Connecticut and Nebraska.

6 In 1883 Ohio's prohibition amendment received a majority of the yes and no votes cast, but not the majority of all the votes cast at the election as required by the Ohio constitution. (Throughout this book, the 1883 Ohio referendum will be considered a failure.) In 1884 Iowa drys had to settle for statutory prohibition because the state Supreme Court invalidated constitutional prohibition on technical grounds. In 1889 Rhode Island voters repealed their state's prohibition amendment just three years after its passage, and South Dakota voters adopted constitutional prohibition in 1889, only to demand its repeal in 1896.

7 New Hampshire's and Vermont's prohibition laws were both passed during the first wave of prohibition agitation (1851–55). Iowa's statutory prohibition law (1884) was effectively nullified in 1894 when the legislature enacted the Mulct Law, establishing a virtual system of licensing.

8 *Congressional Record*, 51st Congress, 1st Session, 107, 526, 8511.

9 L. Edwin Dudley, "The Law and Order Movement: Historical Sketch," *Lend-a-Hand*, March 1892, 200.

10 Ibid., 199. According to the Massachusetts dramshop act of 1875, it was illegal for liquor dealers to sell alcoholic beverages to habitual drunkards and children. For dramshop laws, see Perry R. Duis, *The Saloon: Public Drinking in Chicago and Boston, 1880–1920* (Urbana: University of Illinois Press, 1983), 97–99.

11 Dudley, "The Law and Order Movement," 201.

12 Ernest H. Cherrington, untitled speech, 1911, Ernest H. Cherrington series, Temperance and Prohibition Papers, Ohio Historical Society microfilm, reel 4.

13 The Mississippi Freedom Summer campaign of 1964 was a project sponsored by the Student Non-Violent Coordinating Committee which recruited over one thousand northern white young adults to assist civil rights activists in voter registration campaigns and Freedom Schools. Approximately three hundred additional individuals applied to the project, but for some reason failed to go to Mississippi. For the political differences between the participants and the no-shows, see Doug McAdam, *Freedom Summer* (New York: Oxford University Press, 1988), 186–98. For more on the radicalizing potential of social movements, see Sidney Tarrow, *Power in Movement: Social Movements, Collective Action and Politics*, 2d ed. (Cambridge: Cambridge University Press, 1998), 165–67.

14 Freedom Summer volunteers encountered numerous hostile incidents; four project workers were killed, four were critically wounded, and eighty were beaten. See McAdam, *Freedom Summer*, 96–101.

15 S. E. Nicholson, "The Local-Option Movement," *Annals of the American Academy of Political and Social Sciences* 32 (1908): 475. Though local referenda became increasingly common after the Civil War, the term "local option" refers specifically to local referenda on the liquor question.

16 Although Maine, Kansas, and North Dakota all had constitutional prohibition before 1900, drys in these states had to fend off attempts to repeal or dilute prohibition.

17 For this literature see J. Craig Jenkins, "Resource Mobilization Theory and the Study of Social Movements," *Annual Review of Sociology* 9 (1983): 543–44.

18 The ASL was obsessed with measuring the drys' achievement of tangible goals, and was famous for its maps indicating the dry territory in white and the wet territory in black. In addition, the ASL yearbooks charted other trends which demonstrated dry success, such as the percentage of population under prohibition and the number of dry cities, counties, and state capitals.

19 Similarly, in *The Politics of Transformation*, chapter 4, Zisk finds that organizations pursuing short-range, tangible, incremental goals were more likely to maintain stable or growing memberships than those seeking the transformation of social attitudes.

20 Bureaucratic organization as a key to success is emphasized prominently in William Gamson, *The Strategy of Social Protest* (Belmont, Calif.: Wadsworth, 1990), chapter 7. Although many scholars disagree with Gamson's conclusion, even the strongest advocate of decentralized movement organization would probably agree that movement organizations must be able to coordinate collective action to be effective. For the debate about movement organization, see Tarrow, *Power in Movement*, chapter 8.

21 John D. McCarthy and Mayer N. Zald, "Resource Mobilization and Social Movements: A Partial Theory," in their *Social Movements in an Organizational Society: Collected Essays* (New Brunswick, N.J.: Transaction, 1987), 25–28.

22 John D. McCarthy and Mayer N. Zald, "The Trend of Social Movements in America: Professionalization and Resource Mobilization," in their *Social Movements in an Organizational Society*, 374–89.

23 Anthony Oberschall was one of the first social movement theorists to recognize that existing soli-

darity groups provide a fertile source for recruiting members into a movement. See his *Social Conflict and Social Movements* (Englewood Cliffs, N.J.: Prentice Hall, 1973), 125. For other works on this issue, see Jenkins, "Resource Mobilization Theory," 537–39.

24 Herbert Kitschelt, "Political Opportunity Structures and Political Protest: Anti-Nuclear Movements in Four Democracies," *British Journal of Political Science* 16 (1986): 72–74; Hanspeter Kriesi et al., *New Social Movements in Western Europe: A Comparative Analysis* (Minneapolis: University of Minnesota Press, 1995), 209.

25 With the notable exception of Gamson, whose work does not epitomize the classical resource mobilization approach, resource mobilization theorists fail to define movement success as tangible benefits that meet the movement's goals.

26 Authors who portray the ASL in this fashion include Peter Odegard, *Pressure Politics: The Story of the Anti-Saloon League* (New York: Columbia University Press, 1928); K. Austin Kerr, *Organized for Prohibition: A New History of the Anti-Saloon League* (New Haven: Yale University Press, 1985); and Richard Jensen, *The Winning of the Midwest: Social and Political Conflict, 1888–1896* (Chicago: University of Chicago Press, 1971), 207.

27 Jack S. Blocker, "The Modernity of Prohibitionists: An Analysis of Leadership Structure and Background," in *Alcohol, Reform and Society: The Liquor Issue in Social Context*, ed. Jack S. Blocker (Westport, Conn.: Greenwood, 1979), 149–70.

28 Except for the Washingtonians of the 1840s and the "Gospel Reform" groups of the 1870s, the most significant organizations in the temperance movement were all hierarchical and contained separate departments to perform distinct functions. Such organizations included the American Temperance Society (ATS), the Sons of Temperance, the Independent Order of Good Templars, the Woman's Christian Temperance Union, and the Prohibition party. While these groups were not as professionalized as the ASL, they provided financial support for their workers at some point in their history, and many of their leaders were full-time activists. For example, in the 1830s the ATS employed a full-time secretary, a journal editor, and traveling agents to organize local auxiliaries. Other groups that paid officers, organizers, or lecturers included the Sons (as of 1867), the Good Templars (as of 1867), the WCTU (as of 1879), and the Prohibition party (as of 1900). Finally, though the Protestant churches often squabbled with the temperance movement, the churches remained a source of leadership, workers, and financial and moral support for the movement throughout its history. The ASL may have been the most effective at garnering church support, but other groups (e.g., the Prohibition party) were equally interested in working through the churches.

29 For example, the IOGT peaked in the United States with 367,066 members in 1868 and nonetheless had little impact on prohibition's political fortunes. (See the IOGT's *Right Worthy Grand Lodge Proceedings* for membership figures.)

30 Frances F. Piven and Richard A. Cloward, *Poor People's Movements: Why They Succeed, How They Fail* (New York: Vintage, 1979), xix–xxiv. Disruptive protest activities may include demonstrations, building occupations, acts of civil disobedience, and strikes. See also Gamson, *The Strategy of Social Protest*, chapter 6, for evidence that the success of social movements is linked to disruptive protest, although he does not argue that organization and disruptive protest are incompatible.

31 Lee Ann Banaszak, *Why Movements Succeed or Fail: Opportunity, Culture, and the Struggle for Woman Suffrage* (Princeton, N.J.: Princeton University Press, 1996).

32 Tarrow, *Power in Movement*, 103–4.

33 Kitschelt, "Political Opportunity Structures and Political Protest," 66; Banaszak, *Why Movements Succeed or Fail*, chapter 7. Sometimes confrontational and assimilative strategies are also portrayed as

"high risk" and "low risk." For example, Kriesi et al. assume that confrontational strategies are inherently more costly than assimilative strategies. See their *New Social Movements in Western Europe: A Comparative Analysis* (Minneapolis: University of Minnesota Press, 1995), 46–51.

34 The Women's Crusade (1873–74) was a brief phase of the prohibition movement which was dominated by the use of direct action. During this period, women temperance advocates marched on the saloons where they held pray-ins. For the Women's Crusade, see Jack S. Blocker, *"Give to the Winds Thy Fears": The Women's Temperance Crusade, 1873–1874* (Westport, Conn.: Greenwood, 1985).

35 In fact, the drys typically applied violence and disruptive collective action only when addressing inadequate enforcement efforts. For example, Carrie Nation only picked up her axe after Kansas proved negligent in *enforcing* statewide prohibition. See Robert S. Bader, *Prohibition in Kansas: A History* (Lawrence: University Press of Kansas, 1986), chapter 7.

36 Roberta Ash first advanced the proposition that movements with narrow goals are more likely to succeed in her *Social Movements in America* (Chicago: Markham, 1972), 12. Another analysis of goal definition is Zisk, *The Politics of Transformation*, chapter 4.

37 Gamson, *The Strategy of Social Protest*, 41–50.

38 For example, the national Prohibition party platform of 1888 advocated woman suffrage, civil service reform, preservation of the Sabbath, and arbitration as a means of settling labor disputes. Similarly, the WCTU supported woman suffrage, and sponsored a wide range of social action projects, such as children's aid societies, training schools, shelters for prostitutes, prison reform, and the censorship of "impure" media.

39 Numerous works mention the ASL's single-issue approach as a factor in the organization's success, including Jack S. Blocker, *Retreat from Reform: The Prohibition Movement in the United States, 1890–1913* (Westport, Conn.: Greenwood, 1976); Charles M. Hogan, "Wayne B. Wheeler: Single Issue Exponent" (Ph.D. diss., University of Cincinnati, 1986).

40 Gamson, *The Strategy of Social Protest*, 49. Similarly, Zisk discovers that "while single-issue groups have some advantage over those pursuing multiple goals (mainly on retaining and attracting members), the differences were not great." See her *The Politics of Transformation*, 62–63.

41 For example, in Michigan, where the Prohibition party was active in the 1887 campaign, A. D. P. van Buren notes that party leaders sponsored "non-partisan meetings." See his "Our Temperance Conflict," *Michigan Pioneer Collections* 13 (1888): 405. Only in Washington's amendment campaign of 1889 did prohibition become linked to a radical demand (woman suffrage). See Norman H. Clark, *The Dry Years: Prohibition and Social Change in Washington*, rev. ed. (Seattle: University of Washington Press, 1988), 42–50.

42 For the drys' reliance on nonpartisan organizations to orchestrate their nineteenth-century referenda campaigns, see chapter 6.

43 August F. Fehlandt, *A Century of Drink Reform in the United States* (Cincinnati: Jennings and Graham, 1904), 269–76.

44 For the WCTU and the women's clubs, see Alison M. Parker, *Purifying America: Women, Cultural Reform, and Pro-Censorship Activism, 1873–1933* (Urbana: University of Illinois Press, 1997); Elisabeth Clemens, *The People's Lobby: Organizational Innovation and the Rise of Interest Group Politics in the United States, 1890–1925* (Chicago: University of Chicago Press, 1997), 195–202.

45 Jane Mansbridge, *Why We Lost the ERA* (Chicago: University of Chicago Press, 1986), chapter 13.

46 In ibid., 184–86, Mansbridge claims that the ERA movement temporarily escaped the iron law of involution because there was a good chance of success, the movement depended on actors in dif-

ferent structural roles, and feminism was a potentially inclusive ideology. These three factors, she asserts, are key to understanding the ERA movement's longevity compared with other movements from the 1960s. Since the ERA movement nonetheless failed, it is fair to say that escaping the iron law does not ensure success.

47 Suzanne M. Marilley, *Woman Suffrage and the Origins of Liberal Feminism in the United States, 1820–1920* (Cambridge: Harvard University Press, 1996).

48 Kriesi et al., *New Social Movements*, 208; Edwin Amenta et al., "A Hero for the Aged? The Townshend Movement, the Political Mediation Model, and US Old-Age Policy, 1934–1950," *American Journal of Sociology* 98 (1992): 308–39.

49 Movement success is linked to political crises in Theda Skocpol, *States and Social Revolutions: A Comparative Analysis of France, Russia, and China* (Princeton, N.J.: Princeton University Press, 1979); and Jack Goldstone, "The Weakness of Organization: A New Look at Gamson's *The Strategy of Social Protest*," *American Journal of Sociology* 85 (1980): 1017–42.

50 The impact of unstable political alignments on movement outcomes was first discussed in Peter K. Eisinger, "The Conditions of Protest Behavior in American Cities," *American Political Science Review* 67 (1973): 11–28. On the role of unstable alignments in the American civil rights and women's rights movements, see Piven and Cloward, *Poor People's Movements*, 239–52; Anne N. Costain, *Inviting Women's Rebellion: A Political Process Interpretation of the Women's Movement* (Baltimore: Johns Hopkins University Press, 1992), chapter 7.

51 For an account which explains movement outcomes in terms of state structure, see Kitschelt, "Political Opportunity Structures and Political Protest."

52 For this argument, see Thomas R. Pegram, *Battling Demon Rum: The Struggle for a Dry America, 1800–1933* (Chicago: Ivan R. Dee, 1998), 144–48; Andrew Sinclair, *Prohibition: The Era of Excess* (Boston: Little, Brown, 1962), 119–21; Charles Merz, *The Dry Decade* (Garden City, N.Y.: Doubleday, Doran, 1931), 25–42.

53 Jack S. Blocker, *American Temperance Movements: Cycles of Reform* (Boston: Twayne, 1989), 118.

54 J. Christopher Soper, *Evangelical Christianity in the United States and Great Britain: Religious Beliefs, Political Choices* (New York: New York University Press, 1994), 86.

55 In ibid., 86, Soper suggests that the initiative and referendum, and state constitutional amendment referenda, enabled the ASL to engage in statewide prohibition campaigns. However, constitutional amendment referenda were nothing new, and the drys did not rely on the initiative and referendum (which date back to 1898) as much as one might expect. See chapter 5 for dry use of the initiative and referendum.

56 The referenda in figure 1 refer to propositions that appeared on the ballot as a result of agitation by the prohibitionists; those proposed by their enemies to repeal or dilute statewide prohibition have been excluded.

57 Before 1898 statewide direct legislation could only be enacted in two ways. First, every state constitution (except that of Delaware) included provisions for submitting constitutional amendments and new constitutions to a referendum. By this method, voters could ultimately decide the fate of an amendment or new constitution, but they could not propose constitutional revisions in the first place. Only a constitutional convention could write a new constitution, and only a constitutional convention or state legislature could initiate an amendment. Nonetheless, citizens could petition legislatures and constitutional conventions, and they could elect legislators and convention delegates who were sympathetic to their concerns. Under the second method—the statutory referendum—

the legislature passed a law which only became operative if approved by the state's voters. Like the constitutional referendum, the statutory referendum did not allow citizens to directly initiate a law, but could result from public pressure on the legislature.

58 During the 1880s state lawmakers were responsible for submitting constitutional prohibition to the electorate in fourteen states. In one state, North Carolina, the legislature initiated a statutory referendum on prohibition. Finally, four states—New Hampshire, Washington, South Dakota, and North Dakota—held prohibition referenda that were proposed by constitutional convention. While the drys' success rate in these referenda (31.6%) is respectable by many measures, the radicals were discouraged by it and became less inclined to devote resources to statewide referendum campaigns.

59 In thirteen states, legislatures submitted referenda on constitutional prohibition to the electorate for ratification. In one state, Oklahoma, the state's constitutional convention submitted a referendum on constitutional prohibition to the voters. In four states, lawmakers granted referenda on statutory prohibition. By 1920 nineteen states had enacted the initiative and referendum, but the prohibitionists only used this procedure in twelve states, including Missouri, which also held a constitutional amendment referendum provided for by the state legislature.

60 Five of the forty referenda involved establishing constitutional prohibition in states where the legislature had just adopted statutory prohibition; the other thirty-five referenda sought prohibition in states that lacked state prohibition entirely.

61 Of the thirty states to "go dry" during the Progressive Era, however, eight states adopted statewide prohibition by legislative acts which were not submitted to the electorate. Moreover, in five states, the drys first sought statutory prohibition from the legislature before seeking amendment referenda.

62 Lloyd Sponholtz, "The Initiative and Referendum: Direct Democracy in Perspective, 1898–1920," *American Studies* 14 (1973): 58. David Magleby also notes that groups with low socioeconomic status are often underrepresented in contemporary referendum elections, which "plays a part in the success or failure of propositions for which the outcome is close." See his *Direct Legislation: Voting on Ballot Propositions in the United States* (Baltimore: Johns Hopkins University Press, 1984), 119–20.

63 For the decline in voter turnout after 1896, see Walter D. Burnham, "The Appearance and Disappearance of the American Voter," in his *The Current Crisis in American Politics* (Oxford: Oxford University Press, 1982), 121–65.

64 See Frances F. Piven and Richard A. Cloward, *Why Americans Don't Vote* (New York: Pantheon, 1988), chapter 3, for the demobilization of the American electorate.

65 Indisputably, southern blacks became less likely to vote after encountering violence, poll taxes, and literacy tests in the late nineteenth century. See J. Morgan Kousser, *The Shaping of Southern Politics: Suffrage Restrictions and the One-Party South* (New Haven: Yale University Press, 1974); Jerrold G. Rusk and John J. Stucker, "The Effect of the Southern System of Election Laws on Voting Participation: A Reply to V. O. Key, Jr.," in *The History of American Electoral Behavior*, ed. Joel H. Silbey et al. (Princeton, N.J.: Princeton University Press, 1978), 198–250. Other social groups that were apparently demobilized after 1896 included poor southern whites, immigrants, urban dwellers, and members of the working class. See Burnham, "The Appearance and Disappearance of the American Voter," 136–45, for the sociopolitical consequences of demobilization.

66 U.S. Bureau of the Census, *Historical Statistics of the United States, Colonial Times to 1970* (Washington: Government Printing Office, 1975), 2:1072.

67 The belief that southern blacks voted wet is supported largely by anecdotal evidence. In Tennessee, for instance, the defeat of constitutional prohibition in 1887 was blamed on the black vote. See Paul

Isaac, *Prohibition and Politics: Turbulent Decades in Tennessee, 1885–1920* (Knoxville: University of Tennessee Press, 1965), 57. For evidence that blacks did not always vote as a wet bloc, see Thomas H. Winn, "Liquor, Race and Politics: Clarksville during the Progressive Era," *Tennessee Historical Quarterly* 49 (1990): 207–17. In contrast, the claim that Germans and Catholic immigrants voted wet is better supported. See Ira M. Wasserman, "Prohibition and Ethno-Cultural Conflict: The Missouri Prohibition Referendum of 1918," *Social Science Quarterly* 70 (1989): 886–901; Ira M. Wasserman, "Status Politics and Economic Class Interests: The 1918 Prohibition Referendum in California," *Sociological Quarterly* 31 (1990): 475–84; Jensen, *The Winning of the Midwest*, chapter 4.

68 *International Migrations* (New York: National Bureau of Economic Research, 1929), 1:423–36.

69 U.S. Bureau of the Census, *Religious Bodies: 1906* (Washington: Government Printing Office, 1910), 1:58.

70 In addition to North Carolina and Texas, Tennessee also held a state prohibition referendum in the 1880s.

71 While some scholars use a broader definition of "the South," my use of this term refers specifically to the eleven states which formed the Confederacy, namely, Virginia, North Carolina, South Carolina, Georgia, Alabama, Mississippi, Florida, Texas, Tennessee, Arkansas, and Louisiana.

72 During the Progressive Era, the five states which went dry by referenda included Virginia, South Carolina, North Carolina, Florida, and Texas. The five southern states which achieved statewide prohibition by legislative acts were Georgia, Mississippi, Alabama, Tennessee, and Arkansas.

73 The four referenda in question were held in Alabama (1909), Florida (1910), Texas (1911), and Arkansas (1912).

74 Kitschelt, "Political Opportunity Structures and Political Protest," 66–72. For the impact of élite response and success chances on a movement's repertoire of collective action, see Kriesi et al., *New Social Movements*, 37–52.

75 Doug McAdam, "Conceptual Origins, Current Problems, Future Directions," in *Comparative Perspectives on Social Movements: Political Opportunities, Mobilizing Structures, and Framings*, ed. Doug McAdam et al. (Cambridge: Cambridge University Press, 1996), 29–30.

76 Hogan, "Wayne B. Wheeler," 51; Soper, *Evangelical Christianity in the United States and Great Britain*, 86; Pegram, *Battling Demon Rum*, 111, 113–14; Richard F. Hamm, *Shaping the Eighteenth Amendment: Temperance Reform, Legal Culture, and the Polity, 1880–1920* (Chapel Hill: University of North Carolina Press, 1995), 133.

77 For a discussion of pre-1898 forms of direct legislation, see note 57, above.

78 In Idaho, Utah, and Texas, the drys first won statutory prohibition from the legislature and shortly thereafter triumphed in constitutional amendment referenda.

79 Significantly, the other period of widespread prohibition success in American history, namely the 1850s, was also preceded by a wave of local activism.

80 For the development of local referenda on stock laws, see Ellis P. Oberholtzer, *The Referendum in America* (New York: Charles Scribner's Sons, 1912), 295–300; Steven Hahn, *The Roots of Southern Populism: Yeoman Farmers and the Transformation of the Georgia Upcountry, 1850–1890* (Oxford: Oxford University Press, 1983), chapter 7; Shawn E. Kantor and J. Morgan Kousser, "Common Sense or Commonwealth? The Fence Law and Institutional Change in the Postbellum South," *Journal of Southern History* 59 (1993): 201–42; J. Crawford King, "The Closing of the Southern Range: An Exploratory Study," *Journal of Southern History* 48 (1982): 53–70; Shawn E. Kantor, "Razorbacks, Ticky Cows, and the Closing of the Georgia Open Range: The Dynamics of Institutional Change Uncovered," *Journal of Economic History* 51 (1991): 861–86. For the legal acceptance of local referenda on stock laws, see

Thomas M. Cooley, *A Treatise on the Constitutional Limitations Which Rest upon the Legislative Power of the States of the American Union*, 5th ed. (Boston: Little, Brown, 1883), 148. Only one stock law was declared unconstitutional, a Missouri law from 1873 which was struck down in *Lammert v. Lidwell*, 62 Mo. 188 (1876).

81 Much as comparisons of this sort would help place the prohibition movement in a broader context, this book does not systematically engage in them because of space constraints and a desire to prevent an already complex story from becoming too unwieldy.

82 Banaszak, *Why Movements Succeed or Fail*, chapter 8. According to Banaszak, American suffragists aggressively used organizational, lobbying, and confrontational tactics on a national scale because they overcame the status-quo norm of regional autonomy and operated within a movement network which fostered strong beliefs about the significance of political rights and the efficacy of confrontational techniques. Conversely, their Swiss counterparts used such tactics less extensively because they respected local autonomy and belonged to a movement network which deemphasized the importance of political rights and challenges to the status quo.

83 Hamm, *Shaping the Eighteenth Amendment.*

84 See, e.g., Jeffrey K. Tullis, "Reflections on the Rhetorical Presidency," in *Speaking to the People: The Presidency in Historical Perspective*, ed. Richard J. Ellis (Amherst: University of Massachusetts Press, 1998), 216; and chapters 2, 6, 7, and 8 in this book.

85 In some forms of classic local option, however, the citizenry did not have to initiate local option elections because the law mandated that these elections be held periodically.

86 Rosalind L. Branning, *Pennsylvania Constitutional Development* (Pittsburgh: University of Pittsburgh Press, 1960), 65.

87 See, e.g., *Locke's Appeal*, 72 Pa. (22 F. Smith) 496–97 (1873).

88 In some states, the ASL relied on general state laws which granted the citizenry only indirect control over liquor licensing decisions. For example, in Nebraska the ASL gave up on local option after the legislature refused to pass county option in 1908, 1910, and 1911. Instead, the league exploited the Slocumb Law of 1881, which authorized the granting of liquor licenses by corporate authorities in cities and popularly elected excise commissioners in towns. By turning the elections for excise commissioners and corporate officers into referenda on liquor licensing, and by exploiting municipal initiative and referendum laws, the ASL succeeded in mobilizing Nebraskans who might otherwise have remained uninvolved in the movement, given the state legislature's intransigence. See Robert E. Wenger, "The Anti-Saloon League in Nebraska Politics, 1898–1910," *Nebraska History* 52 (1971): 266–92; John Anderson, "Lincoln, Nebraska, and Prohibition: The Election of May 4, 1909," *Nebraska History* 70 (1989): 184–200.

2 Churches, Lodges, and Dry Organizing

1 David L. Sills, *The Volunteers: Means and Ends in a National Organization* (Glencoe, Ill.: Free Press, 1957), chapter 9; Joseph Gusfield, "Social Structure and Moral Reform: A Study of the WCTU," *American Journal of Sociology* 61 (1955): 221–32; Peter M. Blau, *The Dynamics of Bureaucracy* (Chicago: University of Chicago Press, 1955), 195.

2 Sidney Tarrow, *Power in Movement: Social Movements, Collective Action and Politics*, 2d ed. (Cambridge: Cambridge University Press, 1998), 123–24.

3 The prohibition movement was a branch of the larger temperance movement, which sought to dis-

courage the manufacture, sale, and consumption of alcoholic beverages. Whereas the prohibitionists considered both educational *and* legal efforts to be worthwhile, not every temperance advocate supported state action to ban the Demon Rum.

4 The most established of these early temperance groups was the Massachusetts Society for the Suppression of Intemperance. See Ian Tyrrell, *Sobering Up: From Temperance to Prohibition in Antebellum America, 1800–1860* (Westport, Conn.: Greenwood, 1979), chapter 2.

5 Mark E. Lender and James K. Martin, *Drinking in America: A History* (New York: Free Press, 1982), 46. Lender and Martin base this assertion on estimates that absolute alcohol intake for an individual (aged fifteen or older) averaged 7.1 gallons a year during this period. In contrast, recent estimates of per capita alcohol intake are less than three gallons a year. (See ibid., Appendix.)

6 Ibid., 46–58. See also W. J. Rorabaugh, *The Alcoholic Republic* (New York: Oxford University Press, 1979), for a study of aggregate consumption and drinking practices before 1840.

7 For the early geographical distribution of temperance societies, see the census of temperance organizations in the *Journal of Humanity and Herald of the American Temperance Society*, January–April 1831.

8 Rapid industrialization as a source of the Second Great Awakening and its attendant reforms is emphasized in Paul E. Johnson, *A Shopkeeper's Millennium: Society and Revivals in Rochester, New York, 1815–1837* (New York: Hill and Wang, 1978). For temperance as a byproduct of the Second Great Awakening, see Whitney Cross, *The Burned-Over District: The Social and Intellectual History of Enthusiastic Religion in Western New York, 1800–1850* (Ithaca, N.Y.: Cornell University Press, 1950).

9 Studies show that antebellum temperance agitators typically worked in industries undergoing rapid economic transformations, and therefore that reform advocates were members of a rising middle class, along with artisans who shared their values. See Tyrrell, *Sobering Up*, chapter 4; John S. Gilkeson, *Middle-Class Providence, 1820–1940* (Princeton, N.J.: Princeton University Press, 1986), 23–36; Jill S. Dodd, "The Working Classes and the Temperance Movement in Ante-bellum Boston," *Labor History* 19 (1978): 510–31; W. R. Rorabaugh, "Prohibition as Progress: New York State's License Elections, 1846," *Journal of Social History* 14 (1981): 425–43. This characterization of temperance activists has also been extended to the South in Ian Tyrrell, "Drink and Temperance in the Antebellum South: An Overview and Interpretation," *Journal of Southern History* 48 (1982): 485–510. In the cities, however, temperance leaders were also members of the socioeconomic élite, although many of these men were newcomers to wealth and leadership. See Stuart Blumin, *The Emergence of the Middle Class: Social Experience in the American City, 1760–1900* (Cambridge: Cambridge University Press, 1989), 195–202. For the relationship between sobriety and the ideology of progress, see Tyrrell, *Sobering Up*, chapter 5.

10 Ian Tyrrell, "Women and Temperance in Antebellum America, 1830–1860," *Civil War History* 28 (1982): 129–34; Jed Dannenbaum, "The Origins of Temperance Activism and Militancy Among American Women," *Journal of Social History* 15 (1981): 236–37.

11 The terms "spirituous liquors" and "ardent spirits" refer to alcoholic beverages that are distilled rather than fermented.

12 Tyrrell, *Sobering Up*, chapter 6; John A. Krout, *The Origins of Prohibition* (New York: Alfred A. Knopf, 1925), chapter 8. While total abstinence became a standard position for temperance groups after 1840, the "wine versus grape juice" controversy plagued the Protestant churches after the Civil War.

13 Krout, *The Origins of Prohibition*, 168–72; Tyrrell, *Sobering Up*, 227–29.

14 See chapters 3 and 4 for the antebellum movement's local agitation.

15 Krout, *The Origins of Prohibition*, 170–76.

16 In addition to the fifteen-gallon law, major temperance laws were passed in Mississippi, New Hampshire, Illinois, Tennessee, Rhode Island, and Connecticut.

17 By prohibiting liquor sales in small amounts, anti-liquor activists hoped to abolish barrooms.

18 Robert L. Hampel, *Temperance and Prohibition in Massachusetts, 1813–1852* (Ann Arbor: UMI Research Press, 1982), chapter 6; Tyrrell, *Sobering Up*, 237–39.

19 Of the seven state anti-drink laws enacted in 1838–39, five were repealed after provoking intense opposition.

20 Although one major arm of the benevolent empire focused on foreign missionary work (American Board of Commissioners for Foreign Missions), four significant national groups in the benevolent empire concentrated on domestic proselytizing: the American Bible Society (1816), the American Sunday School Union (1824), the American Tract Society (1825), and the American Home Missionary Society (1826).

21 For the benevolent empire, see Ronald G. Walters, *American Reformers* (New York: Hill and Wang, 1978), chapter 1.

22 In *Sobering Up*, 59, Tyrrell reports that fifteen of the sixteen ATS founders belonged to the American Board of Commissioners for Foreign Missions, and fourteen had participated in the American Tract Society.

23 Walters, *American Reformers*, 31–33.

24 Krout, *The Origins of Prohibition*, 124–31.

25 *Journal of Humanity and Herald of the American Temperance Society*, January–April 1831. That 70.6% of the temperance societies were located in New England, New York, or the Western Reserve is significant because only 31% of the American population resided in these regions, according to the U.S. Census of 1830.

26 Tyrrell, *Sobering Up*, 65–66, 87; Krout, *The Origins of Prohibition*, 111–19; Daniel Dorchester, *The Liquor Problem in All Ages* (New York: Phillips and Hunt, 1888), 222–23, 225, 231–32.

27 *Temperance Manual of the American Temperance Society* (Boston, 1836), 114.

28 H. A. Scomp, *King Alcohol in the Realm of King Cotton, or A History of the Liquor Traffic and of the Temperance Movement in Georgia from 1733 to 1887* (Chicago: Blakely Printing, 1888), 299–308; Krout, *The Origins of Prohibition*, 176–77; Douglas W. Carlson, "Temperance Reform in the Cotton Kingdom," (Ph.D. diss., University of Illinois, 1982), 15–16, 18–19; C. C. Pearson and J. Edwin Hendricks, *Liquor and Anti-Liquor in Virginia, 1619–1919* (Durham: Duke University Press, 1967), 88–89; Joseph R. Gusfield, *Symbolic Crusade: Status Politics and the American Temperance Movement* (Urbana: University of Illinois Press, 1963), 54; and, for a qualification of this argument which nonetheless presents evidence to the same effect, see Tyrrell, "Drink and Temperance in the Antebellum South," 485–91. The South did include evangelical Protestant temperance societies. However, the ATS, its allies, and southern evangelical societies failed to coordinate effective organizing campaigns in the region, leaving southern teetotalers less fully integrated in the larger movement.

29 In the South, the AHMS advocated the ATS's goals during the period 1829–35. After 1840 the AHMS again sponsored temperance activities, but these efforts coincided with the emergence of secular temperance revivals and the Sons of Temperance. See Charles T. Thrift, "The Operations of the American Home Missionary Society in the South, 1826–1861" (Ph.D. diss., University of Chicago, 1936), 164–81, 203, chapter 7.

30 The reasons for the ATS's reconstitution as the ATU are unclear. The *Sixth Report of the American Temperance Society* (1833), 98, reports that the ATS was supposed to be renamed the United States Tem-

perance Union (USTU) and be based in Philadelphia (as opposed to Boston, the ATS's home). Tyrrell suggests that Philadelphia was a more acceptable base for the national movement because of its central location and because it lacked Boston's reputation for abolitionism. Furthermore, the USTU was supposed to be a more truly national organization and to increase internal harmony by basing its representation in the federal system. However, the USTU ultimately became the ATU in 1836, and, though structured by federalism, was based in New York. The ATU was also more radical than the ATS, in that it adopted a total abstinence pledge rather than a pledge to abstain from distilled liquors. See Tyrrell, "Drink and Temperance in the Antebellum South," 486–87; Krout, *The Origins of Prohibition*, 153–60; Tyrrell, *Sobering Up*, 144.

31 George F. Clark, *History of the Temperance Reform in Massachusetts* (Boston: Clarke and Carruth, 1888), 23.

32 Krout, *The Origins of Prohibition*, 131–33, 153–61; Tyrrell, *Sobering Up*, 144, 239.

33 Some of the ATU's defections in the late 1830s may have stemmed from these internal controversies, but the Panic of 1837 may also have reduced the group's financial support. See Tyrrell, *Sobering Up*, 149–50.

34 For factionalism in the abolitionist ranks, see Aileen S. Kraditor, *Means and Ends in American Abolitionism: Garrison and His Critics on Strategy and Tactics, 1834–1850* (New York: Vintage, 1970). For the antebellum peace movement, see Walters, *American Reformers*, 112–21.

35 Tyrrell, *Sobering Up*, chapter 8; Krout, *The Origins of Prohibition*, 200–214; Jed Dannenbaum, *Drink and Disorder: Temperance Reform in Cincinnati from the Washingtonian Revival to the WCTU* (Urbana: University of Illinois Press, 1984), 37–41; Hampel, *Temperance and Prohibition in Massachusetts*, 115–22. The ATU's disdain for the dry fraternal orders largely reflected the unpopularity of the Masons, who had spawned the Antimasons, a political party centered in the northeastern United States and active in the 1820s and early 1830s. Like the Antimasons, the union had a base of support—the evangelical Protestant churches—with serious misgivings about secret societies. Church leaders condemned their secrecy, passwords, and regalia as anti-republican and smacking of intrigue.

36 Antebellum prohibition laws were called "Maine Laws" because Maine pioneered this kind of legislation in 1851.

37 The *American Temperance Union Reports* continued to list five or six southern state temperance societies as affiliates until 1841, but it did not list their officers and left the spaces for their names blank. Similarly, while John H. Cocke of Virginia served as the ATU's president in the years 1836–42, and while three of its twenty vice-presidents represented southern states in the 1840s, the overwhelming majority of the ATU's officers were northerners. See also *American Temperance Union Report for 1840* (New York: American Temperance Union, 1840), 28–34; Krout, *The Origins of Prohibition*, 177.

38 Sara M. Evans and Harry C. Boyte, *Free Spaces: The Sources of Democratic Change in America* (Chicago: University of Chicago Press, 1992), 17–18.

39 For Washingtonian temperance, see Hampel, *Temperance and Prohibition in Massachusetts*, chapters 7 and 8; Dannenbaum, *Drink and Disorder*, chapter 2; Tyrrell, *Sobering Up*, chapter 7; Krout, *The Origins of Prohibition*, chapter 9.

40 *Templar's Magazine*, June 1851, 310–11. Cary exaggerates somewhat, for some Washingtonian societies apparently held weekly meetings and attempted to sustain the reformed. While many local Washingtonian groups survived the decline of the revivals, their decentralized character allowed each to adopt its own form and principles, and it is thus difficult to gauge their combined impact on the temperance movement. By the late 1840s, however, the Sons had clearly created a more solid organization than their precursors.

41 The Sons called their lodges "divisions."

42 Donald W. Beattie, "Sons of Temperance: Pioneers in Total Abstinence and 'Constitutional' Prohibition" (Ph.D. diss., Boston University, 1966), 71–73.

43 Beginning in 1847, the Grand (state) Divisions recorded how many members they expelled annually in the *Journal of the Proceedings of the Grand Division of the Sons of Temperance of North America.*

44 According to teetotalers, "cold water" was the best substitute for liquor.

45 Another selective incentive offered by the Sons was their mutual insurance program. Although the generosity of these benefits peaked in 1854, the Sons' program provided limited disability and death benefits to members until 1916.

46 Beattie, "Sons of Temperance," 88–90. See also *Nashville Union*, 9 July 1846, 2 July 1847, and 24 June 1848, for the Sons' Fourth of July celebrations.

47 Samuel F. Cary, ed., *The National Temperance Offering, and Sons and Daughters of Temperance Gift* (New York: R. Vandien, 1850), 167; Beattie, "Sons of Temperance," 85–87.

48 R. L. Pierce, *A History of the Order of the Sons of Temperance in Ohio* (Cincinnati: George M. Young, 1849), 45–47, 67–68; Nancy R. Siegal, "A Matter of the Public Welfare: The Temperance Movement in Antebellum Cincinnati" (M.A. thesis, University of Cincinnati, 1971), 69; Pearson and Hendricks, *Liquor and Anti-Liquor in Virginia*, 123; Beattie, "Sons of Temperance," 198.

49 Pierce, *History of the Order of the Sons of Temperance in Ohio*, 110–13; Dannenbaum, *Drink and Disorder*, 87.

50 For example, in 1850 the Massachusetts Sons favored prohibiting the sale of both fermented and distilled liquors, as well as the imprisonment of convicted sellers. See the *Quarterly Journal of the Grand Division of the Sons of Temperance, State of Massachusetts*, January 1850, 3, 5. For the Sons' support for prohibition, see Tyrrell, *Sobering Up*, 215–18.

51 *Journal of the Proceedings of the Grand Division of the Sons of Temperance of North America, Ninth Session* (1852), 6–7.

52 *Journal of the Proceedings of the Grand Division of the Sons of Temperance of North America, Fourth Session* (1847), 16–17; *Eighth Session* (1851), 28–29.

53 U.S. Bureau of the Census, *Seventh Census of the United States* (Washington: Robert Armstrong, 1853), xxxviii.

54 Although some northern divisions may have secretly admitted blacks, the National Division refused membership to blacks from 1850 to 1866.

55 While the North Carolina Grand Division endorsed state prohibition in 1852, this group refused to sponsor it in 1854. In addition, several local divisions petitioned for prohibition themselves. See Daniel J. Whitener, *Prohibition in North Carolina, 1715–1945* (Chapel Hill: University of North Carolina Press, 1945), 29–47; Tyrrell, *Sobering Up*, 276–78.

56 *Nashville Union*, 29 April 1853. For similar activity by the Sons in South Carolina and Georgia, see Carlson, "Temperance Reform in the Cotton Kingdom," 251–54, 275. In some southern states, however, the Sons did not advocate the stringent prohibition laws that northern Sons promoted. For the southern Sons' sponsorship of weaker anti-liquor laws, see Pearson and Hendricks, *Liquor and Anti-Liquor in Virginia*, 128–30; Carlson, "Temperance Reform in the Cotton Kingdom," 227–37; James B. Sellers, *The Prohibition Movement in Alabama, 1702 to 1943* (Chapel Hill: University of North Carolina Press, 1943), 33–37.

57 Other temperance fraternal orders, like the Independent Order of Rechabites and the Temple of Honor, were also founded during the antebellum period, but they remained small and usually eschewed politics.

58 Some sources claim that the Templars emerged from the Knights of Jericho, an adjunct of the Sons

designed to appeal to those who were too young to become full-fledged Sons. Other sources assert that the IOGT was an offshoot of the Temple of Honor, which had branched off from the Sons in 1845 to provide more substantial insurance benefits and more intricate rituals than those of the Sons. In either case, the Templars can be considered an indirect descendent of the Sons.

59 Sons who later became Templars included Simeon B. Chase, Nathaniel Curtis, James Black, Samuel D. Hastings, John N. Stearns, B. H. Mills, Gideon T. Stewart, Edward W. Mills, and Isaac Paul. Moreover, anecdotal evidence supports the Sons' contention that both the Templars and the apolitical Temple of Honor were built on the ruins of the Sons in many localities.

60 David M. Fahey, *Temperance and Racism: John Bull, Johnny Reb, and the Good Templars* (Lexington: University Press of Kentucky, 1996), 15–19; *Collected Writings of Jessie Forsyth, 1847–1937: The Good Templars and Temperance Reform on Three Continents*, ed. David M. Fahey (Lewiston, N.Y.: Edwin Mellen, 1988), 16; Joanne J. Brownsword, "Good Templars in Wisconsin, 1854–1880" (M.A. thesis, University of Wisconsin, 1960), 46–55; Theda Skocpol et al., "A Nation of Organizers: The Institutional Origins of Civic Voluntarism in the United States," *American Political Science Review* 94 (2000): 527–46.

61 For Templar activity in the antebellum prohibition campaigns, see Washington Gladden, *Recollections* (Boston: Houghton Mifflin, 1909), 50–51; Isaac N. Peirce, *The History of the Independent Order of Good Templars* (Philadelphia: Daughaday and Becker, 1869), 80–81, 181–84; Francis M. Whitaker, "A History of the Ohio Woman's Christian Temperance Union" (Ph.D. diss., Ohio State University, 1971), 102–4; Gilman Ostrander, *The Prohibition Movement in California, 1848–1933* (Berkeley: University of California Press, 1957), 17. In general, however, the Templars only became popular after the prohibition excitement had subsided.

62 *Cyclopedia of Temperance and Prohibition* (New York: Funk and Wagnalls, 1891), 241.

63 Although the Sons had sponsored the formation of a juvenile auxiliary, the Cadets of Temperance, this organization was not fully incorporated into the order. In contrast, the Juvenile Templars were established in 1871 as an integral part of the IOGT.

64 Before 1866 women could participate in the Sons' short-lived women's auxiliary, the Daughters of Temperance (1843–48), or contribute directly to the Sons as "lady visitors" (1854–66).

65 Fahey, *Temperance and Racism*, 11, 23–26; *Collected Writings of Jessie Forsyth*, 6–8; Whitaker, "A History of the Ohio Woman's Christian Temperance Union," 93–94, 121–24.

66 See chapter 5 for more on the Free Soil party's role in the antebellum prohibition campaigns. The states and territories that passed Maine Laws included Connecticut (1854), Delaware (1855), Indiana (1855), Iowa (1855), Maine (1851), Massachusetts (1852), Michigan (1853), Minnesota (1852), Nebraska (1855), New Hampshire (1855), New York (1855), Rhode Island (1852), and Vermont (1852).

67 Tyrrell, *Sobering Up*, 290–97.

68 Maine Laws had particularly brief lives in Delaware, Indiana, Nebraska, and New York. In Massachusetts, Connecticut, Iowa, and Michigan, though, the legislature often tinkered with the state liquor policy after successful Maine Law campaigns.

69 For the party system's role in the movement's decline after 1855, see D. Leigh Colvin, *Prohibition in the United States* (New York: George H. Doran, 1926), 39–48; Tyrrell, *Sobering Up*, 305–7. For the movement's interaction with the "third party system," see chapter 4.

70 For instance, the Sons' decline after 1851 has been ascribed to rivalries with other fraternal temperance societies and to internal conflicts concerning women and blacks as members, prohibition as a goal, and the order's political alliances. See Beattie, "Sons of Temperance," 313–22, 323–33; Sellers, *The Prohibition Movement in Alabama*, 37; Whitener, *Prohibition in North Carolina*, 30–31.

71 *Journal of the Proceedings of the Grand Division of the Sons of Temperance of North America* (1851–60). The

Sons would briefly top seventy thousand members in 1860 before the Civil War eroded membership further.

72 Ernest H. Cherrington, *The Evolution of Prohibition in the United States of America* (Westerville, Ohio: American Issue, 1920), 163–64.

73 Peirce, *History of the Independent Order of Good Templars*, 272.

74 Clark, *History of the Temperance Reform in Massachusetts*, 23.

75 In the period 1867–89, the Templars only dipped below 200,000 U.S. members in 1886 (when the figure stood at 193,880). For membership data, see the *Independent Order of the Good Templars, Right Worthy Grand Lodge Proceedings* (1860–94); the *International Supreme Lodge Journals* (1894–1920); William W. Turnbull, *The Good Templars: A History of the Rise and Progress of the Independent Order of Good Templars, 1851–1901, Jubilee Volume*, ed. James Yeames (N.p.: IOGT, 1901).

76 For the decline of evangelical leadership, see James R. Turner, "The American Prohibition Movement, 1865–1897" (Ph.D. diss., University of Wisconsin, 1972), chapter 1; Earl C. Kaylor, "The Prohibition Movement in Pennsylvania" (Ph.D. diss., Pennsylvania State University, 1963), 69. Of course, the evangelical National Temperance Society (NTS) sought to do more than merely publish the *National Temperance Advocate* and to operate its publishing house. This society also organized temperance conventions, sponsored black temperance societies in the South, and sometimes promoted modest political action. However, the society lacked a mass base and failed to mobilize its constituency, the evangelical Protestant churches. Moreover, because of low funds the society could barely maintain its publishing arm, never mind expand its activities. For the NTS, see *National Temperance Advocate*; Turner, "The American Prohibition Movement," 20–21, 24–27, 203–7; J. N. Stearns, "The National Temperance Society and Publication House," in *One Hundred Years of Temperance: A Memorial Volume of the Centennial Temperance Conference Held in Philadelphia, Pa., September 1885* (New York: National Temperance Society and Publication House, 1886), 447–62.

77 John J. Ashenhurst, *Recollections of an Octogenarian* (Bowie, Md.: Heritage, 1990), 140–41; "The Church and Temperance," *Union Signal*, 21 February 1884, 8; Editorial, *Union Signal*, 16 July 1891, 1; George W. Bain, "The Next Practical Step to Be Taken in the Temperance Reform," *Union Signal*, 27 August 1891, 3; "The Religious Press and Temperance," *Union Signal*, 3 September 1891, 10–11; "Fossils and Fanatics on Total Abstinence," *Union Signal*, 15 September 1892, 8–9; Jack S. Blocker, *Retreat from Reform: The Prohibition Movement in the United States, 1890–1913* (Westport, Conn.: Greenwood, 1976), 81–84.

78 When capitalized, "Prohibitionist" refers to the Prohibition party and its activists; in contrast, "prohibitionist" refers to a supporter of prohibition as a public policy. This distinction follows contemporary usage.

79 With national constitutional prohibition, however, congressional parties would be merely shifting responsibility for the substantive choice about prohibition to the partisans in the state legislatures, unless the drys used the convention method of ratification. However, all constitutional amendments possessed nonpartisan overtones for the constitutional prohibitionists. As John B. Finch wrote, "The constitution belongs to the whole people. It does not speak of Republicans, Democrats, or Prohibitionists." See his *Prohibition: Constitutional and Statutory* (New York: National Temperance Society and Publishing House, 1889), 4.

80 For this benefit of constitutional prohibition, see J. Ellen Foster, *Constitutional Amendment Manual, Containing Argument, Appeal, Petitions, Forms of Constitutions and General Directions for Organized Work for Constitutional Prohibition* (New York: National Temperance Society and Publishing House, 1882), 24–25; Willard, "Romance versus Reality," *Chautauquan*, November 1884, 89–90; *The Constitutional Prohibi-*

tionist, ed. J. N. Stearns (New York: National Temperance Society and Publishing House, 1889), 3–5; John B. Finch, "Why Constitutional Prohibition," in *The People versus the Liquor Traffic*, 9–11.

81 For contemporary accounts which distinguish between the radical and moderate drys in a similar manner, see A. B. Nettleton, "The Line on Which All Enemies of the Saloon May Unitedly Do Battle," *Proceedings of the National Temperance Congress Held in the Broadway Tabernacle, New York, Wednesday and Thursday, June 11th and 12th, 1890* (New York: Funk and Wagnalls, 1891), 76–78; I. K. Funk, "A Symposium: On What Line May All Enemies of the Saloon Unitedly Do Battle?" *Homiletic Review*, December 1890, 509–13.

82 For contemporary critiques of the Prohibition party, see S. A. Goodwin, *Prohibition Impossible through a Separate Party and Why*, undated pamphlet found in box 3, Howard Hyde Russell Papers, Bentley Historical Library, University of Michigan; Gail Hamilton, "Prohibition in Politics," *North American Review*, March 1885, 509–20; "A Temperance Platform," *Christian Union*, 12 November 1885, 3–4; Editorial, *Law and Order*, 6 December 1884, 73; "The Prohibition Movement," *Methodist Review*, March 1885, 277–80; Daniel Dorchester, "The National League for the Suppression of the Liquor Traffic," in *One Hundred Years of Temperance*, 530–31; Nettleton, "The Line on Which All Enemies of the Saloon May Unitedly Do Battle," 77–78.

83 Frances B. Finch and Frank J. Sibley, *John B. Finch, His Life and Work* (New York: Funk and Wagnalls, 1888), 272; Finch, *Prohibition: Constitutional and Statutory*, 2–3.

84 Colvin, *Prohibition in the United States*, 226. See also Gideon T. Stewart, "How Shall We Best Secure State Prohibition?" in *Proceedings of the Ninth National Temperance Convention Held at Saratoga Springs, N.Y., June 21 and 22, 1881* (New York: National Temperance Society and Publishing House, 1881), 221–28; John B. Finch, "Anti-License with Prohibition," *Union Signal*, 20 September 1883, 5.

85 William H. Armstrong, "The Sons of Temperance: The Pioneer Advocates of Constitutional Prohibition," in *Journal of the Proceedings of the Grand Division of the Sons of Temperance of North America, Forty-Eighth Annual Convention* (1892), 120–26.

86 Turner, "The American Prohibition Movement," 235.

87 Brownsword, "Good Templars in Wisconsin," 102–6; IOGT *Journal of Proceedings of the Twenty-Sixth Annual Session of the Grand Lodge of Illinois* (1879), 13; *Twenty-Eighth Annual Session* (September 1881), 16–17; Daniel E. Clark, "The History of Liquor Legislation in Iowa, 1878–1908," *Iowa Journal of History and Politics* 6 (1908): 503–4.

88 Robert S. Bader, *Prohibition in Kansas: A History* (Lawrence: University Press of Kansas, 1986), 39–62; Turner, "The American Prohibition Movement," 233–34.

89 *Proceedings of the Ninth National Temperance Convention*, 42.

90 *Annual Meeting Minutes of the National Woman's Christian Temperance Union, 1874 Convention*, 30. For the WCTU's condemnation of temperance advocates who eschewed total abstinence, see "Voices on the Temperance Question," *Union Signal*, 19 April 1883, 8–9.

91 James Black, "Is There a Necessity for a Prohibition Party?" in *Centennial Temperance Volume: A Memorial of the International Temperance Conference, Held in June, 1876* (New York: National Temperance Society and Publication House, 1877), 337. For the party's support for candidates "ennobled by the very cause they champion," see Richard F. Hamm, "Administrative and Prison Suasion: Law Enforcement in the American Temperance Movement, 1880–1920," *Contemporary Drug Problems* 21 (1994): 387–91; Nathan F. Woodbury, *Prohibition in Maine: A History of Its Origin, Results, Political Nullification and Final Ratification from 1837 to 1920* (Lewiston, Maine: Journal Printshop and Bindery, 1920), 18–19; Colvin, *Prohibition in the United States*, 400–401.

92 Richard F. Hamm, *Shaping the Eighteenth Amendment*, chapter 1.

93 *Journal of the Proceedings of the Grand Division of the Sons of Temperance of North America, Twenty-First Annual Convention* (1866), 27; *Twenty-Seventh Annual Convention* (1871), 40–41.

94 Turnbull, *Good Templars*, 47; *Independent Order of the Good Templars, Right Worthy Grand Proceedings, Fourteenth Annual Session* (1868), 24–26.

95 Emancipation's impact on the resurgence of temperance is recorded in a number of contemporary accounts, including Gerrit Smith, "Address to the People of the United States," in Colvin's *Prohibition in the United States*, 75–81; John Marsh, *Temperance Recollections, Labors, Defeats, Triumphs: An Autobiography* (New York: Charles Scribner, 1867); J. B. Dunn, "History of the Temperance Movement," in *Centennial Temperance Volume*, 482–83; Dorchester, *The Liquor Problem in All Ages*, 407–8.

96 Whereas Smith joined with prominent Templars in calling for the Prohibition party's formation in 1869, Phillips accepted the gubernatorial nomination in 1870 from the Massachusetts Prohibition party, which was dominated by Templars and boasted a national leader of the Sons. However, neither man adapted easily to the postwar prohibition regime. Smith did not entirely concur with the tactics adopted at the national Prohibition party convention in 1869, and he lent more support to the New York branch than to the national party. (See *Cyclopedia of Temperance and Prohibition*, 610.) Likewise, Phillips equivocated before accepting the Prohibitionist nomination, which led one historian to remark that "he would doubtless have received a larger prohibition vote if he had promptly accepted [the] nomination." (See Clark, *History of the Temperance Reform in Massachusetts*, 151.)

97 *Journal of the Proceedings of the Grand Division of the Sons of Temperance of North America, Twenty-Second Annual Convention* (1867), 43; *Twenty-Fourth Annual Convention* (1869), 29; Beattie, "Sons of Temperance," 334–35; S. B. Chase, "The Independent Order of Good Templars," in *Centennial Temperance Volume*, 615–16; Carlson, "Temperance Reform in the Cotton Kingdom," 592; Pearson and Hendricks, *Liquor and Anti-Liquor in Virginia*, 159–60; Clark, *The Dry Years*, 28–29; E. K. Putnum, "The Prohibition Movement in Idaho, 1863–1934" (Ph.D. diss., University of Idaho, 1979), 54.

98 Theodore Saloutos, *Farmer Movements in the South, 1865–1933* (Lincoln: University of Nebraska Press, 1964), 33–35; Melton A. McClaurin, *The Knights of Labor in the South* (Westport, Conn.: Greenwood, 1978); Sidney H. Kessler, "The Organization of Negroes in the Knights of Labor," *Journal of Negro History* 37 (1952): 260–63.

99 Beattie, "Sons of Temperance," 172–82; Fahey, *Temperance and Racism*, 58–59.

100 For the United Friends of Temperance (1871–88), see Fahey, *Temperance and Racism*, 70–71; Isaac Litton, "The United Friends of Temperance," in *Centennial Temperance Volume*, 740–48; Scomp, *King Alcohol in the Realm of King Cotton*, 625–31; H. A. Ivy, *Rum on the Run in Texas: A Brief History of Prohibition in the Lone Star State* (Dallas: Temperance Publishing, 1910), 19–22; Whitener, *Prohibition in North Carolina*, 54–55; William G. Davis, "Attacking 'The Matchless Evil': Temperance and Prohibition in Mississippi, 1817–1908" (Ph.D. diss., Mississippi State University, 1975), 49, 66–67.

101 Fahey, *Temperance and Racism*, chapters 3–4; Chase, "Independent Order of Good Templars," 621. Instead of chartering black IOGT lodges, some southern Templars sponsored a new all-black temperance order, the United Order of True Reformers. See David M. Fahey, *The Black Lodge in White America: "True Reformer" Browne and His Economic Strategy* (Dayton: Wright University Press, 1994), 13–14; Scomp, *King Alcohol in the Realm of King Cotton*, 598, 603, 613, 616, 618, 722–23.

102 Fahey, *Temperance and Racism*, chapter 4; Thomas F. Parker, *History of the Independent Order of Good Templars from the Origin of the Order to the Session of the Right Worthy Grand Lodge of 1887* (New York: Phillips and Hunt, 1887), 235–49; Scomp, *King Alcohol in the Realm of King Cotton*, 603–21; Clark, *History of the Temperance Reform in Massachusetts*, 121–22; Chase, "Independent Order of Good Templars," 621–22.

The faction that formed the Right Worthy Grand Lodge of the World consisted largely of British Templars. Though the stated reason for the schism was the racial dispute, others have suggested that British ambition also played a part in the splinter group's formation. See Fahey, *Temperance and Racism*, chapter 4; Parker, *History of the Independent Order of Good Templars*, 259.

103 Fahey, *Temperance and Racism*, 70–71; Sellers, *The Prohibition Movement in Alabama*, 45–46; Scomp, *King Alcohol in the Realm of King Cotton*, 608; 632–41. In Alabama, disgruntled Templars formed the all-white Templars of Temperance, rather than the United Friends of Temperance that emerged in other southern states.

104 *Independent Order of the Good Templars, Right Worthy Grand Proceedings, Twenty-Second Annual Session* (1876), 38–39; *Twenty-Fifth Annual Session* (1879), 34–35.

105 Like the Prohibitionists and the WCTU, the Reform Club movement of the late 1870s drew some support from the fraternal orders. For example, an Illinois Templar complained that this movement "submerged some of our Lodges." See IOGT *Journal of Proceedings of the Twenty-Fifth Annual Session of the Grand Lodge of Illinois* (1878), 47; Turner, "The American Prohibition Movement," 202. Like the antebellum Washingtonians, the Reform Club movement convinced Americans to take the pledge by staging temperance revivals led by reformed drunkards, such as Francis Murphy, Henry Reynolds, and Dr. J. K. Osgood. This movement also resembled its precursor in its initial emphasis on moral suasion, its decentralized organizational structure, and its brief life. However, it differed from Washingtonianism in that it featured religious themes; thus, the Reform Club crusade was often referred to as the "gospel temperance" movement.

106 *Collected Writings of Jessie Forsyth*, 468. Forsyth echoes the claims of George F. Cotterill which appear in his "Good Templary in the United States," *American Issue*, June 1909, 14; and Ernest H. Cherrington, *The Standard Encyclopedia of the Alcohol Problem* (Westerville, Ohio: American Issue, 1924–30), 3:1340.

107 Beattie, "Sons of Temperance," 339.

108 The following party leaders also participated in the Templars, the Sons, or both: George W. Bain, George S. Ball, James Black, William J. Boone, John A. Brooks, A. Burgess, Simeon B. Chase, Eugene W. Chafin, Roswell S. Cheves, George C. Christian, George F. Clark, William F. Clark, John F. Cleghorn, Edward H. Conibear, Uriah Copp, Henry D. Cushing, Albert Dodge, Ephraim L. Eaton, Michael J. Fanning, Herman Faris, Walter Farrington, John B. Finch, Hiram H. Giles, Samuel D. Hastings, I. S. Hicks, Samuel W. Hodges, Andrew B. Huckins, Sylvester Johnson, Theodore D. Kanouse, Fannie Woodbury McCormick, J. R. Miller, Edward W. Mills, John R. Moffett, Emmett D. Nichols, Jonathan H. Orne, Hewson L. Peeke, Isaac Newton Peirce, D. R. Pershing, Edwin J. Pinney, Charles Russell, John Russell, Albert E. Shoemaker, Frank J. Sibley, Henry D. Smith, Green Clay Smith, Julius A. Spencer, Adie A. Stevens, Gideon T. Stewart, Oliver W. Stewart, George R. Stuart, Edward B. Sutton, John L. Thomas, Ralph S. Thompson, John T. Ustick, Henry W. Wilbur, Clarence T. Wilson, Andrew G. Wolfenbarger, Albert D. Wood, Nathan F. Woodbury, Ben D. Wright. Similarly, the following WCTU leaders were drawn from the IOGT: Jessie Ackerman, Anna M. Bain, Carrie M. Wagstaff Barr, Laura A. Berry, Martha McClellan Brown, Mrs. H. B. Brown, Mrs. J. A. Brown, Caroline Brown Buell, Helen L. Bullock, Fanny Du Bois Chase, Anna Wood Clark, Ella Donelson Crawford, Mary C. Crossman, Emma Graves Dietrick, Jessie Forsyth, Harriet Schneider French, Georgeanna M. Gardenier, Laura E. Newcomb Harsha, Harriet N. Kneeland Goff, Frances W. Graham, Rozette Hendrix, Eliza Buckley Ingalls, Mrs. L. M. Kenyon, Imogen F. Hanscom La Chance, Louise M. Andrews Lawson, Eugenia St. John Mann, May Morgan McKoon, Emma Molloy, Emma C. Nason, Martha B. Dickinson O'Donnell, Althea G. Coffin Quimby, Anna Raymond, Florence Donaldson Richard, Mrs. B. C. Rude, Eliza Daniel Stewart, Emily Pitt Stevens, Orpha M. Parker Stuart, Mary F. Myers

Thomas, Mrs. Robert Thompson, Ann Thrower, Mrs. T. S. Truair, Ada Van Pelt, Amanda M. Way, Minnie J. Allison Welch. While some of the overlap between these groups is captured in Mark E. Lender, *Dictionary of American Temperance Biography* (Westport, Conn.: Greenwood, 1984), and Cherrington, *The Standard Encyclopedia of the Alcohol Problem*, my data are also derived from the organizations' officer lists as recorded in group proceedings and memoirs.

109 Brownsword, "Good Templars in Wisconsin," 82–88; Turner, "The American Prohibition Movement," 195, 199–200.

110 The Prohibition party welcomed women into its ranks, though its leaders were primarily men. See Colvin, *Prohibition in the United States*, 68, 116, 643–57. Templar women who participated in party affairs included Martha McClellan Brown, Eugenia St. John Mann, Fanny Woodbury McCormick, and Eliza Daniel Stewart.

111 Black, "Is There a Necessity for a Prohibition Party?" 336–37.

112 Colvin, *Prohibition in the United States*, 63, 82; Jack S. Blocker, "The Modernity of Prohibitionists: An Analysis of Leadership Structure and Background," in *Alcohol, Reform and Society: The Liquor Issue in Social Context*, ed. Jack S. Blocker (Westport, Conn.: Greenwood, 1979), 152–54; Paul Kleppner, *The Third Electoral System, 1853–1892: Parties, Voters, and Political Cultures* (Chapel Hill: University of North Carolina Press, 1979), 242–43. For the party's reliance on this network in political campaigns, see Clark, *History of the Temperance Reform in Massachusetts*, 147–56; Putnum, "The Prohibition Movement in Idaho," 60–62, 165–72, 208–9; Clark, *The Dry Years*, 36–37; Ostrander, *The Prohibition Movement in California*, 95; Brownsword, "Good Templars in Wisconsin," 108.

113 Clark, *History of the Temperance Reform in Massachusetts*, 155.

114 Whereas the national IOGT endorsed separate party action in the late 1860s and early 1870s, the national WCTU supported such action in the mid-1880s and 1890s by passing resolutions in the party's favor.

115 *Independent Order of the Good Templars, Right Worthy Grand Lodge Proceedings, Twenty-Second Annual Session* (1876), 38–39; *Twenty-Fifth Annual Session* (1879), 34–35.

116 Blocker, *Retreat from Reform*, 45.

117 Svend Petersen, *A Statistical History of the American Presidential Elections* (New York: Frederick Ungar, 1963), 198.

118 For example, Barbara L. Epstein unequivocally asserts that after the Woman's Crusade, men "left the active role in the [temperance] movement to women." See her *The Politics of Domesticity: Women, Evangelism, and Temperance in Nineteenth-Century America* (Middletown, Conn.: Wesleyan University Press, 1981), 110.

119 In the most extreme cases, some Prohibitionists laid down their lives for their party. See Richard F. Hamm, "The Killing of John R. Moffett and the Trial of J. T. Clark: Race, Prohibition, and Politics in Danville, 1887–1893," *Virginia Magazine of History and Biography* 101 (1993): 375–404. In general, though, they suffered more from social ostracism. As one party member lamented, "I have not only suffered or been punished in business ways for my radical ideals, but lost former friends, received cold nods from those who should have been my friends, and hooted on the street by boys whose fathers enjoyed repeating current falsehoods." See Woodbury, *Prohibition in Maine*, 281; Cherrington, *The Standard Encyclopedia of the Alcohol Problem* 2:626.

120 *Collected Writings of Jessie Forsyth*, 469. Genevieve G. McBride has echoed Forsyth's argument in *On Wisconsin Women: Working for Their Rights from Settlement to Suffrage* (Madison: University of Wisconsin Press, 1993), 79–80.

121 Scholars estimate that women accounted for 25–50% of Templar membership. See Fahey, *Temper-*

ance and Racism, 24; Brownsword, "Good Templars in Wisconsin," 8; Bader, *Prohibition in Kansas*, 28; *Collected Writings of Jessie Forsyth*, 8. For Templar women during the war, see IOGT *Journal of Proceedings of the Ninth Annual Session of the Grand Lodge of Illinois* (1862), 11; Fahey, *Temperance and Racism*, 27; Brownsword, "Good Templars in Wisconsin," 8; Dannenbaum, "The Origins of Temperance Activism," 245; Cherrington, *The Standard Encyclopedia of the Alcohol Problem* 3:1336.

122 Fahey, *Temperance and Racism*, 28–29; *Collected Writings of Jessie Forsyth*, 8; Bader, *Prohibition in Kansas*, 28.

123 Cherrington, *The Standard Encyclopedia of the Alcohol Problem* 3:1340; Frances E. Willard, *Woman and Temperance: Or, The Work and Workers of the Woman's Christian Temperance Union* (Hartford: Park, 1884), 127–35. Templars who attended the union's first convention included Mrs. J. A. Brown, Martha McClellan Brown, Fanny DuBois Chase, Harriet Schneider French, Harriet N. Kneeland Goff, Mrs. L. M. Kenyon, Eliza Daniel Stewart, and Mrs. Robert Thompson.

124 See chapter 3 for more on the Woman's Crusade. Of course, some crusaders already had experience in the anti-liquor movement. For example, Mary C. Crossman, Mrs. J. A. Brown, Amanda M. Way, Orpha M. Parker Stuart, Harriet Schneider French, Amanda Clark, Anna Wood Clark, Martha McClellan Brown, Barbara Hay, Alfretta "Brightie" Ogle, Eliza Daniel Stewart, and Maggie V. Ustick were all Templars. For the Woman's Crusade, see Jack S. Blocker, *"Give to the Winds Thy Fears": The Women's Temperance Crusade, 1873–1874* (Westport, Conn.: Greenwood, 1985); Ruth Bordin, *Woman and Temperance: The Quest for Power and Liberty, 1873–1900* (Philadelphia: Temple University Press, 1981), chapter 2; Dannenbaum, *Drink and Disorder*, chapter 7.

125 The national WCTU endorsed total abstinence at its first convention in 1874, state prohibition in 1876, national prohibition in 1879, and national constitutional prohibition by the early 1880s. See Bordin, *Woman and Temperance*, 37, 55–56, 63, 123.

126 After producing various pledges, the WCTU adopted the following as its official pledge in 1877: "I hereby solemnly promise, God helping me, to abstain from all distilled, fermented and malt liquors, including wine and cider, and to employ all proper means to discourage use and traffic in the same." Meanwhile, the Templar pledge read as follows: "No member shall make, buy, sell, use, furnish, or cause to be furnished to others as a beverage, any Spirituous or Malt Liquors, Wine or Cider; and every member shall discountenance the manufacture, sale, and use thereof, in all proper ways." See *Annual Meeting Minutes of the National Woman's Christian Temperance Union, 1877 Convention*, 172; *Cyclopedia of Temperance and Prohibition*, 241.

127 Though the union and IOGT were both hierarchical democracies, the WCTU's state and local unions possessed more freedom than their Templar counterparts.

128 Chase, "Independent Order of Good Templars," 610. Indeed, the WCTU took the Templar's committee system to new heights of specialization. By 1890 the union's specialized departments numbered about forty, and addressed organizing, outreach, publicity and education, personal and social reform, and alcohol substitution. For these categories, see Janet Z. Giele, *Two Paths to Women's Equality: Temperance, Suffrage, and the Origins of Modern Feminism* (New York: Twayne, 1995), 93–95. For a WCTU department's history, see Alison M. Parker, *Purifying America: Women, Cultural Reform, and Pro-Censorship Activism, 1873–1933* (Urbana: University of Illinois Press, 1997).

129 By the late nineteenth century, the Templars had lodges in Canada, Great Britain, Australia, New Zealand, Malta, France, Portugal, South Africa, Bermuda, Belgium, India, Ceylon, the Honduras, British Guiana, China, Norway, Sweden, Denmark, and Germany, among others. Similarly, the World's WCTU included unions in Canada, England, Scotland, Australia, France, Spain, Japan, China, India, South Africa, Natal, Norway, and Mexico. For the World's WCTU, see Ian Tyrrell, *Woman's World, Woman's Empire: The Woman's Christian Temperance Union in International Perspective, 1880–1930* (Chapel

Hill: University of North Carolina Press, 1991). Significantly, several international Templars later joined the World's WCTU, including Margaret Bright Lucas, Mary Jane Scott Farnham, Sarah Galt Elwood McKee, Katie H. R. Findlay Stuart, and Emma Stockwell Price.

130 During the 1880s Alabama and Tennessee formed separate black unions, variously designated "State Colored WCTU" and "State Union No. 2" in the national union's reports. By 1900 the unions of North Carolina, Georgia, Arkansas, Louisiana, Texas, and Mississippi were similarly segregated. See the *Annual Meeting Minutes of the National Woman's Christian Temperance Union, 1888–1900 Conventions*, Treasurer's Reports; Bordin, *Woman and Temperance*, 83–85; Mary M. Thomas, *The New Woman in Alabama: Social Reforms and Suffrage, 1890–1920* (Tuscaloosa: University of Alabama Press, 1992), 19–20; Anastasia Sims, " 'The Sword of the Spirit': The WCTU and Moral Reform in North Carolina, 1883–1933," *North Carolina Historical Review* 64 (1987): 398.

131 *Annual Meeting Minutes of the National Woman's Christian Temperance Union, 1886 Convention*, 126; *1887 Convention*, Corresponding Secretary's Report.

132 The best source for WCTU membership data is the *Annual Meeting Minutes of the National Woman's Christian Temperance Union*. For a summary of the union's per capita membership in the states, see Giele, *Two Paths to Women's Equality*, 90–92.

133 "Nebraska's Triple Alliance Greeting," *International Good Templar*, 1889, 763–64. See also "Report on Special Mission Work in Rhode Island and Virginia, USA," *Independent Order of the Good Templars, Right Worthy Grand Proceedings, Thirty-Second Annual Session* (1886), 94–95; *Cyclopedia of Temperance and Prohibition*, 104–11.

134 For collaboration among these organizations, see Putnum, "The Prohibition Movement in Idaho," 78; Clark, *The Dry Years*, 51; IOGT *Journal of Proceedings of the Twenty-Fifth Annual Session of the Grand Lodge of Illinois* (1878), 45; *The Standard Encyclopedia of the Alcohol Problem* 4:1787; Frances E. Willard, *Glimpses of Fifty Years: The Autobiography of an American Woman* (Chicago: H. J. Smith, 1889), 384; Cora Cramer, ed., *History, Pennsylvania Woman's Christian Temperance Union* (Quincy, Pa.: Quincy Orphanage, 1937), 171, 190–91, 284–86; *Minutes of the Fifth Annual Convention of the Woman's Christian Temperance Union of California* (1884), 21; *Sixth Annual Convention* (1885), 26–27.

135 Indeed, the WCTU's southern wing seems to have drawn support from the region's missionary society movement, which only developed in the late 1870s. The union's initial weakness in the South probably also reflected the region's conservative attitudes about women. See Bordin, *Woman and Temperance*, 76–85; Thomas, *New Woman in Alabama*, 13–15; Nancy A. Hardesty, " 'The Best Temperance Organization in the Land': Southern Methodists and the WCTU in Georgia," *Methodist History* 28 (1990): 190.

136 Whitaker, "A History of the Ohio Woman's Christian Temperance Union," 121–24; Bordin, *Woman and Temperance*, 123.

137 *Cyclopedia of Temperance and Prohibition*, 162–67, 576 n. 1; Blocker, *Retreat from Reform*, 41–47.

138 John E. Caswell, "The Prohibition Movement in Oregon to the Adoption of Statewide Prohibition in 1914" (M.A. thesis, University of Oregon, 1937), 45–46. For more on IOGT dissension over the Prohibition party in the states, see Brownsword, "Good Templars in Wisconsin," 98–100, 106–7; William E. West, "Dry Crusade: The Prohibition Movement in Colorado, 1858–1933" (Ph.D. diss., University of Colorado, 1971), 107–8. At the national level, similar acrimony surfaced in 1872, when Prohibitionists insisted that the Right Worthy Grand Lodge uphold the party's uncompromising position on moderate anti-liquor policies, a demand that led to the order's retreat from its prior endorsements of the party. See Turner, "The American Prohibition Movement," 199–200.

139 Norton Mezvinsky, "The White Ribbon Reform, 1874–1920," (Ph.D. diss., University of Wisconsin, 1959), 121–38; Bordin, *Woman and Temperance*, 123–30. For a local union's discord over the Prohibition party, see Clark, *History of the Temperance Reform in Massachusetts*, 171–80.

140 *Annual Meeting Minutes of the National Woman's Christian Temperance Union, 1884 Convention*, 69; *1885 Convention*, 55; *Christian Union*, 29 November 1888, 622; *Independent Order of the Good Templars, Right Worthy Grand Proceedings, Thirty-Second Annual Session* (1886), 120–22.

141 Whitener, *Prohibition in North Carolina*, 56; Scomp, *King Alcohol in the Realm of King Cotton*, 624–41; Grace Leab, "Tennessee Temperance Activities, 1870–1899," *East Tennessee Historical Society's Publications* 21 (1949): 53–55.

142 *Independent Order of the Good Templars, Right Worthy Grand Lodge Proceedings, Twenty-First Annual Session* (1875), 24–25; Ivy, *Rum on the Run in Texas*, 19. During the 1870s regional temperance orders also overshadowed the northern secret societies in Mississippi, Arkansas, and Alabama, though the IOGT revived in Alabama during the 1880s. See Davis, "Attacking 'The Matchless Evil,' " 66; George M. Hunt, "A History of the Prohibition Movement in Arkansas" (M.A. thesis, University of Arkansas, 1933), 40, 67; Sellers, *The Prohibition Movement in Alabama*, 46–47, 52–53.

143 For the IOGT's prominence in Virginia, see Pearson and Hendricks, *Liquor and Anti-Liquor in Virginia*, 158–60; "Virginia," *National Temperance Advocate*, February 1880, 28. In fact, the Virginia IOGT steadily climbed from 216 members in 1868 to 8,699 in 1880. See *Independent Order of the Good Templars, Right Worthy Grand Proceedings* (1868–80).

144 Pearson and Hendricks, *Liquor and Anti-Liquor in Virginia*, 170–72.

145 Whitener, *Prohibition in North Carolina*, 56, 61; Paul Isaac, *Prohibition and Politics: Turbulent Decades in Tennessee, 1885–1920* (Knoxville: University of Tennessee Press, 1965), 13, 18.

146 If the Sons' attempt to establish the Prohibition party in North Carolina produced but minuscule vote totals, the IOGT's campaign for constitutional prohibition in 1889 convinced only fifteen hundred voters to petition the legislature for such action. See Whitener, *Prohibition in North Carolina*, 102–3.

147 Ibid., 87–101.

148 "Virginia," *National Temperance Advocate*, February 1880, 28; Pearson and Hendricks, *Liquor and Anti-Liquor in Virginia*, 174–78; "Report on Special Mission Work in Rhode Island and Virginia," 96; Leab, "Tennessee Temperance Activities," 54, 58; Scomp, *King Alcohol in the Realm of King Cotton*, 623; "Georgia," *National Temperance Advocate*, January 1883, 13.

149 Scomp, *King Alcohol in the Realm of King Cotton*, 627. Of the approximately ten state branches of the United Friends of Temperance, only that of Texas seemed politically inclined. See Ivy, *Rum on the Run in Texas*, 20–23.

150 Ivy, *Rum on the Run in Texas*, 634; Litton, "United Friends of Temperance," 740; Fahey, *Temperance and Racism*, 67.

151 Sellers, *The Prohibition Movement in Alabama*, 47.

152 Scomp, *King Alcohol in the Realm of King Cotton*, 634.

153 Unlike their northern colleagues, southern radicals considered statutory prohibition an acceptable substitute for constitutional prohibition, which perhaps reflected their relative moderation.

154 Davis, "Attacking 'The Matchless Evil,' " 178–82.

155 Southern unions which actively promoted constitutional prohibition during the 1880s included those of Louisiana, Mississippi, North Carolina, Tennessee, and Texas. See Whitener, *Prohibition in North Carolina*, 69; Sims, " 'The Sword of the Spirit,' " 404; Larry J. Watson, "Evangelical Protestants and the Prohibition Movement in Texas, 1887–1919" (Ph.D. diss., Texas A&M University, 1993),

64–66; Davis, "Attacking 'The Matchless Evil,'" 191; *Annual Meeting Minutes of the National Woman's Christian Temperance Union, 1885 Convention*, 115–16; *1887 Convention*, 107; *Cyclopedia of Temperance and Prohibition*, 113–14.

156 Alwyn Barr, *Reconstruction to Reform: Texas Politics, 1876–1906* (Austin: University of Texas Press, 1971), 86–88; Davis, "Attacking 'The Matchless Evil,'" 205–14. See also Pearson and Hendricks, *Liquor and Anti-Liquor in Virginia*, 214–15; Hunt, "A History of the Prohibition Movement in Arkansas," 75.

157 In North Carolina's referendum on statutory prohibition in 1881, 77.4% of the electorate voted wet. Similarly, dry constitutional amendments were rejected by 63.1% of the electorate in Texas (1887) and 55.3% in Tennessee (1887).

158 Davis, "Attacking 'The Matchless Evil,'" 171–74, 186, 190–91, 199–205, 211–14.

159 Watson, "Evangelical Protestants and the Prohibition Movement in Texas," 32–38, 46–48.

160 Other church dignitaries who helped lead the South's postbellum anti-liquor movement included Hamilcar H. McNeill, B. F. Riley, David C. Kelley, Elijah Embree Hoss, O. Fitzgerald, John M. Clayton, A. R. Winfield, Warren C. Black, S. A. Steele, Atticus G. Haygood, J. B. Hawthorne, Henry M. Turner, H. Woodsmall, Jesse H. Page, George B. Whitmore, R. H. Whitaker, A. E. Dickinson, F. M. Edwards, J. L. Lemmons, J. R. Wolf.

161 Isaac, *Prohibition and Politics*, 62, 66–67; Cherrington, *The Standard Encyclopedia of the Alcohol Problem* 4:1447; Whitener, *Prohibition in North Carolina*, 82, 109; Sellers, *The Prohibition Movement in Alabama*, 80; Pearson and Hendricks, *Liquor and Anti-Liquor in Virginia*, 205, 215–16. The hostility of southern church leaders toward the Prohibitionists was such that one Methodist cleric was suspended from the ministry after the party nominated him for governor of Tennessee.

162 For the actions of southern church bodies after 1875, see Davis, "Attacking 'The Matchless Evil,'" 91–92; Scomp, *King Alcohol in the Realm of King Cotton*, 726–34, chapter 46; Sellers, *The Prohibition Movement in Alabama*, 57–62; Whitener, *Prohibition in North Carolina*, 62–63, 107–12; Pearson and Hendricks, *Liquor and Anti-Liquor in Virginia*, 201–10; Isaac, *Prohibition and Politics*, 18–27, 74–75; William A. Link, *The Paradox of Southern Progressivism, 1880–1930* (Chapel Hill: University of North Carolina Press, 1992), 45–51; Cherrington, *The Evolution of Prohibition in the United States of America*, 214, 219–20.

163 Scomp, *King Alcohol in the Realm of King Cotton*, 730–31.

164 Pearson and Hendricks, *Liquor and Anti-Liquor in Virginia*, 171–72. Randolph-Macon College was affiliated with the Methodist church. Other southern Christian colleges which served as hubs of anti-liquor activity included Baylor University, the University of the South, and Emory College. Black colleges like Fisk University and Clark University similarly engaged in political temperance efforts. See Watson, "Evangelical Protestants and the Prohibition Movement in Texas," 45; Leab, "Tennessee Temperance Activities," 58–59; Isaac, *Prohibition and Politics*, 36; Hardesty, "'The Best Temperance Organization in the Land,'" 192; "Georgia," *National Temperance Advocate*, February 1881, 29; Scomp, *King Alcohol in the Realm of King Cotton*, 731.

165 "Tennessee," *National Temperance Advocate*, March 1881, 44; Grace Leab, "The Temperance Movement in Tennessee, 1860–1907" (M.A. thesis, University of Tennessee, 1938), 52.

166 Watson, "Evangelical Protestants and the Prohibition Movement in Texas," 45–64; "Texas," *National Temperance Advocate*, October 1883, 173; "Arkansas," *National Temperance Advocate*, December 1880, 190; Isaac, *Prohibition and Politics*, 34–36; Whitener, *Prohibition in North Carolina*, 61–66.

167 Pearson and Hendricks, *Liquor and Anti-Liquor in Virginia*, 172–76, 209; Davis, "Attacking 'The Matchless Evil,'" 100–103, 133–38; Hunt, "A History of the Prohibition Movement in Arkansas," 67–68; Isaac, *Prohibition and Politics*, 73–75; Leab, "The Temperance Movement in Tennessee," 52–54.

168 By 1887 only Tennessee and Alabama lacked general local option laws. However, activists in Ten-

nessee had access to the Four Mile Law, which allowed activists to gradually reduce the number of saloons in their communities.

169 Galloway served as vice-president of the ASL during the years 1900–1906 and belonged to the league's first national executive committee in 1895. See Ernest H. Cherrington, *The History of the Anti-Saloon League* (Westerville, Ohio: American Issue, 1913), 34–35.

170 Davis, "Attacking 'The Matchless Evil,' " chapters 5–8; "National Prohibition Our Final Object: Mississippi Anti-Saloon League Demands State-wide Prohibition as a Step toward It," *American Issue*, 26 July 1907, 10.

171 Frank Foxcroft, "Prohibition in the South," *Atlantic Monthly*, May 1908, 629.

172 Whitener, *Prohibition in North Carolina*, 87–101, 107; Pearson and Hendricks, *Liquor and Anti-Liquor in Virginia*, 178–80.

173 Apparently, local option became less appealing to North Carolina drys after the wets became more successful at winning "no-license" elections. See Whitener, *Prohibition in North Carolina*, 95–96.

174 North Carolina's anti-liquor activists could use this method of banning local saloons because the state's constitution did not explicitly forbid special legislation. See chapter 4 for more on special legislation. The size of dry regions varied, depending on the petitioners' wishes. For example, some churches requested that liquor sales be banned within a radius of one mile, while others asked for two or three miles.

175 Whitener, *Prohibition in North Carolina*, 100. "Local-prohibition-through-special legislation" had such a marginal impact on the number of licensed saloons because most liquor establishments were located in municipalities, far from the petitioners in question.

176 Nicholson, "Local-Option Movement," 3.

177 *Anti-Saloon*, December 1895, 4, 7; "The Lone Star State Leads: The Onward March of Local Option Prohibition in Texas," *American Issue*, 1 August 1902, 1.

178 Howard H. Russell, "The Governor Helps Quietly: Oberlin Wins the Beatty Law," unpublished manuscript, box 2, Howard Hyde Russell Papers; "How the Victory Was Won in Oregon," *American Issue*, 8 July 1904, 6.

179 "Local Option as a Step to State-Wide Prohibition," *American Issue*, 13 September 1907, 8.

180 Cherrington, *The Evolution of Prohibition in the United States of America*, 92–93.

181 For example, during the years 1873–79 the NTS unsuccessfully sought to initiate a congressional investigation of the liquor traffic and its social effects. See Turner, "The American Prohibition Movement," 205–7. Similarly, the National Christian Temperance Alliance, based in Pennsylvania, apparently accomplished little. See Kaylor, "The Prohibition Movement in Pennsylvania," 311–12.

182 Brownsword, "Good Templars in Wisconsin," 62–63.

183 Blocker, *Retreat from Reform*, 10; Blocker, "The Modernity of Prohibitionists," 158.

184 Clara C. Chapin, ed., *Thumb Nail Sketches of White Ribbon Women* (Chicago: Woman's Temperance Publishing Association 1895), 64–67, 103, 108; Mezvinsky, "The White Ribbon Reform," chapter 4; Bordin, *Woman and Temperance*, 9–10, 34–36; Putnum, "The Prohibition Movement in Idaho," 133–35.

185 In 1880 Mary H. Hunt founded the WCTU's Department of Scientific Temperance Instruction in Schools and Colleges and began her campaign for state laws which required temperance instruction in public schools. Because her work was educational, Hunt received support from most temperance groups and won scientific instruction laws in most states. See Mezvinsky, "The White Ribbon Reform," chapter 7; Bordin, *Woman and Temperance*, 135–38; Dorchester, *The Liquor Problem in All Ages*, 663–67.

186 One exception to this rule was James N. Fitzgerald, a cleric who supported the Prohibition party

and became a Methodist Episcopal bishop. However, Fitzgerald "drew considerable criticism upon himself from his denomination for [his partisan] cause." See Cherrington, *The Standard Encyclopedia of the Alcohol Problem* 3:998–99.

187 "A Frank Statement to Members of the Various Political Parties," *Christian Advocate*, 1 October 1885, 1. See also "Why One Subscriber Discontinues," *Christian Advocate*, 29 March 1888, 201; "The Church One—Parties Many," *Christian Advocate*, 18 October 1888, 685; Ostrander, *The Prohibition Movement in California*, 55; *Cyclopedia of Temperance and Prohibition*, 494–95; Blocker, *Retreat from Reform*, 82–83.

188 Ashenhurst, *Recollections of an Octogenarian*, 141.

189 Colvin, *Prohibition in the United States*, 166.

190 Brownsword, "Good Templars in Wisconsin," 65–66.

191 Ibid., chapter 5; Beattie, "Sons of Temperance," 137–62; Siegal, "A Matter of the Public Welfare," 69, 71; Ostrander, *The Prohibition Movement in California*, 34.

192 Philip S. White and Ezra Stiles Ely, *Vindication of the Order of the Sons of Temperance* (New York: Oliver and Brother, 1848), 41.

193 Brownsword, "Good Templars in Wisconsin," 66–67.

194 The secret orders felt justified in supplanting the churches as the leading anti-liquor associations because the churches appeared passive after the 1850s. See Ostrander, *The Prohibition Movement in California*, 35–36.

195 Turner, "The American Prohibition Movement," 24–25; Brownsword, "Good Templars in Wisconsin," 67; Ostrander, *The Prohibition Movement in California*, 55–57, 86.

196 Nancy A. Hardesty, *Women Called to Witness: Evangelical Feminism in the 19th Century* (Nashville: Abingdon, 1984), 153; Mezvinsky, "The White Ribbon Reform," 82–85; Bordin, *Woman and Temperance*, 36–37, 45–46; Ostrander, *The Prohibition Movement in California*, 58, 62.

197 As Bordin notes, Willard's election did not magically transform the WCTU "from a temperance praying band to an activist organization." In fact, during the Wittenmyer years, state and local unions had often participated in political campaigns. (See Bordin, *Woman and Temperance*, 63–64.) However, the national union's emphasis on political issues gradually increased during the Willard years, while Wittenmyer's preference for moral suasion declined in significance.

198 Daniel Dorchester, "The National League for the Suppression of the Liquor Traffic," 533; Francis M. Whitaker, "Ohio WCTU and the Prohibition Amendment Campaign of 1883," *Ohio History* 83 (1974): 100–101.

199 WCTU leaders acknowledged that such a rule had been proposed at the national convention in 1888 but insisted that a large majority had rejected it. For the controversy over the "gag law," see "Temperance News" in *Christian Union*, 1 November 1888, 15 November 1888, 29 November 1888. For another critique of Willard's tactics in aligning the WCTU with the Prohibition party, see Hamilton, "Prohibition in Politics," 510–11.

200 Hardesty, *Women Called to Witness*, 22–23. Of course, southern churches were even more strongly opposed to the WCTU's advocacy of women's rights. See Hardesty, " 'The Best Temperance Organization in the Land,' " 192–94.

201 Ruth Bordin, *Frances Willard: A Biography* (Chapel Hill: University of North Carolina Press, 1986), 160–68; Willard, *Glimpses of Fifty Years*, 617–21; "The Woman's Christian Temperance Union," *Christian Advocate*, 1 November 1888, 717. Even after the 1888 incident, the WCTU continued to fight for the admission of women as General Conference delegates. See C. H. Zimmerman, "Women in Church and State," *Union Signal*, 5 February 1891, 3; "Woman in the General Conference," *Union Signal*, 5 February 1891, 8.

202 Colvin, *Prohibition in the United States*, chapter 15, 236; Henry W. Blair, *The Temperance Movement: Or, The Conflict between Alcohol and Man* (Boston: William Smythe, 1888), chapter 21; Kleppner, *The Third Electoral System*, 211–14; Richard Jensen, *The Winning of the Midwest: Social and Political Conflict, 1888–1896* (Chicago: University of Chicago Press, 1971), 72–73.

203 Blocker, *Retreat from Reform*, 82–83; Dorcas J. Spencer, *A History of the Woman's Christian Temperance Union of Northern and Central California* (Oakland: West Coast Printing, 1911), 54–55.

204 "Local Option or Prohibition? Views of Prominent Men," *Christian Union*, 28 March 1889, 408.

205 *Collected Writings of Jessie Forsyth*, 377.

206 Frances E. Willard, "Michigan's Battle," *Union Signal*, 21 April 1887, 4.

207 In particular, the radicals opposed "high license" laws, which required individuals to pay substantial annual fees for liquor licenses. According to the radicals, such legislation failed to reduce liquor traffic crimes and only granted legal protection to the trade. For such opposition, see *Independent Order of the Good Templars, Right Worthy Grand Lodge Proceedings, Thirtieth Annual Session* (1883), 10; *Thirty-Second Annual Session* (1886), 118–19; *Thirty-Third Annual Session* (1887), 126; "The Attitude of the Woman's Christian Temperance Union toward High License," *Union Signal*, 15 March 1883, 8–9; *Annual Meeting Minutes of the National Woman's Christian Temperance Union, 1883 Convention*, 54–55; *1885 Convention*, 44; Alphonso A. Hopkins, *Wealth and Waste: The Principles of Political Economy in their Application to the Present Problems of Labor, Law, and the Liquor Traffic* (New York: Funk and Wagnalls, 1895), chapter 8; *Cyclopedia of Temperance and Prohibition*, 207–20; Colvin, *Prohibition in the United States*, chapter 13, 190.

208 "High License and a Prohibitory Constitutional Amendment," *Christian Advocate*, 6 March 1884, 1; "The Church One—Parties Many," 608.

209 Blocker, *Retreat from Reform*, 85–88. For the IOGT's radicalism in its declining years, see Putnum, "The Prohibition Movement in Idaho," 58–63; Eugene F. Chafin, "One Standard of Morals," *National Good Templar*, 28 July 1910, 1–2; Orrin H. Graham, "Results of Local Option," *National Good Templar*, 29 December 1910, 1, 5; Thomas Edwards, "The Prohibition Party," *National Good Templar*, 12 January 1911, 1.

210 *Proceedings of the Sixth Annual Meeting of the Citizens' Law and Order League of the United States* (1888), 114–15; "Andrew Paxton Is Dead," *Chicago Tribune*, 13 January 1889, 15.

211 In the years 1849–51 an Irish priest named Father Mathew converted thousands of American Catholics to the temperance cause during his tour of the United States. As a result, Catholics formed several local temperance societies that emphasized total abstinence. After the Civil War most Catholic teetotalers remobilized under the auspices of the Catholic Total Abstinence Union of America, which peaked in the early twentieth century with about seventy thousand members. For that organization, see Joan Bland, *Hibernian Crusade: The Story of the Catholic Total Abstinence Union of America* (Washington: Catholic University Press, 1951); Joseph C. Gibbs, *History of the Catholic Total Abstinence Union of America* (Philadelphia, 1907).

212 Bland, *Hibernian Crusade*, 115–18.

213 Ibid., 81, 96, 104–5.

214 "Liquor to Minors: A Lecture by Bishop Ireland on This Subject, with Reference to the Citizens' League of Chicago," *Chicago Tribune*, 19 February 1884, 9.

215 *Proceedings of the Sixth Annual Meeting of the Citizens' Law and Order League of the United States*, 115.

216 Clark makes a similar argument in *The Dry Years*, 76–77.

217 "The Temperance Question," *Chautauquan*, December 1883, 179–80; "High License and a Prohibitory Constitutional Amendment," 1; A. D. P. van Buren, "Our Temperance Conflict," *Michigan Pioneer Collections* 13 (1888): 405–7.

218 Editorial, *Law and Order*, 7 March 1885, 177. See also J. C. Schaffer, "Suggestions regarding Temperance Work," *Century Magazine*, March 1884, 792–93.

219 *Christian Union*, 10 July 1890, 36. See also "A Temperance Platform," *Christian Union*, 20 August 1885, 2–3; S. K. Strother, "Prohibition in Kansas," *Century Magazine*, March 1884, 793–94.

220 "For Restriction," *Christian Union*, 3 March 1887, 20; L. Edwin Dudley, "Restrictive License in Boston," *Christian Union*, 15 August 1889, 183; Howard Crosby, "Is High License a Remedy?" *Proceedings of the National Temperance Congress Held in the Broadway Tabernacle*, 187–93; Kaylor, "The Prohibition Movement in Pennsylvania," 288.

221 "To Temperance Voters," *Christian Union*, 8 October 1885, 3; "Local Option," *Christian Advocate*, 28 January 1886, 53; "Recent Temperance Elections," *Christian Union*, 27 June 1889, 811; Editorial, *Christian Union*, 13 December 1888, 702.

222 "Ex-Mayor Low on the Saloon in City Politics," *Christian Union*, 29 November 1888, 622.

223 Most "law and order" reformers only proposed state laws which enhanced enforcement efforts. See "The Citizens' Law and Order League of the United States," *Law and Order*, 4 October 1884, 5; *Proceedings of the Sixth Annual Meeting of the Citizens' Law and Order League of Massachusetts* (1888), 7–8.

224 In addition to founding the National League, Daniel Dorchester wrote a history of the temperance movement, *The Liquor Problem in All Ages*, and served on the Committee on Temperance and Prohibition during two General Conferences of the Methodist Episcopal Church. For his prominence in church circles, see "Great Loss to Methodism: Dr. Daniel Dorchester Passes Away," *Boston Globe*, 13 March 1907, 1, 3.

225 From 1880 to 1884 the Prohibition party raised its presidential vote total from 10,364 votes to 150,957. In New York the Prohibitionist candidate polled 25,006 votes while the Republican candidate, James Blaine, lost the state by 1,149 votes (and hence lost the presidency). See Petersen, *A Statistical History of the American Presidential Elections*, 52, 194.

226 Daniel Dorchester, "The National League for the Suppression of the Liquor Traffic," 530–34; "The National League for the Suppression of the Liquor Traffic," *Law and Order*, 31 January 1885, 143; Turner, "The American Prohibition Movement," 305–7; August F. Fehlandt, *A Century of Drink Reform in the United States* (Cincinnati: Jennings and Graham, 1904), 454; Dorchester, *Liquor Problem in All Ages*, 719. During 1885–88 the Anti-Saloon Republicans sought to convince the party to adopt a more hostile posture toward the liquor industry. See chapter 5 for that movement.

227 Dorchester, "National League for the Suppression of the Liquor Traffic," 533; "A National Temperance League," *Law and Order*, 17 January 1885, 125.

228 Turner, "The American Prohibition Movement," 309.

229 Editorial, *Law and Order*, 7 March 1885, 177.

230 Scomp, *King Alcohol in the Realm of King Cotton*, 770; *Cyclopedia of Temperance and Prohibition*, 769. Indeed, all four of the National League's highest ranked officers, Daniel Dorchester (president), J. Ellen Foster (general secretary), Albert H. Plumb (recording secretary), and Joseph D. Weeks (treasurer), publicly advocated constitutional prohibition. See Dorchester, "An Argument for Constitutional Prohibition," 7–9; Albert H. Plumb, "Constitutional Prohibition," in *The Constitutional Prohibitionist*, ed. J. N. Stearns (New York: National Temperance Society and Publishing House, 1889), 10–11; Foster, *Constitutional Amendment Manual*; Kaylor, "The Prohibition Movement in Pennsylvania," 266 n. 41.

231 Fehlandt, *A Century of Drink Reform*, 271; Turner, "The American Prohibition Movement," 310–11.

232 Editorial, *Law and Order*, 7 March 1885, 177.

233 L. Edwin Dudley, "The Law and Order Movement: Historical Sketch," *Lend-a-Hand*, March 1892, 201.

234 For example, Stewart L. Woodford supported the CLOL's efforts though he was neither a teetotaler nor a prohibitionist. See "Address of Gen. Stewart L. Woodford," *Proceedings of the Fourth Annual Meeting of the Citizens' Law and Order League of Massachusetts* (1886), 26. Similarly, three moderate church dignitaries, Howard Crosby, Lyman Abbott, and Phillips Brooks, all participated in the CLOL while maintaining acrimonious relationships with the radical drys.

235 For endorsements and positive accounts of the CLOL, see *Annual Meeting Minutes of the National Woman's Christian Temperance Union, 1884 Convention*, 26; "The L. and O. League," *Christian Union*, 11 February 1886, 4; "The Power of the Citizen," *Albany Evening Journal*, 22 February 1887, 2; "National Law and Order League," *Christian Union*, 3 March 1887, 21; "Mr. Evarts on 'Law and Order,'" *New York Times*, 23 February 1888, 4; *Minutes of the Eleventh Annual Convention of the WCTU of Colorado* (1890), 60; *Minutes of the Twelfth Annual Convention of the WCTU of Colorado* (1891), 59; *Twelfth Annual Report, WCTU of Illinois* (1885), 12; Blair, *The Temperance Movement*, 496–98. For radical critiques of the CLOL, see John B. Finch, "What, Why, and How," in *The People versus the Liquor Traffic*, ed. Charles A. McNully (Milwaukee: Literature Committee, IOGT, 1887), 214–17; J. C. Fernald, "Representative Enforcement of Law," *Statesman*, October 1888, 27–32; A. A. Miner, "The Saloon Evil," *Arena*, May 1894, 828–29.

236 See chapter 3 for more on the CLOL's enforcement efforts.

237 *Proceedings of the Third Annual Meeting of the Citizens' Law and Order League of Massachusetts* (1885), 10; "Illinois," *National Temperance Advocate*, October 1880, 158; Thomas S. Smith, "A Martyr for Prohibition: The Murder of Reverend George C. Haddock," *Palimpsest* 62 (1981): 186–93; J. C. Furnas, *The Life and Times of the Late Demon Rum* (New York: Capricorn, 1965), 262–63; Perry R. Duis, *The Saloon: Public Drinking in Chicago and Boston, 1880–1920* (Urbana: University of Illinois Press, 1983), 99.

238 Washington Gladden, "The Enforcement of Law," *"Unity, Persistency, Victory!" A Souvenir Selection of Anti-Saloon Addresses* (Columbus: Hann and Adair, 1895).

239 For the ASL's pragmatic legal approach, see Hamm, *Shaping the Eighteenth Amendment*, chapter 4.

240 *Proceedings, Third National Anti-Saloon Convention* (Washington: American Anti-Saloon League, 1898), 54; "More Agitation Needed, and Less Attempted Law Enforcement," *American Issue* 7 (May 1900): 11; "Concerning Detective Service," *American Issue*, September 1900, 7; "Our League Work in Connecticut," *American Issue*, 12 July 1901, 2; "Law and Order Organizations," *American Issue*, 30 September 1904, 8. Of course, the ASL ultimately hired agents to root out illicit activities, and its own enforcement efforts sometimes provoked violence. See, e.g., Charles E. Zartman, "The Prohibition Question in Licking County, 1908–1912" (M.A. thesis, Ohio State University, 1938), chapter 3. However, the ASL consistently maintained that the best enforcement was that conducted by the duly constituted authorities.

241 Howard H. Russell, "Report of the State Superintendent," 30 June 1894, 6–7, Ohio Anti-Saloon League series, Temperance and Prohibition Papers, Ohio Historical Society microfilm, reel 3.

242 Though many CLOL officers and activists were old, infirm, or dead when the ASL began organizing nationally, CLOL activists who worked for the ASL included S. Thrasher, Daniel C. Babcock, and Joseph H. Robbins. Meanwhile, some of the CLOL's honorary officers held similar positions in the ASL, including Lorenzo Sweet Coffin, Nelson J. Dingley, Washington Gladden, David H. Goodell, John Ireland, and John D. Long. John Wanamaker, who served on the CLOL's Executive Committee, helped finance the ASL. Finally, Law and Order leagues which later affiliated with the ASL included those from Connecticut, New Hampshire, and Chicago.

243 *Proceedings, Third National Anti-Saloon Convention*, xiv, 54; "Our League Work in Connecticut," *American Issue*, 12 July 1901, 2; "Connecticut," *American Issue*, 9 October 1903, 9. The Connecticut CLOL concen-

trated on law enforcement, the Connecticut Temperance Union on legislative efforts and education. After Connecticut lawmakers established a state police force in 1903, though, the state Law and Order league no longer assisted in enforcement.

244 "A Mistaken Notion concerning the Real Object of the Anti-Saloon League," *American Issue*, 3 October 1902, 6; Norman Dohn, "The History of the Anti-Saloon League" (Ph.D. diss., Ohio State University, 1959), 36–38, 40–42.

245 For Gladden's changing views about prohibition, see chapter 7.

246 While the National League and CLOL represented distinct approaches to the liquor question, the two organizations nonetheless shared some personnel. For example, John D. Long, John Wanamaker, and Daniel Agnew served in honorary positions for both groups.

247 During the late nineteenth century, this "great man" approach was used by numerous reform groups, including the ineffectual NTS. Indeed, the Templar leader S. B. Chase implicitly criticized these organizations for including "vice-presidents with no duties to perform" and "merely honorary or nominal officers." See Chase, "Independent Order of Good Templars," 610.

248 Dudley, "The Law and Order Movement," 201–2.

249 Among the eminent individuals to serve as CLOL national officers were John Wanamaker, merchant; General O. O. Howard, former commissioner, Freedman's Bureau; John Ireland, Roman Catholic archbishop; Lyman Abbott, editor, *Christian Union;* Nelson Dingley, congressman; and Charles C. Bonney, president, Illinois Bar Association.

250 Scomp, *King Alcohol in the Realm of King Cotton*, 770; *Cyclopedia of Temperance and Prohibition*, 454; Dorchester, "The National League for the Suppression of the Liquor Traffic," 530–34.

251 "The International Law and Order League," *Christian Union*, 4 December 1890, 760. As Charles C. Bonney, president of the CLOL, admitted, "in most cases the officers of the national league have learned of the existence of local organizations only from current accounts in the public press." See his "An Appeal for Law and Order," *Statesman*, January 1890, 195.

252 Robert T. Handy, *A Christian America: Protestant Hopes and Historical Realities* (New York: Oxford University Press, 1971), 60–63, 88–92, 95–98; Jerald C. Brauer, *Protestantism in America: A Narrative History* (Philadelphia: Westminster, 1953), 179–84; John A. Smith, "Ecclesiastical Politics and the Founding of the Federal Council of Churches," *Church History* 43 (1974): 350–65.

253 W. H. Pearce, "A Story of Origins: The Ohio Anti-Saloon League," *American Issue*, 2 November 1904, 10; K. Austin Kerr, *Organized for Prohibition: A New History of the Anti-Saloon League* (New Haven: Yale University Press, 1985), 77–78.

254 "New Temperance Methods," *Chautauquan*, May 1882, 498.

255 Cherrington, *The History of the Anti-Saloon League*, 11–12.

256 Pearce, "A Story of Origins," 10; "Ohio," *National Temperance Advocate*, February 1880, p. 28, May 1880, p. 76, December 1880, p. 190, January 1881, p. 13, February 1881, p. 29, March 1881, p. 44.

257 "Ohio," *National Temperance Advocate*, May 1881, p. 28, July 1881, p. 124; Cherrington, *The History of the Anti-Saloon League*, 12.

258 Whitaker, "Ohio WCTU and the Prohibition Amendment Campaign of 1883," 99–102.

259 Louis A. Banks, "The Anti-Saloon League, Origin and Personnel," in *The Passing of the Saloon*, ed. George H. Hammell (Cincinnati: Tower, 1908), 188–91; Pearce, "A Story of Origins," 10–11; Dohn, "The History of the Anti-Saloon League," 23–24.

260 Herrick Johnson, "Principles and Methods in the Temperance Reform," *Anti-Saloon*, October 1894, 8; Dohn, "The History of the Anti-Saloon League," 36–38.

261 *Annual Meeting Minutes of the National Woman's Christian Temperance Union, 1889–1890 Conventions*, Corre-

sponding Secretary's Reports; Harry M. Chalfant, *Father Penn and John Barleycorn* (Harrisburg: Evangelical, 1920), 120.

262 A. J. Kynett, "The Line on Which All Enemies of the Saloon May Unitedly Do Battle," *Proceedings of the National Temperance Congress Held in the Broadway Tabernacle, New York*, 85–89; Turner, "The American Prohibition Movement," 382–83.

263 Cherrington, *The Standard Encyclopedia of the Alcohol Problem*, 4:1487–88; Lender, *Dictionary of American Temperance Biography*, 284; Smith, "Ecclesiastical Politics and the Founding of the Federal Council of Churches," 354. In addition, Kynett founded and led the Committee on Temperance and Prohibition of the General Conferences of the Methodist Episcopal Church.

264 *Proceedings, Sixteenth National Convention of the Anti-Saloon League of America* (Westerville, Ohio: American Issue, 1915), 108–11; Kaylor, "The Prohibition Movement in Pennsylvania," 312–18; Cherrington, *The History of the Anti-Saloon League*, 20–21, 29–30; "Origin of the Anti-Saloon League," *American Issue*, 30 September 1904, 11.

265 "Not Radical Enough—Too Radical," *American Issue*, 7 January 1901, 4.

266 See, for example, "To Our Anxious Friends," *American Issue*, October 1900, 5.

267 "Too Local and Too Optional," *American Issue*, 5 July 1901, 4. See also W. F. M'Cauley, "Overstrained: Objections to Local Option," *American Issue*, 18 April 1902, 6.

268 See, for example, Kerr, *Organized for Prohibition*, 74; Hamm, *Shaping the Eighteenth Amendment*, 123–29; Blocker, *Retreat from Reform*, 154.

269 Indeed, it was only after 1896 that the WCTU began to pull away from its alliance with the Prohibition party. See Mezvinsky, "The White Ribbon Reform," 138–40; Whitaker, "A History of the Ohio Woman's Christian Temperance Union," 397–400; Bordin, *Woman and Temperance*, 133.

270 Clearly, the WCTU suffered financial setbacks during the 1890s which aggravated internal squabbling. In particular, the union failed to underwrite an impressive office building in Chicago, and its leaders disagreed about this project's feasibility. Meanwhile, in 1896 a battle erupted between Prohibitionists who favored a narrow platform focused on prohibition and other party members who supported other reforms. This latter group walked out of the 1896 convention to form the National Prohibition party, which received only 14,003 votes or 0.10% of the presidential vote. Calling itself the Union Reform party in 1900, it polled 5,695 votes, or 0.04% of the popular vote. See Bordin, *Woman and Temperance*, 142–48; Blocker, *Retreat from Reform*, chapter 4; Colvin, *Prohibition in the United States*, 255–57; Petersen, *A Statistical History of the American Presidential Elections*, 64–65, 67–68.

271 *Annual Meeting Minutes of the National Woman's Christian Temperance Union* (1890–1900); Colvin, *Prohibition in the United States*, chapter 18.

272 Whitaker, "History of the Ohio WCTU," 377. For other union critiques of local option, see "The Solid Saloon," *Union Signal*, 12 April 1894, 9; *Union Signal*, 3 May 1894, 1; "Bishop Haygood on Local Option," *Union Signal*, 15 November 1894, 8; *Union Signal*, 12 December 1895, 1; " 'Saloons Must Go': A Friendly Challenge to the Anti-Saloon League," *Union Signal*, 11 February 1897, 10; "The Weakness of Local Option," *Union Signal*, 23 April 1908, 8–9; Frances E. Beauchamp, "Local Option: Fails to Stop or Control Manufacture," *Union Signal*, 11 June 1908, 5–6. In general, however, the WCTU proved to be more friendly than the Prohibition party to the ASL during its early years. See, e.g., Spencer, *A History of the Woman's Christian Temperance Union of Northern and Central California*, 69.

273 *The Voice*, 17 December 1896, 4; Colvin, *Prohibition in the United States*, 387–95; Dohn, "The History of the Anti-Saloon League," 133–36; Ostrander, *The Prohibition Movement in California*, 95–96.

274 Alphonso A. Hopkins, "Local Option," *National Prohibitionist*, 20 May 1909, 10. The Prohibitionists had always opposed local option and continued to do so after 1900. See *Cyclopedia of Temperance and*

Prohibition, 390–400; H. A. Scomp, "Local Option Not Satisfactory," *The Political Prohibitionist for 1888* (New York: Funk and Wagnalls, 1888), 11–12; H. A. Scomp, "The Present Status of the Temperance Cause," *Union Signal*, 30 November 1893, 2–3; Hopkins, *Wealth and Waste*, chapter 20; A. A. Hopkins, *Profit and Loss in Man* (New York: Funk and Wagnalls, 1909), 361–63; Aaron S. Watkins, "The Present Crisis in Non-Partisanism," *American Advance*, 20 May 1911, 7; " 'Local Option': The Truth about It," *American Prohibition Yearbook for 1911*, ed. Charles Jones et al. (Chicago: National Prohibition Press, 1911), 229–34; *American Prohibition Yearbook for 1912*, ed. William E. Johnson et al. (Chicago: National Prohibition Press, 1912), 101–4; Colvin, *Prohibition in the United States*, chapter 20; Dohn, "The History of the Anti-Saloon League," 137–41. Occasionally, however, Prohibitionists would endorse local option. See "A Prohibition Journal on Local Option," *American Issue*, April 1900, 8.

275 For instance, see "Statutory Prohibition," *Union Signal*, 16 December 1897, 11; and the national Prohibition party's platforms for 1892, 1896, and 1900 in Colvin, *Prohibition in the United States*, 247–49, 257–58, 311–16.

276 For the radicals' support of constitutional prohibition during the 1890s, see "Local Option versus Prohibition," *Union Signal*, 22 February 1894, 9; Frances W. Graham and Georgeanna M. Gardenier, *Two Decades: A History of the First Twenty Years' Work of the Woman's Christian Temperance Union of the State of New York* (Oswego, N.Y.: R. J. Oliphant, 1894), 65–66; Whitaker, "A History of the Ohio Woman's Christian Temperance Union," 372–78; "Twenty-Sixth Annual Convention," *Union Signal*, 16 November 1899, 3.

277 Rhode Island's prohibition amendment of 1886 was repealed in 1889; South Dakota lost its 1889 amendment in 1896.

278 " 'Saloons Must Go,' " 10; Colvin, *Prohibition in the United States*, 241–42; Turner, "The American Prohibition Movement," 219–22, 378–79.

279 For the ASL's slow growth before 1905, see the organization's national convention proceedings; Dohn, "The History of the Anti-Saloon League," 88–92; Clark, *The Dry Years*, 83–85; Ostrander, *The Prohibition Movement in California*, 91–97.

280 Jerry Lien, "The Speechmaking of the Anti-Saloon League of America" (Ph.D. diss., University of Southern California, 1968), 156–60; Dohn, "The History of the Anti-Saloon League," 90–91.

281 To be sure, the ASL did recruit some of its leaders from the Prohibition party, and it cooperated with the party in some campaigns. However, the Prohibitionists never approved of the league's methods and often advocated abandoning local option.

282 Howard H. Russell, "The Anti-Saloon League Movement," 3–4, unpublished manuscript, box 1, Howard Hyde Russell Papers; Ostrander, *The Prohibition Movement in California*, 88–89; Handy, *A Christian America*, 148–51, 170–74; Samuel M. Cavert, *Church Cooperation and Unity in America: A Historical Review, 1900–1970* (New York: Association, 1970), 13–18; Smith, "Ecclesiastical Politics and the Founding of the Federal Council of Churches."

283 Kerr, *Organized for Prohibition*, 134–37; Proceedings, National Anti-Saloon League Conventions (1900–1913), State Reports; Dohn, "The History of the Anti-Saloon League," chapters 3–7. With respect to league finances, Odegard notes that from 1911 to 1925, "approximately 98 percent of the income of the national League was received in amounts of less than a hundred dollars," and cites the state leagues' reports to demonstrate that these organizations also received few large donations. See his *Pressure Politics: The Story of the Anti-Saloon League* (New York: Columbia University Press, 1928), 190–91.

284 Mrs. Clinton Smith, "Anti-Saloon League Convention," *Union Signal*, 22 December 1898, 7; A. M. W., "That Local Option Petition," *Union Signal*, 11 January 1906, 6, 14.

285 "WCTU Not Opposed," *Boston Globe*, 24 October 1909.

286 Mayer N. Zald and Roberta Ash, "Social Movement Organizations: Growth, Decay, and Change," *Social Forces* 44 (1966): 327–40; Jo Freeman, "A Model for Analyzing the Strategic Options of Social Movement Organizations," in *Waves of Protest: Social Movements since the Sixties*, ed. Jo Freeman and Victoria Johnson (Lanham, Md.: Rowman and Littlefield, 1999), 234.

287 See speeches on "The Line on Which All Enemies of the Saloon May Unitedly Do Battle," *Proceedings of the National Temperance Congress*, 50–99; Funk, "Symposium: On What Line May All Enemies of the Saloon Unitedly Do Battle?" 509–13; John Woolley, "How to Unite," *Union Signal*, 17 July 1890, 4–5; Herrick Johnson, "Principle and Method in the Temperance Reform," *Union Signal*, 6 July 1893, 3–4; Scomp, "The Present Status of the Temperance Cause," 2–3; Turner, "The American Prohibition Movement," 380–87; "To Temperance Voters," 3; "Local Option," 53; "Recent Temperance Elections," 811.

3 Modular Collective Action in a Federalist System

1 Sidney Tarrow, *Power in Movement: Social Movements, Collective Action and Politics*, 2d ed. (Cambridge: Cambridge University Press, 1998), chapter 2; Mark Traugott, "Recurrent Patterns of Collective Action," in *Repertoires and Cycles of Collective Action*, ed. Mark Traugott (Durham: Duke University Press, 1995), 3–7; Charles Tilly, *Popular Contention in Great Britain, 1758–1834* (Cambridge: Harvard University Press, 1995), 47, 381.

2 Sidney Tarrow, "Cycles of Collective Action: Between Moments of Madness and the Repertoire of Contention," in *Repertoires and Cycles of Collective Action*, 89–115; Charles Tilly, *Popular Contention in Great Britain*; Mark Traugott, "Recurrent Patterns of Collective Action," 7; Tarrow, *Power in Movement*, chapters 2 and 3.

3 Tarrow, *Power and Movement*, chapters 2 and 4; Charles Tilly, *Popular Contention in Great Britain*; Charles Tilly, *The Contentious French* (Cambridge, Mass.: Belknap, 1986).

4 See, for example, Elizabeth Sanders, *Roots of Reform: Farmers, Workers, and the American State, 1877–1917* (Chicago: University of Chicago Press, 1999); Kenneth Finegold and Theda Skocpol, *State and Party in America's New Deal* (Madison: University of Wisconsin Press, 1995); Richard F. Bensel, *Yankee Leviathan: The Origins of Central State Authority in America, 1859–1877* (Cambridge: Cambridge University Press, 1990); Robert Higgs, *Crisis and Leviathan: Critical Episodes in the Growth of American Government* (New York: Oxford University Press, 1987); Stephen Skowronek, *Building a New American State* (Cambridge: Cambridge University Press, 1982); Charles C. Bright, "The State in the United States during the Nineteenth Century," in *Statemaking and Social Movements: Essays in Theory and History*, ed. Charles Bright and Susan Harding (Ann Arbor: University of Michigan Press, 1984).

5 Michael Schwartz, *Radical Protest and Social Structure: The Southern Farmers' Alliance and Cotton Tenancy, 1880–1890* (Chicago: University of Chicago Press, 1976), chapters 16–17; Ira Katznelson, *City Trenches: Urban Politics and the Patterning of Class in the United States* (New York: Pantheon, 1981), chapter 3; Jane Mansbridge, *Why We Lost the ERA* (Chicago: University of Chicago Press, 1986), 13, 129–43; Janet K. Boles, *The Politics of the Equal Rights Amendment: Conflict and the Decision Process* (New York: Longman, 1979), 72–78. See also Jeffrey Ostler, *Prairie Populism: The Fate of Agrarian Radicalism in Kansas, Nebraska, and Iowa, 1880–1892* (Lawrence: University Press of Kansas, 1993), in which he argues that federalism prevented agrarian insurgents from achieving a greater national presence. Meanwhile, Theda Skocpol contends that the labor movement's federated structure interfered with the state labor federations' push for social legislation in her *Protecting Soldiers and Mothers: The Political Origins of Social Policy in the United States* (Cambridge, Mass.: Belknap, 1992), 235–45. For federalism's impact on a

European social movement, see Lee Ann Banaszak, *Why Movements Succeed or Fail: Opportunity, Culture, and the Struggle for Woman Suffrage* (Princeton, N.J.: Princeton University Press, 1996).

6 William Novak, *The People's Welfare: Law and Regulation in Nineteenth-Century America* (Chapel Hill: University of North Carolina Press, 1996), chapter 1; Ballard C. Campbell, *The Growth of American Government: Governance from the Cleveland Era to the Present* (Bloomington: Indiana University Press, 1995), chapter 1.

7 Novak, *The People's Welfare*, chapters 1 and 5.

8 The temperance and nativist Know-Nothing movements were the most truly national of the antebellum movements; regional reform efforts included the antislavery, antimasonry, Sabbatarian, peace, woman's rights, and labor movements.

9 Paul E. Johnson, *A Shopkeeper's Millennium: Society and Revivals in Rochester, New York, 1815–1837* (New York: Hill and Wang, 1978), 130–31.

10 For state liquor laws before 1890, see *Cyclopedia of Temperance and Prohibition* (New York: Funk and Wagnalls, 1891), 272–360.

11 Ian Tyrrell, *Sobering Up: From Temperance to Prohibition in Antebellum America, 1800–1860* (Westport, Conn.: Greenwood, 1979), 227–32. Until 1835 the governor appointed county commissioners in Massachusetts.

12 Although Georgia county courts had jurisdiction over county liquor licensing, state law did not grant them the authority to refuse all licenses. Hence, the county courts of Camden and Liberty applied to the Georgia legislature for the power to ban licenses, and lawmakers complied.

13 *Cyclopedia of Temperance and Prohibition*, 290, 391; Douglas W. Carlson, "Temperance Reform in the Cotton Kingdom" (Ph.D. diss., University of Illinois, 1982), 167.

14 Tyrrell, *Sobering Up*, 231–34; Carlson, "Temperance Reform in the Cotton Kingdom," 164–70; F. R. Lees, *Textbook of Temperance* (Rockland, Maine: Z. Pope Vose, 1869), 204–6; John A. Krout, *The Origins of Prohibition* (New York: Alfred A. Knopf, 1925), 172; Jed Dannenbaum, *Drink and Disorder: Temperance Reform in Cincinnati from the Washingtonian Revival to the WCTU* (Urbana: University of Illinois Press, 1984), 90.

15 Novak, in chapter 5 of *The People's Welfare*, makes much of the use of nuisance law to shut down "disorderly houses." However, for the citizenry's ability to use nuisance law in the antebellum period, see Thomas C. Mackey, *Red Lights Out: A Legal History of Prostitution, Disorderly Houses, and Vice Districts* (New York: Garland, 1987), chapter 3; *Brown v. Perkins*, 78 Mass. 89 (1858).

16 *The Reminiscences of Neal Dow: Recollections of Eighty Years* (Portland, Maine: Evening Express, 1898), 231.

17 Krout, *The Origins of Prohibition*, 173.

18 Robert L. Hampel, *Temperance and Prohibition in Massachusetts, 1813–1852* (Ann Arbor: UMI Research Press, 1982), 57.

19 Carlson, "Temperance Reform in the Cotton Kingdom," 193–205; H. A. Scomp, *King Alcohol in the Realm of King Cotton, or A History of the Liquor Traffic and of the Temperance Movement in Georgia from 1733 to 1887* (Chicago: Blakely Printing, 1888), 328–31.

20 James Schouler, *Constitutional Studies, State and Federal* (New York: Dodd, Mead, 1897), 35, 192, 221.

21 For the shift from private to mass petitioning in England, see Seymour Drescher, *Capitalism and Antislavery: British Mobilization in Comparative Perspective* (New York: Oxford University Press, 1987), 76–77; Tarrow, *Power in Movement*, 38–39.

22 Drescher, *Capitalism and Antislavery*, 76–80.

23 Albert Goodwin, *The Friends of Liberty: The English Democratic Movement in the Age of the French Revolution* (Cambridge: Harvard University Press, 1979).

24 Gilbert H. Barnes, *The Anti-Slavery Impulse, 1830–1844* (New York: D. Appleton-Century, 1933), 29–35, 42–43, 46–48, 140, 142–43, 264 n. 264; William Lee Miller, *Arguing about Slavery: The Great Battle in the United States Congress* (New York: Alfred A. Knopf, 1996), 107–8.

25 Edward Magdol, *The Antislavery Rank and File: A Social Profile of the Abolitionists' Constituency* (Westport, Conn.: Greenwood, 1986), 54; John B. Jentz, "The Anti-Slavery Constituency in Jacksonian New York City," *Civil War History* 27 (1981): 103–4; Barnes, *The Anti-Slavery Impulse*, 109; Miller, *Arguing about Slavery*, 107.

26 Like the temperance and antislavery advocates, the Sabbatarians were based in the "benevolent empire" that emanated from the Second Great Awakening.

27 John R. Bodo, *The Protestant Clergy and Public Issues, 1812–1848* (Princeton, N.J.: Princeton University Press, 1954), 39–48; Charles C. Cole, *The Social Ideas of the Northern Evangelists, 1826–1860* (New York: Columbia University Press, 1954), 107–8; Whitney Cross, *The Burned-Over District: The Social and Intellectual History of Enthusiastic Religion in Western New York, 1800–1850* (Ithaca, N.Y.: Cornell University Press, 1950), 134; Miller, *Arguing about Slavery*, 41.

28 Cross, *The Burned-Over District*, 134; John S. Gilkeson, *Middle-Class Providence, 1820–1940* (Princeton, N.J.: Princeton University Press, 1986), 68–69; Johnson, *A Shopkeeper's Millennium*, 85–88.

29 Barnes, *The Anti-Slavery Impulse*, 35–36; 130–31; Gilbert H. Barnes and Dwight L. Dumond, eds., *Letters of Theodore Dwight Weld, Angelina Grimké Weld, and Sarah Grimké, 1822–1844* (Gloucester, Mass.: Peter Smith, 1965), vi–vii, xii. As the AASS founders noted in their invitation to the Philadelphia convention, "We have before us numerous examples of similar organizations, which, though feeble and obscure, and contemned by public opinion in the outset, have speedily risen to great influence, and have been the means . . . of immense benefit to the human race. Especially is this true of the National Anti-Slavery Society of Great Britain, and of the American Temperance Society." See Barnes and Dumond, *Letters of Theodore Dwight Weld, Angelina Grimké Weld, and Sarah Grimké*, 118.

30 Miller, *Arguing about Slavery*, 73–74; Barnes, *The Anti-Slavery Impulse*, 63.

31 For the Stuart-Weld correspondence, see Barnes and Dumond, *Letters of Theodore Dwight Weld, Angelina Grimké Weld, and Sarah Grimké*. While the British battle over emancipation still raged in the early 1830s, Stuart mailed Weld several pamphlets by British abolitionists "because I want to have my Theodore's soul engaged in a work, to me the most interesting with which I have ever met." Once in the United States, Stuart continued to encourage Weld's abolitionist activities. See ibid., 42–44, 48–49, 74, 151–52, 164–66.

32 Miller, *Arguing about Slavery*, 108–11; 301–3; 323–25. In fact, Weld was the author of the widely used petition "Fathers and Rulers," "the most popular form for 'female petitioner' until 1840." (The petition is printed in Barnes and Dumond, *Letters of Theodore Dwight Weld, Angelina Grimké Weld, and Sarah Grimké*, 175–76.) After Weld lost his voice in 1836, he trained new AASS agents and supervised petitioning efforts.

33 Magdol, *The Antislavery Rank and File*, 53–56. While most would agree that the antislavery petitions of the 1830s contained over a million signatures, scholars still differ about the precise number of signatures collected by the AASS. For the signature debate, see Miller, *Arguing about Slavery*, 304–9.

34 Barnes, *The Anti-Slavery Impulse*, 110.

35 Ibid., chapters 11–13; Miller, *Arguing about Slavery*; Magdol, *The Antislavery Rank and File*, 54–57. Southern state legislatures also rejected antislavery petitions. See, e.g., *Nashville Union*, 26 January 1842.

36 The evangelical reform wave of the 1830s resembled Tarrow's "cycle of protest." Like a protest cycle, this reform wave involved the broad diffusion of conflict, as well as the expansion of the existing

repertoire of contention to include new protest forms like mass petitioning. See Tarrow, *Power in Movement*, chapter 9, for protest cycles.

37 Barnes, *The Anti-Slavery Impulse*, chapters 11–13; Gilkeson, *Middle-Class Providence*, 32–34; David L. Ludlum, *Social Ferment in Vermont, 1791–1850* (Montpelier: Vermont Historical Society, 1948), 75–76, 80–84; George F. Clark, *History of the Temperance Reform in Massachusetts* (Boston: Clarke and Carruth, 1888), 39–41; *Quarterly Proceedings of the Grand Division of the Sons of Temperance, State of Massachusetts*, January 1851, p. 3, April 1851, p. 3, October 1851, p. 7.

38 Miller, *Arguing about Slavery*, 303–5. The WCTU's Ellen Foster echoed this advice in 1882: "Let the [petitioners] go to every building—be it house or shop or store; let every individual over the required age be asked to sign. Let a few petitions be left in places of common resort, such as the post-office or barber-shop, to catch the signatures of those who might otherwise be overlooked." See J. Ellen Foster, *Constitutional Amendment Manual, Containing Argument, Appeal, Petitions, Forms of Constitutions and General Directions for Organized Work for Constitutional Prohibition* (New York: National Temperance Society and Publishing House, 1882), 56. For petitioning by antebellum teetotalers, see Tyrrell, *Sobering Up*, 279–80; Scomp, *King Alcohol in the Realm of King Cotton*, 330–31; *The Reminiscences of Neal Dow: Recollections of Eighty Years* (Portland, Maine: Evening Express, 1898), 261, 286–87.

39 Indeed, in South Carolina alone some petitions sought state prohibition, others to prohibit liquor retailing in small amounts, and still others to hold a referendum on the liquor issue to gauge public opinion. See Carlson, "Temperance Reform in the Cotton Kingdom," 181–85.

40 Krout, *The Origins of Prohibition*, 172–73, 273–85; Carlson, "Temperance Reform in the Cotton Kingdom," 162–63; Daniel Dorchester, *The Liquor Problem in All Ages* (New York: Phillips and Hunt, 1888), 290–93.

41 The ATU's *Reports* discussed the merits of both local option and the prohibition of liquor by the drink in its state affiliates' annual reports. See, e.g., the Report of the Executive Committee, *Fourth Report of the American Temperance Union* (1840). See also *Journal of the American Temperance Union* and the *Temperance Recorder*, 1837–40.

42 In New England states like Rhode Island, for instance, petitioners often requested local option statutes that authorized town meetings to decide on liquor licensing. In Illinois, however, where the licensing power resided in county courts, early local-optionists accordingly modified their proposals for the county system.

43 *The Reminiscences of Neal Dow*, 354–58. National and state union leaders like John Marsh, Stephen H. Tyng, Neal Dow, and Charles Jewett traversed the northern United States in the early 1850s in favor of Maine Laws. For Dow's travels, see ibid., chapter 18, 496–97. The farthest south Dow traveled was Virginia. He declined invitations to speak in Alabama and Louisiana.

44 *Journal of the Proceedings of the Grand Division of the Sons of Temperance of North America, Ninth Session* (1852), 6–7; *Tenth Session* (1853), 6–7, 41–42; Herbert Wiltsee, "The Temperance Movement, 1848–1871," *Papers in Illinois History* (1937): 87–88.

45 *Nashville Union*, 16 June 1855, 19 June 1855.

46 Dorchester, *The Liquor Problem in All Ages*, 283; *Journal of the Proceedings of the Grand Division of the Sons of Temperance of North America, Tenth Session* (1853), 12–14. For the media debate over the Maine Law, see Dannenbaum, *Drink and Disorder*, 128–44.

47 Lees, *Textbook of Temperance*, 222–37; Dorchester, *The Liquor Problem in All Ages*, 299–301; Tyrrell, *Sobering Up*, 260–61; Clark, *History of the Temperance Reform in Massachusetts*, 89–90; Dannenbaum, *Drink and Disorder*, 98–99; Bruce Tap, " 'The Evils of Intemperance Are Generally Conceded': The Temperance Debate in Early Grand Rapids," *Michigan Historical Review* 19 (1993): 32.

48 Carlson, "Temperance Reform in the Cotton Kingdom," 248–50. The Maine Law gained southern support from teetotalers in Tennessee, Georgia, South Carolina, and North Carolina. In contrast, temperance advocates requested weaker anti-liquor laws in Virginia, Louisiana, Texas, Mississippi and Alabama.

49 State legislatures would reject unsigned or disrespectful petitions, however. For a particularly rancorous debate about whether to receive an anonymous petition that favored retaining a stringent Tennessee liquor law, see *Nashville Union*, 10 November 1841. One legislator, who opposed the wishes of the unnamed "Ladies of Nashville," was offended by its "highly insulting" language aimed at those who preferred a more lax liquor policy. Indeed, he suggested that "no *Lady*" would ever use such language, and that the petition must have "emanated with some member of the House." In 1852 the Tennessee Senate similarly came close to rejecting a petition which criticized Senator Pavatt for his activities on the Select Committee on Tippling Houses. See *Nashville Union*, 31 January 1852.

50 *Nashville Union*, 27 November 1851.

51 *Nashville Union*, 18 October 1841. As Mr. Hill's remarks suggest, a significant number of women and ministers signed anti-liquor petitions.

52 Lees, *Textbook of Temperance*, 228; Dorchester, *The Liquor Problem in All Ages*, 299.

53 For example, Tennessee and Massachusetts both had about one million residents in 1850. However, because Tennessee excluded slaves from the electorate, its potential electorate was smaller by sixty thousand.

54 Scomp makes a similar point in his discussion of the collection of temperance pledges by Dabney Jones of Georgia: "Perhaps 3,000 signatures may not seem such a great work after all. [Another temperance lecturer] laboring in cities and crowded centers, could address more than that number each day. But . . . Dabney had no such teeming constituency. Very few towns in Georgia could count more than a few hundred each of population, and ofttimes long stretches of wilderness, or of sparsely inhabited country, must be traversed in going from one town to another." See his *King Alcohol in the Realm of King Cotton*, 440.

55 In Georgia, for example, the teetotalers circulated two separate petitions in 1853: the main petition, to be signed only by voters, and an ancillary petition for the ladies. This arrangement responded to public criticism of a petition in 1839 that had included the names of women. See Carlson, "Temperance Reform in the Cotton Kingdom," 261. In contrast, northern petitioners never discouraged women's signatures, which often accounted for more than a third of those on memorials.

56 Similarly, in North Carolina, the petitions proffered to the 1852–53 legislature included eighteen thousand signatures, only five thousand of which came from women. See C. C. Pearson and J. Edwin Hendricks, *Liquor and Anti-Liquor in Virginia, 1619–1919* (Durham: Duke University Press, 1967), 133–34; Daniel J. Whitener, *Prohibition in North Carolina, 1715–1945* (Chapel Hill: University of North Carolina Press, 1945), 41.

57 Clark, *History of the Temperance Reform in Massachusetts*, 90; Dorchester, *The Liquor Problem in All Ages*, 299.

58 Lees, *Textbook of Temperance*, 222–23.

59 *Nashville Union*, 30 December 1853; "The Prohibitory Amendment Campaign in the Old Bay State," *Union Signal*, 28 March 1889, 12; Peter Odegard, *Pressure Politics: The Story of the Anti-Saloon League* (New York: Columbia University Press, 1928), 151; Ernest H. Cherrington, *The Evolution of Prohibition in the United States of America* (Westerville, Ohio: American Issue, 1920), 322–23; Norman Dohn, "The History of the Anti-Saloon League" (Ph.D. diss., Ohio State University, 1959), 192.

60 As early as 1839, Josiah Flournoy of Georgia combined mass petitioning with electoral pressure on the state legislature. See Carlson, "Temperance Reform in the Cotton Kingdom," 193–205; Scomp,

King Alcohol in the Realm of King Cotton, 328–39; Krout, *The Origins of Prohibition*, 174. Elsewhere, reformers began to apply electoral pressure in the 1840s. See *Reminiscences of Neal Dow*, 313–18; Dannenbaum, *Drink and Disorder*, 90–92; Krout, *The Origins of Prohibition*, 277, 280.

61 *Reminiscences of Neal Dow*, 313. For more on antebellum electoral pressure, see Scomp, *King Alcohol in the Realm of King Cotton*, 321, 328–39; Clark, *History of the Temperance Reform in Massachusetts*, 238–39; John J. Coffey, "A Political History of the Temperance Movement in New York State, 1808–1920" (Ph.D. diss., Pennsylvania State University, 1976), 86–90; Charles H. Bohner, "Rum and Reform: Temperance in Delaware Politics," *Delaware History* 5 (1953): 255–65; Asa E. Martin, "The Temperance Movement in Pennsylvania Prior to the Civil War," *Pennsylvania Magazine of History and Biography* 49 (1925): 218–23; Wiltsee, "The Temperance Movement," 88.

62 Elisabeth Clemens, *The People's Lobby: Organizational Innovation and the Rise of Interest Group Politics in the United States, 1890–1925* (Chicago: University of Chicago Press, 1997), Prologue.

63 See, e.g., S. A. Goodwin, *Prohibition Impossible through a Separate Party and Why*, undated pamphlet found in box 3, Howard Hyde Russell Papers, Bentley Historical Library, University of Michigan, 1–16. For electoral pressure after 1865, see James R. Turner, "The American Prohibition Movement, 1865–1897" (Ph.D. diss., University of Wisconsin, 1972), chapters 5–10; D. Leigh Colvin, *Prohibition in the United States* (New York: George H. Doran, 1926), chapters 7–11, 14, 18–19, 22–24; K. Austin Kerr, *Organized for Prohibition: A New History of the Anti-Saloon League* (New Haven: Yale University Press, 1985), chapters 4–6, 8; W. M. Burke, "The Anti-Saloon League as a Political Force," *Annals of the American Academy of Political and Social Sciences* 32 (1908): 27–37; William G. Davis, "Attacking 'The Matchless Evil': Temperance and Prohibition in Mississippi, 1817–1908" (Ph.D. diss., Mississippi State University, 1975), chapters 4–8; Joe A. Fisher, "The Liquor Question in Nebraska, 1880–1890" (M.A. thesis, Municipal University of Omaha, 1952), 57, 64–68, chapters 7–8; "Michigan," *National Temperance Advocate*, September 1880, 142; "Ohio," *National Temperance Advocate*, July 1881, 124; "The Ohio Campaign," *National Temperance Advocate*, August 1881, 135; "West Virginia," *National Temperance Advocate*, December 1882, 205; "Missouri," *National Temperance Advocate*, August 1883, 141; "Tennessee," *National Temperance Advocate*, October 1883, 173; "Maryland," *National Temperance Advocate*, May 1884, 76.

64 Tyrrell, *Sobering Up*, 279–80; *Reminiscences of Neal Dow*, 261; Cora Cramer, ed., *History, Pennsylvania Woman's Christian Temperance Union* (Quincy, Pa.: Quincy Orphanage, 1937), 6–7, 19, 22–23, 29, 38, 48–49, 75, 83, 90–92, 103, 111, 139, 171, 174, 178, 205, 223, 246, 316; Fisher, "The Liquor Question in Nebraska," 54–56, 71–72; Davis, "Attacking the "Matchless Evil,' " 110, 112; Richard F. Hamm, *Shaping the Eighteenth Amendment: Temperance Reform, Legal Culture, and the Polity, 1880–1920* (Chapel Hill: University of North Carolina Press, 1995), 77.

65 Foster, *Constitutional Amendment Manual*, 56. See also *Reminiscences of Neal Dow*, 286, where Dow asserts that "a most effective agency for the creation of an improved public sentiment was the circulation of petitions from house to house."

66 Banaszak, for one, claims that the woman suffrage movement reduced its reliance on petitioning after 1900. See her *Why Movements Succeed*, 133–36.

67 For the prohibition movement's continued reliance after 1900 on petitioning and variations on this technique (e.g., telegrams and letter-writing), see Cramer, ed., *History, Pennsylvania Woman's Christian Temperance Union*, 6–7, 49, 90–92, 111; Robert S. Bader, *Prohibition in Kansas: A History* (Lawrence: University Press of Kansas, 1986), 175; "Here and There," *Union Signal*, 27 April 1905, 15; "That Local Option Petition," *Union Signal*, 11 January 1906, 6, 14; "Temperance Forces Alert in Iowa," *Union Signal*, 28 February 1907, 12; "Oklahoma: State Prohibition the Goal," *Union Signal*, 14 March 1907,

14; "Missouri WCTU Petitions for Special Legislative Session," *Union Signal*, 19 December 1907, 3; "Michigan Temperance Forces Hopeful," *Union Signal*, 9 January 1908, 3; " 'Wave' Has Reached Old Bay State," *Union Signal*, 12 March 1908, 12; "Prohibition Campaign in Florida," *Union Signal*, 8 April 1909; Adrianna Hungerford, "From the President," *WCTU Messenger*, February 1914, 1; "Ask Boulder Council to Refuse Liquor Licenses," newspaper clipping, 6 December 1907, *Minutes of the Boulder WCTU* 8:59.

68 Major temperance laws were passed in Massachusetts (1838, repealed 1840); Mississippi (1838, repealed 1842), New Hampshire (1838), Illinois (1839), Tennessee (1838, repealed 1846), Rhode Island (1838, repealed 1841), and Connecticut (1839, repealed 1842). Those of Massachusetts, Mississippi and Tennessee prohibited liquor sales in small amounts, while the other four were laws.

69 In incorporated towns, however, the charters typically granted licensing authority to municipal officials. Still, most of Tennessee's population resided in unincorporated territory during the antebellum period.

70 Paul Isaac, *Prohibition and Politics: Turbulent Decades in Tennessee, 1885–1920* (Knoxville: University of Tennessee Press, 1965), 1–4.

71 Like other select committees, this body convened for a limited time and for a special purpose: to issue a report on the liquor problem and propose a legislative solution (if any), before dissolving at the end of the legislative session.

72 *Nashville Union*, 14 October 1837; Isaac, *Prohibition and Politics*, 4–5; Grace Leab, "The Temperance Movement in Tennessee, 1860–1907" (M.A. thesis, University of Tennessee, 1938), 3–4. Like other measures that banned liquor sales in small quantities, Tennessee's "quart law" attacked the state's retail drinking establishments, where much excessive drinking occurred.

73 *Nashville Union*, 11 December 1845, 14 February 1846.

74 Of the petitions reported in the *Nashville Union* during the 1845–46 legislative session, only two memorials are explicitly described as favoring the quart law's repeal. However, some temperance-related petitions are reported in vague terms, (e.g., as being "on the subject of Tippling Houses"), and it is impossible to discern their content. Still, the bulk of the petitions in this session appear to have supported the quart law.

75 *Nashville Union*, 14 February 1846, emphasis in original.

76 *Nashville Union*, 6 January 1846.

77 *Nashville Union*, 10 December 1847.

78 *Nashville Union*, 15 February 1853, 16 February 1853, 23 February 1853, 11 April 1853, 1 June 1853, 5 June 1853, 22 June 1853. In some counties, no major party candidate supported the anti-liquor position and teetotalers responded by nominating their own aspirants for state office.

79 According to Paul H. Bergeron, the leading issues in the Tennessee elections of 1853 were internal improvements and gerrymandering. See his *Antebellum Politics in Tennessee* (Lexington: University Press of Kentucky, 1982), 124. Moreover, after the elections only one candidate complained loudly about the liquor issue's impact on his electoral fate. A candidate for the U.S. Congress, he attributed his defeat to the perception that he was a radical prohibitionist. See *Nashville Union*, 23 August 1853.

80 *Nashville Union*, 22 December 1853.

81 *Nashville Union*, 16 November 1853, 23 November 1853.

82 *Nashville Union*, 2 December 1853, 3 December 1853, 6 December 1853, 7 December 1853, 13 December 1853, 16 December 1853.

83 *Nashville Union*, 13 December 1853.

84 *Nashville Union*, 21 January 1854, 12 February 1854; Isaac, *Prohibition and Politics*, 7.

85 See chapter 5 for the relationship between the antebellum party system and the anti-liquor movement.

86 *Nashville Union*, 21 April 1853. The *Union* was a Democratic party organ.

87 In 1848 the Free Soil party destabilized the North's two-party system. For that party's impact on the antebellum prohibition movement, see chapter 4.

88 *Reminiscences of Neal Dow*, 242–43, 252, 260–61, 336–37, 449–50, 518, 562–63; Frank L. Byrne, *Prophet of Prohibition: Neal Dow and His Crusade* (Madison: State Historical Society of Wisconsin, 1961), 37–38, 45–46; Lees, *Textbook of Temperance*, 224.

89 Byrne, *Prophet of Prohibition*, 76; *Reminiscences of Neal Dow*, 562–63. For the role of select committees elsewhere, see Coffey, "A Political History of the Temperance Movement in New York State," 55–59; Krout, *The Origins of Prohibition*, 262.

90 *Nashville Union*, 9 October 1855.

91 Indeed, the permanence of the liquor question reached national proportions in 1879, when the House of Representatives organized the first national standing committee on temperance, the Alcoholic Liquor Traffic Committee.

92 *Cyclopedia of Temperance and Prohibition*, 476.

93 Coffey, "A Political History of the Temperance Movement in New York State," 97.

94 Frances F. Piven and Richard A. Cloward, *Poor People's Movements: Why They Succeed, How They Fail* (New York: Vintage, 1979); J. Craig Jenkins and Craig M. Eckert, "Channeling Black Insurgency: Elite Patronage and Professional Social Movement Organizations in the Development of the Black Movement," *American Sociological Review* 51 (1986): 812–29.

95 Novak, *The People's Welfare*, 188; Ann-Marie Szymanski, "Dry Compulsions: Prohibition and the Creation of State-Level Enforcement Agencies," *Journal of Policy History* 11 (1999): 115–46; Tyrrell, *Sobering Up*, 293; Daniel E. Clark, "The History of Liquor Legislation in Iowa, 1846–1861," *Iowa Journal of History and Politics* 6 (1908): 80–81; Bohner, "Rum and Reform," 265–66; Allen Steinberg, *The Transformation of Criminal Justice in Philadelphia, 1800–1880* (Chapel Hill: University of North Carolina Press, 1989), 53–54, 131–33.

96 Tyrrell, *Sobering Up*, 293; Clark, *History of the Temperance Reform in Massachusetts*, 83–85; *Cyclopedia of Temperance and Prohibition*, 67; John Fitzgibbon, "King Alcohol: His Rise, Reign and Fall in Michigan," *Michigan History* 2 (1918): 752–53; Tap, " 'The Evils of Intemperance Are Generally Conceded,' " 34, 40–42. Though only widespread by the 1850s, the Carson League and the Temperance Watchmen were founded in the late 1840s to sustain local temperance victories in New York and Massachusetts.

97 Scattered acts of female vigilantism occurred in Illinois, Wisconsin, Pennsylvania, and Ohio, states which debated but never enacted Maine Laws. Furthermore, women from Indiana and Michigan participated in the destruction of liquor stocks just before their states' enactment of Maine Laws in 1855 and 1854. See Dannenbaum, *Drink and Disorder*, 196–200; Jed Dannenbaum, "The Origins of Temperance Activism and Militancy Among American Women," *Journal of Social History* 15 (1981): 242–43; *Nashville Union*, 16 June 1854, 7 January 1855; Ian Tyrrell, "Women and Temperance in Antebellum America, 1830–1860," *Civil War History* 28 (1982): 142–44; Charles E. Canup, "Temperance Movements and Legislation in Indiana," *Indiana Magazine of History* 16 (1920): 23; Cramer, ed., *History, Pennsylvania Woman's Christian Temperance Union*, 119.

98 Dannenbaum, *Drink and Disorder*, 196.

99 Tyrrell, *Sobering Up*, 294; Tyrrell, "Women and Temperance," 142–43.

100 Dannenbaum, *Drink and Disorder*, 197–98, 209 n. 48.

101 Cramer, ed., *History, Pennsylvania Woman's Christian Temperance Union*, 119; *Nashville Union*, 16 June 1854; Dannenbaum, *Drink and Disorder*, 196–99; Tyrrell, "Women and Temperance," 144.

102 Daniel E. Clark, "The History of Liquor Legislation in Iowa," 81.

103 Clark, *History of the Temperance Reform in Massachusetts*, 200.

104 Tyrrell, *Sobering Up*, 294–97; Clark, *History of the Temperance Reform in Massachusetts*, 83–85; Dannenbaum, *Drink and Disorder*, 196–99; Tap, " 'The Evils of Intemperance Are Generally Conceded,' " 40–44.

105 Jack S. Blocker, *"Give to the Winds Thy Fears": The Women's Temperance Crusade, 1873–1874* (Westport, Conn.: Greenwood, 1985), chapters 1–3; Dannenbaum, *Drink and Disorder*, chapter 7; Borden, *Women and Temperance*, chapter 2.

106 Blocker argues that Midwestern women suffered more from the saloon's social effects because they confronted an abundance of retail liquor outlets within small-town settings, which lacked the segregated vice districts of northeastern cities. See his *"Give to the Winds Thy Fears,"* 113–14.

107 Ibid., 133.

108 Ibid., chapter 7; Dannenbaum, *Drink and Disorder*, chapter 7; Ruth Bordin, *Woman and Temperance: The Quest for Power and Liberty, 1873–1900* (Philadelphia: Temple University Press, 1981), chapters 2–3.

109 According to social movement scholars, this shift from disruptive to conventional tactics typically occurs when a group seeks to influence mainstream political institutions and adopts a more formal structure. See, for example, Suzanne Staggenborg, "The Consequences of Professionalization and Formalization in the Pro-Choice Movement," in *Waves of Protest: Social Movements since the Sixties*, ed. Jo Freeman and Victoria Johnson (Lanham, Md.: Rowman and Littlefield, 1999), 120–22.

110 "Law and Order: A National League Formed at Yesterday's Convention," *Boston Globe*, 23 February 1883, 2.

111 Ernest H. Cherrington, *The Standard Encyclopedia of the Alcohol Problem* (Westerville, Ohio: American Issue, 1924–30), 4:1512–13; Perry R. Duis, *The Saloon: Public Drinking in Chicago and Boston, 1880–1920* (Urbana: University of Illinois Press, 1983), 98–99; "The Week," *Christian Union*, 2 June 1887, 26.

112 Charles C. Bonney, "An Appeal for Law and Order," *Statesman*, January 1890, 195.

113 Duis, *The Saloon*, 97–98; L. Edwin Dudley, "The Law and Order Movement: Historical Sketch," *Lend-a-Hand*, March 1892, 260–62. Among other things, saloons could be held liable for any property damage caused by an inebriate, the effects of lost income on an inebriate's family, and liquor's impact on a child's health.

114 Though Paxton's organization was entitled the "Citizens' League for the Suppression of the Sale of Liquor to Minors and Drunkards," it was nonetheless the first group to promote the "law and order" approach later adopted by the national CLOL, and became its Chicago affiliate in 1883.

115 Because the dramshop laws required the aggrieved to initiate lawsuits, and many saloon customers lacked the funds to do so, Chicago and Boston league activists kept vigil at local courts, watching for cases that might lead to dramshop suits. When such cases arose, agents offered potential plaintiffs free legal services. See Duis, *The Saloon*, 98–99.

116 *Proceedings of the Sixth Annual Meeting of the Citizens' Law and Order League of the United States*, 78, 81–87; Citizens' No-License Committee, *Ten No-License Years in Cambridge* (Cambridge, Mass.: Citizen's Committee, 1898), 101–13.

117 *Proceedings of the Sixth Annual Meeting of the Citizens' Law and Order League of the United States*, 53. For more of Gladden's complaints about Ohio's situation, see "Address of Washington Gladden," *Proceedings of the Fourth Annual Meeting of the Citizens' Law and Order League of Massachusetts* (1886), 20, 24–25. On

the difficulties that women faced in using Ohio's civil damage law, see Blocker, *"Give to the Winds Thy Fears,"* 132–33.

118 Indeed, the Michigan Prohibition party condemned the 1887 state legislature for enacting a law, which resulted in a "great loss of time, energy, and money" that was "incurred in the futile effort to close the open saloon in thirty-eight counties in this State under the unconstitutional local option law." See "Pedigree and Pocket Book: The Prohibition Party, in Convention Assembled, Scores the Republicans," *Detroit Free Press*, 28 June 1888, 5.

119 *Proceedings of the Sixth Annual Meeting of the Citizens' Law and Order League of the United States*, 54.

120 Fisher, "Liquor Question in Nebraska," 58.

121 *Proceedings of the Sixth Annual Meeting of the Citizens' Law and Order League of the United States*, 51.

122 Bonney, "An Appeal for Law and Order," 195.

123 Kansas had enacted constitutional prohibition in 1880, but this amendment was often poorly enforced. See Bader, *Prohibition in Kansas*, chapters 6–7.

124 Hamm, *Shaping the Eighteenth Amendment*, chapter 4; "More Agitation Needed, and Less Attempted Law Enforcement," *American Issue* 7 (May 1900): 11; "Put the Emphasis on Agitation and Law Enforcement," *American Issue*, August 1900, 6.

125 "A Statement of What the Anti-Saloon League Undertakes to Do: Detectives, Attorneys and Prosecutions," *American Issue*, 31 May 1901, 1; Charles M. Hogan, "Wayne B. Wheeler: Single Issue Exponent" (Ph.D. diss., University of Cincinnati, 1986), 116–18.

126 Charles E. Zartman, "The Prohibition Question in Licking County, 1908–1912" (M.A. thesis, Ohio State University, 1938), chapter 3; Hogan, "Wayne B. Wheeler," 118–21; Lloyd Sponholtz, "The Politics of Temperance in Ohio, 1880–1912," *Ohio History* 85 (1976): 18–19.

127 Dohn, "The History of the Anti-Saloon League," 59–62.

128 Hamm, *Shaping the Eighteenth Amendment*, 141; "Put the Emphasis on Agitation and Law Enforcement," 6.

129 Hamm, *Shaping the Eighteenth Amendment*, chapters 2–3, 5.

130 Skocpol makes similar points about the implementation of mothers' pensions. See her *Protecting Soldiers and Mothers*, 465–78.

131 H. Kenneth Bechtel, *State Police in the United States: A Socio-Historical Analysis* (Westport, Conn.: Greenwood, 1995), 20–21, 38–45; Szymanski, "Dry Compulsions," 115–46; Leonard F. Fuld, *Police Administration: A Critical Study of Police Organizations in the United States and Abroad* (New York: G. Putnam's Sons, 1910), 416–25; Stanley L. Swart, "Early Efforts at State-Level Law Enforcement: The Failure of Ohio's Supervision of Local Police Authorities, 1902–1925," *Ohio History* 90 (1981): 141–57.

4 Legislative Supremacy and the Definition of Movement Goals

1 To be sure, it was more difficult to alter state constitutions in New England than elsewhere. See James Q. Dealey, *Growth of American State Constitutions* (Boston: Ginn, 1915), 248–52. However, the drys were nevertheless able to secure constitutional amendment referenda in Maine (1884), Rhode Island (1886), New Hampshire (1889), Connecticut (1889), and Massachusetts (1889), suggesting that the barriers to amending these constitutions were not insurmountable.

2 Lee Ann Banaszak, *Why Movements Succeed or Fail: Opportunity, Culture, and the Struggle for Woman Suffrage* (Princeton, N.J.: Princeton University Press, 1996), 31–32.

3 Richard F. Hamm, *Shaping the Eighteenth Amendment: Temperance Reform, Legal Culture, and the Polity, 1880–1920* (Chapel Hill: University of North Carolina Press, 1995), 9–13, chapter 4.

4 As noted in chapter 1, stock law proponents also benefited from devolution and the legal acceptance of this practice. Moreover, as discussed below, the "home rule" movement also profited from greater local autonomy during this period.

5 Theodore J. Lowi and Benjamin Ginsberg, *American Government: Freedom and Power*, 4th ed. (New York: W.W. Norton, 1996), 98–99.

6 Lawrence M. Friedman, "State Constitutions in Historical Perspective," *Annals of the American Academy of Political and Social Science* 496 (1988): 35–39. See also G. Alan Tarr, *Understanding State Constitutions* (Princeton, N.J.: Princeton University Press, 1998), 132–35; Morton Keller, "The Politics of State Constitutional Revision, 1820–1930," in *The Constitutional Convention as an Amending Device*, ed. Kermit L. Hall, Harold M. Hyman, and Leon V. Sigal (Washington: American Historical Association and American Political Science Association, 1987), 68–71; Kermit L. Hall, "The Irony of the Federal Constitution's Genius," in *The Constitution and American Political Development*, ed. Peter F. Nardulli (Urbana: University of Illinois Press, 1992), 244–48.

7 *Report of the Proceedings and Debates in the Convention to Revise the Constitution of the State of Michigan, 1850* (Lansing: R. W. Ingals, 1850), 187. Self-proclaimed temperance men also balked at inserting antiliquor articles in their state constitutions. As a delegate to Ohio's convention of 1850–51 said, "I am well aware of the evils, the crimes, and the misfortunes that follow in the train of intemperance, and I will go as far as any man to sustain the Legislature in every legitimate endeavor to put them down; but I am unwilling to put a power of this kind in the organic law." See *Report of the Debates and Proceedings of the Convention for the Revision of the Constitution of the State of Ohio, 1850–1851* (Columbus: Scott and Bronson, 1851), 2:1325.

8 "Local Option or Prohibition?" *Christian Union*, 28 March 1889, 408. Wet politicians also used this argument to good effect. In 1883, for instance, the pro-liquor Ohio Democrats criticized the Republican legislature for proposing two drink-related amendments, one of which mandated state prohibition. In doing so, they charged that "the Republicans were too eager to make the Constitution elastic and easy to change, when it was meant to be lasting and only subject to change in cases of grave necessity." See Wilfred McCuskey, "The Political Campaign of 1883 in Ohio" (M.A. thesis, Ohio State University, 1948), 29.

9 Keller, "The Politics of State Constitutional Revision," 71–72; Walter F. Dodd, *The Revision and Amendment of State Constitutions* (Baltimore: Johns Hopkins University Press, 1910), 62–65, 125–27; Dealey, *Growth of American State Constitutions*, 40–48; Ellis P. Oberholtzer, *The Referendum in America* (New York: Charles Scribner's Sons, 1912), chapters 4–6.

10 Hall, "The Irony of the Federal Constitution's Genius," 246.

11 Dealey, *Growth of American State Constitutions*, 52–54; Tarr, *Understanding State Constitutions*, 109–13.

12 Tarr, *Understanding State Constitutions*, 109–13; Albert L. Sturm, "The Development of American State Constitutions," *Publius* 12 (1982): 64; Hall, "The Irony of the Federal Constitution's Genius," 246–47; Friedman, "State Constitutions in Historical Perspective," 37.

13 John Locke, *Second Treatise of Government* (Indianapolis: Hackett, 1980), chapters 10–13; M. J. C. Vile, *Constitutionalism and the Separation of Powers* (New York: Oxford University Press, 1967), 63; *Rice v. Foster*, 4 Harr. 489 (1847).

14 Oberholtzer, *The Referendum in America*, chapter 3; Tarr, *Understanding State Constitutions*, 86–120, 117–19.

15 During the 1840s and 1850s, new constitutions which contained bans on the legislature's power to sanction future lotteries included those of New Jersey (1844), Louisiana (1845), Texas (1845), California (1849), Ohio (1851), Indiana (1851), Virginia (1851), Maryland (1851), Iowa (1857), and Kansas (1859).

16 John S. Ezell, *Fortune's Merry Wheel: The Lottery in America* (Cambridge: Harvard University Press, 1960), chapters 7, 10–11, pp. 273–74. In fact, three state constitutions—those of Tennessee (1834), Michigan (1835), and Arkansas (1836)—had abolished the legislature's power to authorize lotteries before the panic of 1837.

17 Ibid., 217; Ernest H. Cherrington, *The Standard Encyclopedia of the Alcohol Problem* (Westerville, Ohio: American Issue, 1924–30), 5:2128. One delegate moved that the convention inquire into "what restrictions may be proper and necessary on the powers of the Legislature in authorizing the issuing of licenses for the sale of ardent spirits," but his resolution was tabled. See *Journal of the Convention of the State of Pennsylvania to Propose Amendments to the Constitution* (Harrisburg: Thompson and Clark, 1837), 1:149.

18 *Report of the Debates and Proceedings of the Convention for the Revision of the Constitution of the State of Ohio* 2:1326. The lottery parallel also surfaced when the Michigan Constitutional Convention of 1850 debated abolishing liquor licensing, and later resurfaced during the postbellum period as well. See *Report of the Proceedings and Debates in the Convention to Revise the Constitution of the State of Michigan*, 770; John B. Finch, *Prohibition: Constitutional and Statutory* (New York: National Temperance Society and Publishing House, 1889), 9; J. Ellen Foster, "Constitutional Prohibition," *Proceedings of the Ninth National Temperance Convention Held at Saratoga Springs, N.Y., June 21 and 22, 1881* (New York: National Temperance Society and Publishing House, 1881), 26; George F. Stewart, contribution to "Prohibitory Law and Personal Liberty," *North American Review*, August 1888, 144.

19 The Michigan convention received thirty-six petitions demanding absolute prohibition of the sale and manufacturing of liquor, while the Ohio gathering recorded 269 anti-liquor memorials, most of which requested the abolition of liquor licensing. See *Report of the Proceedings and Debates in the Convention to Revise the Constitution of the State of Michigan*; *Report of the Debates and Proceedings of the Convention for the Revision of the Constitution of the State of Ohio*, vol. 2.

20 *Report of the Debates and Proceedings of the Convention for the Revision of the Constitution of the State of Ohio*, 2:1308; Siegal, "Matter of Public Welfare," 88–89; *Report of the Proceedings and Debates in the Convention to Revise the Constitution of the State of Michigan*, 413.

21 The Michigan ban on state liquor licensing lasted until 1875; its Ohio analogue survived until 1914. Given their purely negative character, though, neither provision limited liquor sales, and the state legislatures in question ultimately found indirect ways of licensing liquor through taxation.

22 William H. Armstrong, "The Sons of Temperance: The Pioneer Advocates of Constitutional Prohibition," in *Journal of the Proceedings of the Grand Division of the Sons of Temperance of North America, Forty-Eighth Annual Convention* (1892), 121–23; Donald W. Beattie, "Sons of Temperance: Pioneers in Total Abstinence and 'Constitutional' Prohibition" (Ph.D. diss., Boston University, 1966), 216–20.

23 John J. Coffey, "A Political History of the Temperance Movement in New York State, 1808–1920" (Ph.D. diss., Pennsylvania State University, 1976), 122–27. As chapter 5 demonstrates, state legislatures were most likely to submit prohibition amendments to the public when they feared reprisals from dry voters.

24 Ibid., 89, 125–27.

25 Of course, the conventions could have submitted prohibition to the voters as an integral part of the constitution that required their ratification. With prohibition clauses, however, conventions typically forwarded them to the voters as separate amendments.

26 D. Leigh Colvin, *Prohibition in the United States* (New York: George H. Doran, 1926), 109–10.

27 George F. Hoar, *The Constitutional Remedy* (New York: National Temperance Society and Publishing House, 1889), 10–11. See also Finch, *Prohibition: Constitutional and Statutory*, 7; J. Ellen Foster, *Constitu-*

tional Amendment Manual, Containing Argument, Appeal, Petitions, Forms of Constitutions and General Directions for Organized Work for Constitutional Prohibition (New York: National Temperance Society and Publishing House, 1882), 31–32.

28 Tarr, *Understanding State Constitutions*, 113–17; Hall, "The Irony of the Federal Constitution's Genius," 246–52; Dealey, *Growth of American State Constitutions*, 117–21.

29 James Bryce, *The American Commonwealth*, ed. Louis Hacker (New York: Capricorn, 1959), 1:116.

30 J. N. Stearns, "Why Constitutional Prohibition?" in *The Constitutional Prohibitionist*, ed. J. N. Stearns (New York: National Temperance Society and Publishing House, 1889), 3.

31 Tarr, *Understanding State Constitutions*, 115–17; Lawrence M. Friedman, *A History of American Law* (New York: Simon and Schuster, 1973), 305–6.

32 Solon J. Buck, *The Granger Movement: A Study of Agricultural Organization and Its Political, Economic, and Social Manifestations, 1870–1880* (Lincoln: University of Nebraska Press, 1963), 126–31; *Journal of the Constitutional Convention of the State of Illinois, Convened at Springfield, December 13, 1869* (Springfield: State Journal Printing Office, 1870), 1013; Tarr, *Understanding State Constitutions*, 115. Some of the "granger" constitutions directly reflected agrarian discontent; others merely copied the provisions of the Illinois document.

33 Buck, *The Granger Movement*, 194–205.

34 Hall, "The Irony of the Federal Constitution's Genius," 246–47, 250–51; Tarr, *Understanding State Constitutions*, 115–16.

35 Agrarian reformers were not always successful; in 1873, for example, Indiana reformers failed to win legislative approval for an amendment requiring the General Assembly to fix maximum railroad rates. See Charles Kettleborough, *Constitution Making in Indiana* (Indianapolis: Indiana Historical Commission, 1916), 127.

36 Joanne J. Brownsword, "Good Templars in Wisconsin, 1854–1880" (M.A. thesis, University of Wisconsin, 1960), 102–6; IOGT *Journal of Proceedings of the Twenty-Sixth Annual Session of the Grand Lodge of Illinois* (1879), 13, *Twenty-Eighth Annual Session* (1881), 16–17; Daniel E. Clark, "The History of Liquor Legislation in Iowa, 1878–1908," *Iowa Journal of History and Politics* 6 (1908): 503–4; A. D. P. van Buren, "Our Temperance Conflict," *Michigan Pioneer Collections* 13 (1888): 402; Emma L. Thornbrough, *Indiana in the Civil War Era, 1850–1880* (Indianapolis: Indiana Historical Society, 1965), 265.

37 Robert S. Bader, *Prohibition in Kansas: A History* (Lawrence: University Press of Kansas, 1986), 53–54. The Kansas prohibition amendment of 1880 allowed the sale and manufacture of alcohol for medical, scientific, and mechanical purposes.

38 Thomas McDougall et al., *The Liquor Question in the Ohio Campaign of 1883* (Cincinnati: Robert Clarke, 1883), 10.

39 Clark, "The History of Liquor Legislation in Iowa," 523.

40 Finch, *Prohibition: Constitutional and Statutory*, 10–11; Foster, "Constitutional Prohibition," 26.

41 Frances B. Finch and Frank J. Sibley, *John B. Finch, His Life and Work* (New York: Funk and Wagnalls, 1888), 274.

42 Foster, "Constitutional Prohibition," 26; Foster, *Constitutional Amendment Manual*, title page.

43 *Minutes of the Fifth Annual Convention of the Woman's Christian Temperance Union of California* (1884), 68–69.

44 State legislatures receiving petitions for constitutional prohibition during the 1880s included those of Indiana, Connecticut, Ohio, Illinois, New Jersey, Michigan, Mississippi, Pennsylvania, North Carolina, Oregon, West Virginia, California, Missouri, Colorado, Wisconsin, New York, Iowa, Massachusetts, Tennessee, Minnesota, Maine, Kansas, Nebraska, Rhode Island, Maryland, Arkansas, Vermont, and Texas. Meanwhile, prohibitionists pressured constitutional conventions in Pennsylva-

nia (1873), New Hampshire (1889), Washington (1889), North Dakota (1889), South Dakota (1889), and Mississippi (1890) to submit dry amendments to the people for a vote.

45 Anti-liquor activists waged strong campaigns for general laws in Pennsylvania (1870–73, 1876–79), New York (1870–72), New Jersey (1871–73, 1881–82, 1885–88), Texas (1875–76), Arkansas (1879), Ohio (1880–81), Delaware (1880–86), Indiana (1881), Tennessee (1873–82), South Carolina (1880–82), Louisiana (1884), Georgia (1882–85), Florida (1884–85), Mississippi (1883–86), and Virginia (1881–86). In California, Iowa, Connecticut, and Massachusetts, however, state legislatures enacted laws without much support from teetotalers.

46 "Neutrality, Instead of Protection Should Be the Attitude of the Legislature," *American Issue*, 17 January 1902, 1.

47 See, e.g., "The Clark Bill the Issue," *American Issue*, September 1900, 7; "The Vast Significance of the Beal Bill Victory for Local Option," *American Issue*, 4 April 1902, 4; Caswell, "Prohibition Movement in Oregon to the Adoption of Statewide Prohibition in 1914," 62.

48 B. W. Williams, "Methods of Temperance Reform," *Union Signal*, 20 February 1890, 3.

49 H. A. Scomp, "Local Option," *Cyclopedia of Temperance and Prohibition* (New York: Funk and Wagnalls, 1891), 393. See also H. A. Scomp, "Local Option Not Satisfactory," *The Political Prohibitionist for 1888* (New York: Funk and Wagnalls, 1888), 11–12.

50 "Local Option versus Prohibition," *Union Signal*, 22 February 1894, 9.

51 Scomp, "Local Option," 391–93. For Scomp's prediction that "cliques, rings and combinations of all sorts" would labor to repeal Georgia's law of 1885, see H. A. Scomp, *King Alcohol in the Realm of King Cotton, or A History of the Liquor Traffic and of the Temperance Movement in Georgia from 1733 to 1887* (Chicago: Blakely Printing, 1888), 763; Scomp, "Local Option Not Satisfactory," 11–12.

52 See, for example, the liquor laws described in the following: Charles E. Canup, "Temperance Movements and Legislation in Indiana," *Indiana Magazine of History* 16 (1920): 11–12, 22; David M. Ellis et al., *A Short History of New York State* (Ithaca, N.Y.: Cornell University Press, 1957), 309; "An Act to Tax and Regulate Tippling and Tippling Houses, and to Increase the Revenue," *Nashville Union*, 29 January 1846; Douglas W. Carlson, "Temperance Reform in the Cotton Kingdom" (Ph.D. diss., University of Illinois, 1982), 165–70; Daniel J. Whitener, *Prohibition in North Carolina, 1715–1945* (Chapel Hill: University of North Carolina Press, 1945), 35–36; Thomas J. Bailey, *Prohibition in Mississippi, or Anti-Liquor Legislation from Territorial Days, with Its Results in the Counties* (Jackson, 1917), 15–16, 18–19, 22–23; William G. Davis, "Attacking 'The Matchless Evil': Temperance and Prohibition in Mississippi, 1817–1908" (Ph.D. diss., Mississippi State University, 1975), 35–36; James B. Sellers, *The Prohibition Movement in Alabama, 1702 to 1943* (Chapel Hill: University of North Carolina Press, 1943), 10–13, 29–31.

53 John F. Dillon, *Commentaries on the Law of Municipal Corporations*, 3d ed. (Boston: Little, Brown, 1881), 1:54–56; Friedman, *A History of American Law*, 166, 459–60. Upon receiving a charter, a municipality could be sued, own property, and make contracts, and would survive the death of its original inhabitants.

54 George M. Hunt, "A History of the Prohibition Movement in Arkansas" (M.A. thesis, University of Arkansas, 1933), 24–27, 53–54.

55 Ibid., 24, 28–32; Bryce, *The American Commonwealth* 1:603, 605.

56 Canup, "Temperance Movements and Legislation in Indiana," 19–21. For other legislatures' reliance on special legislation, see Asa E. Martin, "The Temperance Movement in Pennsylvania Prior to the Civil War," *Pennsylvania Magazine of History and Biography* 49 (1925): 217–18; Sellers, *Prohibition Movement in Alabama*, 29–30, 37–39; Whitener, *Prohibition in North Carolina*, 48–49; Bailey, *Prohibition*

in *Mississippi*, 18–33; Davis, "Attacking 'The Matchless Evil,' " 36–37, 39–40; H. A. Ivy, *Rum on the Run in Texas: A Brief History of Prohibition in the Lone Star State* (Dallas: Temperance Publishing, 1910), 18; *Cyclopedia of Temperance and Prohibition*, 276, 278, 289–90, 304, 310, 318, 326, 331, 338–39; Cherrington, *The Standard Encyclopedia of the Alcohol Problem*, 78, 196, 1079, 1306, 1452, 1606, 1701, 1784, 2128, 2634; Ernest H. Cherrington, *The Evolution of Prohibition in the United States of America* (Westerville, Ohio: American Issue, 1920), 111, 119, 129.

57 "Report of the Executive Committee," *Fourth Report of the American Temperance Union* (1840), 29.

58 Martin, "The Temperance Movement in Pennsylvania Prior to the Civil War," 216.

59 Cherrington, *The Standard Encyclopedia of the Alcohol Problem* 4:1657.

60 *Reminiscences of Neal Dow*, 278–79.

61 The states that enacted general laws before 1860 included New Hampshire (1838), Rhode Island (1838, repealed 1841, reenacted: 1845), Connecticut (1839, repealed 1842), Illinois (1839), New York (1845, repealed 1847), Michigan (1845), Vermont (1844, repealed 1850), Iowa (1847, repealed 1849, reenacted: 1857, nullified 1857), Delaware (1847, nullified 1847), New Jersey (1847, repealed 1848), Missouri (1851), Louisiana (1852), Indiana (1853, nullified 1853), and Minnesota (1858). Meanwhile, the statute of Ohio (1846, repealed 1847) affected only ten counties, that of Pennsylvania (1846, nullified 1847) only eighteen. A Texas law (1854, nullified 1856) applied the principle to decisions involving the licensing of saloons to sell liquor in small quantities. Finally, when Massachusetts lawmakers authorized the election of county commissioners in 1835, they created a policy of virtual local option. Candidates for county commissioner often ran on "license" and "no-license" platforms, and the outcomes of these elections generally determined county liquor policies.

62 While some states after the war allowed for annual elections (e.g., Massachusetts, Connecticut, and Wisconsin), most other postwar laws only authorized fresh "no-license" elections after a longer interval, such as two, three, or even four years. Anti-liquor activists did not necessarily mind the longer intervals, though, because they allowed communities to thoroughly implement their "no-license" decisions before the wets could petition for a new election.

63 Compare, for example, the accounts of local option in antebellum Michigan with those of postbellum Massachusetts. See *Report of the Proceedings and Debates in the Convention to Revise the Constitution of the State of Michigan*, 432–33; Tap, " 'The Evils of Intemperance Are Generally Conceded,' " 24–26; "Local Option in Massachusetts," in *The Yearbook of the United States Brewers' Association*, 1910 (New York: United States Brewers' Association, 1910), 96–117.

64 In a few states, such as New Jersey and Minnesota, however, antebellum laws stipulated that the voters had to petition for "no-license" elections.

65 For example, many postbellum local option statutes empowered county commissioners to secure evidence for enforcing these laws.

66 Antebellum laws generally imposed fines of less than $20 on dealers who operated in no-license territory. In contrast, postwar measures often included fines that could approach $200, $500, or more, depending on the dealer's prior convictions.

67 For varied interpretations of antebellum "no-license" outcomes, see *Report of the Proceedings and Debates in the Convention to Revise the Constitution of the State of Michigan*, 409–10, 432–34; Tap, " 'The Evils of Intemperance Are Generally Conceded,' " 25–26; John Fitzgibbon, "King Alcohol: His Rise, Reign and Fall in Michigan," *Michigan History* 2 (1918): 57–59; David L. Ludlum, *Social Ferment in Vermont, 1791–1850* (Montpelier: Vermont Historical Society, 1948), 82; John A. Krout, *The Origins of Prohibition* (New York: Alfred A. Knopf, 1925), 276–77, 282; Ian Tyrrell, *Sobering Up: From Temperance to Prohibi-*

tion in *Antebellum America, 1800–1860* (Westport, Conn.: Greenwood, 1979), 242; Jed Dannenbaum, *Drink and Disorder: Temperance Reform in Cincinnati from the Washingtonian Revival to the WCTU* (Urbana: University of Illinois Press, 1984), 93–96.

68 States with long-lived policies included Illinois, New Hampshire, Michigan, and Missouri. For the brevity of most laws, see Cherrington, *The Evolution of Prohibition in the United States of America*, 120–34; Krout, *The Origins of Prohibition*, 275, 282–83.

69 *Parker v. Commonwealth*, 6 Barr 507, 518–19 (1847); Oberholtzer, *The Referendum in America*, 319–21.

70 *Rice v. Foster; Maize v. State*, 4 Ind. 342 (1853); *State v. Swisher*, 17 Tex. 441 (1856); *Geebrick v. State*, 5 Iowa 491 (1857).

71 Friedman, *A History of American Law*, 311. The Pennsylvania, Iowa, Indiana, and Delaware decisions all declared existing statutes void. The Texas case, however, involved a measure which was repealed by the state legislature before *State v. Swisher* was announced.

72 *Maize v. State*, 344, 350.

73 Lloyd Sponholtz, "The Initiative and Referendum: Direct Democracy in Perspective, 1898–1920," *American Studies* 14 (1973): 44, *Rice v. Foster*, 490–91; Oberholtzer, *The Referendum in America*, chapter 8.

74 Bryce, *The American Commonwealth* 1:469, 549–52; Oberholtzer, *Referendum in America*, 83, 158–59, 286; Lee J. Vance, "The Fight for More Anti-Liquor Legislation," *Case and Comment* 23 (1916): 43.

75 *Rice v. Foster*, 491.

76 *Maize v. State*, 347–48.

77 John B. Finch, "What, Why, and How," in *The People versus the Liquor Traffic*, ed. Charles A. McNully (Milwaukee: Literature Committee, IOGT, 1887), 207–9.

78 James R. Turner, "The American Prohibition Movement, 1865–1897" (Ph.D. diss., University of Wisconsin, 1972), 195; Earl C. Kaylor, "The Prohibition Movement in Pennsylvania" (Ph.D. diss., Pennsylvania State University, 1963), 103–4, 119; Whitener, *Prohibition in North Carolina*, 83.

79 Hunt, "A History of the Prohibition Movement in Arkansas," 46–50; Scomp, *King Alcohol in the Realm of King Cotton*, 757–59; C. C. Pearson and J. Edwin Hendricks, *Liquor and Anti-Liquor in Virginia, 1619–1919* (Durham: Duke University Press, 1967), 167–70.

80 Kaylor, "The Prohibition Movement in Pennsylvania," 118–19; Francis M. Whitaker, "A History of the Ohio Woman's Christian Temperance Union" (Ph.D. diss., Ohio State University, 1971), 372–73.

81 Clark, "The History of Liquor Legislation in Iowa," 351–53; *State v. Weir*, 33 Iowa 134 (1871).

82 Paul Isaac, *Prohibition and Politics: Turbulent Decades in Tennessee, 1885–1920* (Knoxville: University of Tennessee Press, 1965), 9; Grace Leab, "Tennessee Temperance Activities, 1870–1899," *East Tennessee Historical Society's Publications* 21 (1949): 57–58.

83 Gilman Ostrander, *The Prohibition Movement in California, 1848–1933* (Berkeley: University of California Press, 1957), 42–52; *Ex Parte Wall* 48 Cal. 279 (1874).

84 *Commonwealth v. Bennett*, 108 Mass. 27 (1871); *State v. Morris Common Pleas*, 36 N. Jersey Law R. 72 (1872); *Anderson v. Commonwealth*, 13 Bush. 485 (1874); *Fell v. State*, 42 Maryland 71 (1874); *State v. Wilcox*, 42 Conn. 364 (1875); *State v. Cooke*, 24 Minn. 247 (1877).

85 To be sure, this test case did not arise under the 1872 general law but instead involved an 1871 law authorizing Philadelphia's 22d Ward to vote on the licensing question. Still, an anti-local option decision in this case would have had a chilling effect on the temperance movement's willingness to use the 1872 law.

86 Kaylor, "The Prohibition Movement in Pennsylvania," 130–38; *Locke's Appeal*, 72 Pa., 22 F. Smith 491 (1873).

87 *The Aurora v. United States*, 7 Cranch 382 (1813). For Agnew's participation in nonpartisan anti-liquor

efforts, see Kaylor, "The Prohibition Movement in Pennsylvania," 138, 253; *Proceedings of the Sixth Annual Meeting of the Citizens' Law and Order League of the United States* (1888), 2, 97.

88 *Locke's Appeal*, 496–98.

89 *Bancroft v. Dumas*, 21 Vt. 456 (1849); *Rice v. Foster*, 493–97; *State v. Swisher*, 444–48; Oberholtzer, *The Referendum in America*, 320–21, 324–28.

90 See *Fell v. State*, 85–89; *State v. Morris Common Pleas; State v. Wilcox*, 374; *Schulherr v. Bordeaux*, 8 South. 201 (1886); *State v. Pond*, 6 S.W. 472–76 (1887); *Gordon v. State*, 23 N.E. 67 (1889); *Feek v. Bloomingdale Township Board*, 47 N.W. 41 (1890); R. L. Starr, "Are Local Option Liquor Laws Unconstitutional?" *Statesman*, September 1889, 329–33; Vance, "The Fight for More Anti-Liquor Legislation," 44.

91 *Commonwealth v. Bennett*, 28–29; Oberholtzer, *The Referendum in America*, 324, 328–34; Vance, "The Fight for More Anti-Liquor Legislation," 44. For Gray's views on historical precedent, see Robert M. Spector, "Legal Historian on the United States Supreme Court: Justice Horace Gray, Jr., and the Historical Method," *American Journal of Legal History* 12 (1968): 181–210.

92 Thomas M. Cooley, *A Treatise on the Constitutional Limitations Which Rest upon the Legislative Power of the States of the American Union*, 5th ed. (Boston: Little, Brown, 1883), 148.

93 See *State v. Wilcox*, 373; *State v. Morris Common Pleas; State v. Cooke*, 249–50; *Anderson v. Commonwealth; Caldwell v. Barrett*, 73 Ga. 606–7 (1884); *Savage v. Commonwealth*, 5 S.E. 566–67 (1888); *Paul v. Gloucester County*, 50 N.J. Law, 21 Vroom 600–607 (1888); *Territory v. O'Connor*, 41 N.W. 753 (1889); *State v. Forkner*, 62 N.W. 776 (1895).

94 *Paul v. Gloucester County*, 600.

95 *Feek v. Bloomingdale Township Board*, 41. See also *Locke's Appeal*, 496–97, *Paul v. Gloucester County*, 609, Vance, "The Fight for More Anti-Liquor Legislation," 44.

96 *Thornton v. Territory*, 3 Wash. T. 428 (1888).

97 Robert C. Kriebel, *Where Saints Have Trod: The Life of Helen Gougar* (West Lafayette, Ind.: Purdue University Press, 1985), 115.

98 *Maize v. State*. Gougar was on the verge of joining the Prohibition party when she researched the question of local option.

99 *Groesch v. State*, 42 Ind. 558–59 (1873).

100 Cooley, *A Treatise on the Constitutional Limitations*, 148.

101 *Feek v. Bloomingdale Township Board*, 42.

102 *State v. Forkner*, 782. For other strong dissents against pro–local option decisions, see *Locke's Appeal*, 501–7; *Fell v. State*, 90–117; *State v. Pond*, 479–502; *Paul v. Gloucester County*, 613–36.

103 Wilfrid M. Kellogg, "Local Option: Its Relation to the Genius of our Government," *Statesman*, August 1889, 269–73; "Local Option versus Prohibition," 9.

104 Whitaker, "A History of the Ohio Woman's Christian Temperance Union," 375–76; L. C. Pitner, "Local Option and Nullification," *Reason*, November 1886, 163–64.

105 See *Feek v. Bloomingdale Township Board*, 43–44; *State v. Pond*, 482–83; *Paul v. Gloucester County*, 627–36.

106 *Maize v. State; Geebrick v. State*.

107 "The Local Question," *Union Signal*, 6 March 1890, 8.

108 John B. Finch, "Why Constitutional Prohibition," in *The People versus the Liquor Traffic*, 5–6; Hoar, "Constitutional Remedy," 6–8; *Union Signal*, 24 April 1884, 1; "How Came the Saloon in Politics?" *Union Signal*, 21 July 1887, 8–9; Colvin, *Prohibition in the United States*, 135–36, 360–61; Kellogg, "Local Option," 269–73.

109 Editorial, *Christian Advocate*, 9 August 1888, 521; "A Great Opportunity," *Christian Advocate*, 30 August 1888, 573.

110 Howard H. Russell, "The Governor Helps Quietly: Oberlin Wins the Beatty Law," unpublished manuscript, box 2, Howard Hyde Russell Papers; "How the Victory Was Won in Oregon," *American Issue*, 8 July 1904, 11; "Not Satisfied," *American Issue*, 11 July 1902, 1–2; "To Confuse Temperance People," 4; *Ohio ex rel. Lloyd v. Dollison*, 68 Ohio 688 (1903); Charles M. Hogan, "Wayne B. Wheeler: Single Issue Exponent" (Ph.D. diss., University of Cincinnati, 1986), 59–67.

111 *Ohio ex rel. Lloyd v. Dollison*. For the Ohio ASL's success in sustaining local option laws, see Hogan, "Wayne B. Wheeler," 77–99.

112 Oberholtzer, *The Referendum in America*, chapters 9–12; Cooley, *A Treatise on the Constitutional Limitations*, 140–42, 148; Dealey, *Growth of American State Constitutions*, 223; Thomas E. Cronin, *Direct Democracy: The Politics of Initiative, Referendum and Recall* (Cambridge: Harvard University Press, 1990), 42.

113 Friedman, *A History of American Law*, 305, 309–10, 459–60; Dealey, *Growth of American State Constitutions*, 224–27; Keller, "Politics of State Constitutional Revision," 75–76; Bryce, *The American Commonwealth* 1:495, 558–60. Examples of cases about local referenda on other issues which cited cases upholding local option on liquor include *State v. Board of Freeholders*, 51 N.J.L. 454 (1889); *Hamilton v. Carroll*, 82 Md. 326 (1896); *Little Rock v. North Little Rock*, 72 Ark. 195 (1904); *Eckerson v. Des Moines*, 137 Iowa 452 (1908). Examples of local option cases which cited cases upholding local referenda on other issues include *Locke's Appeal*, *Fell v. State*, *State v. Forkner*, and *In Re O'Brien*, 29 Mont. 530 (1904).

114 Martin, "Temperance Movement in Pennsylvania Prior to the Civil War," 213–14; Kaylor, "Prohibition Movement in Pennsylvania," 88, 103; 120, 123, 124–25, 130, 135–36, 145; Cora Cramer, ed., *History, Pennsylvania Woman's Christian Temperance Union* (Quincy, Pa.: Quincy Orphanage, 1937), 311. In fact, during the early 1870s, teetotalers who feared that state lawmakers would not pass a general local option law also bombarded them with petitions for local prohibitory acts.

115 Branning, *Pennsylvania Constitutional Development*, 41–43, 55, 65–66, 98.

116 Charles C. Binney, *Restrictions upon Local and Special Legislation in State Constitutions* (Philadelphia: Kay and Brother, 1894), 131–80; Oberholtzer, *Referendum in America*, 84–85.

117 The Alabama, North Carolina, and Virginia legislatures proved amenable to special liquor legislation until the early 1900s. Shortly thereafter, though, Virginia and Alabama ratified new constitutions which restricted special legislation. See Sellers, *Prohibition Movement in Alabama*, 91–93, 97; Whitener, *Prohibition in North Carolina*, 117–27, 146; Pearson and Hendricks, *Liquor and Anti-Liquor in Virginia*, 183.

118 Isaac, *Prohibition and Politics*, 10.

119 Pearson and Hendricks, *Liquor and Anti-Liquor in Virginia*, 170, 173, 183. In fact, when Virginia lawmakers followed up on Stubbs's suggestion four years later, they succeeded in reducing the legislature's workload regarding local prohibitory laws. Between the enactment of local option in 1886 and the ratification in 1902 of a constitution which banned special acts, only twelve Virginia localities won special prohibitory legislation from state lawmakers.

120 Hunt, "History of the Prohibition Movement in Arkansas," 43–44.

121 Kaylor, "Prohibition Movement in Pennsylvania," 178–83; 247–51. Some local-optionists of the 1870s became so closely involved in the state movement that they later directed Pennsylvania's constitutional prohibition campaigns in the 1880s.

122 Turner, "American Prohibition Movement," 195–96; "Local-Option in New Jersey," *Christian Advocate*, 4 April 1889, 209–10; Cherrington, *The Standard Encyclopedia of the Alcohol Problem* 2:783–84; Daniel Dorchester, *The Liquor Problem in All Ages* (New York: Phillips and Hunt, 1888), 492.

123 Joe A. Fisher, "The Liquor Question in Nebraska, 1880–1890" (M.A. thesis, Municipal University of Omaha, 1952), 14–36, 48–49; "Nebraska," *National Temperance Advocate*, December 1880, 190; "Ne-

braska," *National Temperance Advocate*, January 1881, 13–14; A. A. Hopkins, *Profit and Loss in Man* (New York: Funk and Wagnalls, 1909), 323–27.

124 Fisher, "The Liquor Question in Nebraska," 37–38, chapter 7.

125 "The WCTU: The Fourteenth Annual Convention Now in Session at Port Huron," *Detroit Free Press*, 1 June 1887, 4.

126 *Annual Meeting Minutes of the National Woman's Christian Temperance Union, 1880 Convention*, 77–78, *1881 Convention*, lxxxiv–lxxxv.

127 C. C. M'Cabe, "Down with the Rum Traffic," *Christian Advocate*, 23 December 1886, 4.

128 *The Political Prohibitionist for 1888*, 12; *Cyclopedia of Temperance and Prohibition*, 396.

129 See, e.g., the local campaigns described in Citizens' No-License Committee, *Ten No-License Years in Cambridge* (Cambridge, Mass.: Citizen's Committee, 1898), 161–69; William F. Hoehn, *No-License in Quincy* (Quincy, Mass., 1899), 12–13, 79–81; Cramer, ed., *History, Pennsylvania Woman's Christian Temperance Union*; George J. Richman, *History of Hancock County, Indiana* (Greenfield, Ind.: William Mitchell, 1916), 407; Ostrander, *The Prohibition Movement in California*, 62.

130 *Union Signal*, 3 May 1894, 1.

131 Louis A. Banks, "The Anti-Saloon League, Origin and Personnel," in *The Passing of the Saloon*, ed. George H. Hammell (Cincinnati: Tower, 1908), 187–88.

132 For example, see "A Campaign against the Saloon," *Anti-Saloon*, June 1895, 6; "Whiskey Rules Us! How Can You Help Us?" *Anti-Saloon*, December 1895, 7; *Proceedings, 1896 National Anti-Saloon Convention* (Washington: American Anti-Saloon League, 1897), 14–15; "A Leader Needed," *American Issue*, August 1900, 6; "More about the Harrison Township Anti-Saloon Victory," "Mt. Blanchard Goes Dry," *American Issue*, 7 June 1901, 4; "A Word to All Good Citizens," *American Issue*, 7 March 1902, 4.

133 "The WCTU: The Fourteenth Annual Convention Now in Session at Port Huron," 4.

134 Hopkins, *Profit and Loss in Man*, 318–19.

135 "Local Option for Municipalities," *American Issue*, January 1900, 6.

136 A. B. Nettleton, "The Line on Which All Enemies of the Saloon May Unitedly Do Battle," *Proceedings of the National Temperance Congress Held in the Broadway Tabernacle, New York, Wednesday and Thursday, June 11th and 12th, 1890* (New York: Funk and Wagnalls, 1891), 82.

137 Cherrington, *The Standard Encyclopedia of the Alcohol Problem* 4:1702; *Proceedings, Fifth National Anti-Saloon Convention* (Baltimore: American Anti-Saloon League, 1900), 55–56; *Proceedings, Sixth National Anti-Saloon Convention* (Baltimore: American Anti-Saloon League, 1902), 68–69; *Proceedings, Eighth National Anti-Saloon Convention* (Harrisburg: American Anti-Saloon League, 1904), 59–60; Thomas R. Pegram, "Temperance Politics and Regional Political Culture: The Anti-Saloon League in Maryland and the South, 1907–1915," *Journal of Southern History* 63 (1997): 86.

138 *Proceedings, Sixth National Anti-Saloon Convention*, 72, 75.

139 "Local Option in Montana," *American Issue*, 11 March 1904, 7; *In Re O'Brien*.

140 "It Is Legal: Constitutionality of the Brannock Law," *American Issue*, 12 February 1904, 10; Hogan, "Wayne B. Wheeler," 77–99.

141 "Lessons from Town Local Option Contests in Ohio," *American Issue*, 4 July 1902, 4.

142 *Proceedings, Fourteenth National Convention of the Anti-Saloon League of America* (Westerville, Ohio: American Issue, 1912), 110.

143 *Proceedings, Twelfth Annual Convention* (Harrisburg: Anti-Saloon League of America, 1907), 125; *Yearbook of the United States Brewers' Association*, 1910, 25, 54, 152–53; "The Value of the Beal Municipal Local Option Law," *American Issue*, 4 April 1902, 6–7.

144 Samuel J. Barrows, "The Temperance Tidal Wave," in *The Passing of the Saloon*, ed. George H. Hammell (Cincinnati: Tower, 1908), 204, 215.

145 In 1902, for example, the Ohio ASL boasted that the state's new municipal-option law would "give temperance people a uniform law for municipalities that cannot be tampered with by councils." They also argued that it would give drys "a firmer grip on the enforcement of the law, the law being uniform for every municipality." See "The Value of the Beal Municipal Local Option Law," 7.

5 Political Alignments, Party Systems, and Prohibition

1 Doug McAdam, "Conceptual Origins, Current Problems, Future Directions," in *Comparative Perspectives on Social Movements: Political Opportunities, Mobilizing Structures, and Framings*, ed. Doug McAdam et al. (Cambridge: Cambridge University Press, 1996), 26–29.

2 Movement analysts who emphasize the role of political alignments in shaping movement outcomes include Frances F. Piven and Richard A. Cloward, *Poor People's Movements: Why They Succeed, How They Fail* (New York: Vintage, 1979); Frances Fox Piven and Richard A. Cloward, "Toward a Class-Based Realignment of American Politics: A Movement Strategy," *Social Policy* 14 (1983): 2–14; Anne N. Costain, *Inviting Women's Rebellion: A Political Process Interpretation of the Women's Movement* (Baltimore: Johns Hopkins University Press, 1992), 24; Rufus Browning, Dale Rogers Marshall, and David H. Tabb, *Protest Is Not Enough: The Struggle of Blacks and Hispanics for Equality in Urban Politics* (Berkeley: University of California Press, 1984), 240–42; Sidney Tarrow, "Social Protest and Policy Reform: May 1968 and the Loi d'Orientation in France," *Comparative Political Studies* 25 (1993): 592–600.

3 Frances F. Piven and Richard A. Cloward, *Why Americans Don't Vote* (New York: Pantheon, 1988), xxii.

4 In addition, American social movements have also achieved some goals through direct legislation and the actions of unelected officials and judges.

5 For the "new political history" and its rediscovery of political parties, see Richard L. McCormick, *The Party Period and Public Policy: American Politics from the Age of Jackson to the Progressive Era* (New York: Oxford University Press, 1986), Introduction.

6 While several works explore the changing coalitional bases of the party system, some which explicitly discuss the impact of social movements on coalition formation include William E. Gienapp, *The Origins of the Republican Party, 1852–1856* (New York: Oxford University Press, 1987); Paul Kleppner, *The Third Electoral System, 1853–1892: Parties, Voters, and Political Cultures* (Chapel Hill: University of North Carolina Press, 1979); Paul Kleppner, *The Cross of Culture: A Social Analysis of Midwestern Politics, 1850–1900* (New York: Free Press, 1970); Richard Jensen, *The Winning of the Midwest: Social and Political Conflict, 1888–1896* (Chicago: University of Chicago Press, 1971); Michael P. Rogin and John L. Shover, *Political Change in California: Critical Elections and Social Movements, 1890–1968* (Westport, Conn.: Greenwood, 1970); James L. Sundquist, *Dynamics of the Party System: Alignment and Realignment of Political Parties in the United States* (Washington: Brookings Institution, 1983).

7 Well-documented examples of such outsiders include the antebellum antislavery, temperance, and nativist movements, the postbellum labor and agrarian movements, and the civil rights movement of the 1950s and 1960s. For the antebellum period, see Gienapp, *The Origins of the Republican Party*; for the late nineteenth century, see Sundquist, *Dynamics of the Party System*, chapter 6. For the civil rights movement's impact on the party system, see Thomas B. Edsall and Mary Edsall, *Chain Reaction: The Impact of Race, Rights, and Taxes on American Politics* (New York: W. W. Norton, 1992).

8 In its most ambitious form, realignment theory contends that American history can be divided into five or six party systems, separated by "critical realignments," or short periods of explosive elec-

toral change. According to Walter Dean Burnham's formulation, for example, the five party systems were: the Experimental System (1789–1820), the Democratizing System (1828–60), the Civil War System (1860–93), the Industrialist System (1894–1932), and the New Deal System (1932–?). Since first sketching realignment theory in the late 1960s, Burnham has speculated that a sixth party system began in the early 1970s, and has recently suggested that a seventh is in the offing. See his "Party Systems and the Political Process," in *Current Crisis in American Politics: Critical Elections and the Mainsprings of American Politics* (New York: W.W. Norton, 1970); "Realignment Lives: The 1994 Earthquake and Its Implications," in *The Clinton Presidency: First Appraisals*, ed. Colin Campbell and Bert A. Rockman (Chatham, N.J.: Chatham House, 1996).

9 Works which portray movements as "coalitional insiders" include Browning, Marshall, and Tabb, *Protest Is Not Enough*; Duane M. Oldfield, *The Right and the Righteous: The Christian Right Confronts the Republican Party* (Lanham, Md.: Rowman and Littlefield, 1996); Matthew C. Moen, *The Christian Right and Congress* (Tuscaloosa: University of Alabama Press, 1989); Allen D. Hertzke, *Echoes of Discontent: Jesse Jackson, Pat Robertson, and the Resurgence of Populism* (Washington: Congressional Quarterly, 1993); Jo Freeman, "Whom You Know versus Whom You Represent: Feminist Influence in the Democratic and Republican Parties," in *The Women's Movements of the United States and Western Europe: Consciousness, Political Opportunity, and Public Policy*, ed. Mary F. Katzenstein and Carol M. Mueller (Philadelphia: Temple University Press, 1987), 215–44.

10 In addition, the nativist Know Nothings successfully sponsored church property laws and the termination of immigrant militia units in the North. See Tyler Anbinder, *Nativism and Slavery: The Northern Know Nothings and the Politics of the 1850s* (New York: Oxford University Press, 1992), 135–61.

11 For the Christian Right's relationship with the GOP, see Oldfield, *The Right and the Righteous*; Clyde Wilcox, *Onward Christian Soldiers? The Religious Right in American Politics*, 2d ed. (Boulder: Westview, 2000), chapter 3; and the articles in the symposium "The Christian Right and the 1994 Elections," *PS: Political Science and Politics* 28 (1995): 5–23.

12 For this argument, see Richard L. McCormick, *From Realignment to Reform: Political Change in New York State, 1893–1910* (Ithaca, N.Y.: Cornell University Press, 1981). In contrast, an insider movement with no chance of defecting may simply be coopted by the party system. See, e.g., Ostler's discussion of the Iowa Farmers' Alliance in his *Prairie Populism: The Fate of Agrarian Radicalism in Kansas, Nebraska, and Iowa, 1880–1892* (Lawrence: University Press of Kansas, 1993), chapter 9.

13 Though many scholars note that the Democrats remained competitive with the Republicans in gubernatorial elections after 1896, the minority party nonetheless lost every statewide election from 1898 to 1910. Moreover, "in the seven elections from 1898 to 1910, the Republicans had elected forty-nine Congressmen, the Democrats, five." See Rogin and Shover, *Political Change in California*, 24–26.

14 George E. Mowry, *The California Progressives* (Chicago: Quadrangle, 1963), 57–82.

15 Promoted by the Anti-Race Track Gambling League, an ally of the Lincoln-Roosevelt League, this act forbade "wagering or pool selling or bookmaking in any way, shape or form." See Franklin Hichborn, *Story of the Session of the California Legislature of 1909* (San Francisco: James H. Barry, 1909), 52–67; Gerald Woods, "A Penchant for Probity: California Progressives and Disreputable Pleasures," *California Progressivism Revisited*, ed. William Deverell and Tom Sitton (Berkeley: University of California Press, 1994), 101, 106.

16 Of course, not every state was characterized by a one-party regime during the Progressive Era. However, even in states with party systems that were more competitive, one party tended to have a decided advantage.

17 Sundquist, *Dynamics of the Party System*, 41–42.

18 Harry L. Watson, *Liberty and Power: The Politics of Jacksonian America* (New York: Noonday, 1990), 186; Thomas R. Pegram, *Battling Demon Rum: The Struggle for a Dry America, 1800–1933* (Chicago: Ivan R. Dee, 1998), 35–37. In contrast to the Whigs, Democratic party activists often opposed anti-liquor legislation as an illegitimate exercise of state power which extinguished individual liberty. During the Tennessee legislature's debate over liquor legislation in 1846, for instance, Representative Pearce, a Democrat, challenged his colleagues' right "under our institutions, to dictate to a citizen, however humble, what he shall eat, drink, or with what he shall clothe himself." See *Nashville Union*, 17 December 1846.

19 In *Liberalism against Populism: A Confrontation between the Theory of Democracy and the Theory of Social Choice* (Prospect Heights, Ill.: Waveland, 1982), William H. Riker argues that political losers have an incentive to disrupt the status quo by raising new issues that may allow them to become winners. Clearly, the Whigs were the minority party during the antebellum period. However, their losses to the Democrats in presidential elections were narrow, and they averaged 49.35% of the vote during the period 1836–48. Moreover, the Whigs were often the "winners" in states where the temperance movement was strongest. For example, they dominated the governments of Massachusetts, Vermont, and Rhode Island, and they were highly competitive in states like Connecticut, New York, and Ohio.

20 Of the legislatures to enact major temperance laws in the late 1830s, four were controlled by the Whigs (Massachusetts 1838, Tennessee 1838, Rhode Island 1839, Connecticut 1839) and three by the Democrats (Mississippi 1838, New Hampshire 1838, Illinois 1839).

21 In Rhode Island, for example, state liquor licensing was restricted by a local option law (1838), which was repealed in 1841, reinstated in 1845, and subsequently weakened in 1848. See John S. Gilkeson, *Middle-Class Providence, 1820–1940* (Princeton, N.J.: Princeton University Press, 1986), 32–33.

22 For a description of temperance opposition in the 1830s see Ian Tyrrell, *Sobering Up: From Temperance to Prohibition in Antebellum America, 1800–1860* (Westport: Greenwood, 1979), chapter 4.

23 "State prohibition" should not be confused with the repeal of all state licensing laws, the favorite goal of many political teetotalers during this period. Whereas the former banned the sale (and often the manufacture) of all intoxicating liquors under threat of penalty, the latter was often little more than a symbolic divorce between the government and the nefarious liquor traffic. By no longer issuing liquor licenses, a state ceased to condone liquor sales; hence, those who sold liquor in a state could be branded "lawless," but would suffer no legal penalties. The most tangible impact of repeal was often the state's loss of license revenue.

24 For example, most of the participants at the annual meeting of the Vermont Temperance Society in 1844 initially favored state prohibition. However, this group was persuaded to support local option by a state politician, who argued that state prohibition would "have difficulty in passing both houses of the General Assembly." See David L. Ludlum, *Social Ferment in Vermont, 1791–1850* (Montpelier: Vermont Historical Society, 1948), 80–81.

25 During the 1840s, petitioning for prohibition occurred in only a few states (e.g., Maine, Massachusetts, and Rhode Island), and the legislative response was mixed. In Maine, forty thousand petitioners persuaded the legislature in 1846 to outlaw the sale of intoxicating liquors in quantities of less than thirty-eight gallons, thus prohibiting all sales other than those by wholesalers. In 1848 Massachusetts lawmakers rejected a prohibition law which had been unanimously approved by a select committee. Finally, petitioning in Rhode Island resulted in no real progress toward prohibition in the 1840s. See Frank L. Byrne, *Prophet of Prohibition: Neal Dow and His Crusade* (Madison: State Historical Society of Wisconsin, 1961), 38; Robert C. Pitman, *Alcohol and the State* (New York: National

Temperance Society and Publication House, 1877), 287–88; Gilkeson, *Middle Class Providence*, 34.

26 Maine's prohibition statute (1851) forbade the sale and manufacture of all intoxicating liquors, except for those required for mechanical and medicinal purposes.

27 The Free Soil party captured 10.1% of the popular vote in the presidential election of 1848. See Svend Petersen, *A Statistical History of the American Presidential Elections* (New York: Frederick Ungar, 1963), 30.

28 Frederick J. Blue, *The Free Soilers: Third Party Politics, 1848–1854* (Urbana: University of Illinois Press, 1973), chapter 6; Theodore C. Smith, *The Liberty and Free Soil Parties in the Northwest* (New York: Longmans, Green, 1897), 160–62.

29 Blue, *The Free Soilers*, 176–187; Smith, *The Liberty and Free Soil Parties*, chapters 12–14.

30 The Compromise of 1850 was a series of congressional laws that included a more stringent fugitive slave law, the organization of Utah and New Mexico as territories without restriction on slavery, the admission of California as a free state, and the suppression of the slave trade in the District of Columbia. Whereas the first two statutes were deemed favorable to the South, the latter two parts of the compromise were meant to placate the North.

31 Richard H. Sewell, *Ballots for Freedom: Antislavery Politics in the United States, 1837–1860* (New York: Oxford University Press, 1976), 232.

32 Stephen E. Maizlish, *The Triumph of Sectionalism: The Transformation of Ohio Politics, 1844–1856* (Kent, Ohio: Kent State University Press, 1983), 182–83. See also Gienapp, *The Origins of the Republican Party*, 47; Ian Tyrrell, *Sobering Up: From Temperance to Prohibition in Antebellum America, 1800–1860* (Westport, Conn.: Greenwood, 1979), 264; Frank L. Byrne, "Maine Law versus Lager Beer: A Dilemma for Wisconsin's Young Republican Party," *Wisconsin Magazine of History* 42 (1958–59): 116.

33 Gienapp, *The Origins of the Republican Party*, 44–60, 66–67; Paul Goodman, "Moral Purpose and Republican Politics in Antebellum America, 1830–1860," *Maryland Historian* 20 (1989): 28–31.

34 The presence of Free Soilers in ruling coalitions did matter in states like Massachusetts, where an alliance of Free Soilers, Whigs, and a bare majority of Democrats passed a Maine Law in 1852. However, this scenario could not be duplicated in states where the Free Soilers did not hold the legislative balance of power. For example, the Ohio legislature of 1853 contained thirteen Free Soil members, only seven fewer than it had Whigs. However, the Democrats controlled an absolute majority of the seats, and preferred not to alienate Maine Law opponents, who had voted solidly Democratic in 1853. See Kevin Sweeney, "Rum, Romanism, Representation, and Reform: Coalition Politics in Massachusetts, 1847–1853," *Civil War History* 22 (1976): 116–37; Smith, *The Liberty and Free Soil Parties*, 275; Anthony G. Carey, "The Second Party System Collapses: The 1853 Maine Law Campaign in Ohio," *Ohio History* 100 (1991): 129–53.

35 In addition to Delaware (1855), which was a slave state, the northern states and territories that passed Maine Laws included Connecticut (1854), Indiana (1855), Iowa (1855), Maine (1851), Massachusetts (1852), Michigan (1853), Minnesota (1852), Nebraska (1855), New Hampshire (1855), New York (1855), Rhode Island (1852), and Vermont (1852).

36 Emma L. Thornbrough, *Indiana in the Civil War Era, 1850–1880* (Indianapolis: Indiana Historical Society, 1965), 59–67; D. Leigh Colvin, *Prohibition in the United States* (New York: George H. Doran, 1926), 45–46; Charles E. Canup, "Temperance Movements and Legislation in Indiana," *Indiana Magazine of History* 16 (1920): 23; *Journal of the Grand Division of the Sons of Temperance, State of Massachusetts*, July 1850, 4; George F. Clark, *History of the Temperance Reform in Massachusetts* (Boston: Clarke and Carruth, 1888), 238–39; Sweeney, "Rum, Romanism, Representation, and Reform," 128–29.

37 The four states in question were Indiana, Delaware, New York, and New Hampshire. See Charles C. Bohner, "Rum and Reform: Temperance in Delaware Politics," *Delaware History* 5 (1953): 237–69; Anbinder, *Nativism and Slavery*, 142.

38 Anbinder, *Nativism and Slavery*, 43–44; W. Darrell Overdyke, *The Know-Nothing Party in the South* (Baton Rouge: Louisiana State University Press, 1950), 86, 177; Douglas W. Carlson, "Temperance Reform in the Cotton Kingdom" (Ph.D. diss., University of Illinois, 1982), 245–46.

39 Given the paucity of immigrants and Catholics in the South, one might assume that the Know Nothings had little support within this region. However, with the exception of a few states, American gubernatorial candidates in the South generally drew over 40% of the vote in the years 1854–57. See table 4.2.

40 In Alabama, Mississippi, and Georgia, two fleeting party coalitions surfaced after the Compromise of 1850: the Unionists, who supported the bulk of the compromise, and the State's Rights party, which did not. However, the emergence of the compromise as an issue did not produce a multiparty system akin to that of the North. Indeed, the State's Rights parties were dominated by Democrats, and the Unionists combined a majority of the Whigs with some Democrats. Hence, when the Democrats re-formed in all three states by 1853, they were opposed by weak Whig organizations until 1854 and the birth of the Know Nothings. In a fourth state, Arkansas, pro-compromise Democrats briefly joined with the Whigs for the gubernatorial election of 1852. See Michael F. Holt, *The Political Crisis of the 1850s* (New York: John Wiley and Sons, 1978), 91–94.

41 For the southern Know Nothings, see Overdyke, *The Know-Nothing Party in the South*, chapter 5.

42 For example, see Marc W. Kruman, *Parties and Politics in North Carolina, 1836–1865* (Baton Rouge: Louisiana State University Press, 1983), 154–57.

43 Only in North Carolina were Democrats endorsed by the state's anti-liquor forces over the Know Nothings. In Georgia, neither the American nor the Democratic gubernatorial candidate took a strong position on prohibition, and the teetotalers ran their own candidate. Meanwhile, in Alabama and Tennessee, Know Nothing gubernatorial candidates supported local option. See Overdyke, *The Know-Nothing Party in the South*, 85–86; Carlson, "Temperance Reform in the Cotton Kingdom," 244–46, 275–80; James B. Sellers, *The Prohibition Movement in Alabama, 1702 to 1943* (Chapel Hill: University of North Carolina Press, 1943), 36; *Nashville Union*, 24 March 1855, 28 April 1855.

44 *Nashville Union*, 7 May 1852, 11 April 1853, 21 April 1853, 21 September 1854; Carlson, "Temperance Reform in the Cotton Kingdom," 248–50; C. C. Pearson and J. Edwin Hendricks, *Liquor and Anti-Liquor in Virginia, 1619–1919* (Durham: Duke University Press, 1967), 138; Overdyke, *The Know-Nothing Party in the South*, 85. In some cases, the promotion of spiritualism did overlap with temperance and other antebellum causes. For example, the preeminent figure in antebellum spiritualism, Andrew Jackson Davis, endorsed abolitionism, temperance, and woman's rights. For antebellum spiritualism, see Ronald G. Walters, *American Reformers* (New York: Hill and Wang, 1978), 163–71.

45 *Nashville Union*, 21 October 1854, as well as 27 January 1855, 14 April 1855, 13 June 1855, and 26 June 1855; Kruman, *Parties and Politics in North Carolina*, 175; Overdyke, *The Know-Nothing Party in the South*, 203–4; Anbinder, *Nativism and Slavery*, 164–65.

46 Roy R. Glashan, *American Governors and Gubernatorial Elections, 1775–1978* (Westport, Conn.: Meckler, 1979), 40–41.

47 Kruman, *Parties and Politics in North Carolina*, chapter 7.

48 *The Reminiscences of Neal Dow: Recollections of Eighty Years* (Portland, Maine: Evening Express, 1898), 139.

49 Gienapp, *The Origins of the Republican Party*, 434–35, tables 13.32–35.

50 With the exception of a few German Methodists, the German-American community was opposed to prohibition. See Frederick C. Luebke, *Immigrants and Politics: The Germans of Nebraska, 1880–1900* (Lincoln: University of Nebraska Press, 1969), 6, 50; David W. Detjen, *The Germans in Missouri, 1900–1918: Prohibition, Neutrality, and Assimilation* (Columbia: University of Missouri Press, 1985), 27–28.

51 Gienapp, *The Origins of the Republican Party*, 227–28, 235, 278–79, 365–66, 391; Eric Foner, *Free Soil, Free Labor, Free Men: The Ideology of the Republican Party before the Civil War* (New York: Oxford University Press, 1970), 241–42, 247; Byrne, "Maine Law versus Lager Beer," 117–20.

52 John Marsh, *Temperance Recollections, Labors, Defeats, Triumphs: An Autobiography* (New York: Charles Scribner, 1867), 297.

53 Tyrrell, *Sobering Up*, 290–97, 305–7.

54 Daniel Dorchester, *The Liquor Problem in All Ages* (New York: Phillips and Hunt, 1888), 399.

55 For the liquor policies of Republican-led state governments in this period see Robert Cook, *Baptism of Fire: The Republican Party in Iowa, 1838–1878* (Ames: Iowa State University Press, 1994), 87–88, 110; Dale Baum, "Teetotalers Enter Politics: The Massachusetts Prohibitionist Party in the Early 1870s," *Mid-America* 65 (1983): 139; John J. Coffey, "A Political History of the Temperance Movement in New York State, 1808–1920" (Ph.D. diss., Pennsylvania State University, 1976), 125–27; *Cyclopedia of Temperance and Prohibition* (New York: Funk and Wagnalls, 1891), 588.

56 To finance the Civil War, the U.S. government enacted the Internal Revenue Act of 1862, which imposed an extensive system of internal taxes on commodities and transactions. Among other things, the act levied a tax on distilled spirits and malt liquors with a special license for retailers. While the measure affected many industries, its liquor provisions accounted for 18.5% of the act's wartime collections. In 1868, when most taxes were repealed, the government continued to collect liquor taxes, which supplied a substantial portion of total tax revenues. (In 1898, for example, 41.2% of total U.S. tax revenues came from liquor taxes!) See Tun Yuan Hu, *The Liquor Tax in the United States, 1791–1947: A History of the Internal Revenue Taxes Imposed on Distilled Spirits by the Federal Government* (New York: Columbia Graduate School of Business, 1950), chapter 2, appendix 1; Richard F. Hamm, *Shaping the Eighteenth Amendment: Temperance Reform, Legal Culture, and the Polity, 1880–1920* (Chapel Hill: University of North Carolina Press, 1995), chapters 3, 5; *Cyclopedia of Temperance and Prohibition*, 251–57, 634–38.

57 For example, while some Republican lawmakers objected strongly to the federal liquor tax, they nonetheless voted for the Internal Revenue Act as an emergency wartime measure that would be repealed after the war. See Earl C. Kaylor, "The Prohibition Movement in Pennsylvania" (Ph.D. diss., Pennsylvania State University, 1963), 54; Ernest H. Cherrington, *The Evolution of Prohibition in the United States of America* (Westerville, Ohio: American Issue, 1920), 155–56; August F. Fehlandt, *A Century of Drink Reform in the United States* (Cincinnati: Jennings and Graham, 1904), 139–44.

58 Cook, *Baptism of Fire*, 87–88.

59 See chapter 2 for this organizational decline.

60 For example, see the dry campaigns described in Coffey, "A Political History of the Temperance Movement," chapter 3.

61 For Republican equivocation on the liquor question during Reconstruction, see Richard H. Abbott, "Massachusetts: Maintaining Hegemony," and Richard N. Current, "Wisconsin: Shifting Strategies to Stay on Top," in *Radical Republicans in the North: State Politics during Reconstruction*, ed. James C. Mohr (Baltimore: Johns Hopkins University Press, 1976); Daniel E. Clark, "The History of Liquor Legislation in Iowa, 1878–1908," *Iowa Journal of History and Politics* 6 (1908): 42–56; Kaylor, "The Prohibition Movement in Pennsylvania," 122–35, 173–83; Kleppner, *The Third Electoral System*, 131–36. In general, radical prohibitionists saw the GOP as indifferent to their cause during the years 1866–76. In this decade, Republican state legislatures repealed anti-liquor policies in Connecticut (1867, 1872), Massachusetts (1875), and Michigan (1875), and failed to advance the dry cause elsewhere. Moreover, in 1872 the national party inserted the "Raster resolution" in its platform, which stated that the GOP respected "the rights reserved by the people to themselves" and which was interpreted as rejecting

prohibitory policies. See *Cyclopedia of Temperance and Prohibition*, 589–90; George L. Case, "The Prohibition Party: Its Origin, Purpose and Growth," *Magazine of Western History* 9 (1888–89): 375–76; James Black, "Is There a Necessity for a Prohibition Party?" in *Centennial Temperance Volume: A Memorial of the International Temperance Conference, Held in June, 1876* (New York: National Temperance Society and Publication House, 1877), 337–41.

62 Kaylor, "The Prohibition Movement in Pennsylvania," 151–56, 162, 165, 182–83; Clark, *History of the Temperance Reform in Massachusetts*, 148–52; *Cyclopedia of Temperance and Prohibition*, 57, 62, 477.

63 For evidence to this effect, see Baum, "Teetotalers Enter Politics," 140–42; Kleppner, *The Cross of Culture*, 123–24, 318–19.

64 Kleppner, *The Third Electoral System*, 247–52.

65 Kaylor, "The Prohibition Movement in Pennsylvania," 110.

66 Colvin, *Prohibition in the United States*, 78, 84. See also Kleppner, *The Third Electoral System*, 245–47.

67 For the antebellum antislavery parties, see Sewell, *Ballots for Freedom*.

68 Black, "Is There a Necessity for a Prohibition Party?" 334.

69 *Cyclopedia of Temperance and Prohibition*, 30–33; Gideon T. Stewart, "How Shall We Best Secure State Prohibition?" in *Proceedings of the Ninth National Temperance Convention Held at Saratoga Springs, N.Y., June 21 and 22, 1881* (New York: National Temperance Society and Publishing House, 1881), 223, 226–27; Editorial, *The Voice*, 25 September 1884; Jack S. Blocker, *Retreat from Reform: The Prohibition Movement in the United States, 1890–1913* (Westport, Conn.: Greenwood, 1976), 39–40; James R. Turner, "The American Prohibition Movement, 1865–1897" (Ph.D. diss., University of Wisconsin, 1972), 278–79, 311. While they claimed that their party would produce a political "smash-up," the Prohibitionists did not always predict that it would replace the Republican party. See *The Voice*, 17 December 1885, 3.

70 *Cyclopedia of Temperance and Prohibition*, 33; Editorial, *The Voice*, 25 September 1884.

71 Helen M. Gougar, "A Prohibitionist Points the Way Out," *Arena*, May 1894, 833.

72 *Minutes of the National Woman's Christian Temperance Union, 1881 Convention*, Appendix, lxxv–lxxviii; *Cyclopedia of Temperance and Prohibition*, 574; Colvin, *Prohibition in the United States*, 168, 188–89; Blocker, *Retreat from Reform*, 41–44. At the party's National Conference in January 1885, the Prohibitionists decided to focus on developing the party's southern wing.

73 "The Great Prohibition Mass-Meeting," *Christian Union*, 16 June 1887, 24; Colvin, *Prohibition in the United States*, 191.

74 For the Prohibition party's regional strength in national elections, see Blocker, *Retreat from Reform*, 44–46; for the state level, see *Cyclopedia of Temperance and Prohibition*, 562–77.

75 *The Political Prohibitionist for 1888* (New York: Funk and Wagnalls, 1888), 48–49. On occasion, southern drys refused to vote for pro-liquor Democrats, and threw their support behind temperance Republicans. See Paul Isaac, *Prohibition and Politics: Turbulent Decades in Tennessee, 1885–1920* (Knoxville: University of Tennessee Press, 1965), 30–31. In addition, while the region's Republicans typically shied away from endorsing prohibitory policies, some southern Republicans raised the temperance issue to enhance their personal appeal. For example, Tennessee's Republican governor, William G. Brownlow, proposed statewide anti-liquor legislation in 1865, 1867, and 1869. Despite Brownlow's considerable influence in the Radical-led legislature, Republican lawmakers failed to act on his proposals. See Forrest Conklin, "Parson Brownlow—Temperance Advocate, Part II," *Tennessee Historical Quarterly* 39 (1980): 302–5. Finally, after Reconstruction ended and the southern Republicans declined, state GOP conventions occasionally promoted prohibition to disrupt Democratic party unity. For instance, in 1886 the Republican parties of Arkansas, Tennessee, and Texas endorsed the submission of prohibition to a popular vote.

76 As described in chapter 2, many southern teetotalers left northern-based temperance societies because their colleagues appeared overly concerned with the status of black members. Despite remaining distinct from the GOP and northern reform groups, southern drys were still criticized for their adherence to a "northern" cause. As late as the 1880s, for instance, Mississippi wets continued to "wave the bloody shirt," alleging that "prohibition was a 'Yankee institution' and came from where 'the Abolition Party and all the isms start from.' " See William G. Davis, "Attacking 'The Matchless Evil': Temperance and Prohibition in Mississippi, 1817–1908" (Ph.D. diss., Mississippi State University, 1975), 126; Isaac, *Prohibition and Politics*, 53.

77 Pearson and Hendricks, *Liquor and Anti-Liquor in Virginia*, 210–11; *Cyclopedia of Temperance and Prohibition*, 148–51; Grace Leab, "Tennessee Temperance Activities, 1870–1899," *East Tennessee Historical Society's Publications* 21 (1949): 53; *Cyclopedia of Temperance and Prohibition*, 150.

78 Pearson and Hendricks, *Liquor and Anti-Liquor in Virginia*, 212–13; Alwyn Barr, *Reconstruction to Reform: Texas Politics, 1876–1906* (Austin: University of Texas Press, 1971), 87; Daniel J. Whitener, *Prohibition in North Carolina, 1715–1945* (Chapel Hill: University of North Carolina Press, 1945), 82–83.

79 Sellers, *The Prohibition Movement in Alabama*, 74–76, 85; Pearson and Hendricks, *Liquor and Anti-Liquor in Virginia*, 220; George M. Hunt, "A History of the Prohibition Movement in Arkansas" (M.A. thesis, University of Arkansas, 1933), 72–74, 76–77; Denise A. Herd, "Prohibition, Racism and Class Politics in the Post-Reconstruction South," *Journal of Drug Issues* 13 (1983): 82–83; *Cyclopedia of Temperance and Prohibition*, 151; Belle Kearney, *A Slaveholder's Daughter* (New York: Negro Universities Press, 1969), 187–88.

80 Davis, "Attacking 'The Matchless Evil,' " 82–84, 146; 187–99; 202–5; 213–14.

81 *Minutes of the National Woman's Christian Temperance Union* (1886), 82.

82 James B. Cranfill, *Dr. J. B. Cranfill's Chronicle: A Story of Life in Texas, Written by Himself and about Himself* (New York: Fleming H. Revell, 1916), 303–7; Davis, "Attacking 'The Matchless Evil,' " 182–83; 205–11; Whitener, *Prohibition in North Carolina*, 81–82.

83 Petersen, *A Statistical History of the American Presidential Elections*, 194–200; *Cyclopedia of Temperance and Prohibition*, 562–77; *The Political Prohibitionist for 1888*, 83–127; Glashan, *American Governors and Gubernatorial Elections*. The eleven gubernatorial elections in question were held in the following states (with the popular vote percentages listed parenthetically): Connecticut (3.8%), Delaware (35.8%), Michigan (6.6%), Minnesota (4.1%), Nebraska (6.0%), New Jersey (8.6%), Oregon (5.0%), Pennsylvania (4.0%), Rhode Island (9.6%), Texas (6.1%), and Wisconsin (6.0%).

84 Steven J. Rosenstone, Roy L. Behr, and Edward H. Lazarus, *Third Parties in America: Citizen Response to Major Party Failure* (Princeton, N.J.: Princeton University Press, 1984), 8.

85 For arguments against a third party, see D. C. Babcock, "How Shall We Use the Ballot?" in *Proceedings of the Ninth National Temperance Convention*, 162–68. See also Gail Hamilton, "Prohibition in Politics," *North American Review*, June 1885, 509–20. This polemic written against the Prohibition party declares that anti-liquor activists "have always found in the Republican party friends to their cause, often friends to their methods" and have "no need of a third party to enact laws."

86 Nathan F. Woodbury, *Prohibition in Maine: A History of Its Origin, Results, Political Nullification and Final Ratification from 1837 to 1920* (Lewiston, Maine: Journal Printshop and Bindery, 1920), 18.

87 Sellers, *The Prohibition Movement in Alabama*, 85, emphasis in original.

88 See chapter 1 for a discussion of voter turnout in the 1880s.

89 *Cyclopedia of Temperance and Prohibition*, 29–30.

90 Kleppner, *The Cross of Culture*, 5–7.

91 Most historians agree that massive voting irregularities marred the South's elections during the

Gilded Age. However, Jensen argues that corruption was episodic and marginal in the Midwest during the years 1880–1900 in *The Winning of the Midwest*, 34–57.

92 For contemporary accounts of the parties' concern over dry defections, see "Prohibition in Politics," *Chautauquan*, June 1883, 541; "The Prohibition Balance of Power," *Nation*, 10 June 1886, 482–83; "Prohibition as a Solvent of Parties," *Nation*, 16 June 1887, 504.

93 Jensen, *The Winning of the Midwest*, 69–88; Kleppner, *The Third Electoral System*, 255–57.

94 Robert S. Salisbury, *William Windom: Apostle of Positive Government* (Lanham, Md.: University Press of America, 1993), 298.

95 *Cyclopedia of Temperance and Prohibition*, 150; Pearson and Hendricks, *Liquor and Anti-Liquor in Virginia*, 175.

96 In many ways, the Kansas state legislature's submission of constitutional prohibition to the electorate in 1880 was accidental. Fearing the enactment of a modest anti-liquor law, wet state legislators proposed constitutional prohibition as a substitute, with the expectation that it would not receive the required two-thirds vote from state lawmakers. Only after the amendment passed did it become apparent that the 1880 legislature included "a large number of representatives who were prepared to support strong dry legislation." See Robert S. Bader, *Prohibition in Kansas: A History* (Lawrence: University Press of Kansas, 1986), chapter 3.

97 For the constitutional prohibition campaigns of the 1880s, see *Cyclopedia of Temperance and Prohibition*, 97–128; 443–50; Colvin, *Prohibition in the United States*, 135–44, chapter 12; Turner, "The American Prohibition Movement," chapters 6, 7.

98 In addition to losing votes to the Prohibitionists in 1877, the Republicans undoubtedly lost some to the Greenbackers, who won 14.0% of the gubernatorial vote in that year. See Glashan, *American Governors and Gubernatorial Elections*, 92–93.

99 Clark, "The History of Liquor Legislation in Iowa, 1878–1908," 505–8; *Cyclopedia of Temperance and Prohibition*, 105–6; Jensen, *The Winning of the Midwest*, 93–98; Glashan, *American Governors and Gubernatorial Elections*, 92–93.

100 *Cyclopedia of Temperance and Prohibition*, 27; Turner, "The American Prohibition Movement," 316–20, 339–41.

101 Petersen, *Statistical History of the American Presidential Elections*, 52. Indeed, the most spectacular burst of Republican hostility toward the Prohibitionists occurred after the presidential election of 1884. Convinced that the Prohibitionist candidacy of Governor John St. John, a former Republican, had led to the GOP's defeat, angry Republicans burned or hung him in effigy in over one hundred towns across the nation. See Bader, *Prohibition in Kansas*, 76–77; Colvin, *Prohibition in the United States*, 166; Turner, "The American Prohibition Movement," 304. Though many Republicans blamed the Prohibition party for Blaine's defeat, historians have identified other causes, including the personalities of the major party candidates, the GOP's failure to woo Irish voters, and the inclement election-day weather in upstate New York. For a discussion which downplays the Prohibition party's significance, see Coffey, "A Political History of the Temperance Movement," 185–91.

102 Bader, *Prohibition in Kansas*, 78; *The Political Prohibitionist for 1888*, 52, 130–33, 154; *Cyclopedia of Temperance and Prohibition*, 28; Turner, "The American Prohibition Movement," 316–18; Salisbury, *William Windom*, 296–97; *New York Times*, 13 July 1886, 2; *Nation*, 22 July 1886, p. 67, 15 July 1886, p. 44, 29 July 1886, p. 86. During 1886 the Anti-Saloon Republicans held state conventions in New Jersey, Minnesota, Massachusetts, New York, and elsewhere.

103 Apparently, the Anti-Saloon Republicans persuaded the Massachusetts state party to adopt a plank

in favor of submission, but accounts of similar developments in other states have not been located. For Massachusetts, see *New York Times*, 13 July 1886, 2; *Nation*, 22 July 1886, p. 67, 15 July 1886, p. 44.

104 *Cyclopedia of Temperance and Prohibition*, 592.

105 *The Political Prohibitionist for 1888*, 156.

106 Whitener, *Prohibition in North Carolina*, 61–67; Sellers, *The Prohibition Movement in Alabama*, 67–85; "The Texas Campaign," *Nation*, 7 July 1887, 6–7; Barr, *Reconstruction to Reform*, 85–92; Davis, "Attacking 'The Matchless Evil,'" 138–42, 185–96; Isaac, *Prohibition and Politics*, 27–31; Turner, "The American Prohibition Movement," 258–62.

107 Of the jurisdictions that held dry referenda in the 1880s, the sixteen that existed as states before 1889 were Kansas, North Carolina, Iowa, Ohio, Maine, Rhode Island, Michigan, Texas, Tennessee, Oregon, West Virginia, New Hampshire, Massachusetts, Pennsylvania, Connecticut, and Nebraska. However, one of these states (New Hampshire) proposed its amendment through a constitutional convention and is not included in the above discussion. Meanwhile, three of the referenda were submitted by the constitutional conventions of new states (Washington, North Dakota, and South Dakota). Until 1889 these were territories, supervised by territorial governors appointed by the president, and hence lacking an electoral history which could provide comparable data about the electoral competitiveness of the two parties.

108 The ten gubernatorial elections in question were held in the following states (with the dates and popular vote percentages listed parenthetically): Connecticut (1886, 3.8%), Iowa (1877, 4.3%), Massachusetts (1887, 4.1%), Michigan (1886, 6.6%), Nebraska (1888, 6.0%), Ohio (1881, 2.7%), Oregon (1886, 5.0%), Pennsylvania (1886, 4.0%), Rhode Island (1885, 5.4%), and Texas (1886, 6.1%). See *Cyclopedia of Temperance and Prohibition*, 562–77; Glashan, *American Governors and Gubernatorial Elections*.

109 For the liquor question's diminishing appeal as a major party issue after 1890, see Colvin, *Prohibition in the United States*, 243–45; Coffey, "A Political History of the Temperance Movement," 219–22; Isaac, *Prohibition and Politics*, 61–80.

110 Jensen, *The Winning of the Midwest*, 102–21; Larry Engelmann, "Dry Renaissance: The Local Option Years," *Michigan History*, 1975, 70–71; Kleppner, *The Third Electoral System*, 347, 342–356; Paul Kleppner, *Continuity and Change in Electoral Politics, 1893–1928* (New York: Greenwood, 1987), 205–8; Paul Kleppner, *Who Voted? The Dynamics of Electoral Turnout, 1870–1980* (New York: Praeger, 1982), 76–77.

111 "A New Temperance Organization," *Union Signal*, 1 March 1894, 9. See chapter 6 for more on the amendment campaigns of the 1880s.

112 "'Saloons Must Go': A Friendly Challenge to the Anti-Saloon League," *Union Signal*, 11 February 1897, 10; Editorial, *Statesman*, July 1890, 305; Colvin, *Prohibition in the United States*, 241–42; Blocker, *Retreat from Reform*, chapter 4.

113 Such legal and institutional barriers to voting included residency requirements, registration procedures, literacy tests, and poll taxes.

114 At the turn of the century, anti-corruption reforms included the Australian ballot, the short ballot, civil service reform, nonpartisan elections at the local level, the direct election of U.S. senators, the direct primary, the initiative, the referendum, and the recall. Though intended to prevent the railroads and other well-endowed interests from dominating state and local politics, many scholars argue that these reforms ultimately undermined party loyalty.

115 Dewey W. Grantham, *Southern Progressivism: The Reconciliation of Progress and Tradition* (Knoxville: University of Tennessee Press, 1983), 119–21.

116 *Proceedings, Tenth Annual Convention of the Anti-Saloon League* (Harrisburg: Anti-Saloon League of Amer-

ica, 1906), 79–83; K. Austin Kerr, *Organized for Prohibition: A New History of the Anti-Saloon League* (New Haven: Yale University Press, 1985), 106–11; Peter Odegard, *Pressure Politics: The Story of the Anti-Saloon League* (New York: Columbia University Press, 1928), 89–90; Joe Michael Shahan, "Reform and Politics in Tennessee, 1906–1914" (Ph.D. diss., Vanderbilt University, 1981), chapter 8; Isaac, *Prohibition and Politics*, 182–95.

117 Kleppner, *Continuity and Change*, 205–11; Kleppner, *Who Voted?*, 74–78.

118 Odegard, *Pressure Politics*, 81–82.

119 Blocker, *Retreat from Reform*, 156; Kerr, *Organized for Prohibition*, 108, 172. In fact, the league even distrusted the Democrats after 1918, when a Democratic Congress approved the national prohibition amendment. In the mid-1920s, its encyclopedia described this party as "the main reliance of the liquor forces in their efforts to prevent the enactment of prohibitory liquor legislation" both at the national level and "in such States as embrace a large foreign element in their population." See Ernest H. Cherrington, *The Standard Encyclopedia of the Alcohol Problem* (Westerville, Ohio: American Issue, 1924–30), 2:789.

120 After the election of 1896, the following states saw their governments controlled by Republican regimes: California, Connecticut, Delaware, Illinois, Iowa, Kansas, Maine, Massachusetts, Michigan, New Hampshire, North Dakota, Pennsylvania, Rhode Island, South Dakota, Utah, Vermont, West Virginia, and Wisconsin. It should be emphasized, though, that state party politics were considerably more volatile than national party politics. Hence, states like New York, Indiana, and Nebraska continued to sustain highly competitive party systems.

121 After 1914 no state Progressive party mounted a serious independent campaign for governor. See Glashan, *American Governors and Gubernatorial Elections*.

122 In both North Carolina and Tennessee, the GOP remained capable of winning over 40% of the vote in gubernatorial elections during the Progressive Era.

123 Of course, northeastern states like New York, New Jersey, New Hampshire, Vermont, and Massachusetts were also affected by the development of reform politics, but as George Mowry points out, this "new political spirit was never quite so spectacularly successful as it was in the Middle West, the West, and the South." See George E. Mowry, *The Era of Theodore Roosevelt and the Birth of Modern America, 1900–1912* (New York: Harper and Row, 1958), 78.

124 Richard L. McCormick, "The Discovery That Business Corrupts Politics: A Reappraisal of the Origins of Progressivism," in his *The Party Period and Public Policy*, 332.

125 Russell B. Nye, *Midwestern Progressive Politics: A Historical Study of Its Origins and Development, 1879–1950* (East Lansing: Michigan State College Press, 1951), 203–4; Grantham, *Southern Progressivism*, chapter 2; James Wright, *The Progressive Yankees: Republican Reformers in New Hampshire, 1906–1916* (Hanover, N.H.: University Press of New England, 1987), chapter 3; Richard L. McCormick, *From Realignment to Reform: Political Change in New York State, 1893–1910* (Ithaca, N.Y.: Cornell University Press, 1981), chapters 4–8; Mowry, *The California Progressives*, chapter 3. Of course, in some states both parties had politically significant reform wings. See, for example, David R. Berman, *Reformers, Corporations, and the Electorate: An Analysis of Arizona's Age of Reform* (Niwot: University Press of Colorado, 1992); Hoyt L. Warner, *Progressivism in Ohio, 1897–1917* (Columbus: Ohio State University Press, 1964); Carl H. Chrislock, *The Progressive Era in Minnesota, 1899–1918* (St. Paul: Minnesota Historical Society, 1971).

126 "Senate in Line on Local Option," *Chicago Tribune*, 8 May 1908, 4; "Senate Surgeons Cut Up Charter," *Chicago Tribune*, 8 May 1907, 1, 4; Thomas R. Pegram, "The Dry Machine: The Formation of the Anti-Saloon League of Illinois," *Illinois Historical Journal* 83 (1990): 185; Thomas R. Pegram, *Partisans and*

Progressives: Private Interest and Public Policy in Illinois, 1870–1922 (Urbana: University of Illinois Press, 1992), 113–14.

127 Between 1904 and 1910 the GOP stalwarts were so weak that they failed to provide organized opposition to the progressives in the Wisconsin Republican party. Meanwhile, the Milwaukee progressives first asserted significant influence over the state GOP in the Senate primary election of 1908. In 1907, then, the Wisconsin legislature's substantial Republican majorities were dominated by the rurally based progressives, the wing of the GOP most favored by the state ASL. For example, the Wisconsin League supported Republican progressives like Irving L. Lenroot, John M. Nelson, John Strange, Merlin Hull, and William M. Lewis, all of whom were based in rural counties and who leaned toward the dry position. The ASL had also initially supported Robert M. La Follette, also rurally based, and had participated in his campaign in 1906 to defeat the stalwart Republican congressman Joseph W. Babcock. However, the league's support for La Follette evaporated when he placed the support of the wet Milwaukee progressives above all other considerations after 1908. See *Proceedings, Tenth Annual Convention of the Anti-Saloon League*, 96; *Proceedings, Eleventh Annual Convention of the Anti-Saloon League of America* (Harrisburg: Anti-Saloon League of America, 1906), 130; *Proceedings, Twelfth Annual Convention of the Anti-Saloon League of America* (Harrisburg: Anti-Saloon League of America, 1907), 145–46; *Proceedings, Fifteenth National Convention of the Anti-Saloon League of America* (Westerville, Ohio: American Issue, 1914), 339; *Proceedings, Sixteenth National Convention of the Anti-Saloon League of America* (Westerville, Ohio: American Issue, 1915), 538–40; "Thayer Remonstrance Bill," *American Issue*, 28 April 1905, 6–7; Robert S. Maxwell, *Emanuel Philipp: Wisconsin Stalwart* (Madison: State Historical Society of Wisconsin, 1959), 58–69; Herbert F. Margulies, *The Decline of the Progressive Movement in Wisconsin, 1890–1920* (Madison: State Historical Society of Wisconsin, 1968), 42–43, 62, 77, 79–81 (and note 84), 96, 98, 106, 114–16, 125, 128, 266; David L. Brye, *Wisconsin Voting Patterns in the Twentieth Century* (New York: Garland, 1979), 226, 240–41, 375; Padraic M. Kennedy, "Lenroot, La Follette, and the Campaign of 1906," *Wisconsin Magazine of History*, 1959, pp. 164, 173.

128 *Proceedings, Thirteenth National Convention of the Anti-Saloon League of America* (Westerville, Ohio: American Issue, 1910), 167–68; *Proceedings, Sixteenth National Convention of the Anti-Saloon League*, 539. Interestingly, the Wisconsin ASL had supported Frank McGovern when he served as Milwaukee's district attorney. After McGovern became governor, however, the ASL denounced him as the "retail liquor dealers' candidate." See *Proceedings, Tenth Annual Convention of the Anti-Saloon League*, 97; *Proceedings, Eleventh Annual Convention of the Anti-Saloon League*, 130; *Proceedings, Fifteenth National Convention of the Anti-Saloon League*, 339.

129 "Great Gains for Clean Government in Recent Elections," *American Issue*, November 1908, 4–5; "Additional Anti-Saloon Victories in Recent Elections," *American Issue*, December 1908, 2–3; Grantham, *Southern Progressivism*, 56–57, 92, 101–2, chapter 6; Sellers, *The Prohibition Movement in Alabama*, 176–78; Isaac, *Prohibition and Politics*, chapters 9–11; Richard L. Niswonger, *Arkansas Democratic Politics, 1896–1920* (Fayetteville: University of Arkansas Press, 1990), 200–201; Lewis L. Gould, *Progressives and Prohibitionists: Texas Democrats in the Wilson Era* (Austin: University of Texas Press, 1973), 28–57.

130 Dewey W. Grantham, *Hoke Smith and the Politics of the New South* (Baton Rouge: Louisiana State University Press, 1958), 131–237.

131 *Proceedings, Sixteenth National Convention of the Anti-Saloon League*, 409–10; "Georgia Passes State Prohibition Law," *American Issue*, 9 August 1907, 14–15; Grantham, *Southern Progressivism*, 161–62; Lovick P. Winter, "Prohibition in Georgia," *Independent*, 22 August 1907, 422–44; *Thirty-Fourth Annual Report of the Woman's Christian Temperance Union of Massachusetts* (1908), 41.

132 Gilman Ostrander, *The Prohibition Movement in California, 1848–1933* (Berkeley: University of California Press, 1957), 115–16; E. K. Putnum, "The Prohibition Movement in Idaho, 1863–1934" (Ph.D. diss., University of Idaho, 1979), 247–49.

133 Clifton J. Phillips, *Indiana in Transition: The Emergence of an Industrial Commonwealth, 1880–1920* (Indianapolis: Indiana Historical Society, 1968), 100–101; William E. West, "Dry Crusade: The Prohibition Movement in Colorado, 1858–1933" (Ph.D. diss., University of Colorado, 1971), 204.

134 Thomas E. Cronin, *Direct Democracy: The Politics of Initiative, Referendum and Recall* (Cambridge: Harvard University Press, 1990), 51; "Some Opinions about Direct Legislation," *Union Signal*, 3 June 1897, 8–9; Harriet E. Orcutt, "How the WCTU Can Help Procure Direct Legislation," *Union Signal*, 14 April 1898, 4–5; A. A. Brown, "The Initiative and Referendum," *Union Signal*, 27 October 1898, 4; Eltweed Pomeroy, "Direct Legislation, Part I," *Union Signal*, 21 September 1899, 4–5; Eltweed Pomeroy, "Direct Legislation, Part II," *Union Signal*, 28 September 1899, 4–5; Eltweed Pomeroy, "Direct Legislation, Part III," *Union Signal*, 5 October 1899, 4–5; Lucinda B. Chandler, "What Is Direct Legislation? Why Should We Have It?" *Union Signal*, 24 January 1901, 5.

135 Harriet E. Orcutt, "What Is Direct Legislation?" *Union Signal*, 30 December 1897, 4.

136 William E. Johnson, "The Anti-Saloon League's Interest in the Initiative and Referendum," *American Issue*, 27 July 1906, 4. See also "How the Victory Was Won in Oregon," *American Issue*, 8 July 1904, 6; "Recommends the Initiative and Referendum," *American Issue*, 27 September 1907, 5.

137 Nancy K. Tisdale, "The Prohibition Crusade in Arizona" (M.A. thesis, University of Arizona, 1965), 104–9; Berman, *Reformers, Corporations, and the Electorate*, 74–79; Cronin, *Direct Democracy*, 52.

138 Clark, *The Dry Years*, 101–3; Robert W. Cherny, *Populism, Progressivism, and the Transformation of Nebraska Politics, 1885–1915* (Lincoln: University of Nebraska Press, 1981), 110–11; *Proceedings, Fourteenth National Convention of the Anti-Saloon League of America* (Westerville, Ohio: American Issue, 1912), 128–29; Ostrander, *The Prohibition Movement in California*, 104; Dorcas J. Spencer, *A History of the Woman's Christian Temperance Union of Northern and Central California* (Oakland: West Coast Printing, 1911), 94; Tom Sitton, *John Randolph Haynes: California Progressive* (Stanford: Stanford University Press, 1992), 43–44; Cronin, *Direct Democracy*, 51–52; Richard L. Niswonger, *Arkansas Democratic Politics, 1896–1920* (Fayetteville: University of Arkansas Press, 1990), 243–46; Lloyd Sponholtz, "The Initiative and Referendum: Direct Democracy in Perspective, 1898–1920," *American Studies* 14 (1973): 54–55, 58.

139 Blocker, *Retreat from Reform*, 170, 181; Glashan, *American Governors and Gubernatorial Elections* 92–93. In addition to Iowa in 1901, the Prohibition party also ran strong gubernatorial races in Illinois, Indiana, Maine, Massachusetts, Michigan, Minnesota, Pennsylvania, Rhode Island, and South Dakota during the Progressive Era. All these states were characterized by either GOP-dominated regimes or party systems where the Republican party had a decided advantage.

140 To be sure, these amendments' wording varied, and often differed as to the exceptions they would make for liquor used for medicinal, scientific, mechanical, and sacramental purposes. However, they all banned the sale and manufacture of intoxicating liquors, and there is no systematic relationship between the amendments' exceptions and their eventual success. For example, during the 1880s the drys in Connecticut, Washington, and West Virginia explicitly included exemptions for sacramental wines in their amendment proposals and failed to secure constitutional prohibition. In contrast, the prohibitionists of Kansas, Maine, South Dakota, and North Dakota failed to provide for such an exemption, and their amendments were approved by the voters. See *Cyclopedia of Temperance and Prohibition*, 100–102, for the amendments proposed in the years 1880–90.

141 "Indirectly proposed" referenda were those placed on the ballot by either state legislatures or constitutional conventions.

6 The Dynamics of Local Gradualism in the States

1 Ann-Marie Szymanski, "Direct Legislation, State Politics, and American Politics: A Comparison of the Progressive Era and Contemporary American Politics," unpublished paper presented at the Annual Meeting of the New York Political Science Association, 29 April 1995; Sponholtz, "Initiative and Referendum," 43–64.

2 "A Magnificent Poll," *Union Signal*, 13 September 1883, 8.

3 Daniel J. Whitener, *Prohibition in North Carolina, 1715–1945* (Chapel Hill: University of North Carolina Press, 1945), 163.

4 Mrs. T. Holman, "After the Battle," *Union Signal*, 20 October 1887, 4.

5 *Proceedings, Fourteenth National Convention of the Anti-Saloon League of America* (Westerville, Ohio: American Issue, 1912), 140–41.

6 *Cyclopedia of Temperance and Prohibition* (New York: Funk and Wagnalls, 1891), 110.

7 *Proceedings, Sixteenth National Convention of the Anti-Saloon League of America* (Westerville, Ohio: American Issue, 1915), 502.

8 Betty H. Zisk, *Money, Media, and the Grassroots: State Ballot Issues and the Electoral Process* (Newbury Park, Calif.: Sage, 1987), 139.

9 *Cyclopedia of Temperance and Prohibition*, 111; A. D. P. Van Buren, "Our Temperance Conflict," *Michigan Pioneer Collections* 13 (1888): 405.

10 Larry D. Engelmann, "O Whiskey: The History of Prohibition in Michigan" (Ph.D. diss., University of Michigan, 1971), 245.

11 K. Austin Kerr, *Organized for Prohibition: A New History of the Anti-Saloon League* (New Haven: Yale University Press, 1985), 244; Peter Odegard, *Pressure Politics: The Story of the Anti-Saloon League* (New York: Columbia University Press, 1928), 122–26.

12 The Templars, Sons, and WCTU provided membership data in the minutes of their national meetings. The Prohibition party's national vote can be found in Svend Petersen, *A Statistical History of the American Presidential Elections* (New York: Frederick Ungar, 1963), 194–200.

13 Robert S. Bader, *Prohibition in Kansas: A History* (Lawrence: University Press of Kansas, 1986), 46–51; *Cyclopedia of Temperance and Prohibition*, 104–5.

14 Daniel E. Clark, "The History of Liquor Legislation in Iowa, 1878–1908," *Iowa Journal of History and Politics* 6 (1908): 512–14.

15 "Ohio," *National Temperance Advocate*, September 1883, 157; Francis M. Whitaker, "Ohio WCTU and the Prohibition Amendment Campaign of 1883," *Ohio History* 83 (1974): 95–97; Ernest H. Cherrington, *The History of the Anti-Saloon League* (Westerville, Ohio: American Issue, 1913), 12.

16 For instance, Maine's constitutional prohibition campaign in 1884 was conducted by a state campaign committee, uniting the WCTU, the IOGT, and others. Similarly, campaigns in other states were led by the Oregon State Temperance Alliance (1887), the Tennessee Temperance Alliance (1887), the Non-Partisan Prohibition Amendment Organization (Texas, 1887), the State Amendment Committee (Michigan, 1887), a Non-Partisan League (West Virginia, 1888), the State Temperance Alliance (Washington, 1889), the State Prohibition Amendment Campaign Committee (Pennsylvania, 1889), Prohibition Amendment Committee (New Hampshire, 1889), the Constitutional Campaign Committee (Massachusetts, 1889), and the Non-Partisan Prohibition League (Nebraska, 1890). In the campaign for constitutional prohibition in Connecticut in 1889, however, the temperance organizations worked independently (yet amicably). Similarly, the campaign in Rhode Island in 1886 was

coordinated by two organizations: the WCTU; and an association of the Rhode Island Temperance Union, the IOGT, and other groups.

17 Jenny B. Beauchamp, "Plan of Work for Texas Amendment Campaign," *Union Signal*, 30 June 1887, 5; Sybal Hazel, "Statewide Prohibition Campaigns in Texas" (M.A. thesis, Texas Technological College, 1942), 24–27; Mary M. Clardy, "San Antonio and the Liquor Traffic," *Union Signal*, 1 September 1887, 5.

18 Earl C. Kaylor, "The Prohibition Movement in Pennsylvania" (Ph.D. diss., Pennsylvania State University, 1963), 265, 278; Mrs. N. H. Knox, "The Defeat of Constitutional Prohibition in New Hampshire," *Union Signal*, 28 March 1889, 5; Anna E. Bussell, "New Hampshire: After the Battle," *Union Signal*, 28 March 1889, 10–11; Elisabeth Gordon, "The Amendment Defeated in Massachusetts, April 22," *Union Signal*, 2 May 1889, 4. For the Maine campaign of 1884 and its precinct-style organization, see Willard, "Romance versus Reality," *Chautauquan*, November 1884, 88–91.

19 Frances E. Willard, "Little Rhody at the Fore," *Union Signal*, 29 April 1886, 5.

20 *Cyclopedia of Temperance and Prohibition*, 105; Bader, *Prohibition in Kansas*, 58; "South Dakota's Conflict," *Union Signal*, 7 November 1889, 5.

21 Bader, *Prohibition in Kansas*, 46; *Minutes of the National Woman's Christian Temperance Union, 1885 Convention*, 158. As in the Progressive Era, small donors provided the bulk of these funds. For example, the national union generally recorded contributions of one dollar in its collections for campaign work among Nebraska's "foreigners." See Sophia F. Grubb, "Nebraska Campaign Fund," *Union Signal*, 1 May 1890, 5; Sophia F. Grubb, "Work among Foreigners," *Union Signal*, 12 June 1890, 12.

22 C. H. Smith, "From South Dakota," *Union Signal*, 9 May 1889, 5.

23 Knox, "The Defeat of Constitutional Prohibition in New Hampshire," 5.

24 Bussell, "New Hampshire," 10–11.

25 Harry M. Chalfant, *Father Penn and John Barleycorn* (Harrisburg: Evangelical, 1920), 117–19.

26 William E. Johnson, "The Story of West Virginia's Great Fight," *American Issue*, January 1913, 4–5, 10; *Proceedings, Fifteenth National Convention of the Anti-Saloon League of America* (Westerville, Ohio: American Issue, 1914), 190–92, 336–37; D. Leigh Colvin, *Prohibition in the United States* (New York: George H. Doran, 1926), 347–48; Ernest H. Cherrington, *The Standard Encyclopedia of the Alcohol Problem* (Westerville, Ohio: American Issue, 1924–30), 6:2830–31.

27 Jerry Lien, "The Speechmaking of the Anti-Saloon League of America" (Ph.D. diss., University of Southern California, 1968), 175–76.

28 Cherrington, *The Standard Encyclopedia of the Alcohol Problem* 3:1183; Barbara J. Howe, "West Virginia Women's Organizations, 1880s–1930 or 'Unsexed Termagents . . . Help the World Along,'" *West Virginia History* 49 (1990): 83–84.

29 G. K. Renner, "Prohibition Comes to Missouri, 1910–1919," *Missouri Historical Review* 63 (1968): 377–81.

30 According to the U.S. Census, about 10% of Missouri's industrial output was derived from the liquor industry in 1909. In contrast, the liquor industry generally accounted for less than 6% of most states' industrial output. See also Renner, "Prohibition Comes to Missouri," 366–71; "Anheuser-Busch Is Scared," *Chicago Tribune*, 17 April 1909, 2.

31 Mary M. Thomas, *The New Woman in Alabama: Social Reforms and Suffrage, 1890–1920* (Tuscaloosa: University of Alabama Press, 1992), 36–38; James B. Sellers, *The Prohibition Movement in Alabama, 1702 to 1943* (Chapel Hill: University of North Carolina Press, 1943), 136–47.

32 See, e.g., Magleby, *Direct Legislation: Voting on Ballot Propositions in the United States* (Baltimore: Johns Hopkins University Press, 1984), 147; Daniel Lowenstein, "Campaign Spending and Ballot Propo-

sitions: Recent Experience, Public Choice Theory and the First Amendment," *UCLA Law Review* 29 (1982): 518.

33 John R. Owens and Larry L. Wade, "Campaign Spending on California Ballot Propositions, 1924–1984: Trends and Voting Effects," *Western Political Quarterly* 39 (1986): 685–89.

34 Colvin, *Prohibition in the United States*, 203–8.

35 Ibid., 204.

36 Colvin's allegations mirror those of the *Cyclopedia of Temperance and Prohibition*.

37 Washington Gladden, "The Saloon in Politics, Letter of Washington Gladden," *Chautauquan*, January 1888, 229. Although Gladden later served as an ASL vice-president, he rejected prohibition before 1905. See the discussion of Gladden in chapter 7.

38 The "Committee of Fifty," cited in Joseph Rowntree and Arthur Sherwell, *The Temperance Problem and Social Reform* (New York: Truslove, Hanson and Comba, 1900), 111.

39 Ernest H. Crosby, "The Saloon as a Political Power," *Forum*, May 1889, 328.

40 Colvin, *Prohibition in the United States*, 203–10; *Cyclopedia of Temperance and Prohibition*, 382, 445.

41 Kate C. Bushnell, "What South Dakota Is Doing," *Union Signal*, 5 September 1889, 5; *Cyclopedia of Temperance and Prohibition*, 126.

42 J. R. Wolf, "The Fight for Prohibition in Texas," *Christian Advocate*, 2 June 1887, 5.

43 Clinton B. Fisk, "The Saloon in Politics, Letter of Clinton B. Fisk," *Chautauquan*, January 1888, 231.

44 See Odegard, *Pressure Politics*, chapters 7, 9, for the fund-raising efforts of the ASL and the USBA.

45 Instead of working closely with the NWLDA to forestall prohibition, the brewers sought to promote beer, low in alcohol, as a temperance drink that would decrease the incidence of drunkenness (which the brewers felt was chiefly caused by hard liquor). See, e.g., Kerr, *Organized for Prohibition*, chapter 7. This conflict probably did not interfere with the willingness of these groups to contribute financially toward the defeat of statewide dry referenda, however. For example, the USBA often participated in state pro-liquor efforts, and in 1915 reported that it had assisted the wets in at least twenty-six states. See Odegard, *Pressure Politics*, 258–59.

46 For a state-level account of the liquor industry's capacity to unite and raise money, see Gilman Ostrander, *The Prohibition Movement in California, 1848–1933* (Berkeley: University of California Press, 1957), 131–33.

47 See, e.g., "Ohio Wets Spend Money like Water," *American Issue* (Ohio Edition), 20 November 1914, 2; "More than Half a Million Spent by Ohio Wets," *American Issue* (Ohio Edition), 19 November 1915, 3.

48 *Proceedings, Sixteenth National Convention of the Anti-Saloon League*, 531.

49 The $130,000 figure includes spending by prominent drys to pay for extra copies of the *Virginian*. Any assistance from the national ASL was included in the $80,000, and there are no other recorded expenditures distributed by an agency other than the Virginia League. See C. C. Pearson and J. Edwin Hendricks, *Liquor and Anti-Liquor in Virginia, 1619–1919* (Durham: Duke University Press, 1967), 282–83.

50 For example, WCTU members received only $532 combined for travel expenses, and otherwise petitioned and campaigned at their own expense. See Engelmann, "O Whiskey," 245–46; "Michigan's Campaign in Full Swing," *American Issue* (Ohio Edition), 8 September 1916, 2. For another stingy, volunteer-based dry campaign, see Ostrander, *The Prohibition Movement in California*, 127–31.

51 Whitener, *Prohibition in North Carolina*, 163–68.

52 Kerr, *Organized for Prohibition*, 171; James A. White, "Report of J. A. White, State Campaign Manager before the State Committee on October 1, 1918," 4–5, Temperance and Prohibition Papers microfilm edition, Ohio Anti-Saloon League Series, roll 2.

53 Francis M. Whitaker, "A History of the Ohio Woman's Christian Temperance Union" (Ph.D. diss., Ohio State University, 1971), 372–78, 414–20; "Our Allies and Helpers: The WCTU and the Beal Law," *American Issue*, 18 April 1902, 1.

54 As elsewhere, WCTU membership data are derived from the *Annual Meeting Minutes of the National Woman's Christian Temperance Union.*

55 Joseph R. Gusfield, *Symbolic Crusade: Status Politics and the American Temperance Movement* (Urbana: University of Illinois Press, 1963), 102.

56 Ibid., 110.

57 Ibid., 103–4.

58 While this chapter discusses urban states, radical unions also tended to mobilize fewer new members than their more moderate counterparts in rural states. For example, the extremist Mississippi WCTU lost 82.7% of its membership during the years 1900–1919, whereas its gradualist counterpart in Tennessee grew by 491.7% in these years. For the strategic orientation of these two unions, see Davis, "Attacking 'The Matchless Evil,'" chapters 7–8; Paul Isaac, *Prohibition and Politics: Turbulent Decades in Tennessee, 1885–1920* (Knoxville: University of Tennessee Press, 1965), chapters 4–8.

59 In 1878 Frances Willard was elected president of the Illinois WCTU, a position she relinquished in 1879 to become the national union's president.

60 Mary Earhart, *Frances Willard: From Prayers to Politics* (Chicago: University of Chicago Press, 1944), 153–54; Ruth Bordin, *Frances Willard: A Biography* (Chapel Hill: University of North Carolina Press, 1986), 102.

61 Initially, Willard advocated forming a prohibition party called the "Home Protection" party. After persuading the Prohibitionists to adopt "Prohibition Home Protection party" as their name in 1882, Willard and her supporters then fused with the existing National Prohibition party. By 1884 Willard and her supporters were fully integrated into the party, and it resumed its previous name.

62 Earhart, *Frances Willard*, 212–13; Frances E. Willard, *Glimpses of Fifty Years: The Autobiography of an American Woman* (Chicago: H. J. Smith, 1889), 376–79.

63 *Union Signal*, 21 November 1889, 10.

64 Apart from her position on woman's suffrage, Wittenmyer had opposed Willard's plan for apportioning WCTU representation in the national body, her preference for relatively autonomous state and local affiliates, and her desire to broaden the union's agenda beyond temperance.

65 Mark E. Lender, *Dictionary of American Temperance Biography* (Westport, Conn.: Greenwood, 1984), 528–29; Kaylor, "The Prohibition Movement in Pennsylvania," 213–14, 252–53; Earhart, *Frances Willard*, 304. In 1888, for example, Wittenmyer opposed the WCTU's support for female representation in the General Conference of the Methodist Episcopal Church.

66 Indeed, in 1884 two leaders of the Pennsylvania union—Ellen M. Watson and Mrs. Joseph D. Weeks—objected loudly to partisan prohibition at the national convention. In 1885 they were joined by Wittenmyer and seven other Pennsylvania activists in signing a protest against the national WCTU's partisan leanings. Frances L. Swift, president of the Pennsylvania WCTU (1881–89), was among the signatories. See *Minutes of the National Woman's Christian Temperance Union, 1885 Convention*, 45; "Political Action in the National," *Union Signal*, 22 November 1888, 8.

67 Some county unions approved of partisan prohibition; others split into two warring camps over this issue; and still others emphatically declared their nonpartisanship. See Cora Cramer, ed., *History, Pennsylvania Woman's Christian Temperance Union* (Quincy, Pa.: Quincy Orphanage, 1937), 74; *Union Signal*, 27 December 1888, 10–11, 26 September 1889, 11.

68 The Pennsylvania state convention took place in October; at the national convention in November, Iowa's delegates walked out, claiming that nonpartisan members were unwelcome in the national WCTU.

69 *Union Signal*, 24 October 1889, 1, 14 November 1889, 10; Chalfant, *Father Penn and John Barleycorn*, 193–94.

70 In 1890 the Non-partisan WCTU was organized at the national level (with Ann Wittenmyer as president, 1896–98), the Woman's Christian Temperance Alliance (also nonpartisan) in Pennsylvania (led by Ellen M. Watson during the 1890s).

71 Cramer, ed., *History, Pennsylvania Woman's Christian Temperance Union*, 104; *Union Signal*, 20 October 1887, 1; *Union Signal*, 18 October 1888, 1; *Union Signal*, 24 October 1889, 1. In fact, the Pennsylvania WCTU's closest political ally during the 1880s was the Constitutional Amendment Association, a nonpartisan group devoted to persuading state lawmakers to submit constitutional prohibition to the electorate. See Kaylor, "The Prohibition Movement in Pennsylvania," 264–65.

72 See, e.g., "Miss Brehm in Part," *Union Signal*, 8 December 1904, 15–16. Among others, the following union leaders were also Prohibition party activists after 1900: Marie C. Brehm, L. Belle Goodman, Emily Hill, Ella S. Stewart, and Lulu E. Miner. Furthermore, the union often invited Prohibitionists, such as Daniel A. Poling, to address state gatherings. See "Illinois President's Address," *Union Signal*, 17 October 1901, 7; "Ticket in Field for Prohibition," *Chicago Tribune*, 3 February 1907, 6; "Liquor Foes Make Ticket," *Chicago Tribune*, 10 September 1908, 4; "Answers Attack on Prohibition," *Chicago Tribune*, 13 October 1913, 5; "Drys in Near Riot, Down Mullvihill," *Chicago Tribune*, 12 May 1910, 4; Cherrington, *The Standard Encyclopedia of the Alcohol Problem* 1:399.

73 The Illinois WCTU's most positive statement on local option was issued in 1901, when the ASL was sponsoring the Rankin Bill, a stringent county option measure. In discussing the bill, the group emphasized that it stood "for nothing short of total prohibition," but rejoiced in "every movement to crush out the liquor business." See "Illinois' Local Option Bill," *Union Signal*, 18 April 1901, 9.

74 "Rum Debate On: Talk Is Vitriolic," *Chicago Tribune*, 20 February 1907, 7; "Crusade by 10,000 Wars on Saloons," *Chicago Tribune*, 14 February 1911, 4; "8,000 'Lobby' for Anti-Saloon Bill," *Chicago Tribune*, 15 February 1911, 3.

75 "State Drys Praise 'Tribune,'" *Chicago Tribune*, 13 May 1910, 3; "Local Option vs. Prohibition," *American Issue*, 6 June 1907, 12; "'Drys' Fix Slate for August Vote," *Chicago Tribune*, 14 June 1908, 6; William H. Anderson, "Local Option Is Fundamentally Option to Prohibit—A Ghost Laid," *American Issue*, October 1908, 6, 15, 16; "The Fruits of Local Option in Illinois," *American Prohibition Yearbook for 1911*, ed. Charles Jones et al. (Chicago: National Prohibition, 1911), 232–33.

76 Mary E. Kuhl, "Illinois," *Annals of the American Academy of Political and Social Sciences* 32 (1908): 513; *Minutes of the National Woman's Christian Temperance Union, 1910 Convention*, 126.

77 "State Drys Praise 'Tribune,'" 3; "Women Will Urge Deneen to Abolish Vice Districts," *Chicago Tribune*, 7 May 1910, 9; "State-Wide Campaign Launched in Illinois," *Union Signal*, 26 May 1910, 12.

78 *Proceedings, Sixteenth National Convention of the Anti-Saloon League*, 417; Ernest H. Cherrington, *Anti-Saloon Yearbook, 1915* (Westerville, Ohio: American Issue, 1915), 136.

79 *Minutes of the National Woman's Christian Temperance Union, 1915 Convention*, 132.

80 "Liquor Foes Are Divided: Anti-Saloon Men Will Not Support State Wide Prohibition," *Chicago Tribune*, 19 April 1910, 4.

81 "State Drys Praise 'Tribune,'" 3; "Divided on 'Dry State' Plan: Chafin Faction in Convention to Oppose Petitioning Legislature," *Chicago Tribune*, 10 May 1910, 7.

82 " 'Drys' Plan Funeral Parade in Battle against Liquor," *Chicago Tribune*, 3 July 1908, 7; "Women Will Urge Deneen to Abolish Vice Districts," 9; "WCTU Members Fight Principal," *Chicago Tribune*, 14 April 1911, 5. "WCTU Demands Clean Marriage," *Chicago Tribune*, 12 October 1913, 6; "Mormon Question Stirs State WCTU Meeting," *Chicago Tribune*, 14 October 1913, 9.

83 "Results of Local Option Elections," *Union Signal*, 16 April 1908, 3, 14; "The Women's Part in Election Campaigns," *Union Signal*, 23 April 1908, 2. In 1913 the Illinois legislature gave women the right to vote in some municipal contests, including "no-license" elections. See "WCTU Will Make Use of Power of the Ballot," *Chicago Tribune*, 10 October 1913, 8.

84 For example, the local option drive in Chicago in 1911 was directed by the Illinois ASL and the Young People's Civic League. See "Organize Forces for Saloon War," *Chicago Tribune*, 12 November 1911, 1; Cherrington, *The Standard Encyclopedia of the Alcohol Problem* 1:261.

85 Thomas R. Pegram, "The Dry Machine: The Formation of the Anti-Saloon League of Illinois," *Illinois Historical Journal* 83 (1990): 181–86.

86 While Marie C. Brehm joined the WCTU in 1891 and became state recording secretary in 1895, Helen L. Hood had been active in the state union as early as 1883. See Cherrington, *The Standard Encyclopedia of the Alcohol Problem* 1:399; "Illinois," *Union Signal*, 22 March 1883, 11.

87 Rebecca B. Chambers, "Pennsylvania," *Union Signal*, 9 March 1905, 5.

88 Kaylor, "The Prohibition Movement in Pennsylvania," 331, 332–33; "Changes in Pennsylvania Officiary," *Union Signal*, 17 October 1907, 14; "Pennsylvania's Local Option Campaign," *Union Signal*, 26 March 1908, 12; "Pennsylvania Hopes for Local Option," *Union Signal*, 4 February 1909, 12; "Keystone State Convention," *Union Signal*, 28 October 1909, 14; "Law-Making in Pennsylvania," *Union Signal*, 29 June 1911, 12; Cramer, ed., *History, Pennsylvania Woman's Christian Temperance Union*, 111; "Woman's Christian Temperance Union in Action," 246; *Minutes of the National Woman's Christian Temperance Union, 1910 Convention*, 124–25.

89 Kaylor, "The Prohibition Movement in Pennsylvania," 358–71; Chalfant, *Father Penn and John Barleycorn*, chapter 14; Cramer, ed., *History, Pennsylvania Woman's Christian Temperance Union*, 5–6, 25–26, 34, 38, 52, 66, 83, 90–92, 111, 116, 139–40, 151–53, 165, 167, 171–72, 175, 178, 181, 184, 212, 224, 227, 254, 292–93, 303, 316, 319; *Minutes of the National Woman's Christian Temperance Union, 1912 Convention*, 144–45; "Hoist by Their Own Petard," *Union Signal*, 19 May 1910, 14; "Pennsylvania Presents Petition," *Union Signal*, 16 February 1911, 11; "Pennsylvania Stirring," *Union Signal*, 30 March 1911, 13.

90 Chalfant, *Father Penn and John Barleycorn*, 150; "Hoist by Their Own Petard," 14.

91 Other new unions which lobbied the licensing courts included the New Rehoboth and Drexel Hill unions. See Cramer, ed., *History, Pennsylvania Woman's Christian Temperance Union*, 6, 76, 116.

92 Ibid., 227. For other counties, see ibid., 52, 140, 165; "Pennsylvania Presents Petition," 11.

93 For example, Pennsylvania newspapers reported instances of cooperation between the union and the ASL, and noted when the WCTU was involved in remonstrance campaigns. See Kaylor, "The Prohibition Movement in Pennsylvania," 327, 333; "Pennsylvania Uses Remonstrance System by Written Protest against Saloons," *American Issue*, 16 March 1906, 9. In addition, Harry M. Chalfant, editor of the Pennsylvania ASL's newspaper, credited the WCTU with much remonstrance work. See his *Father Penn and John Barleycorn*, 137–38, 141, 148–49, 200–201.

94 Before 1916 the WCTU and the ASL occasionally marched in the same parades, but the media failed to mention other instances of cooperation. Beginning in 1916, however, the two organizations, along with the Prohibition party and twenty other organizations, formed the Dry Chicago Federation, which sought a dry Chicago by 1918. See "March, Sing, Pray, to Banish Liquor," *Chicago Tribune*, 27 September 1908, 1, 3; "Vice Crusaders March in the Rain to Throttle Sin," *Chicago Tribune*, 29 Sep-

tember 1912, 1, 2; "Fight for Dry Chicago by 1918 Begins at Once," *Chicago Tribune*, 10 November 1916, 3.

95 See, for example, "Renews Defense of Grant," *Chicago Tribune*, 15 October 1909, 3; "Women Will Urge Deneen to Abolish Vice Districts," 9; "State Drys Praise 'Tribune,' " 3.

96 Cherrington, *The Standard Encyclopedia of the Alcohol Problem* 4:1727.

97 Even if the Chicago wets and "Boss" Penrose of Pennsylvania had been more amenable to the antiliquor cause, however, the ASL would not have sponsored a referendum had it felt that the electorate was not thoroughly educated on the liquor issue. See, e.g., "Liquor Foes Are Divided," 4.

98 Engelmann, "O Whiskey," 291–92.

99 Apparently, Van Etten was part of the Reform Club movement of the late 1870s. This movement induced Americans to take the pledge by staging temperance revivals led by reformed drunkards, such as Francis Murphy, Henry Reynolds and Dr. J. K. Osgood.

100 Van Buren, "Our Temperance Conflict," 402.

101 "Michigan," *National Temperance Advocate*, September 1880, 142; *National Temperance Advocate*, June 1881, 108; *Cyclopedia of Temperance and Prohibition*, 111.

102 "Michigan," *National Temperance Advocate*, January 1881, 13. In particular, Lutheran and Roman Catholic parishes had failed to adopt "unfermented wine" in their services. Since many wets adhered to these two faiths, the Michigan prohibitionists apparently thought that they could win constitutional prohibition without their support.

103 John Fitzgibbon, "King Alcohol: His Rise, Reign and Fall in Michigan," *Michigan History* 2 (1918): 755; *Cyclopedia of Temperance and Prohibition*, 111.

104 *The Political Prohibitionist for 1888* (New York: Funk and Wagnalls, 1888), 121; Roy R. Glashan, *American Governors and Gubernatorial Elections, 1775–1978* (Westport, Conn.: Meckler, 1979), 152–53; Fitzgibbon, "King Alcohol," 755–57; *Cyclopedia of Temperance and Prohibition*, 111.

105 During the 1880s the average margin of victory in Michigan gubernatorial elections was 3.8%, which was far below the national average of 17.2%. See Glashan, *American Governors and Gubernatorial Elections*.

106 Fitzgibbon, "King Alcohol," 757.

107 The amendment campaign of 1887 united the Michigan branches of the Sons, the IOGT, the WCTU, and the Prohibition party, as well as the local Reform Clubs inspired by the temperance orators Francis Murphy and Henry A. Reynolds. Given that the referendum vote was nonpartisan, dry leaders worked easily together for constitutional prohibition. See, for example, "The Conflict in Michigan," *Christian Advocate*, 24 March 1887, 1.

108 W. W. Washburn, "The Recent Temperance Campaign in Michigan," *Christian Advocate*, 5 May 1887, 296; "Cold Water Champions," *Detroit Free Press*, 12 February 1887, 5; *Minutes of the National Woman's Christian Temperance Union, 1887 Convention*, 124–25; *Cyclopedia of Temperance and Prohibition*, 111; "Speakers for the Michigan Amendment Campaign," *Union Signal*, 3 March 1887, 5; "Michigan," *Union Signal*, 14 April 1887, 3; "Michigan: After the Battle," *Union Signal*, 21 April 1887, 10; "Major Hilton in Michigan," *Union Signal*, 28 April 1887, 3.

109 Van Buren, "Our Temperance Conflict," 403. Other sources report the referendum vote totals as slightly different. For example, Rowntree and Sherwell, *The Temperance Problem and Social Reform*, 715, report the vote as 184,281 votes against prohibition, 178,636 in favor. Similarly, Cherrington cites a wet victory of 184,281 to 178,638 in his Ernest H. Cherrington, *The Evolution of Prohibition in the United States of America* (Westerville, Ohio: American Issue, 1920), 231. In any event, sources agree that the wets' margin of victory was between 5,500 and 6,000.

110 "Causes of the Failure of Prohibition in Michigan," *Christian Advocate*, 5 May 1887, 286; A. R. Moors,

"An Important Cause of the Failure of the Prohibition Amendment to Pass in Michigan," *Christian Advocate*, 2 June 1887, 4; Frances E. Willard, "Michigan's Battle," *Union Signal*, 21 April 1887, 4–5; *Cyclopedia of Temperance and Prohibition*, 111; "Some Queer Things Are Shown by the Michigan Returns," *Union Signal*, 28 April 1887, 3; Fitzgibbon, "King Alcohol," 758–59.

111 Willard, "Michigan's Battle," 5; *Cyclopedia of Temperance and Prohibition*, 111; Editorial, *Statesman*, June 1889, 176–77.

112 Washburn, "The Recent Temperance Campaign in Michigan," 296.

113 Ibid., 296.

114 Willard, "Michigan's Battle," 5. See also "Michigan," *Union Signal*, 14 April 1887, 3.

115 For the radicals' rejection of "high" licensing policies, see n. 206 to chapter 2.

116 "Causes of the Failure of Prohibition in Michigan," 286.

117 Ibid., 286; *Cyclopedia of Temperance and Prohibition*, 111; Fitzgibbon, "King Alcohol," 758.

118 *Detroit Free Press*, 19 May 1887, 5; *Christian Union*, 2 June 1887, 26.

119 *Detroit Free Press*, 1 June 1887, 4.

120 *Detroit Free Press*, 28 June 1888, 5; *Christian Union*, 5 July 1888, 24; Colvin, *Prohibition in the United States*, 190.

121 Van Buren, "Our Temperance Conflict," 405.

122 Ibid., 403.

123 In 1899 the Michigan legislature raised the petitioning requirement from 25% of qualified voters to 33%.

124 In fact, the absence of reform groups from the local option debate led the Michigan press to conclude that "there is no [public] demand whatever for the passage of a local option law by the Legislature." See the excerpt from the *Lansing Journal* in the *Detroit Free Press*, 25 May 1887, 4.

125 Larry Engelmann, "Dry Renaissance: The Local Option Years," *Michigan History*, 1975, 70. Significantly, Michigan's state and local WCTU reports from the 1890s ignore the state's county option law. Instead, they consistently reaffirm the Michigan union's loyalty to the Prohibition party.

126 See, e.g., *Proceedings, Third National Anti-Saloon Convention* (Washington: American Anti-Saloon League, 1898), 68.

127 William G. Hubbard, "Michigan," *American Issue*, 30 November 1900, 8.

128 *Proceedings, Seventh National Anti-Saloon Convention* (Baltimore: American Anti-Saloon League), xxxvii.

129 *Proceedings, Sixteenth National Convention of the Anti-Saloon League*, 446–47.

130 *Proceedings, Sixth National Anti-Saloon Convention* (Baltimore: American Anti-Saloon League, 1902), 72.

131 "Why Township and Ward Option in Michigan?" *American Issue*, 17 June 1904, 6; "Larger Local Option for Michigan," *American Issue*, 9 September 1904, 2–3; "Detroit Citizens Going to Lansing," *Detroit Free Press*, 28 March 1905, 12; "Local Option," *Detroit Free Press*, 23 November 1907, 7; Dora Stockman, "WCTU Forces Active in Michigan," *Union Signal*, 5 January 1905, 13; Engelmann, "O Whiskey," 173.

132 "Local Option in Bond Law," *Detroit Free Press*, 28 October 1907, 1, 6; "One Word Does It All," *Detroit Free Press*, 28 October 1907, 6; "Local Option by Indirection," *Detroit Free Press*, 28 October 1907, 4; "Temperance Victories in Michigan," *Union Signal*, 23 April 1908, 2.

133 "Larger Local Option for Michigan," 2; "Petition to Go to Legislature," *Detroit Free Press*, 14 March 1905, 11; *Proceedings, Ninth Annual Anti-Saloon Convention*, 66; *Proceedings, Eleventh Annual Convention of the Anti-Saloon League of America* (Harrisburg: Anti-Saloon League of America, 1906), 99–100; *Proceedings, Twelfth Annual Convention of the Anti-Saloon League of America* (Harrisburg: Anti-Saloon League of America, 1907), 108–9; *Proceedings, Sixteenth National Convention of the Anti-Saloon League*, 447.

134 *Proceedings, Eleventh Annual Convention of the Anti-Saloon League*, 99–100; *Proceedings, Twelfth Annual Convention of the Anti-Saloon League*, 110.

135 For the union's support of constitutional prohibition after 1900, see "State Effort for Prohibition," *Union Signal*, 15 March 1906, 13; "Michigan: Prohibitory Amendment Campaign On," *Union Signal*, 14 March 1907, 12; "Michigan in Line," *Union Signal*, 15 August 1907, 14; "Michigan Temperance Forces Hopeful," *Union Signal*, 9 January 1908, 3; "Michigan Constitutional Convention," *Union Signal*, 6 February 1908, 12.

136 "Michigan," *American Issue*, March 1900, 11; "WCTU Notes," *Union Signal*, 19 February 1903, 11; " 'Our Peaceful War' in Michigan," *Union Signal*, 7 May 1903, 2; "Thirty New Unions in Michigan," *Union Signal*, 9 June 1904, 11.

137 Stockman, "WCTU Forces Active in Michigan," 13; "Michigan Legislature Is Considering Remonstrance Law," *Union Signal*, 21 March 1907, 14.

138 "Prohibition Hearing in Michigan," *Union Signal*, 12 December 1907, 2; Engelmann, "O Whiskey," 161.

139 *Thirty-First Annual Convention of the WCTU of the Sixth District of Michigan* (1908), 36–37; *Thirty-Second Annual Convention of the WCTU of the Sixth District of Michigan* (1909), 41; *Thirty-third Annual Convention of the WCTU of the Sixth District of Michigan* (1910), 48; *Twenty-Sixth Annual Convention of the WCTU of Gennessee County, Michigan* (1908), 202; *Twenty-Seventh Annual Convention of the WCTU of Gennessee County, Michigan* (1909), 213; *Twenty-Eighth Annual Convention of the WCTU of Gennessee County, Michigan* (1910), 133, 137, 147; *Nineteenth Annual Meeting of the WCTU of Ingham County, Michigan* (1908), 30–31; *Annual Meeting Minutes of the National Woman's Christian Temperance Union, 1908 Convention*, 159, *1909 Convention*, 146, *1910 Convention*, 141–42; "Temperance Victories in Michigan," 2; "Making the Map White in Michigan," *Union Signal*, 15 April 1909, 3; "Ten New Dry Counties in Michigan," *Union Signal*, 28 April 1910. For the wet perspective on these county option campaigns, see *Yearbook of the United States Brewers' Association*, 1910, 54–76.

140 "The Michigan Anti-Saloon League Extends Greeting," 12 October 1908, Ernest H. Cherrington series, Temperance and Prohibition Papers, Ohio Historical Society microfilm, reel 1; *Proceedings, Twelfth Annual Convention of the Anti-Saloon League*, 108; *Proceedings, Fourteenth National Convention of the Anti-Saloon League*, 122. For the Michigan drys' reliance on small donors during the local option years, see Engelmann, "O Whiskey," 161–62; *Annual Meeting Minutes of the National Woman's Christian Temperance Union, 1908 Convention*, 159.

141 Engelmann, "O Whiskey," 100.

142 Ernest H. Cherrington, *Anti-Saloon Yearbook*, 1916 (Westerville, Ohio: American Issue, 1916), 224; Ernest H. Cherrington, *Anti-Saloon Yearbook*, 1918 (Westerville, Ohio: American Issue, 1918), 219.

143 "Enthusiastic Michigan Convention," *Union Signal*, 25 June 1908, 11; "Victories Bring Enthusiasm," *Union Signal*, 8 July 1909, 5; *Annual Meeting Minutes of the National Woman's Christian Temperance Union, 1908 Convention*, 159.

144 Engelmann, "O Whiskey," 170, 136, 260–62; *Proceedings, Fifteenth National Convention of the Anti-Saloon League*, 299; James Shermerhorn, "Why the Detroit Times Went Dry," *American Issue*, 8 January 1916, 10–11. For correspondence about the Local Option Press Association, see folder entitled "Local Option campaign and enforcement, June–December 1909," box 2, Marshall L. Cook Papers, Bentley Historical Library, University of Michigan.

145 Forty Michigan counties were dry by 1910; seven years later, forty-four counties had adopted a "no-license" position through the county option law. During the years 1910–17, though, several coun-

ties experienced challenges to their dry status and underwent new elections biennially. See Engelmann, "Dry Renaissance," 76–80; Ernest H. Cherrington, *Anti-Saloon Yearbook, 1912* (Westerville, Ohio: American Issue, 1912), 174–75; Cherrington, *Anti-Saloon Yearbook, 1918*, 216–21.

146 " 'State-Wide Prohibition' Michigan's Slogan," *Union Signal*, 4 May 1911, 2; *Annual Meeting Minutes of the National Woman's Christian Temperance Union, 1911 Convention*, 135. Some of the WCTU's resources were also diverted to woman's suffrage referenda in 1912 and 1913. State and local union reports indicate that WCTU members devoted considerable time and money to winning these campaigns. See, e.g., *Annual Meeting Minutes of the National Woman's Christian Temperance Union, 1912 Convention*, 137, *1913 Convention*, 142–43.

147 Engelmann, "O Whiskey," 161, 132–33, 171–72; *Proceedings, Fourteenth National Convention of the Anti-Saloon League*, 122–23; Cherrington, *Anti-Saloon Yearbook, 1912*, 174–77; George W. Morrow to Junius E. Beal, 20 May 1910, Correspondence, May 1910, box 2, Junius E. Beal Papers, Bentley Historical Library, University of Michigan.

148 "Michigan's State-Wide Campaign," *American Issue*, December 1912, 10; *Proceedings, Sixteenth National Convention of the Anti-Saloon League*, 448; Ernest H. Cherrington, *Anti-Saloon Yearbook, 1913* (Westerville, Ohio: American Issue, 1913), 137–38; *Yearbook of the United States Brewers' Association, 1913* (New York: United States Brewers' Association, 1914), 35–37; Cherrington, *Standard Encyclopedia of the Alcohol Problem* 4:1765.

149 Engelmann, "O Whiskey," 199–200, 221; *Thirty-Sixth Annual Convention of the WCTU of the Sixth District of Michigan* (1913), 71; *Grand Rapids South Union Minutes* 5:59, 76; *Thirty-first Annual Convention of WCTU of Gennessee County, Michigan* (1913).

150 "Michigan," *American Issue*, 20 March 1915, 4–5, 24 April 1915, 5; *Proceedings, Sixteenth National Convention of the Anti-Saloon League*, 448–49; Engelmann, "O Whiskey," 227–36.

151 Engelmann, "O Whiskey," 244–55; Larry D. Engelmann, "Billy Sunday: 'God, You've Got a Job on Your Hands in Detroit,' " *Michigan History* 55 (1971): 1–21; *Thirty-Third Annual Convention of the WCTU of Gennessee County* (1915), 250–51; *Thirty-Fourth Annual Convention of the WCTU of Gennessee County, Michigan* (1916), 271–72; *Twenty-Seventh Annual Convention of the WCTU of Ingham County, Michigan* (1916), 96; *Thirty-Sixth Annual Convention of the WCTU of the Seventh District of Michigan* (1916); *Twenty-Seventh Annual Convention of the WCTU of the Twelfth District of Michigan* (1916); *Thirty-Eighth Annual Convention of the WCTU of the Sixth District of Michigan* (1915), 72; *Thirty-Ninth Annual Convention of the WCTU of the Sixth District of Michigan* (1916); "Michigan's Campaign in Full Swing," 2; "Out for Prohibition: Michigan's Well-Known Citizen Favors Dry State," *American Issue* (Ohio Edition), 6 October 1916, 3.

152 Engelmann, "O Whiskey," 263–75, 294.

153 "Drys Victorious in Four Wet States," *American Issue* (Ohio Edition), 10 November 1916, 1; "Big Cities Are Now Aiding Drys Ousting Saloons," *American Issue* (Ohio Edition), 17 November 1916, 1; "Dry Landslide Increased by Full Returns of the Election," *American Issue* (Ohio Edition), 17 November 1916, 4; "Prohibition Victories All Over Nation," *Christian Science Monitor*, 10 November 1916, 1, 5; "Over Half of States Put in Dry Column," *Chicago Tribune*, 9 November 1916, 1–2; "Four More 'Dry' States," *Literary Digest*, 25 November 1916, 1389–90.

154 Kerr similarly notes that the WCTU's national network was so well developed that its national legislative superintendent "could contact a member in every county in the nation to begin agitation as needed." See his *Organized for Prohibition*, 158–59.

155 Engelmann, "O Whiskey," 298–301. Specifically, Engelmann found a correlation of .50224 between the 1910 urban population per county and opposition to prohibition. Moreover, he found a .39273 correlation between the percentage of foreign born per county and opposition to prohibition.

156 Jane Mansbridge, *Why We Lost the ERA* (Chicago: University of Chicago Press, 1986), chapter 13.

157 William H. Anderson, "The Need of Illinois," *American Issue*, 23 January 1903, 3.

158 Ernest H. Cherrington, *Anti-Saloon Yearbook, 1909* (Columbus: Anti-Saloon League of America, 1909), 168.

159 "Liquor Foes Are Divided," 4.

7 Turning Moderates into Radicals

1 "Senate in Line on Local Option," *Chicago Tribune*, 8 May 1907, 4.

2 Ernest H. Cherrington, *The Evolution of Prohibition in the United States of America* (Westerville, Ohio: American Issue, 1920), 368–79.

3 *Proceedings, Fifteenth National Convention of the Anti-Saloon League of America* (Westerville, Ohio: American Issue, 1914), 35–36; Cherrington, *The Evolution of Prohibition in the United States*, 251–52.

4 "Out for Prohibition: Michigan's Well-Known Citizen Favors Dry State," *American Issue* (Ohio Edition), 6 October 1916, 3.

5 Fred M. Jackson, "Birmingham's Experience," *Independent*, 22 July 1909, 169.

6 Stephen Monahan, "Local Option a Failure," *Independent*, 22 July 1909, 169–70. For contemporary assessments of local option's effectiveness after 1900, see Ernest H. Cherrington, *The Anti-Saloon Yearbook, 1911* (Westerville, Ohio: American Issue, 1911), 96–228; *Yearbook of the United States Brewers' Association, 1910*; Charles Roberts, *The Working of Local Option in the Cities: The Policy of No-License in the State of Massachusetts, USA* (Manchester, England: United Kingdom Alliance, 1907); Amy F. Acton, *Local Option in Massachusetts* (New York: Charities Publication Committee, 1911).

7 "Local Option as a Step to State-Wide Prohibition," 8; Ernest H. Cherrington, *Anti-Saloon Yearbook, 1909* (Columbus: Anti-Saloon League of America, 1909); "The Anti-Saloon League and the Principle upon Which It Works," *American Issue* (Ohio Edition), 5 May 1916, 4.

8 When characterizing the ASL's adherents, analysts have generally portrayed them as middle-class, native-born evangelical Protestants mobilized into the league by clergymen. Indeed, Odegard wrote in 1928 that "the churches constitute the backbone of the [ASL]" and described them as the key components of the league's dry machine. See Peter Odegard, *Pressure Politics: The Story of the Anti-Saloon League* (New York: Columbia University Press, 1928), 15–35; Robert A. Hohner, "The Prohibitionists: Who Were They?" *South Atlantic Quarterly* 68 (1969): 494–505; K. Austin Kerr, *Organized for Prohibition: A New History of the Anti-Saloon League* (New Haven: Yale University Press, 1985), 91–93. For denominational support of prohibition, see Robert T. Handy, *A Christian America: Protestant Hopes and Historical Realities* (New York: Oxford University Press, 1971), 89–90, 148–50.

9 Richard Jensen, *The Winning of the Midwest: Social and Political Conflict, 1888–1896* (Chicago: University of Chicago Press, 1971), 87.

10 Kerr, *Organized for Prohibition*, chapter 7.

11 D. Leigh Colvin, *Prohibition in the United States* (New York: George H. Doran, 1926), 368–79.

12 Washington Gladden, *Recollections* (Boston: Houghton Mifflin, 1909), 50–51; Jacob H. Dorn, *Washington Gladden: Prophet of the Social Gospel* (Columbus: Ohio State University Press, 1966), 14–15; Ernest H. Cherrington, *The Standard Encyclopedia of the Alcohol Problem* (Westerville, Ohio: American Issue, 1924–30), 3:1110; Mark E. Lender, *Dictionary of American Temperance Biography* (Westport, Conn.: Greenwood, 1984), 189.

13 Gladden, *Recollections*, 54–64; 118–21; Dorn, *Washington Gladden*, 10–13, 33–35, chapter 6.

14 Dorn, *Washington Gladden*, chapters 7–8; Henry F. May, *Protestant Churches and Industrial America* (New

York: Harper and Brothers, 1949), 170–76; Gladden, *Recollections*, 248–58, 294–315; Hoyt L. Warner, *Progressivism in Ohio, 1897–1917* (Columbus: Ohio State University Press, 1964), 43–45.

15 *Proceedings of the Sixth Annual Meeting of the Citizens' Law and Order League of the United States* (1888), 53; Dorn, *Washington Gladden*, 308–12.

16 Washington Gladden, "The Saloon in Politics, Letter of Washington Gladden," *Chautauquan*, January 1888, 229; "Address of Washington Gladden," *Proceedings of the Fourth Annual Meeting of the Citizens' Law and Order League of Massachusetts* (1886), 23.

17 Washington Gladden, "After the Election," 14 October 1883, Washington Gladden Papers, sermon 234, roll 18, 12.

18 Washington Gladden, *Applied Christianity: Moral Aspects of Social Questions* (New York: Houghton Mifflin, 1886), 182–85.

19 Washington Gladden, "Hurricane Reform," *Century Magazine*, December 1883, 316–18; James Brand, "That 'Hurricane Reform,'" and Washington Gladden, "Comment," *Century Magazine*, May 1884, 147–50; Dorn, *Washington Gladden*, 309–10 n. 20.

20 For Brand's role in organizing the Ohio ASL, see Banks, "Anti-Saloon League, Origin and Personnel," 190; Pearce, "Story of Origins"; Ernest H. Cherrington, *The History of the Anti-Saloon League* (Westerville, Ohio: American Issue, 1913), 19–20.

21 Gladden, "Comment," 149; Washington Gladden, "The Enforcement of Law," *"Unity, Persistency, Victory!" A Souvenir Selection of Anti-Saloon Addresses* (Columbus: Hann and Adair, 1895), 15–16; Gladden, *Moral Gains and Losses of the Temperance Reformation* (Charlottesville, Va.: Progress, 1895).

22 Norman Dohn, "The History of the Anti-Saloon League" (Ph.D. diss., Ohio State University, 1959), 91–92.

23 Washington Gladden, "Sowing the Wind," Washington Gladden Papers, sermon 518, roll 24, 37–38; Dorn, *Washington Gladden*, 315–16 n. 36.

24 Frederic H. Wines and John Koren, *The Liquor Problem in Its Legislative Aspects* (Boston: Houghton Mifflin, 1897), v–viii. Among others, the Committee of Fifty also included Seth Low, (ex-mayor of New York and president of Columbia University), Charles W. Eliot (president of Harvard University), Jacob H. Schiff (banker and philanthropist), and Richard T. Ely (economics professor, University of Wisconsin).

25 Ibid., 86–95, 130–36; "The Committee of Fifty's Investigation," *Union Signal*, 12 August 1897, 8.

26 "Libel on Dr. Gladden," *American Issue*, 1 November 1901, 7.

27 Washington Gladden, *Social Salvation* (New York: Houghton Mifflin, 1902), 164–71; Washington Gladden, "The Municipal Church: The Crying Need of It, and a Program of Its Possible Work," *Century Magazine*, August 1910, 498; Dorn, *Washington Gladden*, 285.

28 Local option "ought to be extended not only to townships and municipalities," Gladden insisted, "but to wards or other subdivisions of cities, so that each neighborhood may determine for itself whether [the liquor] traffic shall be permitted within its boundaries." See his *Social Salvation*, 164–66.

29 Kerr, *Organized for Prohibition*, 109–10.

30 Warner, *Progressivism in Ohio*, 111–15, 157–66. In particular, Gladden had witnessed the death of a pet cause, municipal "home rule," at the hands of Cox and the Republican state legislature in 1902.

31 Dorn, *Washington Gladden*, 339; *Proceedings, Twelfth Annual Convention of the Anti-Saloon League of America* (Harrisburg: Anti-Saloon League of America, 1907), 124.

32 For the sense that prohibition was on the march in these years, see Samuel J. Barrows, "The Tem-

perance Tidal Wave," in *The Passing of the Saloon*, ed. George H. Hammell (Cincinnati: Tower, 1908), 204–15.

33 Cherrington, *Anti-Saloon Yearbook, 1909*, 15, 46–47; Dorn, *Washington Gladden*, 315–16 n. 36.

34 Handy, *A Christian America*, 171; Richard D. Knudten, *The Systematic Thought of Washington Gladden* (New York: Humanities, 1968), 36; Ernest H. Cherrington, *Anti-Saloon Yearbook, 1913* (Westerville, Ohio: American Issue, 1913), 264; *Proceedings, Fifteenth National Convention of the Anti-Saloon League*, 2.

35 James H. Timberlake, *Prohibition and the Progressive Movement* (Cambridge: Harvard University Press, 1963), 167–68; Warner, *Progressivism in Ohio*, 384.

36 Lamar T. Beman, ed., *Selected Articles on Prohibition of the Liquor Traffic* (White Plains, N.Y.: H. W. Wilson, 1917), lvi.

37 Dorn, *Washington Gladden*, 432.

38 Timberlake, *Prohibition and the Progressive Movement*, 23–30.

39 Eleanor H. Woods, *Robert A. Woods: Champion of Democracy* (Freeport, N.Y.: Books for Libraries, 1929), chapter 27; *Dictionary of American Biography* (New York: Charles Scribner, 1936), 10:504.

40 Robert A. Woods, "Drunkenness," *Harvard Theological Review* 7 (1914): 506. See also Robert A. Woods, "Winning the Other Half: National Prohibition a Leading Social Issue," *Survey*, 30 December 1916, 350.

41 Perry R. Duis, *The Saloon: Public Drinking in Chicago and Boston, 1880–1920* (Urbana: University of Illinois Press, 1983), 284; William I. Cole, "Criminal Tendencies," in *The City Wilderness*, ed. Robert A. Woods (Boston: Houghton Mifflin, 1898), 156.

42 Robert A. Woods, "The Total Drift," in *The City Wilderness*, 294.

43 Woods, *Robert A. Woods*, 250–51; Robert A. Woods, "Work and Wages," in *City Wilderness*, 108–9; Robert A. Woods, "Traffic in Citizenship," in *Americans in Process*, ed. Robert A. Woods (Boston: Houghton Mifflin, 1902), 173; Robert A. Woods, "Social Workers' Temperance Bill," *Survey*, 12 March 1910, 924–26; "Bill Is Attacked: Bar and Bottle Bill Attracts Great Crowd to State House," *Boston Globe*, 2 March 1911; Timberlake, *Prohibition and the Progressive Movement*, 65.

44 Woods, *Robert A. Woods*, 252–53; Duis, *The Saloon*, 284, 289–90. By denying wholesale licenses to retailers, the Bar and Bottle Bill was designed to prevent saloonkeepers from selling bottles to customers, who often took liquor home for consumption. Furthermore, the measure would reduce the number of saloons because it stripped them of a profitable source of revenue (wholesaling) which had propped up some marginal retailers.

45 "Bill Is Attacked"; "Favor 'Bar and Bottle Bill,' " *Boston Globe*, 21 February 1910.

46 "500 People at Hearing: Bar and Bottle Repeal Bill Drew Big Crowd," *Boston Globe*, 1 March 1911, 2; Woods, *Robert A. Woods*, 254–55; *Proceedings, Fourteenth National Convention of the Anti-Saloon League of America* (Westerville, Ohio: American Issue, 1912), 121.

47 Woods, "Social Workers' Temperance Bill," 924, 926.

48 Woods, *Robert A. Woods*, 253, 297.

49 Reformers like Woods were particularly disturbed about the buying of rounds, or "treating," which they felt was a major source of drunkenness.

50 Duis, *The Saloon*, 284; Woods, *Robert A. Woods*, 286–90; Michael E. Hennessy, *Four Decades of Massachusetts Politics, 1890–1935* (Freeport, N.Y.: Books for Libraries, 1971), 202.

51 Duis, *The Saloon*, 276–77, 284–86, 290–91; Woods, *Robert A. Woods*, 292–94.

52 Duis, *The Saloon*, 280–81, 285.

53 Hennessy, *Four Decades of Massachusetts Politics*, 229.

54 Woods, *Robert A. Woods*, 294–95.

55 Ibid., 296–97, 322–30; Woods, "Winning the Other Half," 349–52; Ernest H. Cherrington, *Anti-Saloon Yearbook, 1918* (Westerville, Ohio: American Issue, 1918), 211, 430, 447; Ernest H. Cherrington, *Anti-Saloon Yearbook, 1919* (Westerville, Ohio: American Issue, 1919).

56 Woods, *Robert A. Woods*, 322–24, 330; Woods, "Winning the Other Half," 352; Timberlake, *Prohibition and the Progressive Movement*, 66.

57 Miles C. Everett, "Chester Harvey Rowell, Pragmatic Humanist and California Progressive" (Ph.D. diss., University of California, Berkeley, 1966), 91–92, 109, 143–45, 220–21.

58 Gilman Ostrander, *The Prohibition Movement in California, 1848–1933* (Berkeley: University of California Press, 1957), 110; Everett, "Chester Harvey Rowell," 219–20.

59 Everett, "Chester Harvey Rowell," 160–77, 218; Ostrander, *The Prohibition Movement in California*, 101.

60 Everett, "Chester Harvey Rowell," 160–61, 217, 222–27.

61 Ibid., 219–21.

62 Franklin Hichborn, *Story of the Session of the California Legislature of 1911* (San Francisco: James H. Barry, 1911), 203; Everett, "Chester Harvey Rowell," 125, 222.

63 Ostrander, *The Prohibition Movement in California*, 114–16; Cherrington, *Standard Encyclopedia of the Alcohol Problem* 2:481–82; *Proceedings, Fourteenth National Convention of the Anti-Saloon League*, 106, 144–45; Spencer C. Olin Jr., *California's Prodigal Sons: Hiram Johnson and the Progressives, 1911–1917* (Berkeley: University of California Press, 1968), 54.

64 Hichborn, *Story of the Session of the California Legislature of 1911*, 203–4.

65 Dorcas J. Spencer, *A History of the Woman's Christian Temperance Union of Northern and Central California* (Oakland: West Coast Printing, 1911), 100–101; *Proceedings, Sixteenth National Convention of the Anti-Saloon League of America* (Westerville, Ohio: American Issue, 1915), 388–89; Franklin Hichborn, *Story of the Session of the California Legislature of 1913* (San Francisco: James H. Barry, 1913), 323–24.

66 Ostrander, *The Prohibition Movement in California*, 101, 111–12, 134; *Proceedings, Fifteenth National Convention of the Anti-Saloon League*, 277.

67 Ostrander, *The Prohibition Movement in California*, 110, 119, 122–24; Cherrington, *Standard Encyclopedia of the Alcohol Problem* 2:482.

68 Ostrander, *The Prohibition Movement in California*, 111, 134–40; Cherrington, *Standard Encyclopedia of the Alcohol Problem* 2:483; Cherrington, *Anti-Saloon Yearbook, 1913*, 42; Ernest H. Cherrington, *Anti-Saloon Yearbook, 1918* (Westerville, Ohio: American Issue, 1918), 152–55; Everett, "Chester Harvey Rowell," 222.

69 Cherrington, *Anti-Saloon Yearbook, 1918*, 443; Ostrander, *The Prohibition Movement in California*, 111, 141, 149; Cherrington, *Standard Encyclopedia of the Alcohol Problem* 2:482.

70 Ostrander, *The Prohibition Movement in California*, 111, 160; Everett, "Chester Harvey Rowell," 222.

71 See, for example, Timberlake, *Prohibition and the Progressive Movement*, 161–65; J. Morgan Kousser, *The Shaping of Southern Politics: Suffrage Restrictions and the One-Party South* (New Haven: Yale University Press, 1974), 220–26.

72 Kerr, *Organized for Prohibition*, 183–91.

73 As in California, radical drys in Missouri and Colorado initiated dry amendments that the ASL believed were premature. Both amendments were rejected by the voters. See West, "Dry Crusade," 259–83; *Proceedings, Thirteenth National Convention of the Anti-Saloon League of America* (Westerville, Ohio: American Issue, 1910), 121–22; *Proceedings, Fourteenth National Convention of the Anti-Saloon League*, 125–26; "Another Lid Bill in Missouri," *Chicago Tribune*, 5 March 1909, 12.

74 Colvin, *Prohibition in the United States*, 369, 379, 393–94.

1 Peter M. Blau, *The Dynamics of Bureaucracy* (Chicago: University of Chicago Press, 1955), 195; David L. Sills, *The Volunteers: Means and Ends in a National Organization* (Glencoe, Ill.: Free Press, 1957), 256–64.

2 K. Austin Kerr, *Organized for Prohibition: A New History of the Anti-Saloon League* (New Haven: Yale University Press, 1985), chapter 9; Richard Hamm, "Southerners and the Shaping of the Eighteenth Amendment, 1914–1917," *Georgia Journal of Southern Legal History* 1 (1991): 81–107; Ernest H. Cherrington, *The Standard Encyclopedia of the Alcohol Problem* (Westerville, Ohio: American Issue, 1924–30), 6:2777–83.

3 Ann-Marie Szymanski, "Dry Compulsions: Prohibition and the Creation of State-Level Enforcement Agencies," *Journal of Policy History* 11 (1999): 134–39.

4 Larry D. Engelmann, *Intemperance: The Lost War against Liquor* (New York: Free Press, 1979), 78–82, 125–37, 149–71; Cherrington, *Standard Encyclopedia of the Alcohol Problem* 6:2620; Jimmie L. Franklin, *Born Sober: Prohibition in Oklahoma, 1907–1959* (Norman: University of Oklahoma Press, 1971), 78–105; Kerr, *Organized for Prohibition*, 248–49.

5 Robert A. Woods, "Winning the Other Half: National Prohibition a Leading Social Issue," *Survey*, 30 December 1916, 352. For the dynamics of repeal, see David E. Kyvig, *Repealing National Prohibition* (Chicago: University of Chicago Press, 1979); Kenneth D. Rose, *American Women and the Repeal of Prohibition* (New York: New York University Press, 1996); Thomas R. Pegram, *Battling Demon Rum: The Struggle for a Dry America, 1800–1933* (Chicago: Ivan R. Dee, 1998), chapter 8.

6 Nina Eliasoph, *Avoiding Politics: How Americans Produce Apathy in Everyday Life* (Cambridge: Cambridge University Press, 1998).

7 Martin Luther King, *Stride toward Freedom: The Montgomery Story* (New York: Harper and Brothers, 1958), 36–37.

8 Gerald N. Rosenberg, *The Hollow Hope: Can the Courts Bring About Social Change?* (Chicago: University of Chicago Press, 1991), chapters 4–6.

9 Taylor Branch, *Parting the Waters: America in the King Years, 1954–63* (New York: Simon and Schuster, 1988), 145; Adam Fairclough, *To Redeem the Soul of America: The Southern Christian Leadership Conference and Martin Luther King, Jr.* (Athens: University of Georgia Press, 1987), 11–28, 42–43. Fairclough notes, however, that the Montgomery boycott organizers were initially unaware of the Baton Rouge boycott. Nevertheless, they consciously imitated its use of carpools to sustain their campaign once it got off the ground. See, e.g., King, *Stride toward Freedom*, 75.

10 Fairclough, *To Redeem the Soul of America*, 11–12; King, *Stride toward Freedom*, 40–41, 63.

11 In February 1956, the third month of the boycott, civil rights leaders in Montgomery filed a federal lawsuit against bus segregation, even though they publicly accepted the "first come, first served" principle as a condition for ending the boycott until April. The boycott ended in November, when the Supreme Court affirmed a lower court decision invalidating Alabama's bus segregation laws. See Branch, *Parting the Waters*, chapter 5; Fairclough, *To Redeem the Soul of America*, 20–21, 43; King, *Stride toward Freedom*, 151–53.

12 King, *Stride toward Freedom*, 86.

13 David J. Garrow, *Bearing the Cross: Martin Luther King, Jr., and the Southern Christian Leadership Conference* (New York: William Morrow, 1986), 87, 112.

14 Rosenberg, *Hollow Hope*, 112–16.

15 Robert F. Burk, *The Eisenhower Administration and Black Civil Rights* (Knoxville: University of Tennes-

see Press, 1984), 155; Doug McAdam, *Political Process and the Development of Black Insurgency* (Chicago: University of Chicago Press, 1982).

16 Garrow, *Bearing the Cross*, 81, 85.

17 Doug McAdam, *Political Process and the Development of Black Insurgency* (Chicago: University of Chicago Press, 1982), 136–38; Fairclough, *To Redeem the Soul of America*, 43.

18 Fairclough, *To Redeem the Soul of America*, 42–43.

19 Garrow, *Bearing the Cross*, 115, 121, 124. For the SCLC's failure to register a significant number of voters during the late 1950s, see ibid., 111, 115, 118, 120; Fairclough, *To Redeem the Soul of America*, 43–51.

20 Rosenberg, *Hollow Hope*, 133–35.

21 McAdam, *Political Process*, 152–53, 206–8; Branch, *Parting the Waters*, 272–84, chapters 11, 12; Fairclough, *To Redeem the Soul of America*, 57–62; 143–44.

22 Garrow, *Bearing the Cross*, 224–30; 370–72, 378–79; Fairclough, *To Redeem the Soul of America*, 137–38, chapter 9; McAdam, *Political Process*, 174–79.

23 Garrow, *Bearing the Cross*, 93.

24 Fairclough, *To Redeem the Soul of America*, 135; Branch, *Parting the Waters*, 878.

25 McAdam, *Political Process*, 157–60, 186–91, 192–94, 227.

26 Matthew C. Moen, *The Christian Right and Congress* (Tuscaloosa: University of Alabama Press, 1989), 83–86.

27 Clyde Wilcox, *Onward Christian Soldiers? The Religious Right in American Politics*, 2d ed. (Boulder: Westview, 2000), 35.

28 Moen, *The Christian Right and Congress*, chapter 9; Allen D. Hertzke, *Echoes of Discontent: Jesse Jackson, Pat Robertson, and the Resurgence of Populism* (Washington: Congressional Quarterly, 1993), 145–50; Duane M. Oldfield, *The Right and the Righteous: The Christian Right Confronts the Republican Party* (Lanham, Md.: Rowman and Littlefield, 1996), chapters 4–5; Wilcox, *Onward Christian Soldiers*, 35–41.

29 Matthew C. Moen, *The Transformation of the Christian Right* (Tuscaloosa: University of Alabama Press, 1992), 22–23; Hertzke, *Echoes of Discontent*, 119–20, 144–45; Oldfield, *The Right and the Righteous*, chapters 4–5.

30 Moen, *The Transformation of the Christian Right*, 27–28.

31 Robert Booth Fowler et al., *Religion and Politics in America: Faith, Culture, and Strategic Choices*, 2d ed. (Boulder: Westview, 1999), 145–48, 152–53; Wilcox, *Onward Christian Soldiers*, chapters 2–3; Oldfield, *The Right and the Righteous*, chapter 6.

32 Other Christian Right organizations include Concerned Women for America, Focus on the Family, the Traditional Values Coalition, and the American Family Association.

33 John C. Green et al., "Evangelical Realignment: The Political Power of the Christian Right," *Christian Century* 112 (1995): 676–79; Oldfield, *The Right and the Righteous*, chapters 5–6. The Christian Coalition has suffered some organizational setbacks since 1995, especially since Reed left the group. See Wilcox, *Onward Christian Soldiers*, 44–45, 63.

34 Oldfield, *The Right and the Righteous*, chapter 6.

35 John C. Green, "The Christian Right and the 1994 Elections: A View from the States," *Political Science and Politics* 28 (1995): 6.

36 Ibid., 5.

37 Douglas A. Blackmon, "For Heaven's Sake: Racial Reconciliation Becomes a Priority for the Religious Right," *Wall Street Journal*, 23 June 1997, A1, A8.

38 Of course, mainstream environmental organizations like the Sierra Club and the Audubon Society

maintain state and local chapters as well as national offices. However, these locally based affiliates are relatively autonomous.

39 Mark Dowie, *Losing Ground: American Environmentalism at the Close of the Twentieth Century* (Cambridge: MIT Press, 1995), 105, chapter 6; Paul Lichterman, *The Search for Political Community: American Activists Reinventing Commitment* (Cambridge: Cambridge University Press, 1996), 136–138; Sherry Cable and Charles Cable, *Environmental Problems, Grassroots Solutions: The Politics of Grassroots Environmental Conflict* (New York: St. Martin's, 1995), 70–75, 103–8; Jim Schwab, *Deeper Shades of Green: The Rise of Blue-Collar and Minority Environmentalism in America* (San Francisco: Sierra Club, 1994), 54–55, 385–93; Philip D. Brick and R. McGreggor Cawley, "Knowing the Wolf, Tending the Garden," in *A Wolf in the Garden: The Land Rights Movement and the New Environmental Debate*, ed. Philip D. Brick and R. McGreggor Cawley (Lanham, Md.: Rowman and Littlefield, 1996), 5.

40 David Vogel, "The 'New' Social Regulation in Historical and Comparative Perspective," in *Regulation in Perspective: Historical Essays*, ed. Thomas K. McCraw (Cambridge: Harvard University Press, 1981), 169–75.

41 Dowie, *Losing Ground*, chapters 2–3.

42 Ibid., ix; Ron Arnold, "Overcoming Ideology," in *A Wolf in the Garden*, 25.

43 "Environmental Groups: As Green Turns Brown," *Economist*, 5 March 1994, 27–28; Keith Schneider, "Big Environment Hits the Recession," *New York Times*, 1 January 1995, F4; Dowie, *Losing Ground*, 175–76.

44 Kenneth A. Gould et al., *Local Environmental Struggles: Citizen Activism in the Treadmill of Production* (Cambridge: Cambridge University Press, 1996).

45 Brick and Cawley, "Knowing the Wolf, Tending the Garden," 4–10; Kirk Emerson, "Taking the Land Rights Movement Seriously," in *Wolf in the Garden*; Dowie, *Losing Ground*, chapter 4; James Risen, "Conservative Land-Use Groups Gain in Vote," *New York Times*, 31 January 2001.

46 Dowie, *Losing Ground*, 133, 208, 220, 251–54; Schwab, *Deeper Shades of Green*, xv, 390–92, 412–13; Lichterman, *The Search for Political Community*, 26–27.

47 Dowie, *Losing Ground*, 130–31, 140–55; Robert D. Bullard, *Dumping in Dixie: Race, Class, and Environmental Quality* (Boulder: Westview, 1990), chapter 1; Penina M. Glazer and Myron P. Glazer, *The Environmental Crusaders: Confronting Disaster and Mobilizing Community* (University Park: Pennsylvania State University Press, 1998); Schwab, *Deeper Shades of Green*; Cable and Cable, *Environmental Problems*, 106.

48 For local environmental campaigns, see Schwab, *Deeper Shades of Green*, chapters 1–9; Bullard, *Dumping in Dixie*, chapter 3; Gould et al., *Local Environmental Struggles*, chapters 2–4; Cable and Cable, *Environmental Problems*, 96–102; Glazer and Glazer, *The Environmental Crusaders*, chapters 2–5.

49 Betty Zisk, *The Politics of Transformation: Local Activism in the Peace and Environmental Movements* (Westport, Conn.: Praeger, 1992), 16. In a similar vein, Gould et al. point out that autonomous local environmental groups are sometimes in direct conflict with each other. See their *Local Environmental Struggles*, 202–3.

50 Dowie, *Losing Ground*, 125–40; Cable and Cable, *Environmental Problems*, 108–12.

51 Indeed, the name "Western Bloc" referred to the geographical bloc of eighteen western states where state constitutions allow voters to enact laws by the initiative. For the Western Bloc, see Laura Tallian, *Direct Democracy: An Historical Analysis of the Initiative, Referendum and Recall Process* (Los Angeles: People Lobby's, 1977), chapter 13; David D. Schmidt, *Citizen Lawmakers: The Ballot Initiative Revolution* (Philadelphia: Temple University Press, 1989), 64–73.

52 Patricia A. Wood, "The Environmental Movement: Its Crystallization, Development, and Impact,"

in *Social Movements: Development, Participation, and Dynamics*, ed. James L. Wood and Maurice Jackson (Belmont, Calif.: Wadsworth, 1982), 211–12.

53 The People's Lobby, one of the primary architects of the Western Bloc, offers this advice in a chapter entitled "For States Not Having Direct Legislation," in Tallian's *Direct Democracy*.

54 Fairclough, *To Redeem the Soul of America*, 136; Garrow, *Bearing the Cross*, 275–76.

55 Ernest H. Cherrington, *Anti-Saloon Yearbook, 1909* (Columbus: Anti-Saloon League of America, 1909), 171, 176–77.

56 Oldfield, *The Right and the Righteous*, chapter 6.

57 Cable and Cable, *Environmental Problems*, 121.

58 As Zisk's recent study demonstrates, over one third of local green groups (in a sample of seven metropolitan areas) rely on both hierarchical structures and majoritarian processes of decision making; in addition, a majority uses conventional tactics like lobbying, litigation, and electoral activities. See her *The Politics of Transformation*, chapters 4–8.

59 Local environmental groups which employ consensual (or near consensual) decision making include the local committees of the U.S. Greens, anti-nuclear power groups, affiliates of Earth First, and some local chapters of mainstream environmental organizations (e.g., Greenpeace and the Sierra Club). In contrast, larger, more professionalized groups (e.g., the local affiliates of national organizations) usually operate by majority vote, though many claim to seek widespread support before a vote is taken. See ibid., chapter 5; Dowie, *Losing Ground*, 154; Lichterman, *The Search for Political Community*, chapter 2. For the use of disruptive protest by grassroots Greens, see Lichterman, *The Search for Political Community*, 195–99; Cable and Cable, *Environmental Problems*, 108; Zisk, *The Politics of Transformation*, chapter 8; Dowie, *Losing Ground*, 209–11.

60 Zisk, *The Politics of Transformation*, 173–74; Lichterman, *The Search for Political Community*, 203–8.

61 Dowie, *Losing Ground*, 140–57, 168–73, 219–21, 230–31, 233–34; Schwab, *Deeper Shades of Green*, 385–92; Cable and Cable, *Environmental Problems*, 75; Lichterman, *The Search for Political Community*, 140–43.

62 Robert C. Mitchell, "Silent Spring, Solid Majorities," *Public Opinion* 2 (1979): 19–20; Ronald G. Faich and Richard Gale, "The Environmental Movement: From Recreation to Politics," *Pacific Sociological Review* 14 (1971): 270–87; Paul Mohai, "Public Concern and Elite Involvement in Environmental Issues," *Social Science Quarterly* 66 (1985): 820–38; Schwab, *Deeper Shades of Green*, 388; Dowie, *Losing Ground*, 146; Cable and Cable, *Environmental Problems*, 70, 73–74.

63 Schwab, *Deeper Shades of Green*, 389–92, 412–13; Dowie, *Losing Ground*, 146–47, 152–55, 168.

64 Dowie, *Losing Ground*, 6.

65 Cable and Cable, *Environmental Problems*, 107; Schwab, *Deeper Shades of Green*, chapters 1–9; Dowie, *Losing Ground*, 126–40.

66 Gould et al., *Local Environmental Struggles*, 195–99.

67 Jack S. Blocker, *Retreat from Reform: The Prohibition Movement in the United States, 1890–1913* (Westport, Conn.: Greenwood, 1976).

68 Jack S. Blocker, "The Modernity of Prohibitionists: An Analysis of Leadership Structure and Background," in *Alcohol, Reform and Society: The Liquor Issue in Social Context*, ed. Jack S. Blocker (Westport, Conn.: Greenwood, 1979), 158–62; Howard H. Russell, "The Anti-Saloon League Movement," 3–4, unpublished manuscript, box 1, Howard Hyde Russell Papers, 3–4; Norman Dohn, "The History of the Anti-Saloon League" (Ph.D. diss., Ohio State University, 1959), chapter 2; Earl C. Kaylor, "The Prohibition Movement in Pennsylvania" (Ph.D. diss., Pennsylvania State University, 1963), chapter 10; "A Hoary-Headed Old Falsehood," *American Issue*, 27 September 1901, 4.

69 "A Hoary-Headed Old Falsehood," *American Issue*, 27 September 1901, 3–4; Howard H. Russell, "Our

League, God's Plan," 11, unpublished manuscript, box 1, Howard Hyde Russell Papers; Not Radical Enough—Too Radical," *American Issue*, 7 January 1901, 4; Kaylor, "The Prohibition Movement in Pennsylvania," 310–24; Dohn, "The History of the Anti-Saloon League," chapter 2. For the growth of local interdenominational cooperation during the late nineteenth century, see Robert T. Handy, *A Christian America: Protestant Hopes and Historical Realities* (New York: Oxford University Press, 1971), 170–71; Samuel M. Cavert, *Church Cooperation and Unity in America: A Historical Review, 1900–1970* (New York: Association, 1970), 257–59.

70 James F. Findlay, Jr., *Church People in the Struggle: The National Council of Churches and the Black Freedom Movement, 1950–1970* (New York: Oxford University Press, 1993); Wilcox, *Onward Christian Soldiers*, 45–57, chapter 5.

71 Wilcox, *Onward Christian Soldiers*, 44, 143.

Selected Bibliography

In addition to the materials listed here, two major sources include the microfilm edition of the Temperance and Prohibition Papers and the Howard Hyde Russell Papers at the Bentley Historical Library, University of Michigan. For a fuller accounting of the sources consulted, see the endnotes.

Newspapers, Journals, and Yearbooks

The American Issue (1900–1920)

The American Prohibition Yearbook (1907–15)

Anti-Saloon (1894–95)

The Anti-Saloon Yearbook (1908–20)

The Boston Globe (various years, 1900–1915)

The Century Magazine (various years)

The Chautauquan (1880–90)

The Chicago Tribune (various years)

The Christian Advocate (1880–90)

The Christian Union (1880–90)

The Detroit Free Press (various years)

The International Good Templar (1889–95)

Journal of Humanity and Herald of the American Temperance Society (1831)

Law and Order (1884–85)

The Nashville Union (1837–58; name varies)

The Nation (1880–95)

The National Temperance Advocate (1880–95)

The New York Times (various years)

The Union Signal (1882–1920)

The Voice (various years)

The Yearbook of the United States Brewers' Association (1909–19)

Proceedings

Independent Order of the Good Templars, Right Worthy Grand Lodge Proceedings (1860–94)

International Supreme Lodge Journals (1894–1920)

Journal of the Convention of the State of Pennsylvania to Propose Amendments to the Constitution. 2 vols. Harrisburg: Thompson and Clark, 1837.

Journal of the Proceedings of the Grand Division of the Sons of Temperance of North America (1844–1920)

Proceedings of the Annual Meetings of the Citizens' Law and Order League of Massachusetts (1883–91)

Proceedings of the National Temperance Congress Held in the Broadway Tabernacle, New York, Wednesday and Thursday, June 11th and 12th, 1890. New York: Funk and Wagnalls, 1891.

Proceedings, National Conventions of the Anti-Saloon League of America (1896–1921; title varies)

Proceedings of the Ninth National Temperance Convention Held at Saratoga Springs, N.Y., June 21 and 22, 1882. New York: National Temperance Society and Publishing House, 1881.

Proceedings of the Sixth Annual Meeting of the Citizens' Law and Order League of the United States (1888)

Reports of the American Temperance Union (1837–51)

Report of the Debates and Proceedings of the Convention for the Revision of the Constitution of the State of Ohio, 1850–1851. 2 vols. Columbus: Scott and Bronson, 1851.

Report of the Proceedings and Debates in the Convention to Revise the Constitution of the State of Michigan, 1850. Lansing: R. W. Ingals, 1850.

Books and Pamphlets

Abrams, Richard. *Conservatism in the Progressive Era: Massachusetts Politics, 1900–1912.* Cambridge: Harvard University Press, 1964.

Anbinder, Tyler. *Nativism and Slavery: The Northern Know Nothings and the Politics of the 1850s.* New York: Oxford University Press, 1992.

Ashenhurst, John J. *Recollections of an Octogenarian.* Bowie, Md.: Heritage, 1990.

Bader, Robert S. *Prohibition in Kansas: A History.* Lawrence: University Press of Kansas, 1986.

Bailey, Thomas J. *Prohibition in Mississippi, or Anti-Liquor Legislation from Territorial Days, with Its Results in the Counties.* Jackson, 1917.

Banaszak, Lee Ann. *Why Movements Succeed or Fail: Opportunity, Culture, and the Struggle for Woman Suffrage.* Princeton, N.J.: Princeton University Press, 1996.

Barnes, Gilbert H. *The Anti-Slavery Impulse, 1830–1844.* New York: D. Appleton-Century, 1933.

Barnes, Gilbert H., and Dwight L. Dumond, eds. *Letters of Theodore Dwight Weld, Angelina Grimké Weld, and Sarah Grimké, 1822–1844.* Gloucester, Mass.: Peter Smith, 1965.

Barr, Alwyn. *Reconstruction to Reform: Texas Politics, 1876–1906.* Austin: University of Texas Press, 1971.

Bechtel, H. Kenneth. *State Police in the United States: A Socio-Historical Analysis.* Westport, Conn.: Greenwood, 1995.

Beck, Warren A. *New Mexico: A History of Four Centuries.* Norman: University of Oklahoma Press, 1962.

Beman, Lamar T., ed. *Selected Articles on Prohibition of the Liquor Traffic.* White Plains, N.Y.: H. W. Wilson, 1917.

Bergeron, Paul H. *Antebellum Politics in Tennessee.* Lexington: University Press of Kentucky, 1982.

Berman, David R. *Reformers, Corporations, and the Electorate: An Analysis of Arizona's Age of Reform.* Niwot: University Press of Colorado, 1992.

Blair, Henry W. *The Temperance Movement; or, The Conflict between Alcohol and Man.* Boston: William Smythe, 1888.

Bland, Joan. *Hibernian Crusade: The Story of the Catholic Total Abstinence Union of America.* Washington: Catholic University Press, 1951.

Blocker, Jack S. *Retreat from Reform: The Prohibition Movement in the United States, 1890–1913.* Westport, Conn.: Greenwood, 1976.

——. *"Give to the Winds Thy Fears": The Women's Temperance Crusade, 1873–1874.* Westport, Conn.: Greenwood, 1985.

——. *American Temperance Movements: Cycles of Reform.* Boston: Twayne, 1989.

Blocker, Jack S., ed. *Alcohol, Reform and Society: The Liquor Issue in Social Context.* Westport, Conn.: Greenwood, 1979.

Blue, Frederick J. *The Free Soilers: Third Party Politics, 1848–1854.* Urbana: University of Illinois Press, 1973.

Blumin, Stuart. *The Emergence of the Middle Class: Social Experience in the American City, 1760–1900.* Cambridge: Cambridge University Press, 1989.

Bordin, Ruth. *Woman and Temperance: The Quest for Power and Liberty, 1873–1900.* Philadelphia: Temple University Press, 1981.

——. *Frances Willard: A Biography.* Chapel Hill: University of North Carolina Press, 1986.

Branning, Rosalind L. *Pennsylvania Constitutional Development.* Pittsburgh: University of Pittsburgh Press, 1960.

Brick, Philip D., and R. McGreggor Cawley, eds. *A Wolf in the Garden: The Land Rights Movement and the New Environmental Debate.* Lanham, Md.: Rowman and Littlefield, 1996.

Browning, Rufus P., et al. *Protest Is Not Enough: The Struggle of Blacks and Hispanics for Equality in Urban Politics.* Berkeley: University of California Press, 1984.

Branch, Taylor. *Parting the Waters: America in the King Years, 1954–63.* New York: Simon and Schuster, 1988.

Bryce, James. *The American Commonwealth.* 3d edition. 2 vols. New York: Macmillan, 1910.

Brye, David L. *Wisconsin Voting Patterns in the Twentieth Century, 1900 to 1950.* New York: Garland, 1979.

Buck, Solon J. *The Granger Movement: A Study of Agricultural Organization and Its Political, Economic, and Social Manifestations, 1870–1880.* Lincoln: University of Nebraska Press, 1963.

Bullard, Robert D. *Dumping in Dixie: Race, Class, and Environmental Quality.* Boulder: Westview, 1990.

Burnham, Walter D. *Critical Elections and the Mainsprings of American Politics.* New York: W. W. Norton, 1970.

——. *The Current Crisis in American Politics.* Oxford: Oxford University Press, 1982.

Burton, Robert E. *Democrats of Oregon: The Pattern of Minority Politics, 1900–1956.* Eugene: University of Oregon, 1970.

Byrne, Frank L. *Prophet of Prohibition: Neal Dow and His Crusade.* Madison: State Historical Society of Wisconsin, 1961.

Cable, Sherry, and Charles Cable. *Environmental Problems, Grassroots Solutions: The Politics of Grassroots Environmental Conflict.* New York: St. Martin's, 1995.

Centennial Temperance Volume: A Memorial of the International Temperance Conference, Held in June, 1876. New York: National Temperance Society and Publication House, 1877.

Chalfant, Harry M. *Father Penn and John Barleycorn.* Harrisburg: Evangelical, 1920.

Chapin, Clara C., ed. *Thumb Nail Sketches of White Ribbon Women.* Chicago: Woman's Temperance Publishing Association, 1895.

Cherny, Robert W. *Populism, Progressivism, and the Transformation of Nebraska Politics, 1885–1915.* Lincoln: University of Nebraska Press, 1981.

Cherrington, Ernest H. *The History of the Anti-Saloon League.* Westerville, Ohio: American Issue, 1913.

——. *The Evolution of Prohibition in the United States of America.* Westerville, Ohio: American Issue, 1920.

——. *Standard Encyclopedia of the Alcohol Problem.* 6 vols. Westerville, Ohio: American Issue, 1924–30.

Chrislock, Carl H. *The Progressive Era in Minnesota, 1899–1918.* St. Paul: Minnesota Historical Society, 1971.

Citizens' No-License Committee. *Ten No-License Years in Cambridge.* Cambridge, Mass.: Citizen's Committee, 1898.

Clark, George F. *History of the Temperance Reform in Massachusetts.* Boston: Clarke and Carruth, 1888.

Clark, Norman H. *The Dry Years: Prohibition and Social Change in Washington.* Rev. ed. Seattle: University of Washington Press, 1988.

Clemens, Elisabeth. *The People's Lobby: Organizational Innovation and the Rise of Interest Group Politics in the United States, 1890–1925.* Chicago: University of Chicago Press, 1997.

Colvin, D. Leigh. *Prohibition in the United States: A History of the Prohibition Party and the Prohibition Movement.* New York: George H. Doran, 1926.

Cometti, Elizabeth, and Festus P. Summers, ed. *The Thirty-Fifth State: A Documentary History of West Virginia.* Morgantown: West Virginia University Library, 1966.

Cook, Robert. *Baptism of Fire: The Republican Party in Iowa, 1838–1878.* Ames: Iowa State University Press, 1994.

Cooley, Thomas M. *A Treatise on the Constitutional Limitations which Rest Upon the Legislative Power of the States of the American Union.* 5th ed. Boston: Little, Brown, 1883.

Costain, Anne N. *Inviting Women's Rebellion: A Political Process Interpretation of the Women's Movement.* Baltimore: Johns Hopkins University Press, 1992.

Cramer, Cora, ed. *History, Pennsylvania Woman's Christian Temperance Union.* Quincy, Pa.: Quincy Orphanage, 1937.

Cronin, Thomas E. *Direct Democracy: The Politics of Initiative, Referendum, and Recall.* Cambridge: Harvard University Press, 1989.

Cross, Whitney. *The Burned-Over District: The Society and Intellectual History of Enthusiastic Religion in Western New York, 1800–1850.* Ithaca, N.Y.: Cornell University Press, 1950.

Cyclopedia of Temperance and Prohibition. New York: Funk and Wagnalls, 1891.

Dannenbaum, Jed. *Drink and Disorder: Temperance Reform in Cincinnati from the Washingtonian Revival to the WCTU.* Urbana: University of Illinois Press, 1984.

Dealey, James Q. *Growth of American State Constitutions.* Boston: Ginn, 1915.

Detjen, David W. *The Germans in Missouri, 1900–1918: Prohibition, Neutrality, and Assimilation.* Columbia: University of Missouri Press, 1985.

Dillon, John F. *Commentaries on the Law of Municipal Corporations.* 3d ed. 2 vols. Boston: Little, Brown, 1881.

Dodd, Walter F. *The Revision and Amendment of State Constitutions.* Baltimore: Johns Hopkins University Press, 1910.

Dorchester, Daniel. *The Liquor Problem in All Ages.* New York: Phillips and Hunt, 1888.

Dorn, Jacob H. *Washington Gladden: Prophet of the Social Gospel.* Columbus: Ohio State University Press, 1966.

Dow, Neal. *The Reminiscences of Neal Dow: Recollections of Eighty Years.* Portland, Maine: Evening Express, 1898.

Dowie, Mark. *Losing Ground: American Environmentalism at the Close of the Twentieth Century.* Cambridge: MIT Press, 1996.

Downing, Sybil, and Robert E. Smith. *Tom Patterson: Colorado Crusader for Change.* Niwot: University Press of Colorado, 1995.

Drescher, Seymour. *Capitalism and Antislavery: British Mobilization in Comparative Perspective.* New York: Oxford University Press, 1987.

Duis, Perry R. *Public Drinking in Chicago and Boston: 1880–1920.* Urbana: University of Illinois Press, 1983.

Earhart, Mary. *Frances Willard: From Prayers to Politics.* Chicago: University of Chicago Press, 1944.

Eliasoph, Nina. *Avoiding Politics: How Americans Produce Apathy in Everyday Life.* Cambridge: Cambridge University Press, 1998.

Engelmann, Larry D. *Intemperance: The Lost War against Liquor.* New York: Free Press, 1979.

Epstein, Barbara L. *The Politics of Domesticity: Women, Evangelism, and Temperance in Nineteenth-Century America.* Middletown, Conn.: Wesleyan University Press, 1981.

Evans, Sara M., and Harry C. Boyte. *Free Spaces: The Sources of Democratic Change in America.* Chicago: University of Chicago Press, 1992.

Ezell, John S. *Fortune's Merry Wheel: The Lottery in America.* Cambridge: Harvard University Press, 1960.

Fahey, David M. *Temperance and Racism: John Bull, Johnny Reb, and the Good Templars.* Lexington: University Press of Kentucky, 1996.

——. *The Black Lodge in White America: "True Reformer" Browne and His Economic Strategy.* Dayton: Wright University Press, 1994.

Fairclough, Adam. *To Redeem the Soul of America: The Southern Christian Leadership Conference and Martin Luther King, Jr.* Athens: University of Georgia Press, 1991.

Fehlandt, August F. *A Century of Drink Reform in the United States.* Cincinnati: Jennings and Graham, 1904.

Finch, Frances B., and Frank J. Sibley. *John B. Finch, His Life and Work.* New York: Funk and Wagnalls, 1888.

Finch, John B. *Prohibition: Constitutional and Statutory.* New York: National Temperance Society and Publishing House, 1889.

Foner, Eric. *Free Soil, Free Labor, Free Men: The Ideology of the Republican Party before the Civil War.* New York: Oxford University Press, 1970.

Forsyth, Jessie. *The Collected Writings of Jessie Forsyth, 1847–1937: The Good Templars and Temperance Reform on Three Continents.* Ed. David M. Fahey. Lewiston, N.Y.: Edwin Mellen, 1988.

Foster, J. Ellen. *Constitutional Amendment Manual, Containing Argument, Appeal, Petitions, Forms of Constitutions and General Directions for Organized Work for Constitutional Prohibition.* New York: National Temperance Society and Publishing House, 1882.

Fowler, Robert B., et al. *Religion and Politics in America: Faith, Culture, and Strategic Choices.* 2d ed. Boulder: Westview, 1999.

Franklin, Jimmie L. *Born Sober: Prohibition in Oklahoma, 1907–1959.* Norman: University of Oklahoma Press, 1971.

Freeman, Jo, and Victoria Johnson, eds. *Waves of Protest: Social Movements since the Sixties.* Lanham, Md.: Rowman and Littlefield, 1999.

Friedman, Lawrence M. *A History of American Law.* New York: Simon and Schuster, 1973.

Gamson, William. *The Strategy of Social Protest.* Belmont, Calif.: Wadsworth, 1990.

Garrow, David J. *Bearing the Cross: Martin Luther King, Jr., and the Southern Christian Leadership Conference.* New York: William Morrow, 1986.

Gibbs, Joseph C. *History of the Catholic Total Abstinence Union of America.* Philadelphia, 1907.

Giele, Janet Z. *Two Paths to Women's Equality: Temperance, Suffrage, and the Origins of Modern Feminism.* New York: Twayne, 1995.

Gienapp, William E. *The Origins of the Republican Party, 1852–1856.* New York: Oxford University Press, 1987.

Gilkeson, John S. *Middle Class Providence, 1820–1940.* Princeton, N.J.: Princeton University Press, 1986.

Gladden, Washington. *Applied Christianity: Moral Aspects of Social Questions.* New York: Houghton Mifflin, 1886.

——. *Moral Gains and Losses of the Temperance Reformation.* Charlottesville, Va.: Progress, 1895.

——. *Social Salvation.* New York: Houghton Mifflin, 1902.

——. *Recollections.* Boston: Houghton Mifflin, 1909.

Glashan, Roy. *American Governors and Gubernatorial Elections, 1775–1975*. Stillwater, Minn.: Croxside, 1975.

Glazer, Penina M., and Myron P. Glazer. *The Environmental Crusaders: Confronting Disaster and Mobilizing Community*. University Park: Pennsylvania State University Press, 1998.

Gould, Kenneth A., et al. *Local Environmental Struggles: Citizen Activism in the Treadmill of Production*. Cambridge: Cambridge University Press, 1996.

Gould, Lewis L. *Progressives and Prohibitionists: Texas Democrats in the Wilson Era*. Austin: University of Texas Press, 1973.

Graham, Frances, and Gorgeanna M. Gardenier. *Two Decades: A History of the First Twenty Years' Work of the Woman's Christian Temperance Union of the State of New York*. Oswego, N.Y.: R. J. Oliphant, 1894.

Grantham, Dewey W. *Hoke Smith and the Politics of the New South*. Baton Rouge: Louisiana State Press, 1958.

——. *Southern Progressivism: The Reconciliation of Progress and Tradition*. Knoxville: University of Tennessee Press, 1983.

Gusfield, Joseph R. *Symbolic Crusade: Status Politics and the American Temperance Movement*. Urbana: University of Illinois Press, 1963.

Hamm, Richard F. *Shaping the Eighteenth Amendment: Temperance Reform, Legal Culture, and the Polity, 1880–1920*. Chapel Hill: University of North Carolina Press, 1995.

Hammell, George M., ed. *The Passing of the Saloon*. Cincinnati: Tower, 1908.

Hampel, Robert L. *Temperance and Prohibition in Massachusetts, 1813–1852*. Ann Arbor: UMI Research Press, 1982.

Handy, Robert T. *A Christian America: Protestant Hopes and Historical Realities*. New York: Oxford University Press, 1971.

Hardesty, Nancy A. *Women Called to Witness: Evangelical Feminism in the 19th Century*. Nashville: Abingdon, 1984.

Hennessy, Michael E. *Four Decades of Massachusetts Politics, 1890–1935*. Freeport, N.Y.: Books for Libraries, 1971.

Hertzke, Allen D. *Echoes of Discontent: Jesse Jackson, Pat Robertson, and the Resurgence of Populism*. Washington: Congressional Quarterly, 1993.

Hichborn, Franklin. *Story of the Session of the California Legislature of 1909*. San Francisco: James H. Barry, 1909.

——. *Story of the Session of the California Legislature of 1911*. San Francisco: James H. Barry, 1911.

——. *Story of the Session of the California Legislature of 1913*. San Francisco: James H. Barry, 1913.

Hoar, George F. *The Constitutional Remedy*. New York: National Temperance Society and Publishing House, 1889.

Hoehn, William F. *No-License in Quincy*. Quincy, Mass., 1899.

Holt, Michael F. *The Political Crisis of the 1850s*. New York: John Wiley and Sons, 1978.

Hopkins, Alphonso A. *Wealth and Waste: The Principles of Political Economy in their Application to the Present Problems of Labor, Law, and the Liquor Traffic*. New York: Funk and Wagnalls, 1895.

——. *Profit and Loss in Man*. New York: Funk and Wagnalls, 1909.

Hu, Tun Huan. *The Liquor Tax in the United States, 1791–1947: A History of the Internal Revenue Taxes Imposed on Distilled Spirits by the Federal Government*. New York: Columbia Graduate School of Business, 1950.

Isaac, Paul E. *Prohibition and Politics: Turbulent Decades in Tennessee, 1885–1920*. Knoxville: University of Tennessee Press, 1965.

Ivy, H. A. *Rum on the Run in Texas: A Brief History of Prohibition in the Lone Star State*. Dallas: Temperance, 1910.

Jensen, Richard. *The Winning of the Midwest: Social and Political Conflict, 1888–1896*. Chicago: University of Chicago Press, 1971.

Johnson, Paul E. *A Shopkeeper's Millennium: Society and Revivals in Rochester, New York, 1815–1937*. New York: Hill and Wang, 1978.

Kallenbach, Joseph E., and Jessamine S. Kallenbach. *American State Governors, 1776–1976.* 3 vols. Dobbs Ferry, N.Y.: Oceana, 1977.

Katznelson, Ira. *City Trenches: Urban Politics and the Patterning of Class in the United States.* New York: Pantheon, 1981.

Kerr, K. Austin. *Organized for Prohibition: A New History of the Anti-Saloon League.* New Haven: Yale University Press, 1985.

Kettleborough, Charles. *Constitution Making in Indiana.* Indianapolis: Indiana Historical Commission, 1916.

King, Martin Luther. *Stride toward Freedom: The Montgomery Story.* New York: Harper and Brothers, 1958.

Kleppner, Paul. *The Third Electoral System, 1853–1892: Parties, Voters, and Political Cultures.* Chapel Hill: University of North Carolina Press, 1979.

——. *Who Voted? The Dynamics of Electoral Turnout, 1870–1980.* New York: Praeger, 1982.

——. *Continuity and Change in Electoral Politics, 1893–1928.* New York: Greenwood, 1987.

Knudten, Richard D. *The Systematic Thought of Washington Gladden.* New York: Humanities, 1968.

Kousser, J. Morgan. *The Shaping of Southern Politics: Suffrage Restrictions and the One-Party South.* New Haven: Yale University Press, 1974.

Kraditor, Aileen S. *Means and Ends in American Abolitionism: Garrison and His Critics on Strategy and Tactics, 1834–1850.* New York: Vintage, 1969.

Kriebel, Robert C. *Where Saints Have Trod: The Life of Helen Gougar.* West Lafayette, Ind.: Purdue University Press, 1985.

Kriesi, Hanspieter, et al. *New Social Movements in Western Europe: A Comparative Analysis.* Minneapolis: University of Minnesota Press, 1995.

Krout, John A. *The Origins of Prohibition.* New York: Alfred A. Knopf, 1925.

Kruman, Marc W. *Parties and Politics in North Carolina, 1836–1865.* Baton Rouge: Louisiana State University Press, 1983.

Lees, F. R. *Textbook of Temperance.* Rockland, Maine: Z. Pope Vose, 1869.

Lender, Mark E. *Dictionary of American Temperance Biography.* Westport, Conn.: Greenwood, 1984.

—— and James K. Martin. *Drinking in America: A History.* New York: Free Press, 1982.

Lichterman, Paul. *The Search for Political Community: American Activists Reinventing Commitment.* Cambridge: Cambridge University Press, 1996.

Link, William A. *The Paradox of Southern Progressivism, 1880–1930.* Chapel Hill: University of North Carolina Press, 1992.

Ludlum, David M. *Social Ferment in Vermont, 1791–1850.* Montpelier: Vermont Historical Society, 1948.

Luebke, Frederick C. *Immigrants and Politics: The Germans of Nebraska, 1880–1900.* Lincoln: University of Nebraska Press, 1969.

Magdol, Edward. *The Antislavery Rank and File: A Social Profile of the Abolitionists' Constituency.* Westport, Conn.: Greenwood, 1986.

Magleby, David. *Direct Legislation: Voting on Ballot Propositions in the United States.* Baltimore: Johns Hopkins University Press, 1984.

Maizlish, Stephen E. *The Triumph of Sectionalism: The Transformation of Ohio Politics, 1844–1856.* Kent, Ohio: Kent State University Press, 1983.

Mansbridge, Jane. *Why We Lost the ERA.* Chicago: University of Chicago Press, 1986.

Margulies, Herbert F. *The Decline of the Progressive Movement in Wisconsin, 1890–1920.* Madison: State Historical Society of Wisconsin, 1968.

Marilley, Suzanne M. *Woman Suffrage and the Origins of Liberal Feminism in the United States, 1820–1920.* Cambridge: Harvard University Press, 1996.

Marsh, John. *Temperance Recollections, Labors, Defeats, Triumphs: An Autobiography*. New York: Charles Scribner, 1867.

Maxwell, Robert S. *Emanuel Philipp: Wisconsin Stalwart*. Madison: State Historical Society of Wisconsin, 1959.

May, Henry F. *Protestant Churches and Industrial America*. New York: Harper and Brothers, 1949.

McAdam, Doug. *Political Process and the Development of Black Insurgency*. Chicago: University of Chicago Press, 1982.

——. *Freedom Summer*. New York: Oxford University Press, 1988.

McBride, Genevieve G. *On Wisconsin Women: Working for Their Rights from Settlement to Suffrage*. Madison: University of Wisconsin Press, 1993.

McCarthy, John D. and Mayer N. Zald. *Social Movements in an Organizational Society: Collected Essays*. New Brunswick, N.J.: Transaction, 1987.

McCormick, Richard L. *The Party Period and Public Policy: American Politics from the Age of Jackson to the Progressive Era*. New York: Oxford University Press, 1986.

Mertz, Charles. *The Dry Decade*. Garden City, N.Y.: Doubleday, Doran, 1931.

Miller, William L. *Arguing about Slavery: The Great Battle in the United States Congress*. New York: Alfred A. Knopf, 1996.

Moen, Matthew C. *The Christian Right and Congress*. Tuscaloosa: University of Alabama Press, 1989.

——. *The Transformation of the Christian Right*. Tuscaloosa: University of Alabama Press, 1992.

Mohr, James C., ed. *Radical Republicans in the North: State Politics during Reconstruction*. Baltimore: Johns Hopkins University Press, 1976.

Mowry, George E. *The Era of Theodore Roosevelt and the Birth of Modern America, 1900–1912*. New York: Harper and Row, 1958.

——. *The California Progressives*. Chicago: Quadrangle, 1963.

Niswonger, Richard L. *Arkansas Democratic Politics, 1896–1920*. Fayetteville: University of Arkansas Press, 1990.

Novak, William J. *The People's Welfare: Law and Regulation in Nineteenth-Century America*. Chapel Hill: University of North Carolina Press, 1996.

Nye, Russel B. *Midwestern Progressive Politics: A Historical Study of Its Origins and Development, 1870–1950*. East Lansing: Michigan State College Press, 1951.

Oberholtzer, Ellis P. *The Referendum in America*. New York: Charles Scribner's Sons, 1912.

Odegard, Peter H. *Pressure Politics: The Story of the Anti-Saloon League*. New York: Columbia University Press, 1928.

Oldfield, Duane M. *The Right and the Righteous: The Christian Right Confronts the Republican Party*. Lanham, Md.: Rowman and Littlefield, 1996.

Olin, Spencer C. *California's Prodigal Sons: Hiram Johnson and the Progressives, 1911–1917*. Berkeley: University of California Press, 1968.

Ostler, Jeffrey. *Prairie Populism: The Fate of Agrarian Radicalism in Kansas, Nebraska, and Iowa, 1880–1892*. Lawrence: University Press of Kansas, 1993.

Overdyke, W. Darrell. *The Know-Nothing Party in the South*. Baton Rouge: Louisiana State University Press, 1950.

Parker, Alison M. *Purifying America: Women, Cultural Reform, and Pro-Censorship Activism, 1873–1933*. Urbana: University of Illinois Press, 1997.

Parker, Thomas F. *History of the Independent Order of Good Templars from the Origin of the Order to the Session of the Right Worthy Grand Lodge of 1887*. New York: Phillips and Hunt, 1887.

Pearson, C. C., and J. Edwin Hendricks. *Liquor and Anti-Liquor in Virginia, 1619–1919.* Durham: Duke University Press, 1967.

Pegram, Thomas R. *Partisans and Progressives: Private Interest and Public Policy in Illinois, 1870–1922.* Urbana: University of Illinois Press, 1992.

——. *Battling the Demon Rum: The Struggle for a Dry America, 1800–1933.* Chicago: Ivan R. Dee, 1998.

Peirce, Isaac N. *The History of the Independent Order of Good Templars.* Philadelphia: Daughaday and Becker, 1869.

Petersen, Svend. *A Statistical History of the American Presidential Elections.* New York: Frederick Unger, 1963.

Phillips, Clifton J. *Indiana in Transition: The Emergence of an Industrial Commonwealth, 1880–1920.* Indianapolis: Indiana Historical Society, 1968.

Pierce, P. R. L. *A History of the Order of the Sons of Temperance in Ohio.* Cincinnati: George M. Young, 1849.

Pitman, Robert C. *Alcohol and the State.* New York: National Temperance Society and Publishing House, 1877.

Piven, Frances Fox, and Richard A. Cloward. *Poor People's Movements: Why They Succeed and How They Fail.* New York: Vintage, 1979.

——. *Why Americans Don't Vote.* New York: Pantheon, 1988.

The Political Prohibitionist for 1888. New York: Funk and Wagnalls, 1888.

Rogin, Michael P., and John L. Shover. *Political Change in California: Critical Elections and Social Movements, 1890–1968.* Westport, Conn.: Greenwood, 1970.

Roper, William L., and Leonard J. Arrington. *William Spry: Man of Firmness, Governor of Utah.* Salt Lake City: University of Utah Press, 1971.

Rorabaugh, W. R. *The Alcoholic Republic.* New York: Oxford University Press, 1979.

Rosenberg, Gerald N. *The Hollow Hope: Can the Courts Bring about Social Change?* Chicago: University of Chicago Press, 1991.

Rosenstone, Steven J., et al. *Third Parties in America: Citizen Response to Major Party Failure.* Princeton, N.J.: Princeton University Press, 1984.

Rowntree, Joseph, and Arthur Sherwell. *The Temperance Problem and Social Reform.* New York: Truslove, Hanson and Comba, 1900.

Salisbury, Robert S. *William Windom: Apostle of Positive Government.* Lanham, Md.: University Press of America, 1993.

Sarasohn, Stephen B., and Vera H. Sarasohn. *Political Party Patterns in Michigan.* Detroit: Wayne State University Press, 1957.

Scomp, H. A. *King Alcohol in the Realm of King Cotton, or A History of the Liquor Traffic and of the Temperance Movement in Georgia from 1733 to 1887.* Chicago: Blakely, 1888.

Sellers, James B. *The Prohibition Movement in Alabama, 1702 to 1943.* Chapel Hill: University of North Carolina Press, 1943.

Sewell, Richard H. *Ballots for Freedom: Antislavery Politics in the United States, 1837–1860.* New York: Oxford University Press, 1976.

Schmidt, David D. *Citizen Lawmakers: The Ballot Initiative Revolution.* Philadelphia: Temple University Press, 1989.

Schouler, James. *Constitutional Studies, State and Federal.* New York: Dodd, Mead, 1897.

Schwab, Jim. *Deeper Shades of Green: The Rise of Blue-Collar and Minority Environmentalism in America.* San Francisco: Sierra Club, 1994.

Sinclair, Andrew. *Prohibition: The Era of Excess.* Boston: Little, Brown, 1962.

Sitton, Tom. *John Randolph Haynes: California Progressive.* Stanford: Stanford University Press, 1992.

Skocpol, Theda. *States and Social Revolutions: A Comparative Analysis of France, Russia, and China.* Princeton, N.J.: Princeton University Press, 1979.

———. *Protecting Soldiers and Mothers: The Political Origins of Social Policy in the United States*. Cambridge, Mass.: Belknap, 1992.

Smith, Theodore C. *The Liberty and Free Soil Parties in the Northwest*. New York: Longmans, Green, 1897.

Smith, W. A. *A History of the Anti-Saloon League of Illinois*. Chicago: Anti-Saloon League of Illinois, 1925.

Soper, J. Christopher. *Evangelical Christianity in the United States and Great Britain: Religious Beliefs, Political Choices*. New York: New York University Press, 1994.

Spencer, Dorcas J. *A History of the Woman's Christian Temperance Union of Northern and Central California*. Oakland: West Coast, 1889.

Stearns, J. N., ed. *The Constitutional Prohibitionist*. New York: National Temperance Society and Publishing House, 1882.

Sullivan, John L. *Official Manual of the State of Missouri for the Years 1917–1918*. Jefferson City, Mo.: Hugh Stevens, 1917.

Sundquist, James L. *Dynamics of the Party System: Alignment and Realignment of Political Parties in the United States*. Washington: Brookings Institution, 1983.

Tallian, Laura. *Direct Democracy: An Historical Analysis of the Initiative, Referendum and Recall Process*. Los Angeles: People Lobby's, 1977.

Tarr, G. Alan. *Understanding State Constitutions. Princeton: Princeton University Press, 1998.*

Tarrow, Sidney. *Power in Movement: Social Movements, Collective Action and Politics*. 2d ed. Cambridge: Cambridge University Press, 1998.

Thomas, Mary M. *The New Woman in Alabama: Social Reforms and Suffrage, 1890–1920*. Tuscaloosa: University of Alabama Press, 1992.

Thornbrough, Emma L. *Indiana in the Civil War Era, 1850–1880*. Indianapolis: Indiana Historical Society, 1965.

Tilly, Charles. *The Contentious French*. Cambridge: Harvard University Press, 1986.

———. *Popular Contention in Great Britain, 1758–1834*. Cambridge: Harvard University Press, 1995.

Timberlake, James. *Prohibition and the Progressive Movement, 1900–1920*. Cambridge: Harvard University Press, 1963.

Traugott, Mark, ed. *Repertoires and Cycles of Collective Action*. Durham: Duke University Press, 1995.

Turnbull, William W. *The Good Templars: A History of the Rise and Progress of the Independent Order of Good Templars, 1851–1901, Jubilee Volume*. Ed. James Yeames. N.p.: Independent Order of Good Templars, 1901.

Tyrrell, Ian. *Sobering Up: From Temperance to Prohibition in Antebellum America*. Westport, Conn.: Greenwood, 1979.

———. *Woman's World, Woman's Empire: The Woman's Christian Temperance Union in International Perspective, 1880–1930*. Chapel Hill: University of North Carolina Press, 1991.

Vander Meer, Philip R. *The Hoosier Politician: Officeholding and Political Culture in Indiana, 1896–1920*. Urbana: University of Illinois Press, 1985.

Walters, Ronald G. *American Reformers*. New York: Hill and Wang, 1978.

Warner, Hoyt L. *Progressivism in Ohio, 1897–1917*. Columbus: Ohio State University Press, 1964.

Watson, Harry L. *Liberty and Power: The Politics of Jacksonian America*. New York: Noonday, 1990.

Wesser, Robert F. *A Response to Progressivism: The Democratic Party and New York Politics, 1902–1918*. New York: New York University Press, 1986.

Wilcox, Clyde. *Onward Christian Soldiers? The Religious Right in American Politics*.2d ed. Boulder: Westview, 2000.

Willard, Frances E. *Woman and Temperance; or, The Work and Workers of the Woman's Christian Temperance Union*. Hartford: Park, 1884.

———. *Glimpses of Fifty Years: The Autobiography of an American Woman*. Chicago: H. J. Smith, 1889.

Wines, Frederic H., and John Koren. *The Liquor Problem in its Legislative Aspects.* Boston: Houghton Mifflin, 1897.

Woodbury, Nathan F. *Prohibition in Maine: History of Its Origin, Results, Political Nullification and Final Ratification from 1837 to 1920.* Lewiston, Maine: Journal Printshop and Bindery, 1920.

Woods, Eleanor. *Robert A. Woods: Champion of Democracy.* Freeport, N.Y.: Books for Libraries, 1929.

Woods, Robert A., ed. *The City Wilderness.* Boston: Houghton Mifflin, 1898.

——, ed. *Americans in Process.* Boston: Houghton Mifflin, 1910.

Wright, James. *The Progressive Yankees: Republican Reformers in New Hampshire, 1906–1916.* Hanover, N.H.: University Press of New England, 1987.

Zisk, Betty H. *Money, Media, and the Grassroots.* Newbury Park, Calif.: Sage, 1987.

——. *The Politics of Transformation: Local Activism in the Peace and Environmental Movements.* Westport, Conn.: Praeger, 1992.

Articles and Book Chapters

Anderson, John. "Lincoln, Nebraska, and Prohibition: The Election of May 4, 1909." *Nebraska History* 70 (1989): 184–200.

Baum, Dale. "Teetotalers Enter Politics: The Massachusetts Prohibitionist Party in the Early 1970s." *Mid-America* 65 (1983): 137–54.

Bohner, Charles H. "Rum and Reform: Temperance in Delaware Politics." *Delaware History* 5 (1953): 237–69.

Burran, James A. "Prohibition in New Mexico, 1917." *New Mexico Historical Review* 48 (1973): 133–49.

Byrne, Frank L. "Maine Law versus Lager Beer: A Dilemma of Wisconsin's Young Republican Party." *Wisconsin Magazine of History* 42 (1958–59): 115–20.

Canup, Charles E. "Temperance Movements and Legislation in Indiana." *Indiana Magazine of History* 16 (1920): 3–37, 112–51.

Carey, Anthony G. "The Second Party System Collapses: The 1853 Maine Law Campaign in Ohio." *Ohio History* 100 (1991): 129–53.

Case, George L. "The Prohibition Party: Its Origin, Purpose and Growth." *Magazine of Western History* 9 (1888–89): 115–24, 243–49, 373–79, 555–64, 705–14.

Clark, Daniel E. "The History of Liquor Legislation in Iowa, 1846–1861." *Iowa Journal of History and Politics* 6 (1908): 55–87.

——. "The History of Liquor Legislation in Iowa, 1861–1878." *Iowa Journal of History and Politics* 6 (1908): 339–74.

——. "The History of Liquor Legislation in Iowa, 1878–1908." *Iowa Journal of History and Politics* 6 (1908): 503–605.

——. "Recent Liquor Legislation in Iowa." *Iowa Journal of History and Politics* 15 (1917): 42–69.

Clifford, Deborah P. "The Women's War against Rum." *Vermont History* 52 (1984): 141–60.

Conklin, Forrest. "Parson Brownlow—Temperance Advocate, Part II." *Tennessee Historical Quarterly* 39 (1980): 292–309.

Dannenbaum, Jed. "The Origins of Temperance Activism and Militancy among American Women." *Journal of Social History* 15 (1981): 235–52.

Dodd, Jill S. "The Working Classes and the Temperance Movement in Ante-bellum Boston." *Labor History* 19 (1978): 510–31.

Dudley, L. Edwin. "The Law and Order Movement: Historical Sketch." *Lend-a-Hand*, March 1892, 193–205, 257–69.

Eisinger, Peter K. "The Conditions of Protest Behavior in American Cities." *American Political Science Review* 67 (1973): 11–28.

Engelmann, Larry D. "Billy Sunday: 'God, You've Got a Job on Your Hands in Detroit.'" *Michigan History* 55 (1971): 1–21.

———. "Dry Renaissance: The Local Option Years, 1889–1917." *Michigan History* 59 (1975): 69–90.

Fitzgibbon, John. "King Alcohol: His Rise, Reign and Fall in Michigan." *Michigan History* 2 (1918): 737–80.

Foxcroft, Frank. "Prohibition in the South." *Atlantic Monthly*, May 1908, 627–32.

Freeman, Jo. "Whom You Know versus Whom You Represent: Feminist Influence in the Democratic and Republican Parties." In *The Women's Movements of the United States and Western Europe: Consciousness, Political Opportunity, and Public Policy*. Ed. Mary F. Katzenstein and Carol M. Mueller. Philadelphia: Temple University Press, 1987.

Friedman, Lawrence M. "State Constitutions in Historical Perspective." *Annals of the American Academy of Political and Social Science* 496 (1988): 33–42.

Gladden, Washington. "Hurricane Reform." *Century Magazine*, December 1883, 316–18.

———. "Comment." *Century Magazine*, May 1884, 149–50.

———. "The Enforcement of Law." In *"Unity, Persistency, Victory!" A Souvenir Selection of Anti-Saloon Addresses*. Columbus: Hann and Adair, 1895.

———. "The Municipal Church: The Crying Need of It, and a Program of Its Possible Work." *Century Magazine*, August 1910, 493–99.

Goldstone, Jack. "The Weakness of Organization: A New Look at Gamson's *The Strategy of Social Protest*." *American Journal of Sociology* 85 (1980): 1017–42.

Goodman, Paul. "Moral Purpose and Republican Politics in Antebellum America, 1830–1860." *Maryland Historian* 20 (1989): 5–39.

Green, John C. "The Christian Right and the 1994 Elections: A View from the States." *Political Science and Politics* 28 (1995): 5–8.

Green, John C., et al. "Evangelical Realignment: The Political Power of the Christian Right." *Christian Century* 112 (1995): 676–79.

Gusfield, Joseph. "Social Structure and Moral Reform: A Study of the WCTU." *American Journal of Sociology* 61 (1955): 221–32.

Hall, Kermit L. "The Irony of the Federal Constitution's Genius." In *The Constitution and American Political Development*. Ed. Peter F. Nardulli. Urbana: University of Illinois Press, 1992.

Hamm, Richard F. "The Killing of John R. Moffett and the Trial of J. T. Clark: Race, Prohibition and Politics in Danville, 1887–1893." *Virginia Magazine of History and Biography* 101 (1993): 375–404.

Hardesty, Nancy A. "'The Best Temperance Organization in the Land': Southern Methodists and the WCTU in Georgia." *Methodist History* 28 (1990): 187–94.

Haynes, John E. "Reformers, Radicals, and Conservatives." In *Minnesota in a Century of Change: The State and Its People since 1900*. Ed. Clifford E. Clark. St. Paul: Minnesota Historical Press, 1989.

Herd, Denise A. "Prohibition, Racism and Class Politics in the Post-Reconstruction South." *Journal of Drug Issues* 13 (1983): 77–94.

Hohner, Robert A. "The Prohibitionists: Who Were They?" *South Atlantic Quarterly* 68 (1969): 491–505.

Howe, Barbara J. "West Virginia Women's Organizations, 1880s–1930 or 'Unsexed Termagants . . . Help the World Along.'" *West Virginia History* 49 (1990): 81–102.

Jenkins, J. Craig. "Resource Mobilization Theory and the Study of Social Movements." *Annual Review of Sociology* 9 (1983): 527–53.

Jentz, John B. "The Anti-Slavery Constituency in New York City." *Civil War History* 27 (1981): 101–22.

Keller, Morton. "The Politics of State Constitutional Revision, 1820–1920." In *The Constitutional Convention as an Amending Device.* Ed. Kermit Hall et al. Washington: American Historical Association and American Political Science Association, 1987.

Kennedy, Padraic M. "Lenroot, La Follette, and the Campaign of 1906." *Wisconsin Magazine of History* (1959): 163–74.

Kitschelt, Herbert. "Political Opportunity Structures and Political Protest: Anti-Nuclear Movements in Four Democracies." *British Journal of Political Science* 16 (1986): 57–85.

Leab, Grace. "Tennessee Temperance Activities, 1870–1899." *East Tennessee Historical Society's Publications* 21 (1949): 52–68.

Lowenstein, Daniel. "Campaign Spending and Ballot Propositions: Recent Experience, Public Choice Theory and the First Amendment." *UCLA Law Review* 29 (1982): 505–641.

Martin, Asa E. "The Temperance Movement in Pennsylvania Prior to the Civil War." *Pennsylvania Magazine of History and Biography* 49 (1925): 195–230.

McAdam, Doug. "Conceptual Origins, Current Problems, Future Directions." In *Comparative Perspectives on Social Movements: Political Opportunities, Mobilizing Structures, and Framing.* Ed. Doug McAdam et al. Cambridge: Cambridge University Press, 1996.

Mitchell, Robert C. "Silent Spring, Solid Majorities." *Public Opinion* 2 (1979): 19–20.

Mohai, Paul. "Public Concern and Elite Involvement in Environmental Issues." *Social Science Quarterly* 66 (1985): 820–38.

Nicholson, S. E. "The Local-Option Movement." *Annals of the American Academy of Political and Social Sciences* 32 (1908): 471–75.

Owens, John R. and Larry L. Wade. "Campaign Spending on California Ballot Propositions, 1924–1984." *Western Political Quarterly* 39 (1986): 675–89.

Pegram, Thomas R. "The Dry Machine: The Formation of the Anti-Saloon League of Illinois." *Illinois Historical Journal* 83 (1990): 173–86.

Piven, Frances F., and Richard A. Cloward. "Toward a Class-Based Realignment of American Politics: A Movement Strategy." *Social Policy* 14 (1983): 2–14.

Renner, G. K. "Prohibition Comes to Missouri, 1910–1919." *Missouri Historical Review* 62 (1968): 363–97.

Rorabaugh, W. R. "Prohibition as Progress: New York State's License Elections, 1846." *Journal of Social History* 14 (1981): 425–43.

Rusk, Jerrold G., and John J. Stucker. "The Effect of the Southern System of Election Laws on Voting Participation: A Reply to V. O. Key, Jr." In *The History of American Electoral Behavior.* Ed. Joel H. Silbey et al. Princeton, N.J.: Princeton University Press, 1978.

Shipps, Jan. "Utah Comes of Age Politically: A Study of the State's Politics in the Early Years of the Twentieth Century." *Utah Historical Quarterly* 35 (1967): 91–111.

Sims, Anastasia. " 'The Sword of the Spirit': The WCTU and Moral Reform in North Carolina, 1883–1933." *North Carolina Historical Review* 64 (1987): 394–415.

Smith, John A. "Ecclesiastical Politics and the Founding of the Federal Council of Churches." *Church History* 43 (1974): 350–65.

Smith, Thomas S. "A Martyr for Prohibition: The Murder of George C. Haddock." *Palimpsest* 62 (1981): 186–93.

Sponholtz, Lloyd. "The Initiative and Referendum: Direct Democracy in Perspective, 1898–1920." *American Studies* 14 (1973): 43–64.

——. "The Politics of Temperance in Ohio, 1880–1912." *Ohio History* 85 (1976): 4–27.

Stickle, Warren E. "The Applejack Campaign of 1919: 'As Wet' as the Atlantic Ocean." *New Jersey History* (1971): 5–22.

Swart, Stanley L. "Early Efforts at State-Level Law Enforcement: The Failure of Ohio's Supervision of Local Police Authorities, 1902–1925." *Ohio History* 90 (1981): 141–57.

Sweeney, Kevin. "Rum, Romanism, Representation, and Reform: Coalition Politics in Massachusetts." *Civil War History* 22 (1976): 116–37.

Szymanski, Ann-Marie. "Dry Compulsions: Prohibition and the Creation of State-Level Enforcement Agencies," *Journal of Policy History* 11 (1999): 115–46.

Tap, Bruce. " 'The Evils of Intemperance are Universally Conceded': The Temperance Debate in Early Grand Rapids." *Michigan Historical Review* 19 (1993): 17–45.

Tarrow, Sidney. "Social Protest and Policy Reform: May 1968 and the *Loi d'Orientation* in France." *Comparative Political Studies* 25 (1993): 579–607.

Tyrrell, Ian. "Women and Temperance in Antebellum America, 1830–1860." *Civil War History* 28 (1982): 128–52.

——. "Drink and Temperance in the Antebellum South: An Overview and Interpretation." *Journal of Southern History* 48 (1982): 485–510.

Van Buren, A. D. P. "Our Temperance Conflict." *Michigan Pioneer Collections* 13 (1888): 388–407.

Vogel, David. "The 'New' Social Regulation in Historical and Comparative Perspective" in *Regulation in Perspective: Historical Essays*. Ed. Thomas K. McCraw. Cambridge: Harvard University Press, 1981.

Wasserman, Ira M. "Prohibition and Ethno-Cultural Conflict: The Missouri Prohibition Referendum of 1918." *Social Science Quarterly* 70 (1989): 886–901.

——. "Status Politics and Economic Class Interests: The 1918 Prohibition Referendum in California." *Sociological Quarterly* 31 (1990): 475–84.

Wenger, Robert E. "The Anti-Saloon League in Nebraska Politics, 1898–1910." *Nebraska History* 52 (1971): 266–92.

Whitaker, Francis M. "Ohio WCTU and the Prohibition Amendment Campaign of 1883," *Ohio History* 83 (1974): 84–102.

Winn, Thomas H. "Liquor, Race and Politics: Clarksville during the Progressive Era." *Tennessee Historical Quarterly* 49 (1990): 207–17.

Wood, Patricia A. "The Environmental Movement: Its Crystallization, Development, and Impact." In *Social Movements: Development, Participation, and Dynamics*. Ed. James L. Wood and Maurice Jackson. Belmont, Calif.: Wadsworth, 1982.

Woods, Gerald. "A Penchant for Probity: California Progressives and Disreputable Pleasures." In *California Progressivism Revisited*. Ed. William Deverell and Tom Sitton. Berkeley: University of California, 1994.

Woods, Robert A. "Social Workers' Temperance Bill." *Survey*, 12 March 1910, 924–26.

——. "Drunkenness." *Harvard Theological Review* 7 (1914): 497–506.

——. "Winning the Other Half: National Prohibition a Leading Social Issue." *Survey*, 30 December 1916, 349–52.

Unpublished Dissertations and Theses

Aagard, Robert G. "The Prohibition Movement in Wyoming." M.A. thesis, University of Wyoming, 1966.

Appleton, Thomas H. " 'Like Banquo's Ghost': The Emergence of the Prohibition Issue in Kentucky Politics." Ph.D. diss., University of Kentucky, 1981.

Beattie, Donald W. "Sons of Temperance: Pioneers in Total Abstinence and 'Constitutional' Prohibition." Ph.D. diss., Boston University, 1966.
Brownsword, Joanne J. "Good Templars in Wisconsin, 1854–1880." M.A. thesis, University of Wisconsin, 1960.
Carlson, Douglas W. "Temperance Reform in the Cotton Kingdom." Ph.D. diss., University of Illinois, 1982.
Caswell, John E. "The Prohibition Movement in Oregon to the Adoption of Statewide Prohibition in 1914." M.A. thesis, University of Oregon, 1937.
Coffey, John J. "A Political History of the Temperance Movement in New York, 1808–1920." Ph.D. diss., Pennsylvania State University, 1976.
Davis, William G. "Attacking 'The Matchless Evil': Temperance and Prohibition in Mississippi, 1817–1908." Ph.D. diss., Mississippi State University, 1975.
Dohn, Norman. "The History of the Anti-Saloon League." Ph.D. diss., Ohio State University, 1959.
Dyer, Bruce T. "A Study of the Forces Leading to the Adoption of Prohibition in Utah in 1917." M.S. thesis, Brigham Young University, 1958.
Engelmann, Larry D. "O Whiskey: The History of Prohibition in Michigan." Ph.D. diss., University of Michigan, 1971.
Everett, Miles C. "Chester Harvey Rowell, Pragmatic Humanist and California Progressive." Ph.D. diss., University of California at Berkeley, 1966.
Fisher, Joe A. "The Liquor Question in Nebraska, 1880–1890." M.A. thesis, Municipal University of Omaha, 1952.
Hazel, Sybal. "Statewide Prohibition Campaigns in Texas." M.A. thesis, Texas Technological College, 1942.
Hogan, Charles M. "Wayne Wheeler: Single Issue Exponent." Ph.D. diss., University of Cincinnati, 1986.
Hunt, George M. "A History of the Prohibition Movement in Arkansas." M.A. thesis, University of Arkansas, 1933.
Kaylor, Earl C. "The Prohibition Movement in Pennsylvania, 1865–1920." Ph.D. diss., Pennsylvania State University, 1963.
Leab, Grace. "The Temperance Movement in Tennessee, 1860–1907." M.A. thesis, University of Tennessee, 1938.
McCuskey, Wilfred. "The Political Campaign of 1883 in Ohio." M.A. thesis, Ohio State University, 1948.
Mezvinsky, Norton. "The White Ribbon Reform, 1874–1920." Ph.D. diss., University of Wisconsin, 1959.
Putnum, Edison K. "The Prohibition Movement in Idaho, 1863–1934." Ph.D. diss., University of Idaho, 1979.
Shahan, Joe M. "Reform and Politics in Tennessee: 1906–1914." Ph.D. diss., Vanderbilt University, 1981.
Siegel, Nancy R. "A Matter of Public Welfare: The Temperance Movement in Ante-bellum Cincinnati." M.A. thesis, University of Cincinnati, 1971.
Thrift, Charles T. "The Operations of the American Home Missionary Society in the South, 1826–1861." Ph.D. diss., University of Chicago, 1936.
Tisdale, Nancy K. "The Prohibition Crusade in Arizona." M.A. thesis, University of Arizona, 1965.
Turner, James R. "The American Prohibition Movement, 1865–1897." Ph.D. diss., University of Wisconsin, 1972.
Watson, Larry J. "Evangelical Protestants and the Prohibition Movement in Texas, 1887–1919." Ph.D. diss., Texas A&M University, 1993.
West, William E. "Dry Crusade: The Prohibition Movement in Colorado, 1853–1933." Ph.D. diss., University of Colorado, 1971.

Whitaker, Francis M. "A History of the Ohio Woman's Christian Temperance Union." Ph.D. diss., Ohio State University, 1971.

Zartman, Charles E. "The Prohibition Question in Licking County, 1908–1912." M.A. thesis. Ohio State University, 1938.

Court Cases

The Aurora v. United States, 7 Cranch 382 (1813).

Caldwell v. Barrett, 73 Ga. 604 (1884).

Commonwealth v. Bennett, 108 Mass. 27 (1871).

Eckerson v. Des Moines, 137 Iowa 452 (1908).

Ex Parte Wall, 48 Cal. 279 (1874).

Feek v. Bloomingdale Township Board, 47 N.W. 37 (1890).

Fell v. State, 42 Md. 71 (1874).

Geebrick v. State, 5 Iowa 491 (1857).

Gordon v. State, 23 N.E. 63 (1889).

Groesch v. State, 42 Ind. 547 (1873).

Hamilton v. Carroll, 82 Md. 326 (1896).

In Re O'Brien, 29 Mont. 530 (1904).

Lammert v. Lidwell, 62 Mo. 188 (1876).

Little Rock v. North Little Rock, 72 Ark. 195 (1904).

Locke's Appeal, 72 Pa. (22 P. F. Smith) 491 (1873).

Maize v. State, 4 Ind. 342 (1853).

Ohio ex rel Lloyd v. Dollison, 68 Ohio 688 (1903).

Parker v. Commonwealth, 6 Barr 507 (1847).

Paul v. Gloucester County, 50 N.J. Law (21 Vroom) 585 (1888).

People v. Collins, 3 Mich. 343 (1854).

Rice v. Foster, 4 Harr. 479 (1847).

Savage v. Commonwealth, 5 S.E. 565 (1888).

Schulherr v. Bordeaux, 8 South. 201 (1886).

State v. Board of Freeholders, 51 N.J.L. 454 (1889).

State v. Cooke, 24 Minn. 247 (1877).

State v. Forkner, 62 N.W. 772 (1895).

State v. Morris Common Pleas, 36 N. Jersey Law R. 72 (1872).

State v. Parker, 26 Vt. 357 (1854).

State v. Pond, 6 S.W. 469 (1887).

State v. Swisher, 17 Tex. 441 (1856).

State v. Weir, 33 Iowa 134 (1871).

State v. Wilcox, 42 Conn. 364 (1875).

Territory v. O'Connor, 41 N.W. 746 (1889).

Thornton v. Territory, 3 Wash. T. 428 (1888).

Index

Ann-Marie Szymanski is Assistant Professor of Political Science at the University of Oklahoma.

Library of Congress Cataloging-in-Publication Data
Szymanski, Ann-Marie E.
Pathways to prohibition : radicals, moderates, and social movement outcomes / by Ann-Marie E. Szymanski.
Includes bibliographical references and index.
ISBN 0-8223-3181-0 (cloth)
ISBN 0-8223-3169-1 (pbk.)
1. Prohibition—United States—History. 2. Temperance—United States—History. 3. Social movements—United States—History. I. Title.
HV5089.S983 2003 363.4'1'0973—dc21 2003004911